Middle School 2-2

중간고사 완벽대비

적중 100

영어 기출 문제집

중 **2**

비상 | 김진완

KB087119

Best Collection

구성과 특징

교과서의 주요 학습 내용을 중심으로 학습 영역별 특성에 맞춰 단계별로 다양한 학습 기회를 제공하여 단원별 학습능력 평가는 물론 중간 및 기말고사 시험 등에 완벽하게 대비할 수 있도록 내용을 구성

Words & Expressions

Step1 Key Words 단원별 핵심 단어 설명 및 풀이
Key Expression 단원별 핵심 숙어 및 관용어 설명
Word Power 반대 또는 비슷한 뜻 단어 배우기
English Dictionary 영어로 배우는 영어 단어

Step2 실력평가 단원별 수시평가 대비 주관식, 객관식 문제풀이

Step3 서술형 대비 학업성취도 및 수행능력평가 대비 서술형 문제풀이

Conversation

Step1 핵심 의사소통 의사소통에 필요한 주요 표현 방법 요약
핵심 Check 기본적인 표현 방법 및 활용능력 확인

Step2 대화문 익히기 상황에 따른 대화문 활용 및 연습

Step3 기본평가 시험대비 기초 학습 능력 평가

Step4 실력평가 단원별 수시평가 대비 주관식, 객관식 문제풀이

Step5 서술형 대비 학업성취도 및 수행능력평가 대비 서술형 문제풀이

Grammar

Step1 주요 문법 단원별 주요 문법 사항과 예문을 알기 쉽게 설명
핵심 Check 기본 문법사항에 대한 이해 여부 확인

Step2 기본평가 시험대비 기초 학습 능력 평가

Step3 실력평가 단원별 수시평가 대비 주관식, 객관식 문제풀이

Step4 서술형 대비 학업성취도 및 수행능력평가 대비 서술형 문제풀이

Reading

Step1 구문 분석 단원별로 제시된 문장에 대한 구문별 분석과 내용 설명
확인문제 문장에 대한 기본적인 이해와 인지능력 확인

Step2 확인학습A 빈칸 채우기를 통한 문장 완성 능력 확인

Step3 확인학습B 제시된 우리말을 영어로 완성하여 작문 능력 키우기

Step4 실력평가 단원별 수시평가 대비 주관식, 객관식 문제풀이

Step5 서술형 대비 학업성취도 및 수행능력평가 대비 서술형 문제풀이
교과서 구석구석 교과서에 나오는 기타 문장까지 완벽 학습

Composition

|영역별 핵심문제|
단어 및 어휘, 대화문, 문법, 독해 등 각 영역별 기출문제의 출제 유형을 분석하여 실전에 대비하고 연습할 수 있도록 문제를 배열

|서술형 실전 및 창의사고력 문제|
학교 시험에서 점차 늘어나는 서술형 시험에 집중 대비하고 고득점을 취득하는데 만전을 기하기 위한 학습 코너

|단원별 예상문제|
기출문제를 분석한 후 새로운 시험 출제 경향을 더하여 새롭게 출제될 수 있는 문제를 포함하여 시험에 완벽하게 대비할 수 있도록 준비

|단원별 모의고사|
영역별, 단계별 학습을 모두 마친 후 실전 연습을 위한 모의고사

on the textbook

교과서 파헤치기

- **단어Test1~2** 영어 단어 우리말 쓰기와 우리말을 영어 단어로 쓰기
- **대화문Test1~2** 대화문 빈칸 완성 및 전체 대화문 쓰기
- **본문Test1~5** 빈칸 완성, 우리말 쓰기, 문장 배열연습, 영어 작문하기 복습 등 단계별 반복 학습을 통해 교과서 지문에 대한 완벽한 습득
- **구석구석지문Test1~2** 지문 빈칸 완성 및 전문 영어로 쓰기

이책의 차례 **Contents**

Lesson 5

Explore Your Feelings!

🎤 의사소통 기능

- 좋지 않은 감정을 느끼게 된 원인 묻기
  A: You look down today. What's the matter?
  B: I got a haircut but it's too short.

- 고민을 해결할 방법 제안하기
  A: I've gained weight lately.
  B: I think you should exercise regularly.

🎤 언어 형식

- 현재완료
  They **have been** best friends since childhood.

- 목적격 관계대명사
  I'm sure there is a reason **that** we don't know about.

Key Words

- **advice**[ədváis] 명 조언
- **advise**[ədváiz] 동 조언하다, 충고하다
- **alone**[əlóun] 부 홀로, 혼자
- **avoid**[əvɔ́id] 동 피하다
- **bar**[bɑːr] 명 (특정 음식이나 음료를 파는) 전문점
- **contact**[kɑ́ntækt] 명 접촉, 닿음
- **difficult**[dífikʌlt] 형 어려운
- **elementary**[éləméntəri] 형 초보의, 초급의
- **explain**[ikspéin] 동 설명하다
- **fear**[fiər] 명 두려움, 공포
- **fight**[fait] 동 싸우다
- **forgive**[fərgív] 동 용서하다
- **haircut**[héərkʌt] 명 이발, 머리 깎기
- **hate**[heit] 동 싫어하다
- **hurt**[həːrt] 동 다치게 하다, 아프게 하다
- **limit**[límit] 명 한계, 제한
- **line**[lain] 명 (연극, 영화의) 대사
- **matter**[mǽtər] 명 문제
- **mean**[miːn] 동 의도하다, 작정하다
- **messy**[mési] 형 어질러진, 더러운
- **mirror**[mírər] 명 거울
- **pack**[pæk] 동 싸다, 꾸리다
- **reason**[ríːzn] 명 이유, 까닭
- **repeat**[ripíːt] 동 반복하다
- **share**[ʃɛər] 동 공유하다, 나누다
- **since**[sins] 전 ~부터, ~ 이후
- **snack**[snæk] 명 간식
- **solve**[sɑlv] 동 풀다, 해결하다
- **stand**[stænd] 동 참다, 견디다
- **stuff**[stʌf] 명 물건
- **suggestion**[səgdʒéstʃən] 명 제안
- **toothache**[túːθeik] 명 치통
- **upset**[ʌ́pset] 형 속상한, 마음이 상한
- **wise**[waiz] 형 현명한
- **worry**[wə́ːri] 동 걱정하다 명 걱정
- **yell**[jel] 동 소리치다, 소리 지르다
- **yet**[jet] 부 아직

Key Expressions

- **face a problem** 문제에 직면하다
- **focus on** ~에 집중하다
- **gain weight** 체중이 늘다
- **in the end** 결국, 마침내
- **let it go** 그쯤 해 두다, 내버려 두다
- **lunch break** 점심시간
- **make a mistake** 실수하다
- **on purpose** 고의로, 일부러
- **point out** 지적하다
- **put ~ down** ~을 깎아내리다
- **set an alarm** 자명종을 맞추다
- **shut down** (기계가) 멈추다, 정지하다
- **stay up late** 늦게까지 자지 않고 있다
- **up and down** 좋다가 나쁘다가 하는
- **wake up** 잠에서 깨다
- **work out** 해결하다

Word Power

※ 서로 반대되는 뜻을 가진 어휘

☐ **easy** 쉬운 ↔ **difficult** 어려운

☐ **hate** 싫어하다 ↔ **like** 좋아하다

☐ **wise** 현명한 ↔ **stupid** 어리석은

☐ **upset** 속상한, 마음이 상한 ↔ **relieved** 안도하는

☐ **messy** 어질러진, 더러운 ↔ **clean** 깔끔한

☐ **avoid** 피하다 ↔ **face** 맞서다

☐ **pack** 싸다, 꾸리다 ↔ **unpack** (꾸러미, 짐을) 풀다

☐ **alone** 혼자 ↔ **together** 함께

☐ **limited** 한정된 ↔ **limitless** 무한의, 무제한의

☐ **on purpose** 고의로 ↔ **by accident** 우연히

☐ **elementary** 초급의, 초보의 ↔ **advanced** 상급의, 고등의

☐ **gain weight** 체중이 늘다 ↔ **lose weight** 체중이 줄다

English Dictionary

☐ **advice** 조언
→ an opinion or a suggestion about what somebody should do in a particular situation
누군가가 특정한 상황에서 해야 하는 것에 대한 의견 또는 제안

☐ **avoid** 피하다
→ to keep away from somebody/something; to try not to do something
누군가 또는 무언가로부터 멀리하다; 무언가를 하지 않으려고 하다

☐ **contact** 접촉
→ the state of touching something
무언가를 만지는 상태

☐ **elementary** 초급의
→ in or connected with the first stages of a course of study
학업 과정에서 첫 번째 단계에 관련된

☐ **forgive** 용서하다
→ to stop feeling angry with somebody who has done something to harm, annoy or upset you
당신에게 해롭게 하거나 화나게 하거나 또는 불안하게 하는 무언가를 한 사람에게 화내는 감정을 그만두다

☐ **hate** 싫어하다
→ to dislike something very much
무언가를 매우 싫어하다

☐ **hurt** 다치게 하다
→ to cause physical pain to somebody/yourself; to injure somebody/yourself
누군가 또는 당신 자신에게 신체적 고통을 야기하다; 누군가 또는 당신 자신을 부상을 입히다

☐ **line** 대사
→ the words spoken by an actor in a play or film/movie
연극 또는 영화에서 배우에 의해 이야기되는 말

☐ **messy** 어질러진, 더러운
→ dirty and/or untidy
더러운, 그리고[또는] 정돈되지 않은

☐ **repeat** 반복하다
→ to say or write something again or more than once
무언가를 다시 또는 한번 이상 말하거나 쓰다

☐ **share** 공유하다
→ to have or use something at the same time as somebody else
다른 누군가와 동시에 무언가를 갖거나 사용하다

☐ **suggestion** 제안
→ an idea or a plan that you mention for somebody else to think about
다른 누군가가 그것에 관해 생각하도록 당신이 언급한 의견 또는 계획

☐ **toothache** 치통
→ a pain in one of your teeth
치아의 아픔

☐ **yell** 소리 지르다
→ to shout loudly, for example because you are angry, excited, frightened or in pain
예를 들어 당신이 화가 나거나, 흥분하거나, 깜짝 놀라거나 고통을 당하고 있기 때문에 크게 소리 지르다

서답형

01 다음 짝지어진 단어의 관계가 같도록 빈칸에 알맞은 말을 쓰시오.

easy : difficult = like : h_____

중요

02 다음 중 밑줄 친 부분의 뜻풀이가 바르지 <u>않은</u> 것은?

① I didn't want to go there <u>alone</u>. 혼자, 홀로
② The sport is dangerous because there is a lot of body <u>contact</u>. 접촉
③ You can overcome your <u>fear</u> of water. 두려움
④ Susan will <u>forgive</u> the rude boy. 용서하다
⑤ I can't memorize my <u>lines</u> at all. 선

서답형

03 다음 우리말에 맞게 빈칸에 알맞은 말을 쓰시오.

(1) 밤에 혼자 다니지 마세요.
➡ Don't walk round _____ at night.
(2) 내가 무대에 섰을 때, 나는 대사를 잊어버렸다.
➡ When I was on the stage, I forgot my _____.
(3) 여기 제한 속도는 60km/h이다.
➡ The speed _____ is 60km/h here.
(4) 저는 여섯 살 때 이후부터 여기에 살고 있습니다.
➡ I've lived here _____ I was six years old.

04 다음 영영풀이가 가리키는 것을 고르시오.

an opinion or a suggestion about what somebody should do in a particular situation

① matter
② fear
③ mirror
④ stuff
⑤ advice

서답형

05 다음 우리말에 맞게 주어진 단어를 사용하여 영작하시오.

(1) 나는 추위를 별로 잘 참지 못한다. (very, stand)
➡ _____
(2) 그들은 그 문제에 대해 이야기했다. (matter)
➡ _____
(3) 제게 조언 좀 주세요. (some, please)
➡ _____
(4) 그녀가 내게 먼저 물어보지 않고 내 물건을 사용해서 나는 화가 났다. (stuff, upset)
➡ _____
_____

06 다음 주어진 문장의 밑줄 친 stand와 같은 의미로 쓰인 것은?

I can't <u>stand</u> his arrogant attitude.

① You don't have to <u>stand</u>. Just sit down.
② Let's <u>stand</u> up and talk about it now.
③ The old buildings <u>stand</u> in front of the library.
④ Can you <u>stand</u> the pain?
⑤ Tall trees <u>stand</u> on the riverside.

01 다음 빈칸에 들어갈 말을 〈보기〉에서 찾아 쓰시오.

> a pain in one of your teeth

➡ _____

2 다음 우리말에 맞게 빈칸에 알맞은 말을 쓰시오.

(1) 우리의 점심시간은 12시부터 1시까지이다.
➡ Our _____ is from twelve to one.

(2) 나는 너의 조언을 받아들여 집에 일찍 들어갔다.
➡ I took your _____ and went home early.

(3) 난 그녀의 마음을 아프게 하고 싶지 않다.
➡ I don't want to _____ her feelings.

03 다음 문장의 빈칸에 들어갈 말을 〈보기〉에서 골라 쓰시오.

> ┤ 보기 ├
>
> gain weight / in the end / focus on / on purpose

(1) He broke his glasses _____.
(2) You can _____ because of lack of sleep.
(3) We should _____ the changes in the global market.
(4) _____, I accepted his suggestion.

4 다음 우리말을 주어진 단어를 이용하여 영작하시오.

(1) 그는 때때로 사람들을 깎아 내린다. (puts)
➡ _____

(2) 그녀는 항상 내 실수들을 지적한다. (points)
➡ _____

(3) 잠자리에 들기 전에 자명종을 맞춰라. (set)
➡ _____

05 다음 우리말과 일치하도록 주어진 어구를 배열하여 완성하시오.

(1) 내 보고서의 몇몇 실수들을 지적해 주어 고마워요.
(you / mistakes / my / in / report / out / pointing / thank / for / some)
➡ _____

(2) 여기 여러분의 대본이 있으니 대사를 연습하세요.
(your / practice / so / your / here / scripts / are / lines)
➡ _____

(3) 내가 전화한 이유는 토요일 계획에 대해 묻기 위해서였다.
(for / the reason / to / the plans / ask / called / I / Saturday / was / about)
➡ _____
_____

(4) 화재의 위험을 피하기 위해 조치를 취하는 것은 중요하다.
(avoid / is / to / it / important / to / take / the risk / fire / measures / of)
➡ _____
_____

Conversation

1 좋지 않은 감정을 느끼게 된 원인 묻기

A You look down today. What's the matter? (너 오늘 침울해 보여. 무슨 일 있어?)

B I got a haircut but it's too short. (머리를 잘랐는데 너무 짧아.)

■ "What's the matter?"는 상대방의 기분이 언짢아 보일 때 무슨 일이 있는지 혹은 좋지 않은 기분의 원인을 묻고자 할 때 사용된다. 예를 들어, 상대방의 기분이 안 좋아 보일 때 "What's the matter? You look upset."과 같이 말한다.

좋지 않은 감정을 느끼게 된 원인 묻기

- What's wrong? (무슨 일이에요?)
- Is something the matter? (무슨 문제가 있나요?)
- Is there something wrong? (무슨 일이에요?)
- Why do you look so sad[mad]? (왜 그렇게 슬퍼[화나] 보이니?)
- What's the problem with you? (무슨 일이야?)

핵심 Check

1. 다음 우리말과 일치하도록 빈칸에 알맞은 말을 쓰시오.

   (1) **A:** You look so _____. _____? (매우 초조해 보여. 무슨 일이야?)

   B: I dropped my mom's new glasses and broke them. (내가 엄마의 새 안경을 떨어뜨렸는데 그게 깨졌어.)

   (2) **A:** _____? (왜 그렇게 슬퍼 보이니?)

   B: I didn't pass the test. I don't know what to do. (시험을 통과하지 못했어. 나는 무엇을 해야 할지 모르겠어.)

   (3) **A:** You don't look good today. Is there something _____? (너 오늘 좋아 보이지 않아. 무슨 일이야?)

   B: I can't sleep well at night. _____? (밤에 잠을 잘 잘 수 없어. 내가 무엇을 해야 할까?)

② 고민을 해결할 방법 제안하기

A I've gained weight lately. (나는 최근에 체중이 늘었어.)

B I think you should exercise regularly. (내 생각에 네가 규칙적으로 운동을 해야 할 것 같아.)

■ "I think you should ～."는 뭔가 고민하고 있거나 어려움을 겪고 있는 사람에게 그 문제에 대한 해결책을 제안할 때 사용된다. 예를 들어, 친구와 말다툼을 한 후 고민하고 있는 친구에게 문제를 해결할 방안을 제시하고 싶다면 "I think you should talk to your friend first."와 같이 말할 수 있다.

고민을 해결할 방법 제안하기

- Why don't you talk to your father first? (먼저 아빠와 이야기해 보는 게 어때?)
- How about playing a video game? (비디오 게임을 하는 것이 어때?)
- If I were you, I'd go to bed first and think about it later. (내가 너라면 나는 먼저 잠자리에 들고 나중에 생각할래.)
- What about setting an alarm before you go to bed? (잠자리에 들기 전에 알람을 맞추는 게 어때?)
- I recommend writing a letter to your friend. (나는 네 친구에게 편지 쓰는 걸 추천해.)
- I advise you to meet her personally. (나는 네가 개인적으로 그녀를 만나보는 것을 권해.)

핵심 Check

2. 다음 우리말과 일치하도록 빈칸에 알맞은 말을 쓰시오.

(1) **A:** My face turns red when I'm in front of many people. (저는 많은 사람들 앞에 서면 얼굴이 빨개져요.)

 B: _____ take a deep breath first. (내 생각에 네가 먼저 깊게 숨을 쉬어야 할 것 같아.)

(2) **A:** I'm really bad at making eye contact. (저는 정말로 눈을 마주치는 것을 잘 못해요.)

 B: I _____ you to practice looking into your own eyes in the mirror. (나는 네가 거울에서 네 눈을 보는 것을 연습하길 충고해.)

(3) **A:** I want a better style. (나는 더 나은 스타일을 원해요.)

 B: _____ look for magazines with fashion tips? (패션 정보가 있는 잡지를 찾아보는 게 어때?)

Listen & Talk 1-B

Jane: You look tired. ❶What's the matter?

Mike: I didn't have breakfast this morning. I'm so hungry.

Jane: Oh, ❷that's too bad. We still have two more hours ❸until lunch break.

Mike: Our school should have a snack bar. Then, we could have a quick breakfast or snacks.

Jane: I think so, too. How can we ❹make that suggestion?

Mike: We can post it on the suggestion board.

Jane: 너 피곤해 보인다. 무슨 일 있어?

Mike: 오늘 아침에 밥을 못 먹었어. 너무 배가 고파.

Jane: 오, 안됐다. 점심시간까지 아직 두 시간도 더 남았는데.

Mike: 우리 학교도 매점이 있어야 돼. 그러면 간단히 아침이나 간식을 먹을 수 있잖아.

Jane: 내 생각도 그래. 어떻게 하면 우리가 그 제안을 할 수 있을까?

Mike: 우리는 이걸 제안 게시판에 올릴 수 있어.

❶ 상대방의 기분이 언짢아 보일 때 무슨 일이 있는지 혹은 좋지 않은 기분의 원인을 묻고자 한다. What's the problem with you? 등으로 바꾸어 쓸 수 있다.

❷ 유감을 나타내는 표현으로 I'm sorry to hear that. 등으로 바꾸어 쓸 수 있다.

❸ until: ~까지, ~이 되기까지

❹ make a suggestion: 제안을 하다

Check(√) True or False

(1) There isn't a snack bar in Jane's school. T ☐ F ☐

(2) Mike is going to have lunch with Jane soon. T ☐ F ☐

Communication

Solomon: Hello, you're ❶on the air.

Amy: Hi, Solomon. I'm Amy.

Solomon: Hi, Amy. What's the matter?

Amy: I ❷hate sharing my room with my little sister. She uses my ❸stuff without asking me first. What should I do?

Solomon: Hmm.... I think you should tell her your feelings. And you should also make some rules with your sister.

Amy: Oh, I'll try ❹that. Thanks for the advice.

Solomon: 안녕하세요. (방송에) 연결되었습니다.

Amy: 안녕하세요, Solomon. 전 Amy라고 해요.

Solomon: 안녕하세요, Amy. 무슨 일 있어요?

Amy: 전 여동생이랑 제 방을 같이 쓰는 게 싫어요. 그 애는 제게 먼저 물어보지도 않고 제 물건을 쓰거든요. 제가 어떻게 해야 할까요?

Solomon: 흠.... 제 생각엔 당신의 기분을 여동생에게 말해야 할 것 같아요. 그리고 여동생과 몇 가지 규칙을 만들어 봐요.

Amy: 오, 그렇게 할게요. 조언 감사해요.

❶ on the air: 방송 중에

❷ hate은 to부정사와 동명사 모두를 목적어로 취할 수 있다.

❸ stuff: 물건

❹ that은 Solomon의 조언으로 제시된 여동생에게 기분을 이야기하는 것과 여동생과 몇 가지 규칙을 만들어 보는 것을 가리킨다.

Check(√) True or False

(3) Amy is upset because of her little sister. T ☐ F ☐

(4) Solomon thinks that Amy should share her stuff with her little sister. T ☐ F ☐

Listen & Talk 1-A-1

M: You don't look so happy today. What's the matter?

W: I wore my sister's favorite T-shirt. But I got grape juice on ❶it.

M: Oh, no. Did you tell your sister?

W: No, ❷not yet. I don't know ❸what to do.

❶ it은 her sister's favorite T-shirt를 가리킨다.
❷ not yet: 아직 (∼ 않다)
❸ what to do = what I should do

Listen & Talk 1-A-2

Sora: David, you look ❶down today. What's the matter?

David: I got a haircut but it's too short. I look ❷ funny.

Sora: ❸Take off your hat and let me see. (*pause*) Oh, it looks fine.

David: Really? I guess ❹I'm just not used to it yet.

❶ down: 우울한(= depressed, gloomy)
❷ funny: 우스꽝스러운, 우스운, cf. fun: 즐거운, 재미있는
❸ take off: ∼을 벗다
❹ be used to ∼: ∼에 익숙하다

Listen & Talk 2 A-1

Sujin: I don't know how to do better in math. Can you give me some ❶advice?

Jake: How do you study for tests?

Sujin: I just solve a lot of problems.

Jake: Well, don't solve everything. I think you should ❷focus on the ❸ones you got wrong.

❶ advice: 조언, cf. advise: 조언하다
❷ focus on: ∼에 집중하다
❸ ones는 problems를 가리킨다.

Listen & Talk 2 A-2

Emily: I was late for class again. I just can't ❶ wake up in the morning.

Tom: Do you ❷set an alarm?

Emily: Yeah, but I ❸turn ❹it off and go back to sleep.

Tom: I think you should put ❹it far from your bed. That way, you'll have to ❺get out of bed.

❶ wake up: 잠에서 깨다
❷ set an alarm: 자명종을 맞추다
❸ turn off: ∼을 끄다 (↔ turn on: ∼을 켜다)
❹ it은 alarm을 가리킨다.
❺ get out of ∼: ∼에서 나오다

Listen & Talk 2 B

Eric: Ms. Morris, I just can't ❶stop playing computer games. What should I do?

Ms. Morris: Well, ❷why don't you use a special program? When you set a time limit, the computer ❸shuts down at that time.

Eric: Oh, that's a good idea.

Ms. Morris: And I think you should move the computer out of your room and into the living room.

Eric: I think I should. Thank you for the advice, Ms. Morris.

❶ stop+동명사: ∼하던 것을 멈추다, cf. stop+to부정사: ∼하기 위해 멈추다
❷ why don't you ∼?: ∼하는 게 어때?
❸ shut down: (기계가) 멈추다, 정지하다

Conversation **13**

● 다음 우리말과 일치하도록 빈칸에 알맞은 말을 쓰시오.

Listen & Talk 1-A-1

M: You _____ _____ so happy today. What's the _____?

W: I _____ my sister's favorite T-shirt. But I _____ grape juice on it.

M: Oh, no. Did you tell your sister?

W: No, not yet. I don't know _____ _____ _____.

Listen & Talk 1-A-2

Sora: David, you _____ _____ today. _____ _____ _____?

David: I got a _____ but it's too short. I look _____.

Sora: _____ _____ your hat and let me see. (*pause*) Oh, it looks fine.

David: Really? I guess I'm just not _____ _____ it yet.

Listen & Talk 1-B

Jane: You look _____. What's the matter?

Mike: _____ _____ _____ _____ _____ _____ _____. I'm so hungry.

Jane: Oh, that's _____ _____. We still have two more hours until _____ _____.

Mike: Our school should have a _____ _____. Then, we could have a quick breakfast or snacks.

Jane: I think so, too. How can we _____ that _____?

Mike: We can _____ it on the suggestion board.

Listen & Talk 2 A-1

Sujin: I don't know _____ _____ _____ better in math. Can you give me some _____?

Jake: How do you study for tests?

Sujin: I just _____ a lot of problems.

Jake: Well, don't _____ everything. I think you should _____ _____ the _____ you _____ wrong.

해석

M: 너 오늘은 별로 행복해 보이지가 않네. 무슨 일 있어?

W: 언니가 가장 좋아하는 티셔츠를 입었어. 그런데 거기에 포도 주스를 쏟았지 뭐야.

M: 오, 저런. 너희 언니에게 말했어?

W: 아니, 아직. 내가 뭘 해야 할지 모르겠어.

Sora: David, 너 오늘 침울해 보여. 무슨 일 있어?

David: 머리를 잘랐는데 너무 짧아. 우스꽝스럽게 보여.

Sora: 모자를 벗으면 내가 한 번 볼게. 오, 괜찮아 보이는데.

David: 정말? 난 아직 익숙해지지 않은 것 같아.

Jane: 너 피곤해 보인다. 무슨 일 있어?

Mike: 오늘 아침에 밥을 못 먹었어. 너무 배가 고파.

Jane: 오, 안됐다. 점심시간까지 아직 두 시간도 더 남았는데.

Mike: 우리 학교도 매점이 있어야 돼. 그러면 간단히 아침이나 간식을 먹을 수 있잖아.

Jane: 내 생각도 그래. 어떻게 하면 우리가 그 제안을 할 수 있을까?

Mike: 우리는 이걸 제안 게시판에 올릴 수 있어.

Sujin: 수학을 더 잘하는 방법을 모르겠어. 나에게 조언을 좀 줄래?

Jake: 시험을 목표로 어떻게 공부해?

Sujin: 난 그냥 많은 문제를 풀어 봐.

Jake: 글쎄, 전부 풀지 마. 내 생각엔 네가 틀린 문제들에 집중해야 할 것 같아.

Listen & Talk 2 A-2

Emily: I was _____ _____ class again. I just can't _____ _____ in the morning.

Tom: Do you _____ _____ _____?

Emily: Yeah, but I _____ _____ _____ and go back to sleep.

Tom: I think you should put it _____ _____ your bed. _____ _____, you'll have to get out of bed.

Emily: 나 또 수업에 늦었어. 난 정말 아침에 못 일어나겠어.
Tom: 자명종은 맞춰 두는 거야?
Emily: 응, 그렇지만 자명종을 끄고 다시 잠들게 돼.
Tom: 내 생각엔 자명종을 침대에서 멀리 떨어진 곳에 두어야 할 것 같아. 그러면 침대에서 일어날 수밖에 없을 거야.

Listen & Talk 2 B

Eric: Ms. Morris, I just can't _____ _____ _____ _____. _____ _____ _____ _____?

Ms. Morris: Well, why don't you use a special program? When you _____ a time _____, the computer _____ _____ at that time.

Eric: Oh, that's a good idea.

Ms. Morris: And _____ _____ _____ _____ move the computer _____ _____ your room and _____ the living room.

Eric: I think I should. Thank you for the _____, Ms. Morris.

Eric: Morris 선생님, 저 컴퓨터 게임하는 것을 멈출 수가 없어요. 제가 어떻게 해야 할까요?
Mr. Morris: 음, 특별한 프로그램을 써 보는 게 어떨까? 네가 시간 제한을 정해 두면 컴퓨터가 그 시간에 맞춰 종료돼.
Eric: 오, 좋은 생각이네요.
Mr. Morris: 그리고 내 생각엔 컴퓨터를 네 방에서 거실로 옮겨 두어야 할 것 같아.
Eric: 제 생각에도 그래야 할 것 같아요. Morris 선생님, 조언해 주셔서 감사합니다.

Communication

Solomon: Hello, you're _____ _____ _____.

Amy: Hi, Solomon. I'm Amy.

Solomon: Hi, Amy. What's the _____?

Amy: I hate _____ my room _____ my little sister. She uses my _____ without asking me first. What should I do?

Solomon: Hmm.... I think you should tell her your _____. And you should also _____ _____ _____ with your sister.

Amy: Oh, _____ _____ _____. Thanks for the advice.

Solomon: 안녕하세요, (방송에) 연결되었습니다.
Amy: 안녕하세요, Solomon. 전 Amy라고 해요.
Solomon: 안녕하세요, Amy. 무슨 일 있어요?
Amy: 전 여동생이랑 제 방을 같이 쓰는 게 싫어요. 그 애는 제게 먼저 물어보지도 않고 제 물건을 쓰거든요. 제가 어떻게 해야 할까요?
Solomon: 흠.... 제 생각엔 당신의 기분을 여동생에게 말해야 할 것 같아요. 그리고 여동생과 몇 가지 규칙을 만들어 봐요.
Amy: 오, 그렇게 할게요. 조언 감사해요.

Conversation 시험대비 기본평가

01 다음 대화가 자연스럽게 이어지도록 순서대로 배열하시오.

> (A) Do you set an alarm?
> (B) I think you should put it far from your bed. That way, you'll have to get out of bed.
> (C) Yeah, but I turn it off and go back to sleep.
> (D) I was late for class again. I just can't wake up in the morning.

➡ _____

[02~04] 다음 대화를 읽고 물음에 답하시오.

Jane: You look tired. What's the matter?
Mike: (A) I didn't have breakfast this morning. I'm so hungry.
Jane: (B) Oh, that's too bad. We still have two more hours until lunch break.
Mike: (C) Then, we could have a quick breakfast or snacks.
Jane: (D) ⓐI think so, too. How can we make that suggestion?
Mike: (E) We can post it on the suggestion board.

02 위 대화의 (A)~(E) 중 주어진 문장이 들어가기에 적절한 곳은?

> Our school should have a snack bar.

① (A)　　　② (B)　　　③ (C)　　　④ (D)　　　⑤ (E)

03 위 대화의 밑줄 친 ⓐ와 바꾸어 쓸 수 있는 것을 모두 고르시오.

① I'm against it.
② I'm with you in what you say.
③ That's not right.
④ I agree with you.
⑤ This won't work.

04 위 대화의 내용과 일치하지 않는 것은?
① Mike는 아침을 먹지 않아 피곤해 보인다.
② Jane과 Mike는 곧 점심을 먹을 예정이다.
③ 학교에 매점이 없다.
④ Mike는 매점이 있다면 간단히 아침이나 간식을 먹을 수 있을 것이라고 생각한다.
⑤ Jane과 Mike는 제안 게시판에 매점 설치 제안을 할 수 있다.

[01~03] 다음 대화를 읽고 물음에 답하시오.

Tom: You don't look so happy today. (A) <u>What's the matter?</u>

Sue: I wore my sister's favorite T-shirt. But I got grape juice on it.

Tom: Oh, no. Did you tell your sister?

Sue: No, not yet. I don't know what to do.

01 위 대화의 밑줄 친 (A)와 바꾸어 쓰기에 <u>어색한</u> 것은?

① What's the problem with you?
② What's wrong?
③ Is there something wrong?
④ Is something the matter?
⑤ What do you do?

 02 위 대화에서 Sue의 심정으로 적절한 것은?

① worried   ② joyful   ③ lonely
④ happy   ⑤ pleased

03 위 대화의 내용과 일치하도록 빈칸을 완성하시오.

Sue looked so worried because she got grape juice on _____.

[04~06] 다음 대화를 읽고 물음에 답하시오.

Jane: You look tired. What's the matter?

Mike: I didn't have breakfast this morning. I'm so hungry.

Jane: Oh, (A)<u>that's too bad.</u> We still have two more hours until lunch break.

Mike: Our school should have a snack bar. Then, we could have a quick breakfast or snacks.

Jane: I think so, too. How can we make that suggestion?

Mike: We can post it on the suggestion board.

서답형
04 위 대화에서 주어진 영영풀이가 나타내는 말을 찾아 쓰시오.

an idea or a plan that you mention for somebody else to think about

➡ _____

서답형
05 How can Jane and Mike make the suggestion?

➡ _____

06 위 대화의 밑줄 친 (A)와 바꾸어 쓸 수 있는 것을 <u>모두</u> 고르시오.

① I'm sorry to hear that.
② but I'm afraid I can't.
③ what a pity!
④ no problem.
⑤ don't mention it.

서답형
07 다음 대화가 자연스럽게 이어지도록 순서대로 배열하시오.

(A) Take off your hat and let me see. (*pause*) Oh, it looks fine.
(B) I got a haircut but it's too short. I look funny.
(C) You look down today. What's the matter?
(D) Really? I guess I'm just not used to it yet.

➡ _____

[08~09] 다음 대화를 읽고 물음에 답하시오.

> Sujin: I don't know how to do better in math. (a)Can you give me some advice?
>
> Jake: How do you study for tests?
>
> Sujin: I just solve a lot of problems.
>
> Jake: Well, don't solve everything. (A)_____
>
> _____

서답형

08 위 대화의 빈칸 (A)에 들어갈 말을 보기에 주어진 단어를 모두 배열하여 완성하시오.

┌─ 보기 ┐
you / should / ones / you / got / the / wrong / think / focus / I / on
└─────────┘

➡ _____

중요

09 위 대화의 밑줄 친 (a)와 바꾸어 쓸 수 없는 것은?

① What should I do?
② Would you give me some tips?
③ Would you advise me?
④ Will you give me a hint as to what I should do?
⑤ What can I do for you?

[10~12] 다음 대화를 읽고 물음에 답하시오.

> Eric: Ms. Morris, I just can't stop ⓐto play computer games. What should I do?
>
> Ms. Morris: Well, (A)why don't you use a special program?(how) When you set a time ⓑlimit, the computer ⓒshuts down at that time.
>
> Eric: Oh, that's a good idea.
>
> Ms. Morris: And I think you should move the computer ⓓout of your room and ⓔinto the living room.
>
> Eric: I think I should. I'll try that. Thank you for the advice, Ms. Morris.

서답형

10 위 대화의 밑줄 친 ⓐ~ⓔ 중 대화의 흐름상 어색한 것을 찾아 바르게 고치시오.

➡ _____

서답형

11 위 대화의 밑줄 친 (A)와 의미가 같도록 주어진 단어를 사용하여 다시 쓰시오.

➡ _____

12 위 대화의 내용과 일치하지 않는 것은?

① Eric은 컴퓨터 게임을 멈추지 못해 고민이다.
② Ms. Morris는 Eric에게 특별한 프로그램을 사용해 볼 것을 추천한다.
③ 특별한 프로그램은 시간을 정해 두면 컴퓨터가 그 시간에 맞춰 종료된다.
④ Ms. Morris는 Eric이 컴퓨터를 거실에서 그의 방으로 옮길 것을 조언한다.
⑤ Eric은 Ms. Morris의 조언을 실행해 볼 것이다.

[13~14] 다음 대화를 읽고 물음에 답하시오.

> Emily: I was late for class again. I just can't wake up in the morning.
>
> Tom: Do you set an alarm?
>
> Emily: Yeah, but I turn it off and go back to sleep.
>
> Tom: I think you should put it far from your bed. That way, you'll have to get out of bed.

서답형

13 Why was Emily late for class?

➡ _____

서답형

14 Why does Tom advise Emily to put an alarm far from the bed?

➡ _____

[01~03] 다음 대화를 읽고 물음에 답하시오.

Solomon: Hello, (A)you're on the air.

Amy: Hi, Solomon. I'm Amy.

Solomon: Hi, Amy. What's the matter?

Amy: I hate sharing my room with my little sister. She uses my stuff without asking me first. What should I do?

Solomon: Hmm.... I think you should tell her your feelings. And you should also make some rules with your sister.

Amy: Oh, I'll try that. Thanks for the advice.

01 위 대화의 밑줄 친 (A)의 의미를 우리말로 쓰시오.

➡ _____

02 Why doesn't Amy like sharing her room with her little sister?

➡ _____

_____

 위 대화의 내용과 일치하도록 빈칸을 완성하시오.

Amy: I'm so upset with my sister who uses my stuff without asking me first. I hate sharing my room with her.

Solomon: If I were you, I'd _____

_____ .

[04~05] 다음 대화를 읽고 물음에 답하시오.

Sujin: I don't know how to do better in math. Can you give me some advice?

Jake: How do you study for tests?

Sujin: I just solve a lot of problems.

Jake: Well, don't solve everything. I think you should focus on the ones you got wrong.

04 What's the matter with Sujin?

➡ _____

05 What is Jake's advice to do better in math?

➡ _____

06 다음 대화를 읽고 대화의 내용과 일치하도록 다음 표를 완성하시오.

Eric: Ms. Morris, I just can't stop playing computer games. What should I do?

Ms. Morris: Well, why don't you use a special program? When you set a time limit, the computer shuts down at that time.

Eric: Oh, that's a good idea.

Ms. Morris: And I think you should move the computer out of your room and into the living room.

Eric: I think I should. Thank you for the advice, Ms. Morris.

⬇

Student Name	Eric
Date	August 24th
Problem	(A) _____ .
Advice	(1) Use a special program to (B) _____ . (2) Move the computer from (C) _____ to (D) _____ .

Grammar

① 현재완료

- I **have read** 500 books since I was six. 여섯 살 이후로 나는 책을 500권 읽었다.
- My father **has never** been to a grocery store. 나의 아버지는 식료품점에 가 본 적이 없다.

■ 현재완료는 과거의 사건이 현재까지 영향을 미칠 때 사용한다. 'have[has]+p.p.'의 형태로, 부정형은 'have[has] not+p.p.'이며, 의문형은 'Have[Has]+주어+p.p. ~?'로 나타낸다.

- The man **has worked** for the company since 2010. 그 남자는 2010년 이래로 그 회사를 위해 일해 왔다.
- **Have** you ever **been** to China? 너는 중국에 가 본 적 있니?

■ 현재완료는 '완료, 경험, 계속, 결과'의 네 가지 용법으로 쓰인다. 완료 용법은 'just, already, yet'과 같은 부사와 주로 함께 쓰이며, 경험은 'ever, never, once, before' 등과 같은 부사와 함께 쓰인다. 'How long ~?'으로 묻는 질문이나 'for+기간', 'since+특정 시점'은 현재완료의 계속 용법에 속한다. 결과 용법은 특별한 부사와 어울리지 않고 과거에 발생한 사건으로 인하여 현재까지 영향을 미치고 있는 상태를 나타낼 때 결과 용법으로 본다.

- The boy **has drunk** the milk already. 그 소년은 벌써 우유를 마셨다. 〈완료〉
- David **has played** ping-pong for an hour. David는 한 시간 동안 탁구를 쳤다. 〈계속〉
- We **have seen** the program several times. 우리는 그 프로그램을 몇 번 본 적이 있다. 〈경험〉
- The girls **have gone** to Busan. 그 소녀들은 부산에 가고 없다. 〈결과〉

*have[has] been to와 have[has] gone to의 사용에 유의하자. '~에 가 본 적이 있다'는 경험은 have[has] been to로 표현하고, '~에 가고 없다'는 결과는 have[has] gone to로 표현한다.

■ 현재완료는 과거의 일이 현재까지 영향을 미칠 때 쓰는 시제이므로 과거를 나타내는 어구인 yesterday, last year, ~ ago 등과 함께 쓸 수 없다.

- Jane has met Tom yesterday. (X)
- Jane met Tom yesterday.　　(○)

핵심 Check

1. 다음 우리말과 일치하도록 빈칸에 알맞은 말을 쓰시오.

(1) Jason은 세 시간 동안 공부하고 있다.

➡ Jason ＿＿＿＿ ＿＿＿＿ for three hours.

(2) 그 비행기는 막 도착했다.

➡ The plane ＿＿＿＿ just ＿＿＿＿.

(3) 나는 어제 이후로 아무것도 하지 않았다.

➡ I ＿＿＿＿ ＿＿＿＿ nothing since yesterday.

② 목적격 관계대명사

- There is a man **whom** my sister likes. 내 여동생이 좋아하는 남자가 있어.
- The flowers **which** you take care of are beautiful. 네가 돌보는 꽃들은 아름다워.

■ 관계대명사는 두 개의 문장을 하나로 이어주는 접속사 역할을 하면서 동시에 (대)명사 역할을 한다. 전치사의 목적어 혹은 동사의 목적어였던 (대)명사를 목적격 관계대명사로 만들어 문장을 하나로 이어준다.

- This is the book **that** Ms. Han recommended. 〈동사의 목적어〉
  이것이 한 선생님이 추천하신 책이다.

- He is the only friend **that** I can rely on. 〈전치사의 목적어〉
  그는 내가 의지할 수 있는 유일한 친구이다.

■ 목적격 관계대명사 who(m), which는 that으로 대체할 수 있으며, 생략 가능하다. 관계대명사가 전치사의 목적어로 사용된 경우 전치사는 동사 뒤에 그대로 두거나, 전치사를 관계대명사 앞으로 보낼 수 있다. 단, 전치사를 관계대명사 앞으로 보낸 경우 관계대명사 that을 쓸 수 없고 관계대명사를 생략할 수 없음에 유의한다.

- Do you konw the woman (**who/whom/that**) Maria is talking to? 너는 Maria가 대화하고 있는 여자를 아니?

- The bag (**which/that**) he brought the other day smells bad. 그가 지난번에 가져온 가방에서 나쁜 냄새가 난다.

- I have the wallet (**which/that**) Tom was looking **for**. Tom이 찾던 지갑을 내가 가지고 있어.
  = I have the wallet **for which** Tom was looking.

- The subject (**which/that**) I am interested **in** is English. 내가 흥미를 느끼는 과목은 영어이다.
  = The subject **in which** I am interested is English.

핵심 Check

2. 다음 우리말과 일치하도록 빈칸에 알맞은 말을 쓰시오.

(1) 네가 만든 그 샌드위치는 맛있어 보인다.
➡ The sandwich _____ _____ _____ looks delicious.

(2) 이것은 그가 나에게 사 준 목걸이야.
➡ This is the necklace _____ _____ _____ for me.

(3) Helen이 함께 온 저 남자를 아니?
➡ Do you know the man _____ _____ _____ _____?

01 다음 문장에서 어법상 <u>어색한</u> 부분을 바르게 고쳐 쓰시오.

(1) When have you left the place?

_____ ➡ _____

(2) Mr. Pang who the children love teach how to swim to them.

_____ ➡ _____

(3) I did this work for a long time until now. So I know about the work well.

_____ ➡ _____

(4) The knife whom you used is very sharp.

_____ ➡ _____

02 적절한 관계사를 이용하여 다음 두 문장을 하나의 문장으로 쓰시오.

star in: ~에서 주연을 맡다

(1) Have you found the pen? You lost it.

➡ _____

(2) Did she take the class? James taught the class.

➡ _____

(3) I want to meet the boy. You speak highly of him.

➡ _____

(4) Molly likes the movie. Tom Cruise starred in the movie.

➡ _____

03 주어진 어구를 바르게 배열하여 다음 우리말을 영어로 쓰시오. 필요하다면 단어를 추가하거나 변형하시오.

(1) 나는 아직 점심을 다 먹지 않았다. (yet / finished / lunch / I / my / haven't)

➡ _____

(2) 그녀는 그 교회에 두 번 가봤어. (two / she / times / been / has / the church)

➡ _____

(3) 나는 내가 가지고 있던 모든 돈을 그녀에게 주었다. (that / I / I / had / all the money / her / gave)

➡ _____

(4) 우리가 제출한 보고서는 어디에 있나요? (in / where / hand / is / which / we / the report)

➡ _____

01 다음 중 빈칸에 들어갈 말로 가장 적절한 것은?

> A: Have you seen her lately?
> B: _____

① Yes, I do. ② No, I don't.
③ Yes, I saw. ④ Yes, I have.
⑤ No, I have.

02 다음 우리말을 영어로 바르게 옮긴 것은?

> 너는 Jamie가 쓴 책을 읽고 싶니?

① Have you wanted to read the book which Jamie has written?
② Do you want to the book that Jamie was writing?
③ Did you wrote the book that Jamie read?
④ Did you read the book that Jamie wrote?
⑤ Do you want to read the book which Jamie wrote?

03 다음 중 빈칸에 들어갈 말로 가장 적절한 것은?

> Tyler has studied Economy _____.

① last year ② the other day
③ since yesterday ④ last week
⑤ a year ago

서답형

04 다음 두 문장을 한 문장으로 쓸 때 빈칸을 완성하시오.

> • I like the dress.
> • You want to buy the dress.

➡ I _____.

05 다음 우리말을 영어로 바르게 옮기지 않은 것은?

① 네가 악수한 그 소년은 누구니?
→ Who is the boy that you shook hands with?
② 나는 그녀를 한 번 만난 적 있어.
→ I have met her once.
③ 그는 그녀를 3년 동안 알아왔습니다.
→ He has known her for three years.
④ 그들은 네가 만든 기계를 좋아해.
→ They like the machine that you made.
⑤ 너는 서울에 가 본 적이 있니?
→ Have you ever gone to Seoul?

06 다음 중 어법상 바르지 않은 것은?

① Katherine likes the music which her friends don't like.
② Kelly has met Julian a few minutes ago.
③ Can you tell me the story that Tom told you?
④ Have you eaten the food before?
⑤ Did you buy the pants that you wanted to buy?

07 다음 중 빈칸에 들어갈 말로 가장 적절한 것은?

> Jina has paid the bill _____ five years.

① since ② already ③ for
④ just ⑤ almost

서답형

08 다음 우리말을 영어로 쓸 때 빈칸에 알맞은 말을 세 단어로 쓰시오.

> 그들은 네가 파티에 초대한 사람들이니?
> ➡ Are they the people _____
>   to the party?

중요

09 다음 빈칸에 들어갈 말이 바르게 짝지어진 것은?

> • _____ you ever met a famous person like Justin Bieber?
> • Brad _____ to Italy. He is enjoying his vacation.

① Have – was   ② Have – has gone
③ Did – have been   ④ Did – went
⑤ Did – want to go

10 다음 두 문장을 하나의 문장으로 바르게 표현한 것은?

> They began to talk about the subject two hours ago. They still talk about it.

① They talked about the subject two hours ago.
② They talked about the subject until now.
③ They have talked about the subject since two hours.
④ They have talked about the subject for two hours.
⑤ They have just talked about the subject.

서답형

11 다음 두 문장을 하나의 문장으로 쓰시오.

> • Tell me about the people.
> • You met them in the hospital.

➡ _____
  _____

12 다음 중 현재완료의 용법이 다른 하나는?

① They have just finished their work.
② He has already signed up for the class.
③ Jena has seen the menu for 20 minutes.
④ Melissa has not passed the test yet.
⑤ Brad has checked the schedule already.

중요

13 다음 중 밑줄 친 부분을 생략할 수 없는 것은?

① The boys that you are looking at are my children.
② The cat that is resting on the chair looks so cute.
③ My car was made in the company that Paul works for.
④ The candy that the girl is eating was made by me.
⑤ The cup that Amelia likes to use is on the shelf.

14 다음 빈칸에 가장 적절한 말을 고르시오.

> Look at the man and the dog _____ are walking together.

① which   ② who   ③ what
④ that   ⑤ whom

서답형

15 주어진 어구를 바르게 배열하여 다음 우리말을 영어로 쓰시오.

> 네가 나에게 보낸 그 편지는 아직 도착하지 않았어.
> (yet / the letter / has / that / not / to me / arrived / sent / you)

➡ _____

16 (A)~(C)에서 어법상 옳은 것끼리 바르게 짝지어진 것은?

> • Ted has used the computer (A)[for / since] he was a high school student.
> • What (B)[did you do / have you done] last weekend?
> • Clara (C)[has painted / painted] the wall twice until now.

① for – did you do – has painted

② for – did you do – painted

③ for – have you done – has painted

④ since – did you do – has painted

⑤ since – have you done – painted

17 다음 중 밑줄 친 부분의 쓰임이 <u>다른</u> 하나는?

① Do you know the girl <u>that</u> is making something with clay?

② The fact <u>that</u> is well known to us is that she is a great cook.

③ I don't know about the party <u>that</u> was planned by Jane.

④ The man likes to see the movie <u>that</u> was filmed at Sydney.

⑤ I don't care about the information <u>that</u> Sarah told us.

18 다음 중 빈칸에 들어갈 말이 바르게 짝지어진 것은?

> The company considers publishing a book _____ David _____ three years ago.

① who – has written

② whose – wrote

③ which – wrote

④ that – has wrote

⑤ that – is writing

서답형

19 다음 주어진 단어를 활용하여 우리말을 영어로 쓰시오.

> 전에 인도에 가 본 적이 있나요? (ever)

➡ _____

20 다음 중 어법상 바르지 <u>않은</u> 것은?

① Maria has learned math for three years.

② Can you give me back the pen that you borrowed from me?

③ Mina has had lunch a few minutes ago.

④ I have made my own jacket once.

⑤ The plants that you have just watered look beautiful.

서답형

21 다음 두 문장을 하나의 문장으로 쓰시오.

> I lost my cap. And I still don't have it.

➡ _____

서답형

22 다음 두 문장을 하나의 문장으로 쓰시오.

> • The I-pad was my birthday present.
> • I got it from my father.

➡ _____

_____

서답형

23 주어진 단어를 바르게 배열하여 문장을 완성하시오.

> The toys (with / that / play / the children) look dirty.

➡ _____

01 주어진 단어를 이용하여 다음 두 문장을 하나의 문장으로 표현하시오.

> It was sunny yesterday. It is still sunny today. (since)

➡ _____

02 다음 우리말에 맞도록 빈칸에 알맞은 말을 써서 문장을 완성하시오.

> 네가 마시고 있는 그 차 어때?
> ➡ How do you like the tea _____
> _____ _____ _____?

03 주어진 단어를 어법에 맞게 빈칸에 각각 쓰시오.

> | ago   for   since |
>
> • Julia has known Karl _____ 2015.
> • We have discussed the problem _____ a couple of hours.
> • Tom and Jane got married sixteen years _____.
> • We have known each other _____ we were young.

04 주어진 어구를 바르게 배열하여 다음 우리말을 영어로 쓰시오.

> 사람들이 찾던 그 실종 소년이 어젯밤 집으로 왔습니다.
> (were / the missing boy / whom / looking / people / for / last night / home / came)

➡ _____

_____

05 다음 대화의 빈칸에 알맞은 말을 쓰시오.

> **A:** How long _____ _____ _____ in this house?
> **B:** We moved into this house two years _____. So we _____ _____ in this house _____ two years.

06 자연스러운 문장이 되도록 관계대명사를 이용하여 하나의 문장으로 연결하시오. that은 사용하지 마시오.

> • What is the name of the man?
> • This is the car.
> • Where is the red sweater?

> • My friend hopes to buy it someday.
> • I put it in my drawer.
> • You want to meet him.

➡ (1) _____

_____

(2) _____

_____

(3) _____

_____

07 다음 우리말을 영어로 쓰시오.

> **A:** 너는 전에 코끼리를 본 적이 있니?
> **B:** 아니, 본 적 없어.

➡ _____

➡ _____

08 다음 문장에서 어법상 틀린 것을 고쳐 문장을 다시 쓰시오.

(1) Have you thrown a party for her yesterday?

➡ _____

(2) I have gone to Boston many times.

➡ _____

(3) The sandwich who he made for us is very delicious.

➡ _____

_____

09 다음 상황을 읽고 한 문장으로 표현하시오.

> Yesterday, Kevin lost his umbrella. So he doesn't have it now.

➡ _____

10 적절한 관계사를 이용하여 다음 두 문장을 한 문장으로 쓸 때 빈칸을 완성하시오.

(1) There isn't much information. You can get it.
➡ There _____ .

(2) I gave Tim the pants. He always liked them.
➡ I _____ .

(3) Is he the man? You respect him very much.
➡ Is _____ ?

11 다음 우리말을 8 단어로 이루어진 영어 문장으로 쓰시오.

> 이것은 우리 아빠가 만드신 책상이야.

➡ _____

12 다음 문장에서 생략 가능한 것을 생략하여 문장을 다시 쓰시오.

(1) The tennis game that he played yesterday was great.

➡ _____

(2) Do you know the boy who is talking with your sister?

➡ _____

(3) The subject which Jane is interested in is history and Korean.

➡ _____

13 다음 빈칸에 알맞은 말을 4 단어로 쓰시오.

> 그녀는 좋아하지 않는 음식에는 손도 대지 않는다.
> ➡ She never touches the food _____
> _____ .

14 다음 상황을 읽고 빈칸에 알맞은 말을 쓰시오.

> I lost my shoes last week. I still don't have them. In other words, I _____ _____ my shoes.

15 우리말에 맞게 빈칸에 알맞은 말을 세 단어로 쓰시오.

> 네가 참석한 파티에 얼마나 많은 사람들이 있었니?
> = How many people were there at the party _____ _____ _____ ?

Reading

Voices in Our Mind

Bella is 15 years old this year and these days her feelings are going up
요즘에

and down. Today, she looks down. Let's listen to Bella's feelings and
우울한

find out why.
= why she looks down today

Day 1

Anger: What a day! I can't believe Jenny yelled at Bella after the
정말 끔찍한 날이야!

school play.

Sadness: Well, that's because Bella forgot her lines on stage.
that's because+원인: 그것은 ~이기 때문이다

Anger: Jenny pointed out the mistake that Bella made. How could she
목적격 관계대명사 (which로 대체 가능)

do that in front of everyone?
'Jenny pointed out the mistake that Bella made'를 가리킴

Joy: But I'm sure Jenny did not mean to hurt Bella. They have been
mean to V: V하는 것을 의도하다   Jenny와 Bella가 초등학교 때부터 지금까지 쭉 가장 친한 친구였다는 의미

best friends since elementary school. Remember?

Anger: That's what I'm saying. A true friend would never put Bella
관계대명사(~하는 것)   If가 없는 가정문에서 주어가 if절을 대신하고 있다.(= If she were a true friend. she)

down like that.
그렇게

Fear: I'm worried that they are not going to be friends anymore.
not ~ anymore: 더 이상 ~ 않다(= no longer)

Joy: Come on, Fear. Don't go too far. We'll see.
도를 넘다   알다

단어	뜻
up and down	좋다가 나쁘다가 하는
yell	소리치다, 소리 지르다
line	(연극, 영화의) 대사
point out	지적하다
make a mistake	실수하다
in front of	~ 앞에서
mean	의도하다, 작정하다
hurt	다치게 하다, 아프게 하다
since	~부터, ~ 이후
put ~ down	~을 깎아내리다

 확인문제

● 다음 문장이 본문의 내용과 일치하면 T, 일치하지 않으면 F를 쓰시오.

1 Bella's feelings are going up and down lately. ☐

2 Jenny yelled at Bella during the school play. ☐

3 Bella couldn't remember her lines on stage. ☐

4 Bella shouted at Jenny in front of others. ☐

5 Bella has known Jenny since elementary school. ☐

Day 2

Anger: I can't forgive Jenny. She didn't say a word to Bella.

Fear: Jenny didn't even look at her. Jenny has never been this cold
　　　　　 심지어　　　　　　　　　　　　　 과거부터 여태껏 이렇게 차가웠던 적이 없었다는 의미의 현재완료 – '경험'

　　　 before.

Sadness: Bella ate alone during lunch today. Poor Bella!
　　　　　　　　　　　　　　　　　　　　　　　 가엾은

Joy: Jenny is Bella's best friend. I'm sure there is a reason that we
　　　　　　　　　　　　　　　　　　　　　　　 목적격 관계대명사(which 대체 가능)

　　　 don't know about.

Anger: I can't stand this any longer. Bella should just go and tell her
　　　　　　　 not ~ any longer: 더 이상 ~ 않다(= no longer)

　　　 about her feelings.

Fear: I don't want Bella to be hurt again. She should let it go.
　　　　　　 want+목적어+to부정사: 목적어가 V하는 것을 원하다　　 그쯤 해 두다. 내버려 두다

Joy: They are good friends. They will work it out.
　　　　　　　　　　　　　　　　　　 └ 해결하다 ┘

Day 3

Joy: Whew! I'm so happy that they are talking again.
　　　　　 I'm so happy that ~: ~하니 참 기쁘다

Anger: Yeah, Bella went to Jenny and talked to her first.

Joy: Jenny didn't avoid Bella on purpose.
　　　　　　　　　　　　　　　 고의로

Sadness: Yeah, Jenny didn't know a way to say sorry.
　　　　　　　　　　　　　　　　 형용사로 쓰인 to부정사로 a way 수식

Fear: I hope Bella doesn't have any more problems like this.
　　　 hope (that): 명사절을 이끄는 접속사 that 생략　　　　　 전치사: ~와 비슷한

Joy: Me, too. But problems are part of growing up. Just like this
　　 나도 그래.　　　　　　　　　　　 동명사: 전치사 of의 목적어　 이번과 꼭 마찬가지로

　　　 time, Bella will face the problems, solve them, and become wiser

　　　 in the end.

확인문제

● 다음 문장이 본문의 내용과 일치하면 T, 일치하지 <u>않으면</u> F를 쓰시오.

1　Jenny said nothing to Bella on the second day. ☐

2　Jenny was cold towards Bella several times. ☐

3　Anger wants Bella to go to Jenny to talk about her feelings. ☐

4　Fear thinks Bella needs to be hurt. ☐

5　Bella and Jenny finally made up. ☐

6　Fear wants Bella not to have any more problems. ☐

---

forgive: 용서하다
alone: 홀로, 혼자
reason: 이유, 까닭
stand: 참다, 견디다
let it go: 그쯤 해 두다, 내버려 두다
work out: 해결하다
avoid: 피하다
on purpose: 고의로, 일부러
grow up: 성장하다
face a problem: 문제에 직면하다
in the end: 결국, 마침내

● 우리말을 참고하여 빈칸에 알맞은 말을 쓰시오.

1 Bella is 15 _____ _____ this year and _____ _____ her feelings are _____ _____ _____ _____.

2 Today, she _____ _____.

3 Let's listen to Bella's _____ and _____ _____ _____.

Day 1

4 Anger: _____ _____ _____! I can't believe Jenny _____ _____ Bella _____ the school play.

5 Sadness: Well, that's _____ Bella _____ her _____ on stage.

6 Anger: Jenny pointed out the mistake _____ _____ _____.

7 How _____ she do that _____ _____ everyone?

8 Joy: But I'm sure Jenny _____ _____ _____ Bella.

9 They _____ _____ best friends _____ elementary school. Remember?

10 Anger: That's _____ I'm _____.

11 A true friend _____ _____ _____ Bella down like that.

12 Fear: I'm worried _____ they are _____ _____ _____ _____ _____ anymore.

13 Joy: Come on, Fear. Don't go _____ _____. We'll _____.

Day 2

14 Anger: I can't _____ Jenny. She didn't _____ _____ _____ to Bella.

15 Fear: Jenny didn't _____ _____ _____ her.

1 Bella는 올해 15세이고 요즘 그 애의 기분은 좋다가 안 좋다가 한다.

2 오늘 그 애는 우울해 보인다.

3 Bella의 감정에 귀 기울여 보고 그 이유를 알아보자.

Day 1

4 Anger: 정말 끔찍한 하루야! 학교 연극이 끝난 후 Jenny 가 Bella에게 소리를 지르다 니 믿을 수가 없어.

5 Sadness: 글쎄, 그건 Bella가 무대에서 그녀의 대사를 잊 어버렸기 때문이잖아.

6 Anger: Jenny는 Bella가 저지 른 실수를 지적했잖아.

7 어떻게 모든 사람 앞에서 그렇 게 할 수가 있니?

8 Joy: 하지만 난 Jenny가 Bella 에게 상처를 주려고 했던 건 아니었다고 확신해.

9 그들은 초등학교 때부터 가장 친한 친구였잖아. 기억하지?

10 Anger: 내 말이 바로 그거야.

11 진정한 친구라면 절대로 그런 식으로 Bella를 깎아내리지 않 을 거야.

12 Fear: 나는 그들이 더 이상 친구 로 지내지 않을까봐 걱정돼.

13 Joy: 자, Fear. 너무 극단적으로 생각하지 마. 곧 알게 되겠지.

Day 2

14 Anger: 난 Jenny를 용서할 수 없어. 그 애는 Bella에게 한마디도 말을 안 했어.

15 Fear: Jenny는 심지어 Bella를 쳐 다 보지도 않았어.

16 Jenny _____ _____ _____ this cold before.

17 Sadness: Bella _____ _____ _____ lunch today. Poor Bella!

18 Joy: Jenny is Bella's _____ _____ .

19 I'm sure there is a reason _____ _____ _____ _____ _____ .

20 Anger: I can't _____ this _____ _____ .

21 Bella should just _____ and _____ her _____ her feelings.

22 Fear: I don't want Bella _____ _____ _____ again.

23 She should _____ _____ _____ .

24 Joy: They are good friends. They will _____ _____ .

Day 3

25 Joy: Whew! I'm so happy _____ they _____ _____ again.

26 Anger: Yeah, Bella went to Jenny and _____ _____ first.

27 Joy: Jenny didn't _____ Bella _____ _____ .

28 Sadness: Yeah, Jenny didn't know _____ _____ _____ sorry.

29 Fear: I hope Bella doesn't have _____ _____ _____ like this.

30 Joy: Me, too. But problems are _____ _____ _____ _____ .

31 _____ _____ this time, Bella will _____ the problems, _____ _____ , and become _____ in the end.

16 Jenny가 전에 이렇게 차가웠던 적이 없었어.

17 Sadness: Bella는 오늘 점심시간에 혼자 밥을 먹었잖아. 가엾은 Bella!

18 Joy: Jenny는 Bella의 가장 친한 친구야.

19 나는 우리가 모르는 어떤 이유가 있다고 확신해.

20 Anger: 나는 더 이상 이 상황을 못 참아.

21 Bella는 일단 가서 Jenny에게 자신의 감정을 말해야 해.

22 Fear: 나는 Bella가 또다시 상처받는 걸 원하지 않아.

23 그 애는 그냥 내버려 두어야 해.

24 Joy: 그 애들은 좋은 친구야. 그 애들이 잘 해낼 거야.

Day 3

25 Joy: 휴! 나는 그 애들이 다시 이야기하게 되어 무척 기뻐.

26 Anger: 그래, Bella가 Jenny에게 가서 그 애에게 먼저 말을 걸었지.

27 Joy: Jenny는 일부러 Bella를 피한 게 아니었어.

28 Sadness: 맞아, Jenny는 사과하는 방법을 몰랐던 거야.

29 Fear: 나는 Bella에게 이번과 같은 문제가 더 이상 없기를 바라.

30 Joy: 나도 그래. 하지만 문제들은 성장의 일부야.

31 이번과 꼭 마찬가지로 Bella는 문제들에 직면하게 될 거고, 그것들을 해결할 거고, 그리고 결국 더 현명해질 거야.

● 우리말을 참고하여 본문을 영작하시오.

1 Bella는 올해 15세이고 요즘 그 애의 기분은 좋다가 안 좋다가 한다.

➡ _____

2 오늘 그 애는 우울해 보인다.

➡ _____

3 Bella의 감정에 귀 기울여 보고 그 이유를 알아보자.

➡ _____

Day 1

4 Anger: 정말 끔찍한 하루야! 학교 연극이 끝난 후 Jenny가 Bella에게 소리를 지르다니 믿을 수가 없어.

➡ _____

5 Sadness: 글쎄, 그건 Bella가 무대에서 그녀의 대사를 잊어버렸기 때문이잖아.

➡ _____

6 Anger: Jenny는 Bella가 저지른 실수를 지적했잖아.

➡ _____

7 어떻게 모든 사람 앞에서 그렇게 할 수가 있니?

➡ _____

8 Joy: 하지만 난 Jenny가 Bella에게 상처를 주려고 했던 건 아니었다고 확신해.

➡ _____

9 그들은 초등학교 때부터 가장 친한 친구였잖아. 기억하지?

➡ _____

10 Anger: 내 말이 바로 그거야.

➡ _____

11 진정한 친구라면 절대로 그런 식으로 Bella를 깎아내리지 않을 거야.

➡ _____

12 Fear: 나는 그들이 더 이상 친구로 지내지 않을까봐 걱정돼.

➡ _____

13 Joy: 자, Fear. 너무 극단적으로 생각하지 마. 곧 알게 되겠지.

➡ _____

Day 2

14 Anger: 난 Jenny를 용서할 수 없어. 그 애는 Bella에게 한마디도 말을 안 했어.

➡ _____

15 Fear: Jenny는 심지어 Bella를 쳐다보지도 않았어.

➡ _____

16 Jenny가 전에 이렇게 차가웠던 적이 없었어.

⇒ _____

17 Sadness: Bella는 오늘 점심시간에 혼자 밥을 먹었잖아. 가엾은 Bella!

⇒ _____

18 Joy: Jenny는 Bella의 가장 친한 친구야.

⇒ _____

19 나는 우리가 모르는 어떤 이유가 있다고 확신해.

⇒ _____

20 Anger: 나는 더 이상 이 상황을 못 참아.

⇒ _____

21 Bella는 일단 가서 Jenny에게 자신의 감정을 말해야 해.

⇒ _____

22 Fear: 나는 Bella가 또다시 상처받는 걸 원하지 않아.

⇒ _____

23 그 애는 그냥 내버려 두어야 해.

⇒ _____

24 Joy: 그 애들은 좋은 친구야. 그 애들이 잘 해낼 거야.

⇒ _____

Day 3

25 Joy: 휴! 나는 그 애들이 다시 이야기하게 되어 무척 기뻐.

⇒ _____

26 Anger: 그래, Bella가 Jenny에게 가서 그 애에게 먼저 말을 걸었지.

⇒ _____

27 Joy: Jenny는 일부러 Bella를 피한 게 아니었어.

⇒ _____

28 Sadness: 맞아, Jenny는 사과하는 방법을 몰랐던 거야.

⇒ _____

29 Fear: 나는 Bella에게 이번과 같은 문제가 더 이상 없기를 바라.

⇒ _____

30 Joy: 나도 그래. 하지만 문제들은 성장의 일부야.

⇒ _____

31 이번과 꼭 마찬가지로 Bella는 문제들에 직면하게 될 거고, 그것들을 해결할 거고, 그리고 결국 더 현명해질 거야.

⇒ _____

[01~06] 다음 글을 읽고 물음에 답하시오.

Bella is 15 years old this year and these days her feelings are going up and down. Today, she looks (A)_____. Let's listen to Bella's feelings and find out why.

Day 1

Anger: What a day! I can't believe Jenny yelled at Bella after the school play.

Sadness: Well, that's because Bella forgot her lines on stage.

Anger: Jenny pointed out the mistake (B)_____ Bella made. How could she do (C)that in front of everyone?

Joy: But I'm sure Jenny did not mean to hurt Bella. They have been best friends (D)_____ elementary school. Remember?

Anger: That's what I'm saying. A true friend would never put Bella down like that.

Fear: I'm worried that they are not going to be friends anymore.

Joy: Come on, Fear. Don't go too far. We'll see.

서답형

01 빈칸 (A)에 알맞은 말을 위 글에서 찾아 쓰시오.

➡ _____

02 다음 중 빈칸 (B)에 들어갈 말로 적절한 것을 모두 고르시오.

① which   ② that   ③ who
④ what   ⑤ whose

서답형

03 밑줄 친 (C)가 의미하는 것을 우리말로 쓰시오.

➡ _____

04 다음 중 빈칸 (D)에 들어갈 말과 다른 말이 들어가는 것은?

① We have known you _____ you were a baby.
② I have studied English _____ 2010.
③ You have sung the same song _____ an hour.
④ They have played the computer game _____ 5 o'clock.
⑤ He has exercised regularly _____ he was in college.

05 다음 중 위 글을 읽고 답할 수 없는 것은?

① How old is Bella?
② How are Bella's feelings these days?
③ What did Jenny do to Bella today?
④ Why did Bella forget her lines on stage?
⑤ What is Joy sure about?

서답형

다음 질문의 답을 위 글에서 찾아 쓰시오.

Q: Why did Jenny yelled at Bella after the school play?

➡ _____

[07~10] 다음 글을 읽고 물음에 답하시오.

Anger: I can't forgive Jenny. She didn't say a word to Bella.

Fear: Jenny didn't even look at ⓐher. (A) Jenny has never been this cold before.

Sadness: Bella ate alone during lunch today. Poor Bella!

Joy: Jenny is ⓑher best friend. I'm sure there is a reason that we don't know about.

Anger: I can't stand this any longer. Bella should just go and tell ⓒher about ⓓher feelings.

Fear: I don't want ⓔher to be hurt again. She should let it go.

Joy: They are good friends. They will work it out.

07 다음 중 밑줄 친 (A)에서 쓰인 현재완료와 그 쓰임이 같은 것은?

① We have just left the restaurant.

② How long have you been here?

③ Helen has never met the mailman.

④ I have lost it, so I don't know where it is.

⑤ Has he finished his project yet?

08 밑줄 친 ⓐ~ⓔ에서 지칭하는 바가 다른 하나는?

① ⓐ　② ⓑ　③ ⓒ　④ ⓓ　⑤ ⓔ

09 다음 중 위 글의 내용과 일치하지 않는 것은?

① Jenny said nothing to Bella.

② Jenny didn't look at Bella even once.

③ Anger doesn't want to bear the situation.

④ Fear thinks Bella should let Jenny go.

⑤ Joy is hopeful about Jenny and Bella.

서답형
10 다음과 같이 풀이되는 말을 위 글에서 찾아 쓰시오.

> to stop being angry with someone and stop blaming

➡ _____

[11~14] 다음 글을 읽고 물음에 답하시오.

Joy: Whew! I'm so happy that they are talking again.

Anger: Yeah, Bella went to Jenny and talked to her first.

Joy: Jenny didn't avoid Bella (A)____ purpose.

Sadness: Yeah, Jenny didn't know a way to say sorry.

Fear: I hope Bella doesn't have any more problems like this.

Joy: Me, too. But problems are (B)성장의 일부. Just like this time, Bella will face the problems, solve them, and become wiser (C)in the end.

중요
11 다음 중 빈칸 (A)에 들어갈 말과 같은 말이 들어가는 것은?

① She is not satisfied _____ the result.

② Don't give _____. You can do it.

③ She will take part _____ the race.

④ He came up _____ a great idea.

⑤ I'm cold. Can you turn _____ the heater?

서답형
12 밑줄 친 우리말 (B)를 영어로 쓰시오. (4단어)

➡ _____

13 다음 중 밑줄 친 (C)를 대신할 수 있는 것은?

① at last　② suddenly

③ fortunately　④ lastly

⑤ lately

서답형
14 Write the reason why Joy is so happy. Fill in the blank with six words.

➡ Joy is happy because _____

_____

[15~19] 다음 글을 읽고 물음에 답하시오.

Bella is 15 years old this year and these days her feelings are going up and down. Today, she looks down. Let's (A)[listen / listen to] Bella's feelings and find out why.

Day 1

Anger: What a day! I can't believe Jenny yelled at Bella after the school play.

Sadness: Well, (B)[that's because / that's why] Bella forgot her ⓐlines on stage.

Anger: Jenny pointed out the mistake that Bella made. How could she do that in front of everyone?

Joy: But I'm sure Jenny did not mean to hurt Bella. They (C)[were / have been] best friends since elementary school. Remember?

Anger: That's what I'm saying. A true friend would never put Bella down like that.

Fear: I'm worried that they are not going to be friends anymore.

Joy: Come on, Fear. Don't go too far. We'll see.

15 (A)~(C)에서 어법상 옳은 것끼리 바르게 짝지은 것은?

① listen – that's because - were
② listen – that's why – were
③ listen – that's because – have been
④ listen to – that's because – have been
⑤ listen to – that's why – have been

서답형

According to the passage, how does Bella feel these days?

➡ _____

서답형

17 What is Fear worried about? Answer in English with a full sentence.

➡ _____

18 다음 중 밑줄 친 ⓐ를 풀이한 말로 가장 적절한 것은?

① a long thin mark which is drawn on a surface
② a line of written words, for example in a play or film
③ a long thin mark that appears on someone's skin as they grow older
④ the edge, outline, or shape of something
⑤ a row of people or things next to each other or behind each other

19 다음 중 위 글의 내용과 일치하지 않는 것은?

① Bella feels depressed today.
② Jenny shouted at Bella.
③ Joy is sure that Jenny intended to hurt Bella.
④ Jenny pointed out Bella's mistake in front of everyone.
⑤ Bella made a mistake on stage.

[20~23] 다음 글을 읽고 물음에 답하시오.

Anger: I can't forgive Jenny. She didn't say a word to Bella.

Fear: Jenny didn't even look at her. Jenny has never been this cold before.

Sadness: Bella ate alone during lunch today. Poor Bella!

Joy: Jenny is Bella's best friend. I'm sure there is a reason (A)that we don't know about.

Anger: I can't stand this any longer. Bella should just go and tell her about her feelings.

Fear: I don't want Bella to be hurt again. She should let it go.

Joy: They are good friends. They will work it out.

20 다음 중 밑줄 친 (A)와 쓰임이 다른 하나는?

① The cheese that you ate is not mine.

② People that participate in the game look happy.

③ The car that he wants to sell is a little old.

④ I will pay you back the money that you lent to me.

⑤ The news that he won first prize is true.

서답형

21 글의 내용에 맞게 빈칸에 알맞은 말을 쓰시오.

Sadness feels sorry for Bella because
_____.

서답형

22 What does Anger want Bella to do about her problem? Answer in English with a full sentence.

➡ _____
_____

23 다음 중 글의 내용과 일치하는 것은?

① Fear doesn't want to bear the situation.

② Fear is afraid that Bella will be hurt again.

③ Joy thinks Bella has to find another good friend.

④ Anger is upset by the fact that Bella ate alone.

⑤ Sadness wants Bella to tell her feelings.

[24~27] 다음 글을 읽고 물음에 답하시오.

Day 3

Joy: Whew! I'm so ⓐhappy that they are talking again.

Anger: Yeah, Bella went to Jenny and talked to her first.

Joy: Jenny didn't ⓑavoid Bella on purpose.

Sadness: Yeah, Jenny didn't know a way to say ⓒsorry.

Fear: I hope Bella doesn't have any more problems like (A)this.

Joy: Me, too. But problems are part of growing up. Just like this time, Bella will ⓓavoid the problems, ⓔsolve them, and become wiser in the end.

24 밑줄 친 ⓐ~ⓔ 중 글의 흐름상 어색한 것은?

① ⓐ   ② ⓑ   ③ ⓒ   ④ ⓓ   ⑤ ⓔ

중요

25 밑줄 친 (A)가 의미하는 것으로 가장 적절한 것은?

① Bella가 Jenny에게 화를 낸 것

② Jenny와 Bella가 서로 이야기하지 않는 것

③ Jenny가 Bella에게 사과하지 않은 것

④ Bella가 Jenny에게 먼저 다가간 것

⑤ Bella가 Jenny를 일부러 피한 것

서답형

26 글의 내용에 맞게 다음 빈칸에 알맞은 말을 쓰시오.

According to Joy, Bella will become
_____ by solving problems with Jenny.

서답형

27 다음은 Jenny에게 Bella가 한 말이다. 빈칸에 알맞은 말을 쓰시오.

We _____ _____ _____ to each other for two days. Now I want to solve the problem between us.

[01~05] 다음 글을 읽고, 물음에 답하시오.

Bella is 15 years old this year and these days her feelings are going up and down. Today, she looks down. Let's listen to Bella's feelings and find out (A)why.

Day 1

Anger: What a day! I can't believe Jenny yelled at Bella after the school play.

Sadness: Well, that's because Bella forgot her lines on stage.

Anger: (B)Jenny pointed out the mistake that Bella made. How could she do that in front of everyone?

Joy: But I'm sure Jenny did not mean to hurt Bella. (C)They became best friends in elementary school. They are still best friends. Remember?

Anger: That's what I'm saying. A true friend would never put Bella down like that.

Fear: I'm worried that they are not going to be friends anymore.

Joy: Come on, Fear. Don't go too far. We'll see.

01 밑줄 친 (A)가 의미하는 것을 완전한 문장으로 쓰시오.

➡ _____

02 밑줄 친 (B)를 두 문장으로 나누어 쓰시오.

➡ _____

➡ _____

03 밑줄 친 문장 (C)를 하나의 문장으로 쓰시오.

➡ _____

04 What mistake did Bella make? Answer in English with a full sentence.

➡ _____

05 다음 물음에 완진한 문징의 영어로 답하시오.

Q: What did Jenny do to Bella after the school play?

➡ _____

[06~08] 다음 글을 읽고 물음에 답하시오.

Day 2

Anger: I can't forgive Jenny. She didn't say a word to Bella.

Fear: Jenny didn't even look at her. Jenny has never been this cold before.

Sadness: Bella ate alone during lunch today. Poor Bella!

Joy: Jenny is Bella's best friend. I'm sure there is a reason that we don't know about.

Anger: I can't stand this any longer. Bella should just go and tell her about her feelings.

Fear: I don't want Bella to be hurt again. She should let it go.

Joy: They are good friends. They will work it out.

06 What did Jenny do to Bella on the second day? Answer in English with a full sentence.

➡ _____

07 위 글의 표현을 이용하여 다음 우리말을 영어로 쓰시오.

> 나는 전에 나의 가장 친한 친구를 용서해 본 적이 있다.

➡ _____

08 다음 물음에 'It's because'를 사용하여 답하시오.

> Q: Why does Sadness say "Poor Bella"?

➡ _____

[09~11] 다음 글을 읽고 물음에 답하시오.

Day 3

Joy: Whew! I'm so happy that they are talking again.

Anger: Yeah, Bella went to Jenny and talked to her first.

Joy: Jenny didn't avoid Bella on purpose.

Sadness: Yeah, Jenny didn't know a way to say sorry.

Fear: I hope Bella doesn't have any more problems like this.

Joy: Me, too. But problems are part of growing up. Just like this time, Bella will face the problems, solve them, and become wiser in the end.

09 다음 질문에 대한 답을 위 글의 내용에 맞게 완성하시오.

> Q: How did Bella make up with Jenny?
> A: _____,
> so they cleared up the misunderstanding.

10 다음 빈칸에 알맞은 말을 쓰시오.

> According to Joy, the problems _____
> _____ _____ help us to become
> wiser.

 11 Fill in the blank with the reason why Jenny avoided Bella.

> Jenny avoided Belly because _____
> _____.

[12~15] 다음 글을 읽고 물음에 답하시오.

Dear Worry Doll,

(A)_____ I'm worried about my terrible math grades. I (B)(have) this problem since last year. I want to do better in math. But when I try to study math, I just can't focus on it. (C)무엇을 해야 할지 모르겠어. I have not had a good night's sleep because of (D)this worry. Can you take my worries away?

 12 다음 두 문장을 하나의 문장으로 바꿔 빈칸 (A)에 쓰시오.

> • I want to tell you a problem.
> • I have a problem.

➡ _____

13 (B)에 주어진 동사를 어법에 맞게 고쳐 쓰시오.

➡ _____

14 to부정사를 이용하여 밑줄 친 우리말 (C)를 영어로 쓰시오.

➡ _____

15 밑줄 친 (D)가 의미하는 것을 위 글에서 찾아 쓰시오.

➡ _____

Wrap up 1

Mr. Jones: Daisy, you're late again.

Daisy: I'm really sorry, Mr. Jones. I stayed up late again last night.

Mr. Jones: Well, I think you should try to go to bed earlier.
  try to+동사원형: ～하려고 노력하다. cf. try ～ing: (시험 삼아) ～해 보다
  You should also pack your bag the night before, so you can save time in
  시간을 절약하다
  the morning.

Daisy: Okay, Mr. Jones. I'll try your advice.

구문해설 • stay up late: 늦게까지 자지 않고 깨어 있다 • pack: (짐을) 싸다 • advice: 조언

Mr. Jones: Daisy, 너 또 지각이구나.

Daisy: Jones 선생님, 정말 죄송해요. 어젯밤에 또 늦게까지 자지 않고 깨어 있었어요.

Mr. Jones: 음, 내 생각엔 넌 더 일찍 잠자리에 들려고 노력해야 할 것 같구나. 또 전날 밤에 가방을 싸 둔다면 아침에 시간을 절약할 수 있어.

Daisy: 알겠어요, Jones 선생님. 조언해 주신 것을 해 볼게요.

Read & Think

Bella: Jenny, I was upset when you pointed out my mistake in front of others.
  때를 나타내는 부사절 접속사   other people
  But I'm sure you didn't mean to hurt my feelings.

Jenny: I'm so sorry, Bella. Thanks for coming up to me first.
  전치사의 목적어(동명사)

구문해설 • upset: 화난 • point out: 지적하다 • mistake: 실수 • in front of: ～ 앞에서
          • others: 다른 사람들 • mean to V: V을 의도하다

Bella: Jenny야, 네가 다른 사람들 앞에서 내 잘못을 지적했을 때 화가 났어. 그렇지만 난 네가 내게 상처를 주려고 일부러 그런 게 아니라고 믿어.

Jenny: Bella야, 미안해. 먼저 내게 와 줘서 고마워.

Think and Write

Dear Worry Doll,

I want to tell you a problem that I have. I'm worried about my terrible math
  목적격 관계대명사
grades. I have had this problem since last year. I want to do better in math.
  현재완료(계속)   since+특정 시점   to부정사를 목적어로 취하는 동사
But when I try to study math, I just can't focus on it. I don't know what to do.
  무엇을 해야 할지(= what I should do)
I have not had a good night's sleep because of this worry. Can you take my
  현재완료 부정문
worries away?

구문해설 • terrible: 끔찍한, 형편없는 • grade: 성적, 점수 • better: 더 나은 • because of: ～ 때문에
          • take A away: A를 없애 주다

걱정 인형에게,

나는 너에게 내가 가진 문제를 말하고 싶어. 나는 나의 끔찍한 수학 성적이 걱정 돼. 나는 작년부터 이 문제를 가지고 있어. 나는 수학을 더 잘하고 싶어. 하지만 내가 수학을 공부하려고 하면, 나는 그것에 집중할 수 없어. 무엇을 해야 할지 모르겠어. 이 걱정 때문에 밤에 잠도 잘 못 자. 내 걱정을 없애 줄 수 있겠니?

영역별 핵심문제

01 다음 영영풀이가 가리키는 것을 고르시오.

> to stop feeling angry with somebody who has done something to harm, annoy or upset you

① give   ② forgive

③ receive   ④ fight

⑤ share

02 다음 중 밑줄 친 부분의 뜻풀이가 바르지 <u>않은</u> 것은?

① A bear can <u>grow up</u> to two meters in height. 성장하다

② I usually <u>gain weight</u> in winter. 체중이 늘다

③ They won the Olympic medal <u>in the end</u>. 결국

④ John pushed me hard <u>on purpose</u>. 실수로

⑤ I'll <u>let it go</u> this time. 내버려두다

03 다음 우리말을 주어진 단어를 이용하여 영작하시오.

(1) 너는 가까이에 있는 문제에 집중해야 한다.
(hand, problem, on)

  ➡ _____

(2) 우리는 또 다시 문제에 직면할 수 있다. (face)

  ➡ _____

(3) 아이들이 요즘은 아주 빠르게 성장한다. (so, these, up, fast)

  ➡ _____

04 다음 짝지어진 단어의 관계가 같도록 빈칸에 알맞은 말을 쓰시오.

> wise : stupid = advanced : _____

05 다음 주어진 문장의 밑줄 친 lines와 같은 의미로 쓰인 것은?

> It is difficult for me to memorize the <u>lines</u> perfectly.

① The red <u>lines</u> refer to the main roads on the map.

② I was embarrassed when I forgot my <u>lines</u>.

③ I'm not good at drawing <u>lines</u> without a ruler.

④ I think the cable <u>lines</u> seem to be damaged.

⑤ I found out just dots and <u>lines</u> on this picture.

06 다음 문장에 공통으로 들어갈 말을 고르시오.

> • I'm sorry, but I didn't _____ it.
> • I hate the man who is _____ about money.
> • Are there any _____s of contacting Mike?

① stand   ② mean

③ check   ④ fight

⑤ point

Conversation

[07~08] 다음 대화를 읽고 물음에 답하시오.

Emily: I was (A)[late / lately] for class again. I just can't wake up in the morning.

Tom: Do you set an alarm?

Emily: Yeah, but I turn it (B)[on / off] and go back to sleep.

Tom: I think you should put it (C)[close to / far from] your bed. That way, you'll have to get out of bed.

07 위 대화의 빈칸 (A)~(C)에 알맞은 말로 짝지어진 것은?

	(A)	(B)	(C)
①	late	on	close to
②	late	off	far from
③	late	off	close to
④	lately	off	far from
⑤	lately	on	close to

08 위 대화의 내용과 일치하지 <u>않는</u> 것은?

① Emily는 전에도 수업에 늦은 적이 있다.
② Emily는 아침에 일어나는 데 어려움을 겪고 있다.
③ Emily는 자명종을 잘못 맞추어 놓는다.
④ Emily는 자명종을 끄고 다시 잠든다.
⑤ Tom은 Emily에게 자명종을 침대에서 멀리 둘 것을 조언한다.

09 다음 대화의 내용과 일치하도록 Amy의 일기를 완성하시오.

Solomon: Hello, you're on the air.
Amy: Hi, Solomon. I'm Amy.
Solomon: Hi, Amy. What's the matter?
Amy: I hate sharing my room with my little sister. She uses my stuff without asking me first. What should I do?
Solomon: Hmm.... I think you should tell her your feelings. And you should also make some rules with your sister.
Amy: Oh, I'll try that. Thanks for the advice.

Mon, 26th Aug, 2019

 I was upset again because my little sister used my stuff without asking me first. I didn't want to (A)_____ anymore. To solve this problem, I called Solomon and asked him to give me his (B)_____. He advised me to (C)_____.
It was a great advice for me and I decided to try that.

10 다음 대화가 자연스럽게 이어지도록 순서대로 배열하시오.

(A) No, not yet. I don't know what to do.
(B) Oh, no. Did you tell your sister?
(C) You don't look so happy today. What's the matter?
(D) I wore my sister's favorite T-shirt. But I got grape juice on it.

➡ _____

[11~12] 다음 대화를 읽고 물음에 답하시오.

Eric: (A) Ms. Morris, I just can't stop playing computer games. What should I do?

Ms. Morris: (B) When you set a time limit, the computer shuts down at that time.

Eric: (C) Oh, that's a good idea.

Ms. Morris: (D) And I think you should move the computer out of your room and into the living room.

Eric: (E) I think I should. Thank you for the advice, Ms. Morris.

11 위 대화의 (A)~(E) 중 주어진 문장이 들어가기에 적절한 곳은?

> Well, why don't you use a special program?

① (A)   ② (B)   ③ (C)   ④ (D)   ⑤ (E)

12 위 대화를 읽고 대답할 수 <u>없는</u> 것은?

① What's the matter with Eric?
② Why can't Eric stop playing computer games?
③ Why does Ms. Morris recommend using a special program?
④ Where will Eric move his computer?
⑤ Where does Eric use his computer?

[13~14] 다음 대화를 읽고 물음에 답하시오.

Sora: David, you look down today. What's the matter?

David: I got a haircut but it's too short. I look funny.

Sora: Take off your hat and let me see. (*pause*) Oh, it looks fine.

David: Really? I guess I'm just not used to it yet.

13 Why did David feel down?

➡ _____

14 What did Sora think about David's haircut?

➡ _____

Grammar

15 다음 중 that이 들어가기에 가장 적절한 곳은?

> The watch (①) you are looking for (②) is (③) on the table (④) in your room (⑤).

①   ②   ③   ④   ⑤

16 다음 우리말을 영어로 바르게 옮기지 <u>않은</u> 것은?

> 그들은 김 선생님이 영어를 가르친 학생들이다.

① They are the students who Mr. Kim taught English.
② They are the students to whom Mr. Kim taught English.
③ They are the students Mr. Kim taught English.
④ They are the students whom Mr. Kim taught English.
⑤ They are the students who taught Mr. Kim English.

17 다음 빈칸에 들어갈 말로 적절한 것을 <u>모두</u> 고르시오.

> The suitcase _____ she brought into this room is similar to mine.

① who   ② which   ③ that
④ whose   ⑤ whom

18 괄호 안의 단어를 바르게 배열하여 문장을 완성하시오.

> The person (about / I / most / whom / care) is not her but you.

➡ _____

19 다음 문장을 읽고 알 수 있는 것을 <u>모두</u> 고르시오.

> Jason has just come back home from his journey.

① Jason has gone on his journey.

② Jason went on a journey.

③ Jason wants to go on his journey.

④ Jason has not arrived at his home yet.

⑤ Jason is at his home now.

20 다음 중 서로 의미가 통하지 <u>않는</u> 것은?

① I didn't see her. I still don't know where she is.
→ I have not seen her lately.

② Paul is the man. I work with him.
→ Paul is the man I work with.

③ I lost my umbrella. But I have it now.
→ I have lost my umbrella until now.

④ The coffee is too hot. June is drinking it.
→ The coffee which June is drinking is too hot.

⑤ Where is the jacket? You have had it since 2010.
→ Where is the jacket you have had since 2010?

21 다음 중 주어진 문장의 현재완료와 쓰임이 같은 것은?

> Mike <u>has visited</u> this place many times.

① Yumi <u>has</u> just <u>read</u> the book.

② He <u>has written</u> many books since 1990.

③ They <u>have watched</u> the movie for an hour.

④ Tom <u>has cleaned</u> his room already.

⑤ We <u>have been</u> to Washington.

22 다음 대화의 빈칸에 알맞은 말을 네 단어로 쓰시오.

> A: Where is Sally?
> B: Oh, _____ her home.
> A: Do you mean she is not here now?
> A: Yes.

23 다음 중 어법상 바르지 <u>않은</u> 것은?

① The bread Susan is baking smells good.

② They have noticed it more than twice until now.

③ How long have you waited for her yesterday?

④ Where are all the guests whom you invited?

⑤ Can you tell me the secret which Katherine told you?

24 다음 두 문장을 하나의 문장으로 쓰시오.

> • I will read the book.
> • I borrowed it from the library.

➡ _____

Reading

[25~28] 다음 글을 읽고 물음에 답하시오.

Bella is 15 years old this year and these days her feelings are going up and down. Today, she looks down. Let's listen to Bella's feelings and find out why.

Day 1

Anger: What a day! I can't believe Jenny yelled at Bella after the school play.

Sadness: Well, that's because Bella forgot her lines on stage.

Anger: Jenny pointed out the mistake (A)<u>that</u> Bella made. How could she do that in front of everyone?

Joy: But I'm sure Jenny did not mean to hurt Bella. They have been best friends since elementary school. Remember?

Anger: That's what I'm saying. A true friend would never put Bella down like that.

Fear: I'm worried that they are not going to be friends anymore.

Joy: Come on, Fear. (B)<u>Don't go too far.</u> We'll see.

25 다음 중 밑줄 친 (A)와 쓰임이 같은 것은?

① Do you think that he is honest?
② Jimmy believes that she stole the bag.
③ This is the man that I admire very much.
④ The fact that she is older than me doesn't matter.
⑤ How do you know that he came back?

26 다음 중 밑줄 친 (B)의 의미로 가장 적절한 것은?

① Don't go farther than I expected.
② Don't think that you can go as far as you want.
③ Bella should run away as far as possible.
④ Don't think that they are not going to be friends anymore.
⑤ Try to be nice to the friends in need.

27 According to the conversation, what did Bella forget on stage? Answer in English with a full sentence.

➡ _____

28 다음 중 위 글을 읽고 답할 수 <u>없는</u> 것은?

① How does Bella look today?
② Who yelled at Bella today?
③ Who pointed out Bella's mistake?
④ Who is Bella's best friend?
⑤ What is the name of the school play?

[29~31] 다음 글을 읽고 물음에 답하시오.

Joy: Whew! I'm so happy that they are talking again.

Anger: Yeah, Bella went to Jenny and talked to her first.

Joy: Jenny didn't avoid Bella (A)<u>on purpose</u>.

Sadness: Yeah, Jenny didn't know a way to say sorry.

Fear: I hope Bella doesn't have any more problems like this.

Joy: Me, too. But problems are part of growing up. Just like this time, Bella will face the problems, solve them, and become wiser in the end.

29 다음 중 밑줄 친 (A)를 대신하여 쓸 수 있는 것은?

① all of sudden   ② by accident
③ intentionally   ④ by mistake
⑤ immediately

30 주어진 어구를 바르게 배열하여 Bella와 Jenny가 처해 있던 문제의 결과를 쓰시오.

Bella and Jenny / each other / with / up / finally / made

➡ _____

31 위 글의 내용과 일치하지 <u>않는</u> 것은?

① Joy feels happy because Bella is talking with Jenny again.
② It was Bella that went to Jenny and talked to her first.
③ Jenny didn't know how to say sorry.
④ Bella doesn't want to face problems like this.
⑤ Problems are part of growth.

[01~02] 다음 대화를 읽고 물음에 답하시오.

> Sujin: I don't know how to do better in math.
> (A)_____
> Jake: How do you study for tests?
> Sujin: I just solve a lot of problems.
> Jake: Well, don't solve everything. (B)I think you should focus on the ones you got wrong.

01 위 대화의 빈칸 (A)에 들어가기에 <u>어색한</u> 것은?

① What should I do to improve my math?
② Would you give me some tips for me?
③ Could you tell me what to do?
④ How can I help you?
⑤ Can you give me some advice?

02 위 대화의 밑줄 친 (B)와 바꾸어 쓰기가 <u>어색한</u> 것은?

① Why don't you focus on the ones you got wrong?
② How about focusing on the ones you got wrong?
③ You had better focus on the ones you got wrong.
④ You need to focus on the ones you got wrong.
⑤ You don't have to focus on the ones you got wrong.

[03~05] 다음 대화를 읽고 물음에 답하시오.

> Jane: You look tired. What's the matter?
> Mike: I didn't have breakfast this morning. I'm so hungry.
> Jane: Oh, that's too bad. We still have two more hours until lunch break.
> Mike: Our school should have a snack bar. Then, we could have a quick breakfast or snacks.
> Jane: I think so, too. How can we make that suggestion?
> Mike: We can post it on the suggestion board.

03 Why doesn't Mike look good?

➡ _____

04 How long should Jane and Mike wait for lunch break?

➡ _____

05 What can Jane and Mike do if there is a snack bar in school?

➡ _____

[06~07] 다음 대화를 읽고 물음에 답하시오.

> Solomon: Hello, you're on the air.
> Amy: Hi, Solomon. I'm Amy.
> Solomon: Hi, Amy. What's the matter?
> Amy: I hate sharing my room with my little sister. She uses my stuff without asking me first. What should I do?
> Solomon: Hmm.... _____ And you should also make some rules with your sister.
> Amy: Oh, I'll try that. Thanks for the advice.

06 위 대화의 빈칸에 들어갈 말을 주어진 단어를 배열하여 완성하시오.

┌─── 보기 ───
│ feelings / you / tell / your / her / I / think / should
└───

➡ _____

07 위 대화를 읽고 알 수 <u>없는</u> 것은?

① Why did Amy call Solomon?

② What's wrong with Amy?

③ Why didn't Amy like sharing her room with her little sister?

④ What is Solomon's advice?

⑤ How will Amy make up with her litter sister?

[08~09] 다음 대화를 읽고 물음에 답하시오.

Julia: Kevin, you look so nervous. What's the matter?

Kevin: I dropped my mom's new glasses and broke them.

Julia: (A)_____ So, your mom also knows about it?

Kevin: Not yet. I can't tell her about it. What should I do?

Julia: Just tell her first before she finds out about it.

08 위 대화에서 나타난 Kevin의 심경으로 적절한 것은?

① relieved   ② lonely

③ worried   ④ surprised

⑤ angry

09 위 대화의 빈칸 (A)에 들어갈 말로 적절한 것을 <u>모두</u> 고르시오.

① I'm very disappointed.

② I'm sorry to hear that.

③ I can't stand it.

④ Oh, that's terrible.

⑤ What a relief!

10 다음 대화가 자연스럽게 이어지도록 순서대로 배열하시오.

(A) Okay, Mr. Jones. I'll try your advice.

(B) Daisy, you're late again.

(C) Well, I think you should try to go to bed earlier. You should also pack your bag the night before, so you can save time in the morning.

(D) I'm really sorry, Mr. Jones. I stayed up late again last night.

➡ _____

다음 중 주어진 문장에 쓰인 현재완료와 쓰임이 <u>다른</u> 것은?

They <u>have</u> not <u>passed</u> the test yet.

① There <u>has</u> just <u>been</u> a car accident.

② Nick <u>has</u> already <u>heard</u> about the news.

③ Karl <u>has</u> just <u>parked</u> his car in the parking lot.

④ Lora <u>has traveled</u> alone many times.

⑤ We <u>have</u> not <u>decided</u> what to do yet.

12 〈보기〉와 같이 하나의 문장을 둘로 나누어 쓰시오.

┤ 보기 ├

Who is the woman whom your sister wants to talk to?

➡ Who is the woman? Your sister wants to talk to her.

(1) Where is the man who you cheered for?

➡ _____

(2) The car that Tony Stark drives in the movie is very expensive.

➡ _____

_____

13 다음 빈칸에 공통으로 들어갈 말로 가장 적절한 것은?

> • This is the key _____ Christine gave to me.
> • I know the boy _____ you met at a dance party.

① who ② which ③ whom
④ whose ⑤ that

14 다음 중 어법상 바르지 <u>않은</u> 것은?

① The train has left already.
② That is the famous building which Antonio Gaudi built.
③ Do you know about the book that Joe is reading it?
④ When did you get the phone call?
⑤ I have not had dinner with her for a month.

다음 밑줄 친 부분 중 생략할 수 <u>없는</u> 것은?

① Everything <u>that</u> he told you is true.
② It is not easy to find the money <u>that</u> someone stole from you.
③ Where is the milk <u>that</u> Mom put in the refrigerator?
④ The information <u>that</u> you found is very valuable to us.
⑤ She wants me to buy a jacket <u>that</u> has many pockets.

16 다음 두 문장을 여섯 단어로 이루어진 하나의 문장으로 표현하시오.

> I lost my cell phone. I still can't find it until now.

➡ _____

주어진 문장과 같은 의미가 되도록 빈칸에 알맞은 말을 쓰시오.

> We began to see this movie two hours ago. And we still see it.
> = We _____ _____ the movie _____ two hours.

[18~21] 다음 글을 읽고, 물음에 답하시오.

> Day 2
> Anger: I can't forgive Jenny. She didn't say a word to Bella.
> Fear: Jenny didn't even look (A)[at / after] her. Jenny has never been this cold before.
> Sadness: Bella ate alone (B)[while / during] lunch today. Poor Bella!
> Joy: Jenny is Bella's best friend. ⓐI'm sure there is a reason that we don't know about.
> Anger: I can't stand this any longer. Bella should just go and tell her about her feelings.
> Fear: I don't want Bella to be hurt again. She should let it go.
> Joy: They are good friends. They will (C)[work it out / work out it].

18 (A)~(C)에서 어법상 옳은 것끼리 바르게 짝지은 것은?

① at – while – work it out
② at – during – work out it
③ at – during – work it out
④ after – during – work out it
⑤ after – while – work it out

19 밑줄 친 문장 ⓐ를 두 문장으로 나누어 쓰시오.

➡ _____

➡ _____

다음 중 위 글의 내용과 일치하지 <u>않는</u> 것은?

① Jenny said nothing to Bella on the second day.

② Jenny has not been this cold to Bella before.

③ Bella didn't have lunch today.

④ Anger wants Bella to tell her feelings to Jenny.

⑤ Joy thinks Bella and Jenny are good friends.

출제율 90%

21 위 글의 내용에 맞게 다음 물음에 완전한 문장의 영어로 답하시오.

Q: What does Fear want for Bella?

➡ _____

[22~24] 다음 글을 읽고 물음에 답하시오.

Day 3

Joy: Whew! I'm so happy that they are talking again.

Anger: Yeah, Bella went to Jenny and talked to her first.

Joy: Jenny didn't avoid Bella on purpose.

Sadness: Yeah, Jenny didn't know a way (A)<u>to say</u> sorry.

Fear: I hope Bella doesn't have any more problems like this.

Joy: Me, too. But problems are part of growing up. Just like this time, Bella will face the problems, solve them, and become wiser in the end.

출제율 100%

22 다음 중 밑줄 친 (A)와 쓰임이 같은 것은?

① Tom went to the office <u>to get</u> the job.

② I want you <u>to make</u> up your mind.

③ David decided <u>to finish</u> the project.

④ I am so happy <u>to see</u> you again.

⑤ I have something <u>to talk</u> to you.

출제율 95%

23 What does Fear hope? Answer in English with a full sentence.

➡ _____

_____

출제율 90%

24 다음 중 위 글의 내용과 일치하지 <u>않는</u> 것은?

①Thanks to Bella's effort, Bella and Jenny were back to being friends. ②Bella told Jenny about her feelings first. ③Owing to Bella's courage, she found out that Jenny avoided her on purpose. ④She just didn't know a good way to say sorry. ⑤Bella will become wiser by solving problems like this.

①　　②　　③　　④　　⑤

[25~26] 다음 글을 읽고 물음에 답하시오.

Dear Worry Doll,

I want to tell you a problem (A)_____ I have. I'm worried about my terrible math grades. (B)_____ I want to do better in math. But when I try to study math, I just can't focus on it. I don't know what to do. I have not had a good night's sleep because of this worry. Can you take my worries away?

출제율 90%

25 다음 중 빈칸 (A)에 들어갈 말로 적절한 것을 <u>모두</u> 고르시오.

① that　　② what　　③ who

④ which　　⑤ whom

출제율 90%

26 다음 두 문장을 하나의 문장으로 바꿔 빈칸 (B)에 쓰시오.

I had this problem last year. I still have it.

➡ _____

[01~03] 다음 대화를 읽고 물음에 답하시오.

Eric: Ms. Morris, I just can't stop playing computer games. (A)제가 어떻게 해야 할까요?(should)

Ms. Morris: Well, why don't you use a special program? When you set a time limit, the computer shuts down at that time.

Eric: Oh, that's a good idea.

Ms. Morris: And I think you should move the computer out of your room and into the living room.

Eric: I thinks I should. Thank you for the advice, Ms. Morris.

01 위 대화의 밑줄 친 (A)의 우리말을 주어진 단어를 사용하여 영작하시오.

➡ _____

02 What happens if Eric sets a time limit using the special program?

➡ _____

03 Where does Ms. Morris advise Eric to move the computer?

➡ _____
_____

04 다음 우리말을 영어로 각각 쓰시오.

(1) 너는 부산에 가 본 적이 있니?
(2) 그녀는 부산에 가고 없습니다.

➡ (1) _____
(2) _____

05 자연스러운 문장이 되도록 관계대명사를 이용하여 하나의 문장으로 바꿔 쓰시오.

- The weight is not that heavy.
- The restaurant is crowded with people.
- The children are very noisy.

- Paul runs it.
- She is lifting it.
- I take care of them.

➡ _____
➡ _____
➡ _____

06 알맞은 질문으로 대화를 완성하시오.

A: _____
B: We have known each other for 10 years.

➡ _____

07 주어진 어구를 바르게 배열하여 다음 우리말을 영어로 쓰시오.

Tom이 바라보고 있는 그 소녀는 Danny의 친구이다.
(Danny's friend / is / is / looking / whom / the girl / at / Tom)

➡ _____

08 다음 우리말에 맞도록 빈칸에 알맞은 말을 네 단어로 쓰시오.

> Jimmy가 쓰고 있는 헬멧은 나의 것과 비슷해.
> = The helmet _____
>   is similar to mine.

09 다음 대화의 빈칸에 알맞은 말을 쓰시오.

> A: How long _____ your brother
>   _____ golf?
> B: He learned golf _____ he was seven
>   years old. So he _____ _____
>   golf _____ five years.

[10~14] 다음 글을 읽고 물음에 답하시오.

Bella is 15 years old this year and these days her feelings are going up and down. Today, she looks down. Let's listen to Bella's feelings and find out why.

Day 1

Anger: What a day! I can't believe Jenny yelled at Bella after the school play.

Sadness: Well, (A)that's because Bella forgot her lines on stage.

Anger: Jenny pointed out the mistake that Bella made. How could she do that in front of everyone?

Joy: But I'm sure Jenny did not mean to hurt Bella. They have been best friends since elementary school. Remember?

Anger: That's what I'm saying. (B)_____
_____

Fear: I'm worried that they are not going to be friends anymore.

Joy: Come on, Fear. Don't go too far. We'll see.

10 밑줄 친 (A)가 의미하는 것을 위 글에서 찾아 쓰시오.

➡ _____

11 주어진 어구를 바르게 배열하여 빈칸 (B)에 들어갈 말을 쓰시오.

> (that / would / down / Bella / like / never
> / put / a true friend)

➡ _____

12 주어진 어구를 바르게 배열하여 다음 대화를 완성하시오.

> A: Bella, why are you so upset?
> B: I am upset because _____
>   _____.
>   And she even shouted loudly.
>   (everyone / Jenny / my mistake / out / in
>   / of / front / pointed)

13 위 글을 읽고 사건의 순서를 바르게 나열하시오.

> ⓐ Jenny yelled at Bella.
> ⓑ Bella was sad because of it.
> ⓒ Bella forgot her lines during the play.

➡ _____

14 다음 우리말에 맞게 빈칸에 알맞은 말을 7 단어로 쓰시오.

> 초등학교 때부터 알아온 Jenny는 나의 가장 친
> 한 친구이다.
> ➡ Jenny _____
>   is my best friend.

01 다음 대화의 내용과 일치하도록 Mike의 일기를 완성하시오.

> **Jane:** You look tired. What's the matter?
>
> **Mike:** I didn't have breakfast this morning. I'm so hungry.
>
> **Jane:** Oh, that's too bad. We still have two more hours until lunch break.
>
> **Mike:** Our school should have a snack bar. Then, we could have a quick breakfast or snacks.
>
> **Jane:** I think so, too. How can we make that suggestion?
>
> **Mike:** We can post it on the suggestion board.

Mon, Sep 23rd, Sunny

I got up late and almost missed the bus. Fortunately, I wasn't late for school. But I felt so tired and hungry because (A)_____ in the morning. Even worse, I had to wait for (B)_____ for lunch break. I thought (C)_____ for hungry students. When I talked about it with Jane, she agreed with my idea. I made a plan to post my idea on (D)_____ soon.

02 주어진 어구와 현재완료 시제를 이용하여 자신과 친구에 관한 여러 가지 이야기를 써 보시오.

argue with a friend	visit one's house	have a snow fight
know him or her since	be to a concert before	

(1) _____

(2) _____

(3) _____

(4) _____

(5) _____

03 다음 Ryan의 글을 읽고 주어진 어휘를 이용하여 빈칸을 채우시오.

> Hi. I'm Ryan. My family moved to New York in 2008 and we still live in New York. I took trip to Spain in 2011 and 2012 with my family. And Cooper, our dog, became a member of our family in 2013. He likes to play with a ball. Also, I became friends with John in 2016. He is my best friend.

(1) Ryan _____ for more than ten years. (live)

(2) Ryan _____ twice. (be)

(3) Ryan _____ 2013. (raise)

(4) Ryan _____ 2016. (know each other)

단원별 모의고사

1 다음 우리말에 맞게 빈칸에 알맞은 말을 쓰시오.

(1) 저는 제안을 하고 싶습니다.
➡ I'd like to make a _____ .

(2) 결코 같은 실수를 반복하지 마라.
➡ Never _____ the same mistake.

(3) 약속을 지키지 못한 걸 용서해 주세요.
➡ Please _____ me for breaking my promise.

2 다음 문장에 공통으로 들어갈 말을 고르시오. (대·소문자 무시)

- I've been busy _____ I came here.
- _____ I'm driving my car, I'll drop by your office.
- _____ when are you a member of the dance club?

① for　　　　② at
③ because　　④ from
⑤ since

3 다음 문장의 빈칸에 들어갈 말을 〈보기〉에서 골라 쓰시오.

┌─ 보기 ─┐
up and down / work out / stay up late / wake up

(1) Did you _____ last night?
(2) Life goes _____ .
(3) I _____ early in the morning.
(4) We can _____ any problem.

4 다음 문장의 빈칸에 들어갈 말을 〈보기〉에서 골라 쓰시오.

┌─ 보기 ─┐
pack / explain / fight / worry / yell

(1) I'll _____ the details of this product.
(2) You should not _____ or run in the museum.
(3) You don't have to _____ about this matter. Everything will be fine.
(4) I have to _____ for my business trip.
(5) My brother and I used to _____ like cat and dog.

[05~06] 다음 대화를 읽고 물음에 답하시오.

Sora: David, you look ⓐdown today. What's the matter?

David: I got a haircut but it's too short. I look funny.

Sora: Take off your hat and let me see. (*pause*) Oh, it looks fine.

David: Really? I guess I'm just not used to it yet.

5 위 대화의 밑줄 친 ⓐdown과 같은 의미로 쓰인 것은?

① Don't look down on me.
② When I feel down, I usually listen to music.
③ You don't need to write it down.
④ I jumped down off the second floor.
⑤ Would you turn the music down?

06 위 대화의 내용과 일치하는 것은?

① Sora needed a haircut.

② The boy really likes his haircut.

③ Sora takes off her hat to show her haircut to David.

④ David doesn't feel good because of his new hairstyle.

⑤ Sora used to have a short haircut.

[07~08] 다음 대화를 읽고 물음에 답하시오.

Solomon: Hello, you're on the air.

Amy: (A) Hi, Solomon. I'm Amy.

Solomon: (B) Hi, Amy. What's the matter?

Amy: (C) She uses my stuff without asking me first. What should I do?

Solomon: (D) Hmm.... I think you should tell her your feelings. And you should also make some rules with your sister.

Amy: (E) Oh, I'll try that. Thanks for the advice.

07 위 대화의 (A)~(E) 중 주어진 문장이 들어가기에 적절한 곳은?

I hate sharing my room with my little sister.

① (A) ② (B) ③ (C) ④ (D) ⑤ (E)

08 위 대화의 내용과 일치하지 <u>않는</u> 것은?

① Amy is talking to Solomon face to face.

② Amy has difficulty sharing her room with her little sister.

③ Amy's sister used Amy's stuff without asking her first.

④ Solomon advises Amy to tell her feelings to her sister.

⑤ Solomon recommends making some rules with her sister to Amy.

09 다음 대화의 내용과 일치하도록 다음 표의 빈칸을 완성하시오.

Jane: You look tired. What's the matter?

Mike: I didn't have breakfast this morning. I'm so hungry.

Jane: Oh, that's too bad. We still have two more hours until lunch break.

Mike: Our school should have a snack bar. Then, we could have a quick breakfast or snacks.

Jane: I think so, too. How can we make that suggestion?

Mike: We can post it on the suggestion board.

⬇

Let's Make a Better School	
Title	Many students are hungry!
Name	Mike, Jane
Suggestion	Some students don't have (A)_____, so they get (B)_____ in the morning. We should (C)_____ _____.

[10~11] 다음 대화를 읽고 물음에 답하시오.

Mr. Jones: Daisy, you're late again.

Daisy: I'm really sorry, Mr. Jones. I stayed up late again last night.

Mr. Jones: Well, I think you should try to go to bed earlier. You should also pack your bag the night before, so you can save time in the morning.

Daisy: Okay, Mr. Jones. I'll try your advice.

10 Why is Daisy late again?

➡ _____

11 According to Mr. Jones, what should Daisy do to save time in the morning?

➡ _____

12 다음 주어진 우리말과 일치하도록 주어진 단어를 모두 배열하여 영작하시오.

(1) 나는 더 이상 그와 일하는 것을 견딜 수 없다.
(stand / him / more / working / any / I / with / can't)

➡ _____

(2) Minho는 영어로 된 대사를 외워야 한다.
(English / lines / memorize / Minho / his / to / in / has)

➡ _____

(3) 나는 그가 내 실수들을 지적했을 때 당황스러웠다.
(mistakes / he / pointed / I / my / was / when / embarrassed / out)

➡ _____

13 다음 빈칸에 알맞은 말이 바르게 짝지어진 것은?

• I have known Chris _____ I was in college.
• They have made the video _____ about three hours.

① for – for
② since – already
③ since – for
④ already – for
⑤ just – since

14 다음 우리말을 영어로 바르게 옮기지 않은 것은?

① 네가 어제 입은 외투는 멋져 보였어.
→ The jacket you wore yesterday looked fancy.
② 이곳에 얼마나 오랫동안 있었던 거야?
→ How long have you been here?
③ 네가 찾던 책이 여기에 있어.
→ The book you were looking for is here.
④ Tina는 그녀의 고향으로 가고 없습니다.
→ Tina has gone to her hometown.
⑤ 나는 네가 말하고 있는 사람을 알지 못해.
→ I don't know the person whom you are talking.

15 다음 중 어법상 바르지 않은 것은?

① There are some rules you have to keep.
② The apple juice which you drank this morning was made by my mom.
③ Ann has never worn the scarf.
④ I ate nothing since yesterday.
⑤ The music that I often listen to is very sad.

16 주어진 어구를 바르게 배열하여 다음 우리말을 영어로 쓰시오.

네가 나에게 사 주었던 그 케이크를 나는 방금 먹었어.
(me / I / for / have / bought / you / just / that / eaten / the cake)

➡ _____

17 주어진 단어를 이용하여 다음 문장을 하나의 문장으로 표현하시오.

I lost my gold necklace. I can't find it. (yet)

➡ _____

[18~20] 다음 글을 읽고 물음에 답하시오.

Bella is 15 years old this year and these days her feelings are going up and down. Today, she looks down. Let's listen to Bella's feelings and find out why.

Day 1
Anger: What a day! I can't believe Jenny yelled at Bella after the school play.
Sadness: Well, that's because Bella forgot her lines on stage.
Anger: Jenny pointed out the mistake that Bella made. How could she do that in front of everyone?

Joy: But I'm sure Jenny did not mean to hurt Bella. They have been best friends since elementary school. Remember?

Anger: That's what I'm saying. A true friend would never put Bella down like that.

Fear: I'm worried that they are not going to be friends anymore.

Joy: Come on, Fear. Don't go too far. We'll see.

18 다음은 Bella의 일기이다. 위 글의 내용과 일치하지 <u>않는</u> 것은?

①I was upset today. ②It was because of Jenny. ③She pointed out the mistake I made during the school play. ④And she even yelled at me during the play. ⑤ There were other people around us. I was so embarrassed.

①   ②   ③   ④   ⑤

19 위 글의 내용에 맞게 대화의 빈칸에 알맞은 말을 쓰시오.

A: Bella, did Jenny point out your mistake in a quiet place?

B: _____ , _____ . _____

_____ .

20 다음 중 위 글의 내용과 일치하지 <u>않는</u> 것은?

① Bella forgot her lines on stage.

② It was Jenny that pointed out the mistake Bella made.

③ Joy believes that Jenny didn't intend to hurt Bella.

④ Jenny looks gloomy because of Bella.

⑤ Anger thinks Jenny is not Bella's true friend.

[21~23] 다음 글을 읽고 물음에 답하시오.

Day 2

Anger: I can't forgive Jenny. She didn't say a word to Bella.

Fear: Jenny didn't even look at her. Jenny has never been this cold before.

Sadness: Bella ate alone during lunch today. Poor Bella!

Joy: Jenny is Bella's best friend. I'm sure there is a reason that we don't know about.

Anger: I can't (A)_____ this any longer. Bella should just go and tell her about her feelings.

Fear: I don't want Bella to be hurt again. She should let it go.

Joy: They are good friends. They will work it out.

21 주어진 영영풀이를 참고하여 빈칸 (A)에 철자 s로 시작하는 단어를 쓰시오.

to be able to accept or deal well with a difficult situation

➡ _____

22 다음 중 둘째 날 일어난 일과 관련이 <u>없는</u> 것은?

① Jenny didn't say a word to Bella.

② Bella was cold toward Jenny.

③ Bella talked to Jenny first.

④ Bella ate lunch alone.

⑤ Jenny didn't look at Bella at all.

23 위 글의 내용에 맞게 다음 물음에 대한 답을 완성하시오.

Q: Why does Joy think Bella and Jenny will work it out?

A: Joy thinks that way because _____

_____ .

Doors to the Wild

 의사소통 기능

- 궁금한 일 표현하기

  A: This flower is bigger than a person.

  B: Yeah. **I'm curious about** the flower.

- 비교해 표현하기

  A: We got a new puppy yesterday.

  B: Oh, he's so small!

  A: Yeah. He's **as small as** my hand.

언어 형식

- 가주어(it) ~ 진주어(to부정사)

  It is dangerous **to stay** alone in such a wild area.

- 원급 비교

  Stella's eyes were **as bright as** stars.

Words & Expressions

Key Words

- **adventurous** [ædvéntʃərəs] 형 모험심이 강한
- **allow** [əláu] 동 허락하다
- **appear** [əpíər] 동 나타나다
- **approach** [əpróutʃ] 동 다가가다, 다가오다
- **attack** [ətæk] 동 공격하다
- **attract** [ətrækt] 동 끌다, ~을 끌어당기다
- **bat** [bæt] 명 박쥐
- **blind** [blaind] 형 눈 먼, 맹인인
- **careless** [kɛ́ərlis] 형 부주의한
- **curious** [kjúəriəs] 형 궁금한, 호기심이 많은
- **dangerous** [déindʒərəs] 형 위험한
- **dead** [ded] 형 죽은
- **dolphin** [dálfin] 명 돌고래
- **feed** [fi:d] 동 밥[우유]을 먹이다, 먹이를 주다
- **female** [fí:meil] 형 암컷의
- **friendship** [fréndʃip] 명 우정
- **giant** [dʒáiənt] 형 거대한
- **ginger** [dʒíndʒər] 명 생강
- **hole** [houl] 명 구멍
- **huge** [hju:dʒ] 형 거대한
- **humorous** [hjú:mərəs] 형 재미있는, 유머러스한

- **insect** [ínsekt] 명 곤충, 벌레
- **language** [lǽŋgwidʒ] 명 언어
- **lifeless** [láiflis] 형 죽은, 생명이 없는
- **probably** [prábəbli] 부 아마
- **pumpkin** [pʌ́mpkin] 명 호박
- **rescue** [réskju:] 명 구조
- **restless** [réstlis] 형 가만히 못 있는
- **seem** [si:m] 동 ~처럼 보이다
- **sense** [sens] 명 감각
- **sheet** [ʃi:t] 명 (종이) 한 장
- **shelter** [ʃéltər] 명 보호소
- **snake** [sneik] 명 뱀
- **strength** [streŋkθ] 명 힘
- **tail** [teil] 명 꼬리
- **thick** [θik] 형 두꺼운
- **throughout** [θru:áut] 전 ~ 동안, ~ 내내
- **tongue** [tʌŋ] 명 혀
- **trunk** [trʌŋk] 명 (코끼리의) 코
- **unbelievably** [ʌnbəlívəbli] 부 믿을 수 없을 정도로
- **whale** [hweil] 명 고래
- **wild** [waild] 형 야생의 명 야생

Key Expressions

- **be born** 태어나다
- **become part of** ~의 일원이 되다
- **care for** ~을 돌보다
- **give a presentation** 발표하다
- **keep one's eyes on** ~에서 눈을 떼지 않다

- **millions of** 수백만의
- **next to** ~ 옆에
- **take a picture of** ~의 사진을 찍다
- **tell the difference** 차이를 구별하다
- **thanks to** ~ 덕분에

Word Power

※ 서로 반대되는 뜻을 가진 어휘

☐ **careful** 주의 깊은 ↔ **careless** 부주의한
☐ **allow** 허락하다 ↔ **prohibit** 금지하다
☐ **safe** 안전한 ↔ **dangerous** 위험한
☐ **giant** 거대한 ↔ **tiny** 작은
☐ **male** 수컷의 ↔ **female** 암컷의
☐ **humorous** 재미있는 ↔ **boring** 지루한

☐ **tail** 꼬리 ↔ **head** 머리
☐ **thick** 두꺼운 ↔ **thin** 얇은
☐ **appear** 나타나다 ↔ **disappear** 사라지다
☐ **attack** 공격하다 ↔ **defend** 방어하다
☐ **alive** 살아 있는 ↔ **dead** 죽은
☐ **believable** 믿을 수 있는 ↔ **unbelievable** 믿을 수 없는

English Dictionary

☐ **allow** 허락하다
→ to let somebody/something do something; to let something happen or be done
누군가나 무언가가 어떤 것을 하게 하다; 무언가가 일어나게 하거나 이루어지게 하다

☐ **approach** 다가가다
→ to come near to somebody/something in distance or time
거리상 또는 시간상으로 누군가나 무언가가 가까이 오다

☐ **blind** 눈 먼, 맹인인
→ not able to see
볼 수 없는

☐ **careless** 부주의한
→ not giving enough attention and thought to what you are doing, so that you make mistakes
당신이 하고 있는 것에 충분한 주의나 생각을 기울이지 않아서 당신이 실수하도록 하는

☐ **curious** 호기심이 많은
→ having a strong desire to know about something
무언가에 대해 알고 싶은 강한 욕구를 가진

☐ **dead** 죽은
→ no longer alive
더 이상 살아 있지 않은

☐ **feed** 먹이를 주다
→ to give food to a person or an animal
사람이나 동물에게 먹을 것을 주다

☐ **friendship** 우정
→ the feeling or relationship that friends have; the state of being friends
친구들이 갖고 있는 감정 또는 관계; 친구인 상태

☐ **insect** 곤충
→ any small creature with six legs and a body divided into three parts
6개의 다리와 3부분으로 나누어지는 몸을 가진 작은 생명체

☐ **rescue** 구조하다
→ to save somebody/something from a dangerous or harmful situation
누군가나 무언가를 위험하거나 해로운 상황으로부터 구하다

☐ **shelter** 보호소
→ a structure built to give protection, especially from the weather or from attack
특히 날씨나 공격으로부터 보호하기 위해 지어진 구조물

☐ **tail** 꼬리
→ the part that sticks out and can be moved at the back of the body of a bird, an animal or a fish
새, 동물, 또는 물고기의 몸통의 뒷부분에서 튀어나와 움직여질 수 있는 부분

☐ **tongue** 혀
→ the soft part in the mouth that moves around, used for tasting, swallowing, speaking, etc.
입안에서 이리저리 움직이는, 맛을 보거나 삼키거나 말을 하는 데 사용되는 부드러운 부분

☐ **trunk** (코끼리의) 코
→ the long nose of an elephant
코끼리의 긴 코

서답형

01 다음 짝지어진 단어의 관계가 같도록 빈칸에 알맞은 말을 쓰시오.

> giant : tiny = thick : _____

02 다음 영영풀이가 가리키는 것을 고르시오.

> not able to see

① deaf　　　　② blind

③ disabled　　 ④ dead

⑤ blank

중요

03 다음 중 밑줄 친 부분의 뜻풀이가 바르지 <u>않은</u> 것은?

① Bears look cute, but they are very <u>dangerous</u>. 위험한

② All the trees were either <u>lifeless</u> or leafless. 생명이 없는

③ I worked <u>throughout</u> the night. ~ 동안

④ Many monkeys <u>appear</u> at your Town Center. 사라지다

⑤ <u>Unbelievably</u>, owls can rotate their heads 270 degrees! 믿을 수 없게도

서답형

04 다음 우리말에 맞게 빈칸에 알맞은 말을 쓰시오.

(1) 코끼리는 음식을 집기 위해 코를 이용한다.
➡ The elephant uses its _____ to pick up food.

(2) 고래는 등으로 물을 내뿜고 있다.
➡ The _____ is spouting water from its back.

(3) 암컷 사자들이 대부분의 사냥을 한다.
➡ _____ lions do most of the hunting.

서답형

05 다음 우리말을 주어진 단어를 이용하여 영작하시오.

(1) 코끼리는 좀처럼 사람들을 공격하지 않는다. (rarely)
➡ _____

(2) 구조팀이 정시에 도착했다. (on)
➡ _____

(3) 이 반지들은 우리의 우정을 상징한다. (symbolize)
➡ _____

06 다음 주어진 문장의 밑줄 친 bat과 같은 의미로 쓰인 것은?

> <u>Bats</u> can fly well in the dark.

① He suddenly struck the man with a baseball <u>bat</u>.

② This <u>bat</u> is made of wood.

③ Do you know how to swing the <u>bat</u>?

④ The sounds made by <u>bats</u> are bounced back to them.

⑤ My father bought me a <u>bat</u> instead of a glove.

중요

07 다음 문장에 공통으로 들어갈 말을 고르시오.

> • I love your _____ of humor.
> • I met the chef suffering from losing his _____ of smell.
> • If you _____ danger, you must start to run.

① sense　　　　② touch

③ feel　　　　　④ idea

⑤ approach

01 다음 짝지어진 단어의 관계가 같도록 빈칸에 알맞은 말을 쓰시오.

safe : dangerous = careful : _____

02 다음 영영풀이가 가리키는 것을 고르시오.

to give food to a person or an animal

① feed   ② fit   ③ seed
④ eat   ⑤ dine

03 다음 우리말에 맞게 빈칸에 알맞은 말을 쓰시오. (한 칸에 한 단어씩 쓸 것.)

(1) 나는 이번 주말에 고양이들을 돌볼 것이다.
   ➡ I'll _____ _____ cats this weekend.
(2) Sue는 Mike에게서 눈을 떼지 못했다.
   ➡ Sue kept _____ _____ on Mike.
(3) 나는 우리 가족의 사진을 찍고 싶다.
   ➡ I want to _____ _____ _____
   of my family.

04 다음 문장의 빈칸에 들어갈 말을 <보기>에서 골라 쓰시오.

┌─ 보기 ├─
probably / seem / feed / female / allow

(1) You _____ to be in a good mood.
(2) We should _____ kids to have thinking time.
(3) _____ gorillas are half the size of the males.
(4) Don't _____ bread to the ducks.
(5) You have _____ heard of Vincent van Gogh.

05 다음 우리말에 맞게 주어진 단어를 사용하여 영작하시오.

(1) 부주의한 운전자는 불이 빨간색으로 바뀐 것을 보지 못했다. (light)
   ➡ _____
(2) 아이들은 그들 주위에 있는 모든 것에 호기심이 있다. (around)
   ➡ _____
(3) 우리 부모님은 내가 컴퓨터 게임하는 것을 허락하지 않을 것이다. (won't)
   ➡ _____
   _____

06 다음 주어진 우리말과 일치하도록 주어진 단어를 모두 배열하여 영작하시오.

(1) 나는 지난 주말에 지역 동물 보호소를 방문했다.
   (last / a / visited / I / animal / weekend / shelter / local)
   ➡ _____
(2) 그는 그때 가만히 있지 않았다.
   (that / he / restless / time / at / was)
   ➡ _____
(3) 우리는 더 모험심을 갖고 강해질 필요가 있다.
   (need / more / we / be / to / and / stronger / adventurous)
   ➡ _____

Conversation

1 궁금한 일 표현하기

A This flower is bigger than a person. 이 꽃은 사람보다 더 크다.

B Yeah. I'm curious about the flower. 응. 나는 이 꽃이 궁금해.

■ "I'm curious about ~."은 놀랍거나 특별한 것에 대하여 호기심이 있다는 것을 표현할 때 사용된다. 예를 들어, 어떤 음식이 맛있어서 그 요리법이 궁금할 경우 "I'm curious about the recipe."와 같이 말한다.

궁금한 일 표현하기

• I wonder what this dish is made of. 나는 이 요리가 무엇으로 만들어졌는지 궁금해.

• I'm interested to know about the amazing dog that can speak English.
나는 영어를 말할 수 있는 이 놀라운 개에 대해 알고 싶어.

• Can someone tell me about the dog that saved a girl from a fire?
누가 나에게 화재로부터 한 소녀를 구한 개에 대해 이야기해 줄 수 있니?

핵심 Check

1. 다음 주어진 우리말과 일치하도록 빈칸을 완성하시오.

(1) **A:** Look at this. This bird laughs like a person. (이것 좀 봐. 이 새는 사람처럼 웃어.)

　　B: Oh, I'm ＿＿＿＿ ＿＿＿＿ the bird. (오. 나는 이 새가 궁금해.)

　　C: Me, too. ＿＿＿＿ ＿＿＿＿ more about it. (나도 그래. 이것에 대해 더 읽어 보자.)

(2) **A:** This horse guided the ＿＿＿＿. (이 말이 맹인들을 안내했어.)

　　B: Oh, I ＿＿＿＿ how he could do it. (오. 나는 어떻게 그가 이것을 했는지 궁금해.)

　　C: So do I. Let's listen to the story more. (나도 그래. 이야기를 더 들어보자.)

(3) **A:** Bees ＿＿＿＿ with each other by dancing. (벌들은 춤을 추며 서로 의사소통을 해.)

　　B: Really? How do they do it? ＿＿＿＿ ＿＿＿＿ ＿＿＿＿ ＿＿＿＿ ＿＿＿＿.
(정말? 그들은 그것을 어떻게 해? 나는 그 방법이 궁금해.)

　　C: Me, too. Let's watch this video and ＿＿＿＿ ＿＿＿＿.
(나도 그래. 이 비디오를 보고 알아보자.)

② 비교해 표현하기

A We got a new puppy yesterday. 우리 어제 새 강아지를 데려왔어.

B Oh, he's so small! 오. 그는 정말 작다.

A Yeah. He's as small as my hand. 응. 그는 내 손만큼 작아.

■ "as ~ as"는 사람이나 사물들의 유사한 특징을 비교할 때 사용된다. 예를 들어, 친구의 동생을 만났을 때 동생의 키가 친구와 거의 비슷하다면 "Your brother is as tall as you."와 같이 말할 수 있다.

비교해 표현하기

• Your shoes and mine are the same. 네 신발과 내 것이 같구나.

• Our math teacher and PE teacher are alike. 우리 수학 선생님과 체육 선생님은 비슷하다.

• Mammoths are similar to elephants. 매머드들은 코끼리들과 비슷하다.

핵심 Check

2. 다음 주어진 우리말과 일치하도록 빈칸을 완성하시오.

(1) **A:** Let's play a guessing game. It's a fruit. (수수께끼 하자. 이것은 과일이야.)

   B: How _____ is it? (얼마나 커?)

   C: It's _____ _____ _____ a basketball. (농구공만큼 커.)

(2) **A:** What _____ is it? (무슨 색이야?)

   B: It's _____ _____ _____ _____ . (장미꽃만큼 붉은색이야.)

   C: I think it's a strawberry. (딸기라고 생각해.)

(3) **A:** The ants can smell things _____ _____ _____ _____ . Aren't they surprising? (개미들은 개만큼 냄새를 잘 맡을 수 있어요. 놀랍지 않나요?)

   B: Yes. I want _____ _____ _____ _____ _____ .
   (네. 나는 그들에 대해 더 알고 싶어요.)

Listen & Talk 1-B

Clare: Do you think we can be friends with lions, Todd?

Todd: No, Clare. I don't think so.

Clare: Well, I watched a video clip about ❶friendship between two men and a lion.

Todd: Really? ❷I'm curious about the story. Can you tell me more?

Clare: The two men raised a baby lion and sent ❸her back into the wild. When the men and the lion met a year later, ❸she remembered them.

Todd: Wow, that's so ❹touching.

Clare: 우리가 사자와 친구가 될 수 있을 거라고 생각해, Todd?

Todd: 아니, Clare. 난 그렇게 생각하지 않아.

Clare: 음, 나 두 남자와 사자 사이의 우정에 대한 동영상을 봤어.

Todd: 정말? 그 이야기가 궁금해. 더 얘기해 줄 수 있어?

Clare: 두 남자가 아기 사자를 길러서 야생으로 돌려보냈대. 일 년 후에 그 남자들과 사자가 만났을 때, 그 사자는 그들을 기억했다는 거야.

Todd: 와, 정말 감동적이구나.

❶ friendship: 우정
❷ 궁금한 것을 나타내는 표현으로 "I'd be interested to know about the story." 또는 "I want to know about the story."로 바꾸어 표현할 수 있다.
❸ her와 she는 a baby lion을 가리킨다.
❹ touching: 감동적인 (= moving)

Check(√) True or False

(1) A baby lion was raised by the two men before going back to the wild. T ☐ F ☐

(2) Clare was moved by a video clip about friendship between two men and a lion. T ☐ F ☐

Communication

Emily: Hello, Dr. Watson. Can you tell us about your study?

Dr. Watson: I study animals ❶that lived millions of years ago.

Emily: Oh, I'm curious about those animals. Were there any interesting ❷ones?

Dr. Watson: Yes, there were many. This is the giant kangaroo. ❸It lived in Australia. ❸It was ❹as heavy as three men and ❸it couldn't jump well.

Emily: That's amazing!

Emily: 안녕하세요, Watson 박사님. 박사님의 연구에 대해 이야기해 주시겠어요?

Dr. Watson: 전 수백만 년 전에 살았던 동물들을 연구합니다.

Emily: 오, 전 그 동물들이 궁금해요. 흥미로운 동물들이 있었나요?

Dr. Watson: 네, 많이 있었죠. 이 동물은 '자이언트 캥거루'입니다. 호주에서 살았어요. 사람 세 명만큼 무거웠고, 잘 뛰지 못했어요.

Emily: 그거 정말 놀랍군요!

❶ that은 주격 관계대명사로 which로 바꾸어 쓸 수 있다.
❷ ones는 animals를 가리킨다.
❸ It은 모두 'the giant kangaroo'를 가리킨다.
❹ 'as+원급+as' 구문으로 '~만큼 …한'을 의미한다.

Check(√) True or False

(3) Emily wanted to know about the animals that lived millions of years ago. T ☐ F ☐

(4) The giant kangaroo was much heavier than three men. T ☐ F ☐

Listen & Talk 1 A-1

Ryan: Judy, did you choose a topic for your science project?

Judy: Not yet. ❶How about you, Ryan?

Ryan: I'm curious about weather change. So I'm thinking about doing the project on ❷that.

Judy: ❷That's an interesting topic!

❶ '너는 어때?'를 의미하며 'What about you?'로 바꾸어 쓸 수 있다.
❷ that은 weather change를 가리킨다.

Listen & Talk 1 A-2

Jane: ❶Look at this picture of a huge flower.

Tom: Wow, ❷it is bigger than a person.

Jane: Yeah. I'm really curious about this flower. It also says here that the flower smells very bad, but ❸insects love the smell.

Tom: Hmm, I wonder why.

❶ Look at: ~을 보다
❷ it은 a huge flower를 가리킨다.
❸ insect: 곤충, 벌레

Listen & Talk 2 A-1

Dylan: Look at this picture, Mina. We got a new puppy yesterday. He's only two weeks old.

Mina: Oh, Dylan, ❶he's so small!

Dylan: Yeah. He's as small as my hand now, but he'll get ❷much bigger in ❸a few months.

Mina: Wow, puppies grow very quickly.

❶ he는 a new puppy를 가리킨다.
❷ much는 비교급을 강조하는 표현으로 even, a lot, still, far 등으로 바꾸어 쓸 수 있다.
❸ a few+셀 수 있는 명사: 조금의, few+셀 수 있는 명사: 거의 없는

Listen & Talk 2 A-2

Kelly: George, ❶that red house over there is my grandparents' house.

George: Wow, the tree by the house is really big.

Kelly: ❷Actually, that tree is as old as me, thirteen years old.

George: How do you know ❸that, Kelly?

Kelly: My grandfather ❹planted the tree in 2004 when I ❺was born.

❶ that은 지시형용사로 '저, 그'를 뜻한다.
❷ actually: 실제로
❸ that은 'That tree is as old as Kelly, thirteen years old.'를 나타낸다.
❹ plant: 심다
❺ be born: 태어나다

Listen & Talk 2 B-2

Toby: Hi, I'm Toby. I'm going to ❶give a presentation about the blue whale. ❷It's ❸the biggest sea animal in the world. How big is ❷it? Well, ❷it's about 30m long. That means ❷it's longer than a basketball court. Another interesting thing is that its ❹tongue is as heavy as an elephant! Surprising, isn't it?

❶ give a presentation: 발표하다
❷ it은 모두 the blue whale을 가리킨다.
❸ the biggest는 '가장 큰'을 의미하며 최상급을 나타낸다.
❹ tongue: 혀

● 다음 우리말과 일치하도록 빈칸에 알맞은 말을 쓰시오.

Listen & Talk 1 A-1

Ryan: Judy, did you choose a _____ for your science project?

Judy: Not yet. How about you, Ryan?

Ryan: _____ _____ _____ _____ _____. So I'm thinking about _____ the project on that.

Judy: That's an interesting topic!

Ryan: Judy, 너 과학 과제로 할 주제 골랐어?
Judy: 아직. 너는 어때, Ryan?
Ryan: 나는 날씨 변화가 궁금하거든. 그래서 난 그것에 관한 과제를 하려고 생각 중이야.
Judy: 주제가 흥미로운걸!

Listen & Talk 1 A-2

Jane: Look at this picture of a _____ flower.

Tom: Wow, it is _____ than a person.

Jane: Yeah. I'm really _____ _____ this flower. It also _____ here that the flower smells very bad, but _____ love the smell.

Tom: Hmm, I wonder _____.

Jane: 이 커다란 꽃 사진을 봐.
Tom: 와, 사람보다 더 크네.
Jane: 그래. 나는 이 꽃이 정말 궁금해. 또 여기에 나와 있는데 그 꽃은 냄새가 매우 고약하지만 벌레들은 그 냄새를 좋아한대.
Tom: 흠, 이유가 궁금하다.

Listen & Talk 1 B

Clare: Do you think we can _____ _____ with lions, Todd?

Todd: No, Clare. I don't _____ _____.

Clare: Well, I watched a video clip about _____ between two men and a lion.

Todd: Really? I'm _____ _____ the story. Can you tell me more?

Clare: The two men _____ a baby lion and sent her _____ into the _____. When the men and the lion met _____ _____ _____, she remembered them.

Todd: Wow, that's so _____.

Clare: 우리가 사자와 친구가 될 수 있을 거라고 생각해, Todd?
Todd: 아니, Clare. 난 그렇게 생각하지 않아.
Clare: 음, 나 두 남자와 사자 사이의 우정에 대한 동영상을 봤어.
Todd: 정말? 그 이야기가 궁금해. 더 얘기해 줄 수 있어?
Clare: 두 남자가 아기 사자를 길러서 야생으로 돌려보냈대. 일 년 후에 그 남자들과 사자가 만났을 때, 그 사자는 그들을 기억했다는 거야.
Todd: 와, 정말 감동적이구나.

Listen & Talk 2 A-1

Dylan: Look at this picture, Mina. We got a new _____ yesterday. He's only two weeks old.

Mina: Oh, Dylan, he's _____ _____!

Dylan: Yeah. He's _____ _____ _____ my hand now, but he'll get _____ _____ in a few months.

Mina: Wow, puppies _____ very quickly.

Dylan: 이 사진 좀 봐, 미나야. 우리 어제 새 강아지를 데리고 왔어. 그 강아지는 2주밖에 안됐어.
Mina: 오, Dylan, 걔 너무 조그맣다!
Dylan: 맞아. 그 애는 지금 내 손만큼 작지만, 몇 달 뒤에는 훨씬 더 커질 거야.
Mina: 와, 강아지들은 정말 빨리 크네.

Listen & Talk 2 A-2

Kelly: George, that red house _____ _____ is my grandparents' house.

George: Wow, the tree by the house is _____ _____ .

Kelly: Actually, that tree is _____ _____ _____ _____ , thirteen years old.

George: How do you know that, Kelly?

Kelly: My grandfather _____ the tree in 2004 when I _____ _____ .

Listen & Talk 2 B

Toby: Hi, I'm Toby. I'm going to _____ _____ _____ about the blue whale. It's _____ _____ sea animal in the world. How big is it? Well, it's about 30m long. That means it's _____ _____ a basketball court. Another interesting thing is that its tongue is _____ _____ _____ an elephant! Surprising, _____ _____ ?

Communication

Emily: Hello, Dr. Watson. Can you tell us about your study?

Dr. Watson: I study animals that lived _____ _____ years ago.

Emily: Oh, I'm _____ about those animals. Were there _____ interesting ones?

Dr. Watson: Yes, there were _____ . This is the giant kangaroo. It lived in Australia. It was _____ _____ _____ three men and it couldn't jump well.

Emily: That's _____ !

해석

Kelly: George, 저기에 있는 빨간 집이 우리 할아버지와 할머니 댁이야.
George: 와, 집 옆에 있는 나무가 굉장히 크네.
Kelly: 사실, 저 나무의 나이는 나랑 같아서 수령이 13년 되었어.
George: 그걸 어떻게 알아, Kelly?
Kelly: 할아버지께서 내가 태어난 해인 2004년에 그 나무를 심으셨거든.

Toby: 안녕하세요, 저는 Toby입니다. 저는 흰긴수염고래에 대해서 발표를 하려고 해요. 그 고래는 세상에서 가장 큰 바다 동물이에요. 얼마나 크냐고요? 음, 길이가 30미터 정도 돼요. 그 말은 그 고래가 농구 경기장보다 길다는 뜻이에요. 또 다른 흥미로운 점은 그 고래의 혀가 코끼리만큼 무겁다는 거예요! 놀랍죠, 그렇지 않나요?

Emily: 안녕하세요, Watson 박사님. 박사님의 연구에 대해 이야기해 주시겠어요?
Dr Watson: 전 수백만 년 전에 살았던 동물들을 연구합니다.
Emily: 오, 전 그 동물들이 궁금해요. 흥미로운 동물들이 있었나요?
Dr Watson: 네, 많이 있었죠. 이 동물은 '자이언트 캥거루'입니다. 호주에서 살았어요. 사람 세 명만큼 무거웠고, 잘 뛰지 못했어요.
Emily: 그거 정말 놀랍군요!

[01~02] 다음 대화를 읽고 물음에 답하시오.

> Ryan: Judy, did you choose a topic for your science project?
>
> Judy: Not yet. How about you, Ryan?
>
> Ryan: I'm curious about weather change. So I'm thinking about doing the project on (a)that.
>
> Judy: _____ (A)

01 위 대화의 빈칸 (A)에 들어갈 말로 나머지와 의도가 다른 것은?

① Sounds like an interesting topic!

② How interesting the topic is!

③ What an interesting topic!

④ I think it should be an interesting topic.

⑤ That's an interesting topic!

02 위 대화의 밑줄 친 (a)가 가리키는 말을 찾아 쓰시오.

➡ _____

[03~04] 다음 글을 읽고 물음에 답하시오.

> Toby: Hi, I'm Toby. I'm going to give a presentation about the blue whale. It's the ___(A)___ (big) sea animal in the world. How big is it? Well, it's about 30m long. That means it's ___(B)___ (long) than a baskctball court. Another interesting thing is that its tongue is as heavy as an elephant! Surprising, isn't it?

03 위 글의 빈칸 (A)와 (B)에 주어진 단어를 알맞은 형태로 쓰시오.

(A) _____ (B) _____

04 위 글의 내용과 일치하지 않는 것은?

① Toby explains the blue whale.

② There is nothing bigger than the blue whale in the sea.

③ The blue whale is 30m long.

④ The basketball court is longer than the blue whale.

⑤ The blue whale's tongue is as heavy as an elephant.

[01~02] 다음 대화를 읽고 물음에 답하시오.

Ryan: Judy, did you choose a topic for your science project?

Judy: Not yet. How about you, Ryan?

Ryan: (A)나는 날씨 변화가 궁금하거든. So I'm thinking about doing the project on that.

Judy: That's an interesting topic!

서답형

01 위 대화의 밑줄 친 (A)의 우리말을 주어진 단어를 모두 배열하여 영작하시오.

┌─ 보기 ┤
curious / weather / about / I'm / change
└─────────────────────────────────

➡ _____

02 위 대화의 내용과 일치하지 <u>않는</u> 것은?

① Judy hasn't decided her topic for the science project.

② Ryan is thinking about weather change for the science project.

③ Ryan is interested in weather change.

④ Judy thinks that the weather change is an interesting topic.

⑤ Judy is interested in weather change.

03 다음 글의 내용과 일치하도록 다음 표의 빈칸을 완성하시오.

Toby: Hi, I'm Toby. I'm going to give a presentation about the blue whale. It's the biggest sea animal in the world. How big is it? Well, it's about 30m long. That means it's longer than a basketball court. Another interesting thing is that its tongue is as heavy as an elephant! Surprising, isn't it?

↓

How big is the blue whale?	
Size	It's the (1)_____ sea animal in the world.
Length	It's (2)_____ long. It's longer than (3)_____ _____.
Interesting point	(4)_____

[04~05] 다음 대화를 읽고 물음에 답하시오.

Jane: Look at this picture of a huge flower.

Tom: Wow, it is bigger than a person.

Jane: Yeah. I'm really curious about this flower. It also says here that the flower smells very bad, but __(A)__ s love the smell.

Tom: Hmm, I wonder why.

서답형

04 위 대화의 빈칸 (A)에 다음 주어진 영영풀이가 나타내는 말을 쓰시오.

any small creature with six legs and a body divided into three part

➡ _____

05 위 대화를 읽고 대답할 수 <u>없는</u> 것은?

① What are Jane and Tom looking at?

② What does Jane want to know about?

③ What is bigger than a person in the picture?

④ Why do insects like the smell of the huge flower?

⑤ How does the huge flower smell?

[06~07] 다음 대화를 읽고 물음에 답하시오.

Dylan: Look at this picture, Mina. We got a new puppy yesterday. He's only two weeks old.

Mina: Oh, Dylan, he's so small!

Dylan: Yeah. He's as (A)[small / smaller] as my hand now, but he'll get (B)[many / much] bigger in a few months.

Mina: Wow, puppies grow very (C)[quick / quickly].

06 위 대화의 괄호 (A)~(C)에 알맞은 말로 바르게 짝지어진 것은?

① small – many – quick

② small – much – quickly

③ smallest – much – quick

④ smaller – much – quickly

⑤ smaller – many – quick

07 위 대화의 내용과 일치하지 <u>않는</u> 것은?

① Dylan은 어제 새 강아지를 얻었다.

② Dylan은 새 강아지를 직접 Mina에게 보여주고 있다.

③ 강아지는 2주 밖에 안됐다.

④ 강아지는 Dylan의 손만큼 작다.

⑤ 강아지는 정말 빨리 큰다.

[08~09] 다음 대화를 읽고 물음에 답하시오.

Clare: Do you think we can be friends with lions, Todd?

Todd: No, Clare. I don't think so.

Clare: Well, I watched a video clip about friendship between two men (A)[and / or] a lion.

Todd: Really? I'm curious about the story. Can you tell me more?

Clare: The two men raised a baby lion and (B)[sending / sent] her back into the wild. When the men and the lion met a year later, she remembered them.

Todd: Wow, ⓐthat's so (C)[touched / touching].

08 위 대화의 괄호 (A)~(C)에 알맞은 말로 바르게 짝지어진 것은?

① and – sending – touched

② and – sent – touching

③ and – sent – touched

④ or – sent – touching

⑤ or – sending – touched

09 위 대화의 밑줄 친 ⓐ가 가리키는 것을 우리말로 쓰시오.

➡ _____

10 다음 대화의 내용과 일치하지 <u>않는</u> 것은?

Kelly: George, that red house over there is my grandparents' house.

George: Wow, the tree by the house is really big.

Kelly: Actually, that tree is as old as me, thirteen years old.

George: How do you know <u>that</u>, Kelly?

Kelly: My grandfather planted the tree in 2004 when I was born.

① The house of Kelly's grandparents is red.

② There is a tree by the red house.

③ The tree is thirteen years old.

④ Kelly's grandfather planted the tree when Kelly was born.

⑤ The tree is as old as Kelly's grandparents.

[01~03] 다음 글을 읽고 물음에 답하시오.

Toby: Hi, I'm Toby. I'm going to give a presentation about the blue whale. It's the biggest sea animal in the world. How big is it? Well, it's about 30m long. That means it's longer than a basketball court. Another interesting thing is that its tongue is as heavy as an elephant! Surprising, isn't it?

01 How long is the blue whale?

➡ _____

02 Which is longer, a blue whale or a basketball court?

➡ _____

03 중요 What is the blue whale's tongue as heavy as?

➡ _____

04 다음 대화의 내용과 일치하도록 빈칸을 완성하시오.

Jane: Look at this picture of a huge flower.
Tom: Wow, it is bigger than a person.
Jane: Yeah. I'm really curious about this flower. It also says here that the flower smells very bad, but insects love the smell.
Tom: Hmm, I wonder why.

↓

Jane found out a flower which is (A)_____ than a person in the (B)_____. Interestingly, the flower smells very bad but (C)_____ are fond of its smell. Tom was curious about why (D)_____ _____ _____.

[05~06] 다음 대화를 읽고 물음에 답하시오.

Clare: Do you think we can be friends with lions, Todd?
Todd: No, Clare. I don't think so.
Clare: Well, I watched a video clip about friendship between two men and a lion.
Todd: Really? I'm curious about the story. Can you tell me more?
Clare: The two men raised a baby lion and sent her back into the wild. When the men and the lion met a year later, she remembered them.
Todd: Wow, that's so touching.

05 중요 What was the video clip Clare watched about?

➡ _____
_____

06 What did the lion remember?

➡ _____

07 고난이도 다음 대화가 자연스럽게 이어지도록 순서대로 배열하시오.

(A) I'm curious about weather change. So I'm thinking about doing the project on that.
(B) Not yet. How about you, Ryan?
(C) That's an interesting topic!
(D) Judy, did you choose a topic for your science project?

➡ _____

Grammar

① 가주어 It

- **It** is good **to read** many books. 많은 책을 읽는 것은 좋다.
- **It** was hard **to stop** the machine. 그 기계를 멈추는 것은 어려웠다.

■ to부정사구가 문장의 주어로 쓰여 주어가 길어진 경우, 주어부를 문장의 맨 뒤로 보내고 이 자리에 It을 쓰는 것이 가주어 It이다.

- **To exercise** early in the morning is helpful.
  = It is helpful **to exercise** early in the morning. 아침 일찍 운동하는 것은 도움이 된다.

■ 가주어 It은 따로 해석하지 않으며 to부정사구를 주어로 해석해야 한다. to부정사구의 부정은 'not+to V'로 나타낸다.

- **It** is wrong **to lie** to your friend. 친구에게 거짓말하는 것은 나쁘다.
- **It** was hard **to remember** all the appointments. 모든 약속을 기억하는 것은 어려웠다.
- **It** is useful **to know** how to use the copy machine. 복사기를 사용하는 방법을 아는 것은 유용하다.
- **It** is necessary **not to skip** meals. 식사를 거르지 않는 것이 필요하다.

■ to부정사구가 주어인 경우 가주어 It을 사용하여 문장을 만드는 것과 마찬가지로, that절이 주어인 경우에도 가주어 It을 사용할 수 있다.

- **That** he should miss his family is natural.
  = **It** is natural **that** he should miss his family. 그가 그의 가족을 그리워하는 것은 당연하다.

핵심 Check

1. 다음 우리말과 일치하도록 빈칸에 알맞은 말을 쓰시오.
   (1) 운동을 규칙적으로 하는 것은 중요하다.
   ➡ _____ is important _____ _____ regularly.
   (2) 놀이공원에 가는 것은 즐겁다.
   ➡ _____ is amusing _____ _____ to the amusement park.
   (3) 걷는 동안 휴대 전화기를 사용하지 않는 것이 중요하다.
   ➡ _____ is important _____ _____ _____ your phone while walking.

② 원급 비교

- Sally is **as** smart **as** Minju. Sally는 민주만큼 똑똑하다.
- They were **as** hungry **as** Tom. 그들은 Tom만큼 배가 고팠다.

- 'as ~ as' 원급 비교는 두 개의 대상을 비교할 때 정도가 같을 경우 사용할 수 있는 표현이다. 'as+형용사/부사의 원급+as'로 '~만큼 …한[하게]'라고 해석한다. 앞에 쓰인 as는 '그러한, 똑같은 정도로'라는 의미의 부사이며, 뒤에 쓰이고 있는 as는 '~와 같이'라는 의미로 접속사이다.
  - Julia came **as** late **as** you. Julia는 너만큼 늦게 왔어.
  - Robert is **as** tall **as** Chuck. Robert는 Chuck만큼 키가 크다.

- 원급 비교의 부정인 'not as[so]+원급+as ~'는 '~만큼 …하지 않은[않게]'라는 의미로, 비교하는 두 대상의 정도가 같지 않을 경우 쓸 수 있다.
  - Your pie was **not as** delicious **as** his pie. 너의 파이는 그의 파이만큼 맛있지 않았어.
  - She doesn't talk **as** loudly **as** Jason. 그녀는 Jason만큼 크게 말하지 않는다.

- 동등 비교를 이용하여 비교의 배수 표현이 가능하다. '배수사(twice, three times)+as+형용사/부사+as'의 형태이며 '~의 몇 배만큼 …한'이라는 의미로 쓰인다.
  - This balloon is **twice as** big **as** that balloon. 이 풍선은 저 풍선보다 두 배만큼 크다.
  - This mountain is **three times as** high **as** Namsan. 이 산은 남산보다 세 배 높다.

- 원급을 이용한 관용 표현을 알아두자. 'as+원급+as possible'은 '가능한 한 ~한[하게]'라고 해석되고 이는 'as+원급+as+주어+can[could]'와 같다.
  - Call me **as** often **as possible**. 가능한 한 자주 전화하렴.

핵심 Check

2. 다음 우리말과 일치하도록 빈칸에 알맞은 말을 쓰시오.
   (1) 그들은 우리만큼 가난하지 않아.
   ➡ They are ＿＿＿ ＿＿＿ ＿＿＿ ＿＿＿ we are.
   (2) 그 치마는 이 바지보다 두 배 비싸.
   ➡ The skirt is ＿＿＿ ＿＿＿ ＿＿＿ these pants.
   (3) 그녀는 나만큼 춤을 잘 춘다.
   ➡ She dances ＿＿＿ ＿＿＿ ＿＿＿ I.

01 다음 문장에서 어법상 <u>어색한</u> 부분을 바르게 고치시오.

(1) It is important to being fair and truthful.

_____ ➡ _____

(2) He is as simply as a child.

_____ ➡ _____

(3) It is essential drive carefully.

_____ ➡ _____

(4) It is three time as expensive as the watch.

_____ ➡ _____

02 다음 우리말에 맞게 빈칸에 알맞은 말을 쓰시오.

(1) 소풍을 가는 것은 친구들과 노는 것만큼 재미있다.
   ➡ Going on a picnic is _____ _____ _____ playing with friends.

(2) 그 강은 나일강만큼 길지 않다.
   ➡ The river is _____ _____ _____ _____ the Nile.

(3) 이 바지는 너의 바지보다 두 배 더 따뜻하다.
   ➡ These pants are _____ _____ _____ _____ yours.

(4) 사탕은 아이스크림만큼 달콤하다.
   ➡ Candies are _____ _____ _____ ice cream.

03 주어진 단어를 바르게 배열하여 다음 우리말을 영어로 쓰시오. 필요하다면 어형을 바꾸시오.

(1) 어려움에 처한 사람들을 돕는 것은 중요합니다.
   (in need / it / people / help / important / is)
   ➡ _____

(2) 서로를 돕는 것은 이득이 된다. (help / it / each / beneficial / is / other)
   ➡ _____

(3) 그는 너만큼 어리석지 않아.
   (are / is / you / foolish / as / he / as / not)
   ➡ _____

(4) 그 영화는 'Amazing Amy'만큼 지루하지 않다.
   (Amazing Amy / is / boring / the movie / as / as / not)
   ➡ _____

01 다음 중 빈칸에 들어갈 말로 알맞지 <u>않은</u> 것은?

> Kathy is as _____ as Polly.

① lovely   ② friendly
③ lonely   ④ diligent
⑤ kindly

02 다음 중 밑줄 친 부분의 쓰임이 <u>다른</u> 하나는?

① <u>It</u> is my favorite hobby to play the violin.
② <u>It</u> was lucky to meet you there.
③ <u>It</u> is under the sofa in the living room.
④ <u>It</u> is hard to play tennis every day.
⑤ <u>It</u> is fun to play computer games.

03 다음 우리말을 영어로 바르게 옮긴 것은?

> 그는 가능한 한 빨리 달렸다.

① He ran as fastly as he could.
② He runs as fastly as he can.
③ He runs as fast as he can.
④ He ran as fast as he can.
⑤ He ran as fast as he could.

서답형

04 주어진 단어를 바르게 배열하여 다음 우리말을 영어로 쓰시오. 필요하다면 단어를 추가하시오.

> 한 시간에 그 퍼즐을 푸는 것은 어렵다.
> (difficult / an hour / in / it / the puzzle / is / solve)

➡ _____

05 다음 중 빈칸에 알맞은 것을 바르게 묶은 것은?

> • It is fun _____ a foreign language.
> • Eating well is _____ sleeping well.

① learn – as important
② learning – as importantly as
③ as learning – as importance
④ to learn – as important as
⑤ to learn – important

06 to부정사를 이용하여 다음 우리말을 영어로 쓸 때, 다섯 번째로 오는 단어는?

> 자전거를 타는 것은 좋은 운동이다.

① good   ② exercise   ③ to
④ ride   ⑤ a

07 다음 중 어법상 <u>틀린</u> 문장은?

① It is my dream to travel around the world.
② Sophia is not as clever as you are.
③ Sunsets are as beautiful as sunrises.
④ It is easy to make them believe it.
⑤ The water in this cup is not as clearer as the water in that cup.

서답형

08 주어진 단어를 활용하여 다음 우리말을 영어로 쓰시오.

> 밤늦게 밖에 혼자 나가는 것은 위험하다.
> (it / outside / late at night)

➡ _____

09 다음 중 표에 관한 내용으로 바르지 <u>않은</u> 것은?

	Age	Height	Weight
Jason	15	170cm	70kg
Mike	14	170cm	64kg
Paul	15	165cm	64kg

① Jason is as old as Paul.

② Mike is not as heavy as Jason.

③ Paul is not as tall as Mike.

④ Jason is as heavy as Paul.

⑤ Mike is as tall as Jason.

10 다음 빈칸에 들어갈 말로 가장 적절한 것은?

It is a pity _____ Helen broke her arm.

① to   ② so   ③ what

④ that   ⑤ which

11 다음 중 우리말 전환이 바르지 <u>않은</u> 것은?

① 네 시계는 내 시계만큼 정확해.

→ Your watch is as accurate as mine.

② 축구를 보는 것은 재미있어.

→ It is fun to watch football.

③ John이 나에게 거짓말을 한 것은 사실이야.

→ It is true John to lie to me.

④ 그는 그녀보다 두 배 많은 물을 가지고 있다.

→ He has two times as much water as she has.

⑤ 그녀의 머리카락은 나만큼 길지 않다.

→ Her hair is not as long as mine.

서답형

12 주어진 단어를 활용하여 다음 두 문장을 하나의 문장으로 표현하시오.

• Alex gets up at 6 a.m. • I get up at 6 a.m., too.

➡ _____ (early)

13 다음 중 어법상 바르지 <u>않은</u> 것은?

①It is ②impolite ③to not pay attention ④to ⑤what others are saying.

①   ②   ③   ④   ⑤

14 다음 중 빈칸에 들어갈 말로 가장 적절한 것은?

Zach is more nervous than Clara. = Clara _____ Zach.

① is as nervous as

② is more nervous than

③ is much more nervous

④ is not as nervous as

⑤ is as nervously as

15 다음 중 밑줄 친 부분의 쓰임이 <u>다른</u> 하나는?

① They wanted to see me <u>to ask</u> some questions.

② It is your duty washing the car every day <u>to keep</u> it clean.

③ Jack went to Paris <u>to study</u> fashion.

④ Polly cooked food for us <u>to make</u> us happy.

⑤ It is necessary <u>to attend</u> the meeting.

16 다음 중 빈칸에 들어갈 말이 바르게 짝지어진 것은?

• It is true _____ Kelvin bought a new car. • You watch TV too much. I don't watch _____ you.

① to – much TV

② that – as many TV as

③ to – TV as much as

④ that – TV as much as

⑤ to – as many TV as

17 다음 우리말을 영어로 바르게 옮긴 것을 고르시오.

> 안전수칙을 따르는 것은 중요합니다.

① It is important to obey rules.
② It is important obey safety rules.
③ It is important to obeying safety rules.
④ It is important to obey safety rules.
⑤ It is important obeyed safety rules.

[서답형]

18 원급 비교를 이용하여 다음 대화의 빈칸에 알맞은 말을 쓰시오.

> A: How tall are you?
> B: I'm 165cm tall.
> A: Oh, then you _____
>   my brother. He is 170cm tall.

[중요]

19 다음 중 서로 의미가 통하지 <u>않는</u> 것은?

① It is not easy to learn French.
    = To learn French is not easy.
② Riding a bike is really exciting.
    = It is really exciting to ride a bike.
③ Your watch is more expensive than mine.
    = My watch is as expensive as yours.
④ It is my job to protect you.
    = Protecting you is my job.
⑤ I think sun flowers are not as pretty as roses.
    = I think roses are prettier than sun flowers.

[서답형]

20 주어진 단어를 활용하여 다음 우리말을 영어로 쓰시오.

> 네가 그녀를 걱정하는 것은 당연해.
> (it / natural / worry about)

➡ _____

[중요]

21 다음 문장과 같은 의미의 문장으로 가장 적절한 것은?

> Kelly works harder than Julia.

① Julia works as hard as Kelly.
② Julia works harder than Kelly.
③ Julia doesn't work hard.
④ Julia doesn't work as hard as Kelly.
⑤ Julia doesn't want to work hard.

[중요]

22 다음 중 어법상 바르지 <u>않은</u> 문장의 개수는?

> ⓐ It is lucky to seeing the man make a speech.
> ⓑ Jim sings as good as Miranda.
> ⓒ Brad makes pies as often as you do.
> ⓓ It is a pity that she made a mistake.
> ⓔ It is difficult find her right suit.

① 1개   ② 2개   ③ 3개   ④ 4개   ⑤ 5개

23 다음 두 문장을 하나의 문장으로 바르게 표현한 것은?

> • David has ten friends.
> • Gloria has five friends.

① David has as many friends as Gloria.
② Gloria has as many friends as David.
③ David hasn't as many friends as Gloria.
④ Gloria hasn't as many friends as David.
⑤ Gloria has more friends than David has.

[서답형]

24 주어진 단어를 활용하여 다음 우리말을 영어로 쓰시오.

> 이 물을 마시는 것은 안전합니다. (it)

➡ _____

01 원급 비교를 이용하여 다음 두 문장을 하나의 문장으로 표현할 때 빈칸에 알맞은 말을 쓰시오.

> Jinsu has three balloons. I have six balloons.
> ➡ I _____ .

02 주어진 단어를 활용하여 다음 우리말을 영어로 쓰시오.

> 이 산의 꼭대기까지 걷는 것이 가능하다.
> (it / the top of this mountain)

➡ _____

03 원급 비교를 이용하여 다음 주어진 문장과 같은 의미가 되도록 빈칸을 완성하시오.

> You have more money than me.
> = I don't have _____ you.

04 다음 문장과 같은 의미의 문장을 완성하시오.

> To wear a helmet is safe.
> = It _____ .

05 다음 빈칸에 알맞은 말을 다섯 단어로 쓰시오.

> Mr. Jackson is 90 years old. Mrs. Jackson is 91 years old. So, Mr. Jackson _____ Mrs. Jackson.

06 다음은 Peter의 자기소개 중 일부이다. 주어진 단어를 활용하여 영어로 쓰시오.

> 안경 없이 무언가를 보는 것은 힘듭니다. 나는 안경이 없으면 박쥐만큼 앞이 보이지 않아요.
> (it / hard / something / without / blind)

➡ _____

_____

07 다음 문장과 같은 의미의 문장을 각각 쓰시오.

(1) That we try to save energy is important.
   ➡ _____

(2) To get there in time is impossible.
   ➡ _____

(3) To hear her singing was difficult.
   ➡ _____

(4) To want to be rich without working hard is foolish.
   ➡ _____
   _____

(5) To play with matches is unsafe.
   ➡ _____

08 다음 글의 빈칸에 알맞은 말을 쓰시오.

> This box weighs 10 grams. A feather weighs 10 grams. So this box _____ a feather. Anyone can move it.

09 주어진 단어를 어법과 내용에 맞게 빈칸에 쓰시오.

이름	Mike	John	Betty
키	168cm	180cm	168cm
몸무게	75kg	75kg	50kg
신발사이즈	280mm	270mm	270mm

(1) Mike _____ John. (tall)

(2) John's shoes _____ Mike's.
   (big)

(3) Betty's shoes _____ John's.
   (big)

(4) John _____ Mike. (heavy)

(5) Mike _____ Betty. (tall)

(6) Betty _____ Mike and John.
   (heavy)

10 주어진 단어를 바르게 배열하여 다음 우리말을 영어로 쓰시오. 필요하다면 단어를 추가하시오.

> 지구에 사는 동물을 보호할 필요가 있다.
> (it / the animals / is / protect / necessary /
> on Earth)

➡ _____

11 다음 대화의 빈칸에 알맞은 말을 세 단어로 쓰시오.

> A: What did you have for lunch?
> B: I ate pizza. It was _____ ice,
>   so I had to heat it.

12 다음 빈칸에 알맞은 말을 다섯 단어로 쓰시오.

> A: Was it _____?
> B: Yes, it was. Answering his questions
>   was not difficult.

13 다음 주어진 단어를 빈칸에 알맞게 채우시오.

> enter a cage   feed the animals
> take a zoo tour   take pets to the zoo

(1) 동물들에게 먹이를 주는 것은 잘못된 것이다.
   ➡ It is _____.

(2) 동물원 관람을 하는 것은 흥미진진하다.
   ➡ It is _____.

(3) 우리에 들어가는 것은 위험하다.
   ➡ It is _____.

(4) 애완동물을 동물원에 데려가는 것은 안전하지
   않다.
   ➡ It is _____.

14 대화의 빈칸에 알맞은 말을 쓰시오.

> A: My rope is one meter long.
> B: Oh, then your rope _____
>   _____ _____ _____ my rope. My
>   rope is 50cm long. But Suji's rope is
>   the same as mine. Her rope _____
>   _____.

15 주어진 단어를 활용하여 다음 대화를 영어로 쓰시오.

> A: 연을 날리는 것은 재미있니?
> B: Yes, it is. Flying a kite _____.
>   응, 그래. 연을 날리는 것은 컴퓨터 게임을 하
>   는 것만큼 재미있어. (fun)

A: _____

B: _____

The Footprints of a Baby Elephant

Date/Time: July 8th / 2:35 p.m.

Notes: Today was my first day in Africa. I took lots of pictures of
넓은 범위 앞에서 쓰이는 전치사 = many
elephants. This morning, I found an elephant group by a small water
~ 옆에
hole. I saw a baby elephant drinking water beside her mother. Her eyes
지각동사+목적어+Ving
were as bright as stars. I gave her a name, Stella. Around noon, I saw
as+원급+as: ~만큼 …한
a group of lions approaching Stella. The elephants stood around Stella
지각동사+목적어+Ving
and made a thick wall. Thanks to them, Stella was safe.
Thanks to+ 명사: ~ 덕분에

Date/Time: July 12th / 7:20 p.m.

Notes: Around sunset, I heard a strange sound. I followed the sound
and found Stella crying next to her mom. She was lying dead and
find+목적어+Ving: 목적어의 상태를 설명하기 위하여 현재분사를 사용   자동사 lie의 주격보어
Stella was alone. It is dangerous to stay alone in such a wild area.
가주어 It   진주어 to V
What's more, it was going to be dark soon. Elephants can't see well at
비인칭 주어(날짜, 날씨, 거리, 명암 등을 나타낼 때)   코끼리가 밤에 잘 볼 수 없는 것은 일반적인 사실이므로 현재시제로 씀
night. So Stella could easily be attacked. I called the elephant shelter
조동사가 있는 수동태
and asked for help. I decided to stay by her until the rescue team came.
to부정사를 목적어로 취하는 동사   시간 부사절 접속사(~할 때까지)

take a picture of ~의 사진을 찍다
hole 구덩이
bright 밝은
approach 다가가다
thick 두꺼운
sunset 해질녘
strange 이상한
follow ~을 따라가다
dead 죽은
dangerous 위험한
wild area 야생 지역
what's more 더욱이
attack ~을 공격하다
shelter 보호소
rescue 구조

확인문제

● 다음 문장이 본문의 내용과 일치하면 T, 일치하지 않으면 F를 쓰시오.

1   The writer gave a name, Stella, to a baby elephant.

2   The writer saw many elephants drink water by the river.

3   The baby elephant was protected by other elephants.

4   Stella's mom was found dead in the morning.

Date/Time: July 12th / 10:40 p.m.

Notes: The night was dark and quiet. I kept my eyes on Stella with
수단을 나타내는 전치사
my night camera. Stella was still next to her mom. She was touching
~옆에(= beside. by)   과거진행형
her mom's lifeless body with her nose. It was sad to see Stella staying
~으로   가주어 It   진주어 to V
close to her mom. I hope Stella stays safe throughout the night.
= I hope (that) 명사절 접속사 생략
Date/Time: July 13th / 6:00 a.m.

Notes: A new elephant group appeared and Stella approached them.
타동사 (approach to ×)
At first, I thought that they would not let Stella in their group. But I
명사절 접속사   ~을 들여놓다
was wrong. An elephant, probably the oldest female allowed Stella to
the+최상급: 가장 ~한   allow+목적어+to V: 목적어가 V하도록 허락하다
become part of the group. The other elephants also seemed to welcome
나머지 모든   ~인 것처럼 보였다
Stella. Unbelievably, one of the female elephants fed Stella. She cared
feed-fed-fed
for Stella as warmly as Stella's mom did. This was such an amazing
as+원급+as: ~만큼 …한   어순: such+a(n)+형용사+명사
moment!

keep one's eyes on ~에서 눈을 떼지 않다

still 여전히

lifeless 죽은, 생명이 없는

throughout ~ 동안, ~ 내내

appear 나타나다

probably 아마도

become part of ~의 일원이 되다

welcome 환영하다, 반기다

unbelievably 믿을 수 없을 정도로

feed 밥[우유]을 먹이다, 먹이를 주다

📎 **확인문제**

● 다음 문장이 본문의 내용과 일치하면 T, 일치하지 <u>않으면</u> F를 쓰시오.

1 It was dark and noisy on the night of July 12. ☐

2 The writer kept watching Stella with his glasses. ☐

3 Stella stayed close to her mother on the night of July 12. ☐

4 A new elephant group approached Stella first. ☐

5 One of the female elephants let Stella in their group. ☐

6 Stella was fed by a female elephant. ☐

7 Some elephants didn't like Stella. ☐

• 우리말을 참고하여 빈칸에 알맞은 말을 쓰시오.

Date/Time: July 8th / 2:35 p.m.

1 Notes: Today _____ _____ _____ day _____ Africa.

2 I _____ lots of _____ elephants.

3 This morning, I _____ an elephant group _____ a small water hole.

4 I _____ a baby elephant _____ water _____ her mother.

5 Her eyes _____ as _____ as stars.

6 I _____ _____ a name, Stella.

7 Around noon, I _____ a group of lions _____ Stella.

8 The elephants _____ _____ Stella and made _____ _____ wall.

9 Thanks to _____, Stella was _____.

Date/Time: July 12th / 7:20 p.m.

10 Notes: _____ sunset, I _____ a strange sound.

11 I _____ the sound and _____ Stella _____ next to her mom.

12 She was _____ _____ and Stella was _____.

13 _____ is dangerous _____ _____ alone _____ such a wild area.

14 _____ _____, _____ was going to be dark soon.

15 Elephants can't _____ _____ at night.

날짜/시간: 7월 8일, 오후 2시 35분

1 기록: 오늘은 내가 아프리카에 온 첫날이었다.

2 나는 코끼리 사진을 많이 찍었다.

3 오늘 아침에 나는 작은 물웅덩이 옆에 있는 한 코끼리 무리를 발견했다.

4 나는 아기 코끼리 한 마리가 엄마 옆에서 물을 마시고 있는 것을 보았다.

5 그 코끼리의 눈이 별처럼 밝았다.

6 나는 그 코끼리에게 Stella란 이름을 붙여 주었다.

7 정오 즈음에 나는 사자 한 무리가 Stella에게 다가가는 것을 보았다.

8 코끼리들은 Stella 주위에 둘러서서 두꺼운 벽을 만들었다.

9 그 코끼리들 덕분에 Stella는 안전했다.

날짜/시간: 7월 12일, 오후 7시 20분

10 기록: 해질녘에 나는 이상한 소리를 들었다.

11 나는 그 소리를 따라갔고 Stella가 자신의 엄마 옆에서 울고 있는 것을 발견했다.

12 엄마는 죽어서 누워 있었고, Stella는 혼자였다.

13 이러한 야생 지역에서 혼자 있는 것은 위험하다.

14 더욱이 곧 어두워질 것이었다.

15 코끼리들은 밤에 잘 볼 수 없다.

16 So Stella could _____ _____ _____ .

17 I called _____ and _____ help.

18 I decided _____ _____ by her _____ the rescue team came.

Date/Time: July 12th / 10:40 p.m.

19 Notes: The night _____ _____ and _____ .

20 I _____ my eyes _____ Stella with my night camera.

21 Stella was _____ _____ _____ her mom.

22 She _____ her mom's lifeless body _____ her nose.

23 _____ was sad _____ Stella _____ close to her mom.

24 I hope Stella _____ _____ throughout the night.

Date/Time: July 13th / 6:00 a.m.

25 Notes: A new elephant group _____ and Stella _____ them.

26 At first, I thought _____ they would not _____ Stella _____ their group.

27 But I was _____ .

28 An elephant, probably _____ allowed Stella _____ _____ part of the group.

29 _____ also seemed to welcome Stella.

30 Unbelievably, one of the female _____ _____ Stella.

31 She cared for Stella _____ Stella's mom _____ .

32 This was _____ _____ _____ moment!

---

16 그래서 Stella는 쉽게 공격을 받을 수 있었다.

17 나는 코끼리 보호소에 전화를 해서 도움을 요청했다.

18 나는 구조대가 올 때까지 Stella 곁에 머물기로 결정했다.

날짜/시간: 7월 12일, 오후 10시 40분

19 기록: 밤은 어둡고 조용했다.

20 나는 야간용 카메라를 이용해서 Stella를 계속 지켜보았다.

21 Stella는 여전히 엄마 곁에 있었다.

22 Stella는 코로 엄마의 죽은 몸을 어루만지고 있었다.

23 Stella가 엄마 가까이에 머물고 있는 것을 보는 것은 슬픈 일이었다.

24 나는 Stella가 밤새도록 안전하게 있기를 바란다.

날짜/시간: 7월 13일, 오전 6시

25 기록: 새로운 코끼리 무리가 나타났고, Stella는 그 무리에 다가갔다.

26 처음에 나는 그 코끼리들이 Stella를 자신의 무리로 받아들이지 않을 것이라고 생각했다.

27 그러나 내 생각이 틀렸다.

28 아마도 가장 나이가 많은 암컷인 듯한 코끼리 한 마리가 Stella가 그 무리의 일원이 되도록 허락했다.

29 다른 코끼리들도 Stella를 반기는 것처럼 보였다.

30 믿을 수 없게도, 암컷 코끼리 중의 한 마리가 Stella에게 젖을 먹였다.

31 그 코끼리는 Stella의 엄마만큼 따뜻하게 Stella를 보살폈다.

32 이것은 너무나 놀라운 순간이었다.

● 우리말을 참고하여 본문을 영작하시오.

날짜/시간: 7월 8일, 오후 2시 35분

1 기록: 오늘은 내가 아프리카에 온 첫날이었다.

➡ _____

2 나는 코끼리 사진을 많이 찍었다.

➡ _____

3 오늘 아침에 나는 작은 물웅덩이 옆에 있는 한 코끼리 무리를 발견했다.

➡ _____

4 나는 아기 코끼리 한 마리가 엄마 옆에서 물을 마시고 있는 것을 보았다.

➡ _____

5 그 코끼리의 눈이 별처럼 밝았다.

➡ _____

6 나는 그 코끼리에게 Stella란 이름을 붙여 주었다.

➡ _____

7 정오 즈음에 나는 사자 한 무리가 Stella에게 다가가는 것을 보았다.

➡ _____

8 코끼리들은 Stella 주위에 둘러서서 두꺼운 벽을 만들었다.

➡ _____

9 그 코끼리들 덕분에 Stella는 안전했다.

➡ _____

날짜/시간: 7월 12일, 오후 7시 20분

10 기록: 해질녘에 나는 이상한 소리를 들었다.

➡ _____

11 나는 그 소리를 따라갔고 Stella가 자신의 엄마 옆에서 울고 있는 것을 발견했다.

➡ _____

12 엄마는 죽어서 누워 있었고, Stella는 혼자였다.

➡ _____

13 이러한 야생 지역에서 혼자 있는 것은 위험하다.

➡ _____

14 더욱이 곧 어두워질 것이었다.

➡ _____

15 코끼리들은 밤에 잘 볼 수 없다.

➡ _____

16 그래서 Stella는 쉽게 공격을 받을 수 있었다.

➡ _____

17 나는 코끼리 보호소에 전화를 해서 도움을 요청했다.

➡ _____

18 나는 구조대가 올 때까지 Stella 곁에 머물기로 결정했다.

➡ _____

날짜/시간: 7월 12일, 오후 10시 40분

19 기록: 밤은 어둡고 조용했다.

➡ _____

20 나는 야간용 카메라를 이용해서 Stella를 계속 지켜보았다.

➡ _____

21 Stella는 여전히 엄마 곁에 있었다.

➡ _____

22 Stella는 코로 엄마의 죽은 몸을 어루만지고 있었다.

➡ _____

23 Stella가 엄마 가까이에 머물고 있는 것을 보는 것은 슬픈 일이었다.

➡ _____

24 나는 Stella가 밤새도록 안전하게 있기를 바란다.

➡ _____

날짜/시간: 7월 13일, 오전 6시

25 기록: 새로운 코끼리 무리가 나타났고, Stella는 그 무리에 다가갔다.

➡ _____

26 처음에 나는 그 코끼리들이 Stella를 자신의 무리로 받아들이지 않을 것이라고 생각했다.

➡ _____

27 그러나 내 생각이 틀렸다.

➡ _____

28 아마도 가장 나이가 많은 암컷인 듯한 코끼리 한 마리가 Stella가 그 무리의 일원이 되도록 허락했다.

➡ _____

29 다른 코끼리들도 Stella를 반기는 것처럼 보였다.

➡ _____

30 믿을 수 없게도, 암컷 코끼리 중의 한 마리가 Stella에게 젖을 먹였다.

➡ _____

31 그 코끼리는 Stella의 엄마만큼 따뜻하게 Stella를 보살폈다.

➡ _____

32 이것은 너무나 놀라운 순간이었다.

➡ _____

[01~03] 다음 글을 읽고 물음에 답하시오.

Date/Time: July 8th / 2:35 p.m.
Notes: Today was my first day in Africa. I took lots of pictures of elephants. This morning, I found an elephant group by a small water hole. I saw a baby elephant drinking water beside her mother. Her eyes were as bright as stars. I gave her a name, Stella. Around noon, I saw a group of lions approaching Stella. The elephants stood around Stella and made a thick wall. Thanks to them, Stella was safe.

01 다음 중 위 글에서 찾아볼 수 <u>없는</u> 것은?

① a person who is taking picture of elephants
② an elephant group near a small water hole
③ a group of lions approaching a baby elephant
④ elephants protecting a baby elephant
⑤ a small elephant sucking its mother's milk

02 다음 중 위 글을 읽고 답할 수 있는 것은?

① How did the writer get to Africa?
② When did the writer take notes?
③ What is the writer's name?
④ How many elephants did the writer see?
⑤ How many lions were there?

서답형
03 What did the writer find on the morning of July 8?

➡ _____
_____

[04~07] 다음 글을 읽고 물음에 답하시오.

Date/Time: July 12th / 7:20 p.m.
Notes: Around sunset, I heard a strange sound. I followed the sound and found Stella crying next to her mom. She was lying dead and Stella was alone. It is dangerous ___(A)___ alone in such a wild area. ___(B)___ , it was going to be dark soon. Elephants can't see well at night. So Stella could easily be attacked. I called the elephant shelter and asked for help. I decided to stay by her until the rescue team came.

서답형
04 빈칸 (A)에 들어갈 알맞은 말을 위 글에서 찾아 어법에 맞게 쓰시오.

➡ _____

05 다음 중 빈칸 (B)에 들어갈 말로 적절하지 <u>않은</u> 것은?

① What's more   ② Furthermore
③ However   ④ In addition
⑤ Besides

06 다음 중 위 글의 내용과 일치하지 <u>않는</u> 것은?

① The writer heard a strange sound around sunset.
② The writer found Stella crying on July 12.
③ Stella was left alone in a wild area.
④ Luckily, Stella can see well at night.
⑤ The writer called the elephant shelter to ask for help.

서답형

07 다음과 같이 풀이되는 말을 위 글에서 찾아 쓰시오.

> a building designed to give protection from bad weather, danger, or attack

➡ _____

[08~10] 다음 글을 읽고 물음에 답하시오.

Date/Time: July 12th / 10:40 p.m.

Notes: The night was dark and quiet. I kept my eyes ___(A)___ Stella with my night camera. Stella was still next to her mom. She was touching her mom's lifeless body with her nose. It was sad to see Stella stay close to her mom. I hope Stella stays safe throughout the night.

08 다음 중 빈칸 (A)에 들어갈 말과 같은 말이 들어가는 것은?

① Did you turn _____ all the lights when you went out of the room?

② I am really looking forward _____ visiting the place.

③ Jason was full _____ justice and courage.

④ Put _____ your mask, or you will catch a cold.

⑤ She needs to pick _____ her sister at the airport.

서답형

09 위 글의 내용과 일치하도록 빈칸에 알맞은 말을 쓰시오.

> A: What made you sad?
> B: _____ _____ _____ _____
> _____ _____ _____ made me
> really sad.

중요

10 다음 중 위 글의 내용과 일치하는 것은?

① The writer wasn't interested in Stella at all.

② Stella left her mother as soon as possible.

③ The writer took care of Stella.

④ Stella's mom was dead.

⑤ Stella spent the night in a shelter.

[11~13] 다음 글을 읽고 물음에 답하시오.

Date/Time: July 13th / 6:00 a.m.

Notes: A new elephant group appeared and Stella approached them.

(A) Unbelievably, one of the female elephants fed Stella. She cared for Stella as warmly as Stella's mom did.

(B) An elephant, probably the oldest female allowed Stella to become part of the group.

(C) At first, I thought that they would not let Stella in their group. But I was wrong.

(D) The other elephants also seemed to welcome Stella.

This was _____ⓐ_____!

서답형

11 자연스러운 글이 되도록 (A)~(D)를 바르게 나열하시오.

➡ _____

12 다음 중 빈칸 ⓐ에 들어갈 말로 가장 적절한 것은?

① amazing such a moment

② such amazing a moment

③ such an amazing moment

④ an amazing such moment

⑤ a moment such amazing

13 Which one is TRUE about the passage?

① The new elephant group didn't accept Stella.

② Stella moved near to the new elephant group.

③ All the elephants didn't like Stella except one elephant.

④ Stella didn't want to be part of the group.

⑤ The writer's guess about the elephants was right.

[14~17] 다음 글을 읽고 물음에 답하시오.

Date/Time: July 8th / 2:35 p.m.
Notes: Today was my first day in Africa. I took ___(A)___ pictures of elephants. This morning, I found an elephant group by a small water hole. ① I saw a baby elephant drinking water beside her mother. ② Her eyes were as bright as stars. ③ I gave her a name, Stella. ④ Around noon, I saw a group of lions approaching Stella. ⑤ Thanks to them, Stella was safe.

14 다음 중 빈칸 (A)에 들어갈 말로 적절하지 않은 것은?

① a number of   ② a lot of

③ lots of   ④ many

⑤ much

15 위 글의 ①~⑤ 중 주어진 문장이 들어가기에 가장 적절한 곳은?

The elephants stood around Stella and made a thick wall.

①   ②   ③   ④   ⑤

16 다음 물음에 완전한 문장의 영어로 답하시오.

Q: Where did the writer write this diary?

➡ _____

17 다음 중 위 글의 내용과 일치하지 않는 것은?

① The writer found an elephant group beside a small water hole.

② The writer took many pictures of elephants.

③ The writer decided to call the mother elephant Stella.

④ A group of lions approached Stella.

⑤ The writer found a group of lions around noon.

[18~21] 다음 글을 읽고 물음에 답하시오.

Date/Time: July 12th / 7:20 p.m.
Notes: Around sunset, I heard a strange sound. I followed the sound and found Stella crying next to her mom. She was lying dead and Stella was alone. (A)To stay alone in such a wild area was dangerous. What's more, (B)it was going to be dark soon. Elephants can't see well at night. So Stella could easily be attacked. I called the elephant shelter and asked for help. I decided to stay by her until the rescue team came.

18 위 글의 밑줄 친 (A)와 같은 의미의 문장을 완성하시오.

It _____.

19 다음 중 밑줄 친 (B)와 쓰임이 다른 것은?

① It was Saturday afternoon.

② It is cloudy and windy.

③ It is ten miles to Boston.

④ It is dark outside.

⑤ It is difficult to solve the problem.

서답형

20 According to the passage, why could Stella be attacked easily at night? Use the phrase 'it's because.'

➡ _____

21 다음 중 위 글을 읽고 답할 수 있는 것은?

① What can elephants do well?
② What was Stella doing in the morning?
③ Whom did the writer call?
④ When did the rescue team come?
⑤ What did the writer see around noon?

[22~23] 다음 글을 읽고 물음에 답하시오.

Date: June 15th, 2019
Write about what you saw:
Today, I saw a plant. It is called a pitcher plant. It is bright green and red. It looks like a pitcher. As for its size, it is about 15cm long. It is as long as my hand. (A)벌레잡이 식물이 곤충을 먹는 것을 보는 것은 흥미로워.

22 Which is NOT true about the passage?

① The writer wrote about a pitcher plant.
② A pitcher plant is bright green and red.
③ The writer's hand is about 15cm long.
④ A pitcher plant is two times as long as the writer's hand.
⑤ A pitcher plant eats insects.

서답형

23 주어진 단어를 활용하여 밑줄 친 우리말 (A)를 영어로 쓰시오.

(it / interesting)

➡ _____

[24~26] 다음 글을 읽고 물음에 답하시오.

Date/Time: July 12th / 10:40 p.m.
Notes: The night was dark and quiet. I ①kept my eyes on Stella with my night camera. Stella was still next to her mom. She was touching her mom's lifeless body with her nose. ②It was sad to see Stella ③staying close to her mom. I hope Stella stays ④safely throughout the night.
Date/Time: July 13th / 6:00 a.m.
Notes: A new elephant group ⑤appeared and Stella approached them. At first, I thought that they would not let Stella in their group. But I was wrong. An elephant, probably the oldest female allowed Stella to become part of the group. The other elephants also seemed to welcome Stella. Unbelievably, one of the female elephants fed Stella. She cared for Stella as ___(A)___ as Stella's mom did. This was such an amazing moment!

서답형

24 빈칸 (A)에 warm의 알맞은 어형을 쓰시오.

➡ _____

25 ①~⑤ 중 어법상 바르지 않은 것은?

①　　②　　③　　④　　⑤

26 다음 중 위 글의 내용을 잘못 이해한 사람은?

① Jason: I'm so sorry that Stella's mom was dead.
② Claire: It was so lucky that Stella spent the night safely.
③ Jim: Unlike the writer, I thought the new elephant group would not accept Stella.
④ Brad: The female elephant which fed Stella is so generous.
⑤ David: I am happy to see Stella become part of the new group.

[01~04] 다음 글을 읽고 물음에 답하시오.

Date/Time: July 8th / 2:35 p.m.
Notes: Today was my first day in Africa. I took lots of pictures of elephants. This morning, I found an elephant group by a small water hole. I saw a baby elephant drinking water beside her mother. _____ (A)
I gave her a name, Stella. Around noon, I saw a group of lions approaching Stella. The elephants stood around Stella and made a thick wall. Thanks to them, Stella was safe.

01 원급비교를 이용하여 다음 두 문장을 하나의 문장으로 만들어 빈칸 (A)를 채우시오.

> Her eyes were bright. They were bright like stars.

➡ _____

02 According to the passage, how did the elephant group protect Stella from the lions?

➡ _____

03 다음 대화의 빈칸을 알맞게 채우시오.

> A: When did you _____ _____ _____ _____?
> B: It was around noon.

04 다음은 글쓴이가 아프리카에서 돌아와서 한 말이다. 위 글의 표현을 활용하여 영어로 쓰시오. 주어진 단어를 활용하시오.

> 사자 한 무리가 Stella에게 다가가는 것을 보는 것은 무서웠어. (it / scare)

➡ _____
_____

[05~08] 다음 글을 읽고 물음에 답하시오.

Date/Time: July 12th / 7:20 p.m.
Notes: Around sunset, I heard a strange sound. I followed the sound and found Stella crying next to her mom. She was lying dead and Stella was alone. It is dangerous to stay alone in such a wild area. What's more, it was going to be dark soon. Elephants can't see well at night. So Stella could easily be attacked. I called the elephant shelter and asked for help. _____ (A) _____ until the rescue team came.

05 주어진 단어를 바르게 배열하여 빈칸 (A)에 들어갈 말을 완성하시오.

> (by / stay / I / to / her / decided)

➡ _____

06 According to the passage, what did the writer find when he followed the strange sound? Answer in English with a full sentence.

➡ _____

07 Write the reason why the writer called the elephant shelter and asked for help. Answer in Korean.

➡ _____
_____

08 원급 비교와 주어진 단어를 활용하여 다음 우리말을 8 단어로 이루어진 한 문장의 영어로 쓰시오.

> 나는 밤에 코끼리만큼 잘 볼 수 없다. (blind)

➡ _____

[09~14] 다음 글을 읽고 물음에 답하시오.

Date/Time: July 12th / 10:40 p.m.

Notes: The night was dark and quiet. I kept my eyes on Stella with my night camera. Stella was still next to her mom. She was touching her mom's lifeless body with her nose. ⓐTo see Stella staying close to her mom was sad. I hope Stella stays safe throughout the night.

Date/Time: July 13th / 6:00 a.m.

Notes: A new elephant group appeared and Stella approached them. At first, I thought that ⓑthey would not let Stella in their group. But I was wrong. An elephant, probably the oldest female allowed Stella to become part of the group. The other elephants also seemed to welcome Stella. Unbelievably, one of the female elephants fed Stella. _____(A)_____. This was such an amazing moment!

09 원급 비교를 이용하여 주어진 문장과 같은 의미의 문장을 빈칸 (A)에 쓰시오.

> She cared for Stella warmly like her mother did.

➡ _____

10 밑줄 친 문장 ⓐ와 같은 의미의 문장을 완성하시오.

> It _____.

11 밑줄 친 ⓑ가 가리키는 것을 위 글에서 찾아 쓰시오.

➡ _____

12 According to the passage, what was Stella doing next to her mother during the night? Answer in English with a full sentence.

➡ _____

_____

13 다음 물음에 완전한 문장의 영어로 답하시오.

> Q: What appeared in front of Stella?

➡ _____

14 When Stella approached a new elephant group, what did the writer think at first? Answer in English.

➡ _____

_____

[15~16] 다음 글을 읽고 물음에 답하시오.

Plant Diary

Date: June 15th, 2019

Write about what you saw:

Today, I saw a plant. It is called a pitcher plant. It is bright green and red. It looks like a pitcher. As for its size, it is about 15cm long. It is as long as my hand. It is interesting that the plant attracts insects and eats them.

15 According to the passage, how long is the writer's hand? Answer in English with a full sentence.

➡ _____

16 According to the passage, what does the plant look like?

➡ _____

Read and Think

Some lions tried to attack Stella. The elephant group made a thick wall to
　　　　～하려고 애썼다
protect her.
to부정사의 부사적 용법 – 목적 (～하기 위해서)
Stella was crying next to her dead mother. I watched her all night.
　　　　　　　　　　　　　　　　　　　　　　　　　밤새도록
The oldest female elephant of a new group allowed Stella to become part of
　　　　　　　　　　　　　　allow+목적어+to부정사: 목적어가 V하도록 허락했다
them.

구문해설　• attack: 공격하다　• thick: 두꺼운　• protect: 보호하다　• dead: 죽은
　　　　　• allow: ～을 허락하다

사자 몇 마리가 Stella를 공격하려고 했다. 코끼리 무리는 Stella를 보호하기 위해 두꺼운 벽을 만들었다. Stella는 그녀의 죽은 엄마 옆에서 울고 있었다 나는 밤새도록 그녀를 지켜보았다. 새로운 무리의 가장 나이 많은 암컷 코끼리는 Stella를 그들의 일원이 되도록 허락했다.

Think & Write C

Plant Diary

Date: June 15th, 2019

Write about what you saw:

Today, I saw a plant. It is called a pitcher plant. It is bright green and red. It
　　　　　　　　　　～라고 불린다
looks like a pitcher. As for its size, it is about 15cm long. It is as long as my
look like+명사: ～처럼 보이다　　　　　　　인칭대명사
hand. It is interesting that the plant attracts insects and eats them.
　　　　　가주어　　　　　　진주어

구문해설　• look like: ～처럼 보이다　• pitcher: 항아리　• as for: ～에 대해서 말하자면
　　　　　• about: 대략　• interesting: 흥미로운　• attract: 끌어들이다

식물 일기
날짜: 6월 15일, 2019년
네가 본 것을 써 봐.
오늘, 나는 식물 하나를 봤다. 그것은 벌레잡이 식물이라고 불린다. 그것은 밝은 녹색에 붉은색이다. 그것은 항아리처럼 생겼다. 크기에 대해 말하자면, 그것은 대략 15cm이다. 그것은 내 손만큼 길다. 그 식물이 벌레를 끌어들이고 그것들을 먹는 것은 흥미롭다.

Wrap Up 1

Minho: Look! Isn't that a sea horse?
　　　　　　　　　　　　　부정의문문
Sue: Actually, no. It's a sea dragon.
　　　actual+-ly
Minho: Oh, really? I'm curious about the difference between them.
　　　　　　　　　　～을 궁금해 하다　　　　　　　　= a sea horse and a sea dragon
Sue: Look at the tail carefully. A sea dragon has a straight one, and but a sea
　　　　　　　　　　　　　　　　　　　　　　　　　= tail
horse does not.
뒤에 have a straight tail이 생략되어 있음.
Minho: Oh, I can tell the difference now!
　　　　　　　　= 차이를 구별하다

구문해설　• sea horse: 해마　• sea dragon: 해룡　• tail: 꼬리　• straight: 곧은

Minho: 봐! 저거 해마 아니야?
Sue: 사실은 아니야. 그건 해룡이야.
Minho: 아, 정말? 난 그 둘의 차이점이 궁금해.
Sue: 꼬리를 주의해서 봐. 해룡은 꼬리가 곧지만, 해마는 그렇지 않아.
Minho: 오, 나 이제 차이를 구별할 수 있겠다!

영역별 핵심문제

Words & Expressions

01 다음 영영풀이가 가리키는 것을 고르시오.

> the soft part in the mouth that moves around, used for tasting, swallowing, speaking, etc.

① tongue   ② knee   ③ lap
④ tooth   ⑤ lip

02 다음 중 밑줄 친 부분의 뜻풀이가 바르지 않은 것은?

① He dug a <u>hole</u> in the garden. 구멍
② Jane is using a ladder to <u>approach</u> the sign. 다가가다
③ The <u>thick</u> mud walls block the sunlight. 얇은
④ Tom got a dog from an animal <u>shelter</u>. 보호소
⑤ <u>Wild</u> animals usually avoid human sounds. 야생의

03 다음 우리말에 맞게 빈칸에 알맞은 말을 쓰시오.

(1) 동물 구조 팀이 강가에서 캥거루를 구조했다.
  ➡ An animal _____ team saved a kangaroo from the river.
(2) 긴 꼬리가 치타가 균형을 잡을 수 있도록 도와준다.
  ➡ A long _____ helps the cheetah to keep its balance.
(3) 그녀는 온 힘을 다해 그 밧줄을 당겼다.
  ➡ She pulled on the rope with all her _____.

04 다음 주어진 문장의 밑줄 친 approach와 같은 의미로 쓰인 것은?

> Nobody could <u>approach</u> the President.

① She took the wrong <u>approach</u> to the problem.
② Don't wait for kids to come, <u>approach</u> them first.
③ What is the best <u>approach</u> to the learning of English?
④ His <u>approach</u> was not effective to solve this problem.
⑤ I think the best <u>approach</u> is the conversation.

05 다음 우리말과 일치하도록 주어진 어구를 모두 배열하여 영작하시오.

(1) 작은 소년 옆에 있는 소녀를 아니?
  (the little / the / next / girl / to / you / know / do / boy)
  ➡ _____
(2) 전 세계 수백만의 사람들이 인터넷을 사용한다.
  (use / people / the Internet / the world / millions / around / of)
  ➡ _____
(3) 그녀는 그녀의 딸 사진을 찍는 것을 아주 좋아한다.
  (her / she / daughter / take / of / to / a / picture / loves)
  ➡ _____

06 다음 문장에 들어갈 말을 〈보기〉에서 찾아 순서대로 쓰시오.

┌─── 보기 ├─
receive / give / keep / tell /
appear / attract
└─

- I was asked to (A)_____ a presentation in English class.
- It is hard for me to (B)_____ the difference between two dogs.
- During the game, I had to (C)_____ my eyes on the ball.

Conversation

[07~08] 다음 대화를 읽고 물음에 답하시오.

Jane: ⓐLook at this picture of a huge flower.
Tom: Wow, it is ⓑmore big than a person.
Jane: Yeah. I'm really ⓒcurious about this flower. It also says here that the flower ⓓsmells very bad, but insects love the smell.
Tom: Hmm, I wonder ⓔwhy.

07 위 대화의 ⓐ~ⓔ 중 어법상 어색한 것을 찾아 바르게 고치시오.

➡ _____

08 위 대화의 내용과 일치하지 않는 것은?

① Jane and Tom are looking at the huge flower in the garden.
② The huge flower is bigger than a person.
③ Jane wants to know the huge flower more.
④ The huge flower smells very bad.
⑤ The insects love the smell of the huge flower.

09 다음 주어진 문장 뒤에 대화가 자연스럽게 이어지도록 순서대로 배열하시오.

Do you think we can be friends with lions?

(A) Wow, that's so touching.
(B) No, I don't think so.
(C) Really? I'm curious about the story. Can you tell me more?
(D) Well, I watched a video clip about friendship between two men and a lion.
(E) The two men raised a baby lion and sent her back into the wild. When the men and the lion met a year later, she remembered them.

➡ _____

10 다음 대화를 읽고 Dr. Watson이 소개한 자이언트 캥거루의 특징을 우리말로 간략하게 서술하시오.

Emily: Hello, Dr. Watson. Can you tell us about your study?
Dr. Watson: I study animals that lived millions of years ago.
Emily: Oh, I'm curious about those animals. Were there any interesting ones?
Dr. Watson: Yes, there were many. This is the giant kangaroo. It lived in Australia. It was as heavy as three men and it couldn't jump well.
Emily: That's amazing!

➡ _____
_____

[11~13] 다음 대화를 읽고 물음에 답하시오.

Dylan: Look at this picture, Mina. We got a new puppy yesterday. He's only two weeks old.
Mina: Oh, Dylan, he's so small!
Dylan: Yeah. ⓐ그는 지금 내 손만큼 작다(as, small), but he'll get ___(A)___ bigger in a few months.
Mina: Wow, puppies grow very quickly.

11 위 대화의 빈칸 (A)에 들어갈 말로 <u>어색한</u> 것은?

① much   ② very   ③ a lot

④ far   ⑤ even

12 위 대화의 밑줄 친 ⓐ의 우리말을 주어진 단어를 사용하여 영어로 쓰시오.

➡ _____

13 위 대화를 읽고 대답할 수 <u>없는</u> 것은?

① What did Dylan get yesterday?

② How old is the new puppy?

③ How small is the new puppy now?

④ What is Dylan showing to Mina?

⑤ What should Dylan do to take care of the puppy?

Grammar

14 다음 중 빈칸에 들어갈 말로 가장 적절한 것은?

It is wrong _____ bad things about friends.

① say   ② to say

③ to saying   ④ that

⑤ to

15 다음 중 어법상 바르지 <u>않은</u> 것은?

A: Was ①it fun ②to watching a baseball game?

B: Yes, it ③was. I like ④watching a baseball game ⑤a lot.

①   ②   ③   ④   ⑤

16 다음 중 문장의 전환이 바르지 <u>않은</u> 것은?

① To take a trip to another country is fun.
  = It is fun to take a trip to another country.

② Washing all the dishes is difficult.
  = It is difficult to wash all the dishes.

③ It is good to help people in the poor countries.
  = To help people in the poor countries are good.

④ James is not as thin as Paul.
  = Paul is thinner than James.

⑤ The man is heavier than the woman.
  = The woman is not as heavy as the man.

17 주어진 단어를 활용하여 다음 우리말을 일곱 단어로 이루어진 한 문장의 영어로 쓰시오.

물 없이 사는 것은 불가능하다.
(impossible / live)

➡ _____

18 다음은 남자와 여자 30명씩을 대상으로 선호하는 과일을 물은 설문조사 결과이다. 표를 제대로 분석하지 <u>못한</u> 사람은?

	Apple	Grape	Orange
men	8	14	8
women	8	7	15

① 민수: Men like apples as much as women.

② 은서: Women don't like oranges as much as men.

③ 혜진: Men like grapes two times as much as women.

④ 현우: Men like apples as much as oranges.

⑤ 청아: Men don't like oranges as much as women.

19 주어진 단어를 활용하여 다음 우리말을 7단어로 이루어진 한 문장의 영어로 쓰시오.

> 그녀가 노래 부르는 것을 듣는 것은 어려웠다.
> (difficult / hear / it)

➡ _____

20 다음 중 밑줄 친 부분의 쓰임이 다른 하나는?

① <u>It</u> is my duty to clean my room every day.
② <u>It</u> is interesting that you think her beautiful.
③ <u>It</u> is fun to see them playing together.
④ <u>It</u> was boring to hear him talk.
⑤ <u>It</u> was found on the table.

21 다음 문장을 하나의 문장으로 바르게 표현한 것은?

> James's dog is three years old. My dog is three years old, too.

① James's dog is older than my dog.
② James's dog is not as old as my dog.
③ James's dog is two times as old as my dog.
④ James's dog is as old as my dog.
⑤ My dog is not as old as James's dog.

22 다음 중 빈칸에 들어갈 말로 적절한 것을 고르시오.

> It was exciting _____ a soccer game at the stadium.

① to watching   ② watches
③ watch   ④ watched
⑤ to watch

[23~26] 다음 글을 읽고 물음에 답하시오.

> Date/Time: July 8th / 2:35 p.m.
> Notes: Today was my first day in Africa. I took lots of pictures of elephants. This morning, I found an elephant group by a small water hole. I saw a baby elephant (A)[drinking / to drink] water beside her mother. Her eyes were as (B)[bright / brightly] as stars. I gave her a name, Stella. Around noon, I saw a group of lions approaching Stella. The elephants stood around Stella and made a thick wall. Thanks to (C)[it / them], Stella was safe.

23 (A)~(C)에서 어법상 옳은 것끼리 바르게 짝지은 것은?

① drinking – bright – it
② drinking – brightly – it
③ drinking – bright – them
④ to drink – bright – them
⑤ to drink – brightly – it

24 What name did the writer give to the baby elephant? Answer in English with a full sentence.

➡ _____

25 다음 중 위 글을 읽고 답할 수 <u>없는</u> 것은?

① What did the writer see on his first day in Africa?
② What did the writer find this morning?
③ Where was the group of elephants on the morning of July 8?
④ What was the baby elephant doing beside her mother?
⑤ How many lions were approaching Stella?

26 위 글의 내용에 맞게 빈칸에 알맞은 말을 쓰시오.

> A: Why did the elephants make a thick wall around the baby elephant?
>
> B: It's because they wanted _____
>
> _____ _____ _____ _____
>
> from _____.

27 다음 주어진 문장이 들어가기에 가장 적절한 곳은?

> But I was wrong.

①   ②   ③   ④   ⑤

28 (A)~(C)에서 어법상 옳은 것끼리 바르게 짝지은 것은?

① beside – approached – was

② besides – approached to – was

③ beside – approached – did

④ besides – approached to – did

⑤ beside – approached to – did

[27~30] 다음 글을 읽고 물음에 답하시오.

Date/Time: July 12th / 10:40 p.m.

Notes: The night was dark and quiet. I kept my eyes on Stella with my night camera. Stella was still (A)[beside / besides] her mom. She was touching her mom's lifeless body with her nose. It was sad to see Stella staying close to her mom. I hope Stella stays safe throughout the night.

Date/Time: July 13th / 6:00 a.m.

Notes: A new elephant group appeared and Stella (B)[approached / approached to] them. ① At first, I thought that they would not let Stella in their group. ② An elephant, probably the oldest female allowed Stella to become part of the group. ③ The other elephants also seemed to welcome Stella. ④ Unbelievably, one of the female elephants fed Stella. ⑤ She cared for Stella as warmly as Stella's mom (C)[was / did]. This was such an amazing moment!

29 위 글의 내용에 맞게 빈칸에 알맞은 말을 쓰시오.

> A: It was really surprising that _____
>
> _____ _____ _____ _____
>
> _____ _____.
>
> B: She is really generous. Although Stella was not her baby, she took care of her like Stella's mom.

30 다음 중 위 글의 내용과 일치하지 않는 것은?

① It was dark and quiet on the night of July 12.

② The writer had a night camera.

③ The writer hoped Stella would stay safe.

④ Stella stayed by her mom without touching her.

⑤ The writer didn't expect that the new elephant group would let Stella in their group.

단원별 예상문제

01 다음 문장의 빈칸에 들어갈 말을 〈보기〉에서 골라 쓰시오.

┌─ 보기 ┤

careless / humorous / sheet / blind / wild

(1) We laughed at the comedian's _____ stories.

(2) I'm sorry to hurt your feelings by my _____ words.

(3) It's dangerous to stay alone in a _____ area.

(4) I'm as _____ as a bat without my glasses.

(5) We should prepare a _____ to draw the picture.

02 다음 우리말을 주어진 단어를 이용하여 영작하시오.

(1) 야생 동물은 위험할 수 있다. (be)

➡ _____

(2) 우리는 유머 감각을 가질 필요가 있다. (need)

➡ _____

(3) 동물원에서 동물들에게 먹이를 주지 마라. (don't, feed)

➡ _____

[03~04] 다음 대화를 읽고 물음에 답하시오.

Minho: Look! Isn't that a sea horse?

Sue: Actually, no. It's a sea dragon.

Minho: Oh, really? I'm curious about the difference between them.

Sue: Look at the tail carefully. A sea dragon has a straight one, but a sea horse does not.

Minho: Oh, I can (A)<u>tell</u> the difference now!

03 위 대화의 밑줄 친 (A)tell과 같은 의미로 쓰인 것은?

① Would you <u>tell</u> me the truth?

② Why don't you <u>tell</u> everyone your story?

③ I can't <u>tell</u> you from your twin sister.

④ Don't <u>tell</u> me what to do.

⑤ Many doctors <u>tell</u> us that we should not eat too much.

04 해마와 해룡을 어떻게 구분할 수 있는지 우리말로 설명하시오.

➡ _____

[05~06] 다음 대화를 읽고 물음에 답하시오.

Emily: (A) Hello, Dr. Watson. Can you tell us about your study?

Dr. Watson: (B) I study animals that lived millions of years ago.

Emily: (C) Were there any interesting ones?

Dr. Watson: (D) Yes, there were many. This is the giant kangaroo. It lived in Australia. It was as heavy as three men and it couldn't jump well.

Emily: (E) That's amazing!

05 위 대화의 (A)~(E) 중 주어진 문장이 들어가기에 가장 적절한 곳은?

> Oh, I'm curious about those animals.

① (A) ② (B) ③ (C) ④ (D) ⑤ (E)

06 위 대화의 내용과 일치하지 <u>않는</u> 것은?

① Dr. Watson studies animals which lived millions of years ago.

② Emily wants to know what Dr. Watson studies.

③ The giant kangaroo lived in Australia.

④ The giant kangaroo was not able to jump well.

⑤ The giant kangaroo was heavier than three men.

[07~08] 다음 대화를 읽고 물음에 답하시오.

Kelly: George, (A)[which / that] red house over there is my grandparents' house.

George: Wow, the tree by the house is really big.

Kelly: Actually, that tree is (B)[so / as] old as me, thirteen years old.

George: How do you know that, Kelly?

Kelly: My grandfather (C)[plant / planted] the tree in 2004 when I was born.

07 위 대화의 괄호 (A)~(C)에 알맞은 말을 바르게 쓰시오.

(A) _____ (B) _____ (C) _____

08 위 대화를 읽고 대답할 수 <u>없는</u> 것은?

① What color is the house of Kelly's grandparents?

② What is there by the house of Kelly's grandparents?

③ How old is the tree that Kelly's grandfather planted?

④ When was Kelly born?

⑤ What tree did Kelly's grandfather plant in 2004?

[09~10] 다음 대화를 읽고 물음에 답하시오.

Ryan: Judy, did you choose a topic for your science project?

Judy: Not yet. How about you, Ryan?

Ryan: I'm curious about weather change. So I'm thinking about doing the project on that.

Judy: That's an interesting topic!

09 What are Judy and Ryan talking about?

➡ _____

10 What is Ryan wondering about?

➡ _____

11 다음 중 주어진 문장의 밑줄 친 부분과 그 쓰임이 같은 것은?

<u>It</u> is necessary to say no sometimes.

① <u>It</u> is a long and thin object.

② <u>It</u> is dark and humid.

③ <u>It</u> was interesting to talk with him.

④ <u>It</u> was my parents' wedding anniversary.

⑤ <u>It</u> made me angry and upset.

12 다음 중 어법상 바르지 <u>않은</u> 것은?

① It is dangerous to talk with a stranger.

② Jane earns two times as much money as Tom.

③ That is fun to get along with friends.

④ This pen is as cheap as the pencil.

⑤ It is necessary to start at once.

13 주어진 단어를 활용하여 다음 우리말을 영어로 쓰시오.

> 밤에 그 사물을 보는 것은 가능했다.
> (it / the object)

➡ _____

14 다음 문장과 같은 의미의 문장은?

> Jill knows more people than me.

① I know more people than Jill.
② Jill doesn't know as many people as I do.
③ I don't know as many people as Jill does.
④ Jill knows as many people as I do.
⑤ Jill knows twice as many people as I do.

15 다음 중 어법상 바르지 않은 것은?

> ①It was impossible ②understand him ③because he spoke ④too fast. He spoke ⑤as fast as a train.

①   ②   ③   ④   ⑤

16 주어진 단어를 바르게 배열하여 다음 우리말을 영어로 쓰시오. 필요하면 단어를 추가하시오.

> 이 방은 저 방보다 대략 두 배 더 크다.
> (that one / this room / about / large / as / is / two times)

➡ _____

17 주어진 단어를 활용하여 다음 우리말을 영어로 쓰시오.

> 물고기가 물속에서 수영하는 것을 보는 것은 아주 멋졌다.
> (it / wonderful / fish)

➡ _____

[18~23] 다음 글을 읽고 물음에 답하시오.

> Date/Time: July 12th / 7:20 p.m.
> Notes: Around sunset, I heard a (A)[joyful / strange] sound. I followed the sound and found Stella crying next to her mom. She was lying dead and Stella was alone. ⓐ이러한 야생 지역에서 혼자 있는 것은 위험하다. What's more, it was going to be (B)[dark / bright] soon. Elephants can't see well at night. So Stella could easily be attacked. I called the elephant shelter and asked for help. I decided to stay by her until the rescue team came.
> Date/Time: July 12th / 10:40 p.m.
> Notes: The night was dark and quiet. I kept my eyes on Stella with my night camera. Stella was still next to her mom. She was touching her mom's (C)[lively / lifeless] body with her nose. (D)It was sad to see Stella staying close to her mom. I hope Stella stays safe throughout the night.

18 주어진 단어를 활용하여 밑줄 친 우리말 ⓐ를 영어로 쓰시오.

> (it / stay / such)

➡ _____

✏️ 출제율 100%

19 (A)~(C)에서 글의 흐름상 자연스러운 것끼리 바르게 짝지은 것은?

① joyful – dark – lively
② joyful – bright – lifeless
③ joyful – dark – lifeless
④ strange – dark – lifeless
⑤ strange – bright – lively

✏️ 출제율 90%

20 다음 중 밑줄 친 (D)와 쓰임이 다른 것은?

① It was my fault to give her the message.
② It is his job to make us delicious food.
③ It is used to make cheese and yogurt.
④ It is amazing to see them talking with delight.
⑤ It is interesting that you gave her your diary.

✏️ 출제율 95%

21 Which is NOT true about the passage?

① The writer heard Stella crying in the evening.
② Stella was crying beside her mother.
③ It was the elephant shelter that the writer called.
④ Stella was touching her dead mom with her nose.
⑤ Stella left her mom as soon as it was getting dark.

✏️ 출제율 95%

22 다음 중 위 글을 읽고 찾아볼 수 없는 것을 모두 고르시오.

① a baby elephant crying beside her dead mother
② some elephants protecting Stella at night
③ the writer staying near Stella to watch her
④ the rescue team approaching Stella
⑤ the writer calling the elephant shelter

✏️ 출제율 90%

23 다음 물음에 완전한 문장의 영어로 답하시오.

> **Q**: What did the writer hear around sunset?

➡ _____

[24~25] 다음 글을 읽고 물음에 답하시오.

Plant Diary
Date: June 15th, 2019
Write about what you saw:
Today, I saw a plant. It is called a pitcher plant. It is bright green and red. It looks like a pitcher. As for its size, it is about 15cm long. It is as long as my hand. (A)그 식물이 곤충을 끌어들이고 그것들을 먹는 것은 흥미롭다.

✏️ 출제율 95%

24 주어진 단어를 활용하여 밑줄 친 우리말 (A)를 영어로 쓰시오.

> (it / that / insects)

➡ _____

_____

✏️ 출제율 100%

25 다음 중 위 글을 읽고 답할 수 없는 것은?

① What did the writer see today?
② What is the plant called?
③ What does the plant look like?
④ How does the plant attract insects?
⑤ How long is the writer's hand?

[01~03] 다음 대화를 읽고 물음에 답하시오.

> Kelly: George, that red house over there is my grandparents' house.
> George: Wow, the tree by the house is really big.
> Kelly: Actually, that tree is as ⓐunderline older as me, thirteen years old.
> George: How do you know that, Kelly?
> Kelly: My grandfather planted the tree in 2004 when I ⓑunderline born.

01 위 대화의 밑줄 친 ⓐ와 ⓑ를 어법상 바르게 고쳐 쓰시오.

ⓐ _____ ⓑ _____

02 How old is the tree by the red house?

➡ _____

03 What did Kelly's grandfather do when Kelly was born?

➡ _____

04 주어진 단어를 바르게 배열하여 다음 우리말을 영어로 쓰시오. 필요하면 단어를 추가하시오.

> 학급 친구들에게 친절하게 대하는 것은 중요하다.
> (be / is / it / your / kind / important / classmates / to)

➡ _____

05 괄호 안의 단어를 활용하여 다음 두 문장을 하나의 문장으로 쓰시오.

> • A yellow pencil is only one dollar.
> • A green pencil is only one dollar, too. (cheap)

➡ _____

06 다음 대화의 빈칸에 알맞은 말을 다섯 단어로 쓰시오.

> A: Is it _____?
> B: Sure. Living without electricity is not that easy, but possible.

➡ _____

07 다음 대화를 읽고 주어진 단어를 활용하여 문장을 완성하시오.

> A: When do you usually go to bed, Brian?
> B: I go to bed at 9 p.m. How about you, June?
> A: Oh, I go to bed at 9 p.m., too.

➡ Brian _____ June. (early)

08 다음 대화의 빈칸에 알맞은 말을 쓰시오.

> A: Did you play soccer better than them?
> B: No. I didn't play soccer _____ _____ them. They were very good players.

09 다음 대화를 읽고 빈칸에 알맞은 말을 쓰시오.

> A: I think Helen is sick.
> B: Why do you say so?
> A: Her face looks like a sheet. It is too white.

➡ Helen's face is _____ a sheet.

[10~12] 다음 글을 읽고 물음에 답하시오.

Date/Time: July 8th / 2:35 p.m.
Notes: Today was my first day in Africa. I took ①lots of pictures of elephants. This morning, I found an elephant group by a small water hole. I saw a baby elephant ② drinking water beside her mother. Her eyes were as bright as stars. I gave her a name, Stella. Around noon, I saw a group of lions ③approaching Stella. The elephants stood around Stella and made ④a thick wall. Thanks to them, Stella was ⑤in danger.

10 위 글의 표현을 활용하여 다음 우리말을 영어로 쓰시오.

> 나의 눈은 그녀의 눈만큼 밝지 않아.

➡ _____

⭐ 중요
11 What approached Stella? Answer in English with a full sentence.

➡ _____

12 ①~⑤ 중 글의 흐름상 어색한 것을 바르게 고쳐 쓰시오.

➡ _____

[13~15] 다음 글을 읽고 물음에 답하시오.

Date/Time: July 13th / 6:00 a.m.
Notes: A new elephant group appeared and Stella approached them. At first, I thought that they would not let Stella in their group. But I was wrong. An elephant, probably the oldest female allowed Stella to become part of the group. The other elephants also seemed to welcome Stella. Unbelievably, one of the female elephants fed Stella. (A)그녀는 Stella의 엄마만큼 따뜻하게 Stella를 보살폈다. This was such an amazing moment!

13 주어진 단어를 활용하여 밑줄 친 우리말 (A)를 영어로 쓰시오.

> (care / as / as / Stella's mom / do)

➡ _____
_____

14 위 글의 내용과 일치하도록 빈칸에 알맞은 말을 쓰시오.

> Q: What did the oldest elephant do for Stella?
> A: She let _____ _____
> _____ _____ _____ .

⭐ 중요
15 다음은 아프리카에서 돌아온 글쓴이의 말이다. 글의 내용에 맞게 빈칸에 알맞은 말을 쓰시오.

> When I saw Stella approaching a new elephant group, I thought it was impossible that they _____ _____ _____ _____ their group. But it didn't go as I thought. I was really relieved.

01 다음 대화의 내용과 일치하도록 Mina의 일기를 완성하시오.

Clare: Do you think we can be friends with lions, Todd?

Todd: No, Clare. I don't think so.

Clare: Well, I watched a video clip about friendship between two men and a lion.

Todd: Really? I'm curious about the story. Can you tell me more?

Clare: The two men raised a baby lion and sent her back into the wild. When the men and the lion met a year later, she remembered them.

Todd: Wow, that's so touching.

Mon, Oct 7th, 2019

I was so touched by the story Clare told me today. I didn't think that we could be friends with (A)_____. Then, Clare introduced the video clip about (B)_____ between two men and a lion. When I heard that the baby lion remembered the two men who (C)_____, I felt so moved.

---

02 주어진 어구와 가주어 it을 이용하여 여러 가지 문장을 쓰시오.

---

to see elephants protect a baby elephant

to read that the female elephant took care of Stella

to see the new elephants accept Stella as a group member

---

(1) _____

(2) _____

(3) _____

03 다음 식물에 관하여 읽고 식물 관찰 일지를 완성하시오.

Name: Moss Ball   Color: dark green

Size: about 4cm   An interesting fact: It floats up when it gets enough sunlight.

Plant Diary

Today, I saw a plant. It is called _____. It is _____. It looks _____ a small ball. As for its size, it is _____. It is _____ a ping-pong ball. It is interesting that _____.

단원별 모의고사

01 다음 대화가 자연스럽게 이어지도록 순서대로 배열하시오.

> (A) Oh, Dylan, he's so small!
>
> (B) Wow, puppies grow very quickly.
>
> (C) Yeah. He's as small as my hand now, but he'll get much bigger in a few months.
>
> (D) Look at this picture, Mina. We got a new puppy yesterday. He's only two weeks old.

➡ _____

[02~04] 다음 대화를 읽고 물음에 답하시오.

Emily: Hello, Dr. Watson. Can you tell us about your study?

Dr. Watson: I study animals that lived millions of years ago.

Emily: Oh, I'm curious about those animals. Were there any interesting ones?

Dr. Watson: Yes, there were many. This is the giant kangaroo. It lived in Australia. It was as heavy as three men and it couldn't jump well.

Emily: That's amazing!

02 What does Dr. Watson study?

➡ _____
_____

03 Where did the giant kangaroo live?

➡ _____

04 How heavy was the giant kangaroo?

➡ _____

[05~06] 다음 대화를 읽고 물음에 답하시오.

Clare: Do you think we can be friends with lions, Todd?

Todd: (A) No, Clare. I don't think so.

Clare: (B) Well, I watched a video clip about friendship between two men and a lion.

Todd: (C) Can you tell me more?

Clare: (D) The two men raised a baby lion and sent her back into the wild. When the men and the lion met a year later, she remembered them.

Todd: (E) Wow, that's so touching.

05 위 대화의 (A)~(E) 중 주어진 문장이 들어가기에 적절한 곳은?

> Really? I'm curious about the story.

① (A) ② (B) ③ (C) ④ (D) ⑤ (E)

06 위 대화의 내용과 일치하는 것은?

① Todd thought that people can be friends with lions.

② Clare watched the video clip about friendship of two men.

③ The two men brought up a baby lion in the wild.

④ When the two men met the lion a year later, they were afraid of her.

⑤ Todd is touched by the story about friendship between two men and a lion.

[07~08] 다음 대화를 읽고 물음에 답하시오.

Jane: Look at this picture of a huge flower.

Tom: Wow, it is bigger than a person.

Jane: Yeah. I'm really curious about this flower. It also says here that the flower smells very bad, but insects love the smell.

Tom: Hmm, I wonder why.

07 What is Jane curious about?

➡ _____

08 How does the huge flower smell?

➡ _____

09 다음 문장의 빈칸에 들어갈 말을 〈보기〉에서 골라 쓰시오.

> ┤ 보기 ├
> become part of / give a presentation / thanks to / next to / tell the difference

(1) Can you _____ between the twin?

(2) I want to _____ the dancing club.

(3) Who will _____ first?

(4) The tree _____ the red house is planted by my father.

(5) _____ your help, I could finish my work early.

[10~11] 다음 대화를 읽고 물음에 답하시오.

Kelly: George, that red house over there is my grandparents' house.

George: Wow, the tree by the house is really big.

Kelly: Actually, _____(A)_____, thirteen years old.

George: How do you know that, Kelly?

Kelly: My grandfather planted the tree in 2004 when I was born.

10 위 대화의 빈칸 (A)에 들어갈 말을 〈보기〉에 주어진 단어를 모두 배열하여 영작하시오.

> ┤ 보기 ├
> as / me / is / as / that / tree / old

➡ _____

11 What are Kelly and George talking about?

① the house of Kelly's grandparents
② the tree by the red house
③ the color of the big house
④ how big the tree by the red house is
⑤ how old Kelly's grandparents are

12 다음 대화가 자연스럽게 이어지도록 순서대로 배열하시오.

> (A) That's amazing!
> (B) I study animals that lived millions of years ago.
> (C) Hello, Dr. Watson. Can you tell us about your study?
> (D) Oh, I'm curious about those animals. Were there any interesting ones?
> (E) Yes, there were many. This is the giant kangaroo. It lived in Australia. It was as heavy as three men and it couldn't jump well.

➡ _____

13 다음 중 주어진 문장의 밑줄 친 부분과 쓰임이 같은 것은?

> It was exciting to feed a sea bird.

① They went out to see what was going on.
② She has many friends to talk with.
③ We made a cake to make her happy.
④ It is dangerous to swim in this lake.
⑤ To win the contest, Julia did everything she could.

14 다음 세 사람의 공부 시간을 읽고 형용사 long을 사용하여 세 사람의 공부 시간을 비교하는 문장의 빈칸을 채우시오.

> Clara: I study four hours a day.
> Smith: I study three hours a day.
> Zach: I study two hours a day.

➡ Smith doesn't study _____ _____
_____ Clara. Clara studies _____
_____ _____ _____ Zach.

15 다음 중 어법상 바르지 않은 것은?

① It is necessary to respect other cultures.
② The cheetah runs as fast as a car.
③ She is as tall as her mother.
④ It is amusing that he makes so many jokes.
⑤ Have so much food as you want.

16 다음 중 빈칸에 들어갈 말이 바르게 짝지어진 것은?

> • To train children to be polite is important.
> = (A)_____ is important (B)_____ children to be polite.
> • Please send me the e-mail as soon as possible.
> = Please send me the e-mail as soon as (C)_____.

① That – train – you do
② That – to train – you can
③ It – train – you can
④ It – to train – you do
⑤ It – to train – you can

17 주어진 어구를 활용하여 다음 우리말을 영어로 쓰시오.

> 그의 말을 듣는 것은 중요해. 그의 의견은 너의 의견만큼 중요하기 때문이야.
> (It / what he says / It's because / opinion)

➡ _____

_____

[18~25] 다음 글을 읽고 물음에 답하시오.

Date/Time: July 8th / 2:35 p.m.
Notes: Today was my first day in Africa. I took lots of pictures of elephants. This morning, I found an elephant group by a small water hole. ① I saw a baby elephant drinking water beside her mother. Her eyes were as bright as stars. ② I gave her a name, Stella. ③ The elephants stood around Stella and made a thick wall. _____(A)_____ them, Stella was safe.
Date/Time: July 12th / 7:20 p.m.
Notes: Around sunset, I heard a strange sound. ④ I followed the sound and found Stella crying next to her mom. ⑤ She was lying dead and Stella was alone. (a)It is dangerous to stay alone in such a wild area. What's more, it was going to be dark soon. Elephants can't see well at night. So Stella could easily be attacked. I called the elephant shelter and asked for help. I decided to stay by her _____(B)_____ the rescue team came.

18 ①~⑤ 중 주어진 문장이 들어가기에 가장 적절한 곳은?

> Around noon, I saw a group of lions approaching Stella.

①   ②   ③   ④   ⑤

19 다음 중 빈칸 (A)에 들어갈 말로 가장 적절한 것은?

① Despite   ② Instead of
③ Thanks to   ④ In spite of
⑤ Apart from

20 다음 중 글의 흐름상 빈칸 (B)에 들어갈 말로 가장 적절한 것은?

① if   ② because   ③ or
④ until   ⑤ since

21 다음 중 밑줄 친 (a)와 쓰임이 같은 것은?

① It is under your bed.
② It was fun to play with the dogs.
③ It is a rocket.
④ It was quite dark outside.
⑤ It can't be true.

22 다음은 글쓴이가 코끼리 보호소에 전화한 내용이다. 글의 내용에 맞게 빈칸에 알맞은 말을 쓰시오.

> A: Hi. This is _____ _____ _____.
>   How can I help you?
> B: Hello. I'm calling you because of a baby elephant. She is _____ now.
> A: Oh, it is dangerous _____ _____ _____ in the wild.
> B: Yes. It's going to be _____ soon, so I'm very worried about her.

23 Which is NOT true about the passage?

① The writer saw a group of elephant on the first day in Africa.
② Stella was drinking water next to her mother.
③ Stella's eyes shone brightly like stars.
④ The elephant group saved the baby elephant by making a thick wall.
⑤ Stella's mom was dead because she was attacked by lions.

24 What did the writer see in the elephant group? Answer in English with eight words.

➡ _____

25 다음은 글쓴이와 통화한 코끼리 보호소 직원의 말이다. 원급 비교와 주어진 단어를 이용하여 영어로 쓰시오.

> 우리가 가능한 한 빨리 그곳에 갈게요.
> (be there / soon)

➡ _____

Art around Us

의사소통 기능

- 구체적인 종류나 장르 묻기

  A: **What Kind of** music are you going to play?

  B: I'm going to play rock music.

- 둘 중에 더 좋아하는 것 말하기

  A: There are two kinds of *Mona Lisas*. Which do you prefer?

  B: I **prefer** Botero's *Mona Lisa* **to** da Vinci's.

언어 형식

- 사역동사

  It will **make** you **wonder** about the painting more.

- 간접의문문

  Do you know **where Icarus is**?

교과서
Words & Expressions

Key Words

- **artist**[ɑ́:rtist] 명 예술가, 미술가
- **artwork**[ɑ́rtwərk] 명 예술 작품
- **brush**[brʌʃ] 명 붓
- **canvas**[kǽnvəs] 명 화폭, 캔버스
- **classical**[klǽsikəl] 형 클래식의
- **comedy**[kɑ́mədi] 명 희극, 코미디
- **despite**[dispáit] 전 ~에도 불구하고
- **detail**[ditéil] 명 세부 사항
- **direct**[dirékt] 동 ~로 향하다, 겨냥하다
- **direction**[dirékʃən] 명 방향
- **exhibit**[igzíbit] 동 전시하다
- **feather**[féðər] 명 깃털
- **flat**[flæt] 형 납작한
- **frog**[frɔːg] 명 개구리
- **hip-hop**[híphɑp] 명 (음악) 힙합
- **landscape**[lǽndskèip] 명 풍경
- **maze**[meiz] 명 미로
- **melt**[melt] 동 녹다
- **modern**[mɑ́dərn] 형 현대의
- **myth**[miθ] 명 신화
- **notice**[nóutis] 동 ~을 알아차리다

- **novel**[nɑ́vəl] 명 소설
- **novelist**[nɑ́vəlist] 명 소설가
- **pop**[pɑp] 명 팝 음악
- **prefer**[prifə́:r] 동 더 좋아하다
- **prince**[prins] 명 왕자
- **produce**[prədjú:s] 동 생산하다
- **production**[prədʌ́kʃən] 명 생산
- **promise**[prɑ́mis] 동 약속하다
- **queen**[kwi:n] 명 왕비, 여왕
- **real**[rí:əl] 형 진짜의, 현실적인
- **rock**[rɑk] 명 록 음악
- **seaside**[sísaid] 명 해변, 바닷가
- **since**[sins] 접 ~ 때문에, ~이므로
- **stick**[stik] 동 (몸의 일부를) 밀다, 내밀다
- **teen**[ti:n] 명 십 대
- **tourist**[túərist] 명 관광객
- **tragedy**[trǽdʒədi] 명 비극
- **version**[və́:rʒən] 명 (어떤 것의) 변형
- **wax**[wæks] 명 밀랍, 왁스
- **wing**[wiŋ] 명 날개
- **wonder**[wʌ́ndər] 동 궁금해하다

Key Expressions

- **glance at** ~을 힐끗 보다
- **loot at** ~을 보다
- **move on** ~로 이동하다, 넘어가다
- **prefer A to B** A를 B보다 더 좋아하다

- **right away** 즉시, 바로
- **soap bubble** 비눗방울
- **stay away from** ~을 가까이하지 않다
- **take a look** ~을 보다

Word Power

※ 서로 반대되는 뜻을 가진 어휘

- □ **ancient** 고대의 ↔ **modern** 현대의
- □ **noticed** 알아차려진 ↔ **unnoticed** 눈에 띄지 않는
- □ **melt** 녹다 ↔ **freeze** 얼다
- □ **comedy** 희극 ↔ **tragedy** 비극
- □ **ask** 묻다 ↔ **answer** 대답하다
- □ **cheap** 싼 ↔ **expensive** 비싼

- □ **prince** 왕자 ↔ **princess** 공주
- □ **direct** 직접적인 ↔ **indirect** 간접적인
- □ **king** 왕 ↔ **queen** 왕비, 여왕
- □ **produce** 생산하다 ↔ **consume** 소비하다
- □ **real** 진짜의 ↔ **fake** 가짜의
- □ **entire** 전체의 ↔ **partial** 일부의

English Dictionary

- □ **artist** 예술가
  → someone who produces art
  예술을 만들어 내는 사람

- □ **canvas** 화폭, 캔버스
  → a piece of thick cloth used by artists for painting on, usually with oil paints, or the painting itself
  보통 유성 물감으로 그 위에 그림을 그리기 위해, 또는 그림 자체를 위해 미술가에 의해 사용되는 두꺼운 천 조각

- □ **detail** 세부 사항
  → a single piece of some information of fact about something
  무언가에 관한 사실에 대한 하나의 정보

- □ **direction** 방향
  → the way something or someone moves, faces, or is aimed
  무언가 또는 누군가가 움직이거나 마주하거나 또는 목표로 하는 길

- □ **feather** 깃털
  → one of the light soft things that cover a bird's body
  새의 몸을 덮고 있는 가볍고 부드러운 것들 중 하나

- □ **landscape** 풍경
  → an area of countryside, especially in relation to its appearance
  특히 외관과 관련된 시골 지역

- □ **melt** 녹다
  → to change from a solid to a liquid by applying heat
  열을 가함으로써 고체에서 액체로 변하다

- □ **myth** 신화
  → an ancient story, especially one invented in order to explain natural or historical events
  특히 자연적이거나 역사적인 사건을 설명하기 위해 만들어진 고대의 이야기

- □ **notice** 알아차리다
  → to see or become conscious of something or someone
  무언가 또는 어떤 사람을 보거나 의식하게 되다

- □ **seaside** 해변, 바닷가
  → an area that is close to the sea
  바다에 가까운 지역

- □ **stick** 내밀다
  → to put it in a position where other people can see a part of your body
  다른 사람들이 당신의 신체의 일부를 볼 수 있는 자리에 놓다

- □ **tragedy** 비극
  → a very sad event, especially one involving death
  특히 죽음과 관련된 매우 슬픈 사건

- □ **wing** 날개
  → one of the parts of a bird's or insect's body that it uses for flying
  날기 위해 사용하는 새나 곤충의 신체 부분 중의 하나

- □ **wonder** 궁금해하다
  → to want to know more about something because it interests you
  당신에게 흥미를 불러일으키기 때문에 어떤 것에 대해 더 알고 싶어지다

서답형

01 다음 짝지어진 단어의 관계가 같도록 빈칸에 알맞은 말을 쓰시오.

| increase : decrease = _____ : freeze |

02 다음 영영풀이가 가리키는 것을 고르시오.

| an ancient story, especially one invented in order to explain natural or historical events |

① myth
② article
③ novel
④ essay
⑤ poem

03 다음 중 밑줄 친 부분의 뜻풀이가 바르지 <u>않은</u> 것은?

① He doesn't use a <u>brush</u> when he draws.
붓
② My boss will tell you about the <u>details</u>.
세부 사항
③ I like to watch the <u>comedy</u> show on Sundays. 희극
④ Our attention <u>directed</u> to the result of the race. 향했다
⑤ Jane looks young and beautiful <u>despite</u> her age. ~ 때문에

서답형

04 다음 우리말에 맞게 빈칸에 알맞은 말을 쓰시오.

(1) 우리는 멈춰서 그 가게를 보았다.
➡ We stopped and _____ a look at the store.
(2) 그녀는 버스 정류장에서 나를 힐끗 보았다.
➡ She _____ at me at the bus station.
(3) 나는 종종 미술 작품을 보러 박물관에 간다.
➡ I often go to the museum to see _____.
(4) 아이들이 비눗방울을 가지고 놀고 있다.
➡ The kids are playing with _____
_____.

서답형

05 다음 문장의 빈칸에 들어갈 말을 〈보기〉에서 골라 쓰시오.

보기
| wings / details / wax / myth / landscape |

(1) A tiger and a bear appear in the _____ of Dangun.
(2) I looked down on the peaceful _____ from the hill.
(3) My boss will tell you about the _____.
(4) They made _____ dolls of many actors.
(5) Airplanes have _____ like birds.

06 다음 주어진 문장의 밑줄 친 notice와 같은 의미로 쓰인 것은?

| I didn't <u>notice</u> the mistakes in this movie. |

① I didn't <u>notice</u> whether she was there or not.
② This <u>notice</u> was on my front door.
③ We received the <u>notice</u> two weeks ago.
④ All rules cannot be changed without any <u>notice</u>.
⑤ Will you post up a <u>notice</u> on the board?

Words & Expressions 서술형 시험대비

01 다음 짝지어진 단어의 관계가 같도록 빈칸에 알맞은 말을 쓰시오.

> king : queen = prince : _____

02 다음 우리말에 맞게 빈칸에 알맞은 말을 쓰시오.

(1) 산꼭대기 위의 눈은 절대 녹지 않는다.
➡ The snow on the top of the mountain
never _____.

(2) 나는 당신을 나의 전시회에 초대하고 싶어요.
➡ I'd like to invite you to my _____.

(3) 어떤 새들은 다채로운 깃털을 갖고 있다.
➡ Some birds have colorful _____.

03 다음 문장의 빈칸에 들어갈 말을 〈보기〉에서 골라 쓰시오.

> ┤ 보기 ├
> notice / landscape / seaside / promise / stick

(1) From the hill, she looked down on the peaceful _____.

(2) I didn't _____ that Ted was there.

(3) Don't _____ your arm out of the car window.

(4) My dad _____d to buy me new shoes.

(5) We are going on a picnic at the _____ this Sunday.

04 다음 우리말을 주어진 단어를 이용하여 영작하시오.

(1) 나는 그가 왜 나를 그의 파티에 초대했는지 궁금하다. (invite)
➡ _____

(2) 새 자동차의 생산이 다음 달에 시작될 것이다. (car, start)
➡ _____

(3) 처음에 아무도 나를 알아차리지 못했다. (nobody)
➡ _____

05 다음 영영풀이가 가리키는 말을 쓰시오.

> to change from a solid to a liquid by applying heat

➡ _____

06 다음 우리말과 일치하도록 주어진 단어를 모두 배열하여 영작하시오.

(1) 폭풍우 치는 동안 창문 가까이 가지 마라.
(during / stay / a storm / windows / from / away)
➡ _____

(2) 제가 당신의 영화표를 봐도 될까요?
(take / movie / I / at / your / may / look / a / ticket)
➡ _____

(3) 나는 경찰에 바로 신고했다.
(police / right / called / I / away / the)
➡ _____

Words & Expressions 113

Conversation

1 구체적인 종류나 장르 묻기

A What kind of music are you going to play? 어떤 종류의 음악을 연주할 거니?

B I'm going to play rock music. 나는 록 음악을 연주할 거야.

■ "What kind of ~?"는 어떤 대상의 종류나 유형에 대해서 구체직으로 묻고자 할 때 사용된다. 예를 들어, 어떤 식당에서 먹을 수 있는 음식의 종류가 무엇인지 궁금할 때 "What kind of food does the restaurant serve?"와 같이 물을 수 있다.

구체적인 종류나 장르 묻기

• What sort of traditional food do you like? 어떤 종류의 전통 음식을 좋아하니?

• What type of person is the new math teacher? 새로 오신 수학 선생님은 어떤 사람인가요?

• To which category does this game belong? 이 게임은 어느 범주에 속하나요?

핵심 Check

1. 다음 우리말과 일치하도록 빈칸에 알맞은 말을 쓰시오.

(1) A: ＿＿＿＿ ＿＿＿＿ ＿＿＿＿ ＿＿＿＿ do you like? (어떤 종류의 콘서트를 좋아하니?)

　　 B: I like a rock concert. (나는 록 콘서트를 좋아해.)

(2) A: What sort of ＿＿＿＿ ＿＿＿＿ ＿＿＿＿ ＿＿＿＿ ＿＿＿＿ ＿＿＿＿?

　　 (어떤 종류의 영화를 보고 싶니?)

　　 B: I want to see a comedy movie. (나는 코미디 영화를 보고 싶어.)

(3) A: What ＿＿＿＿ of person is the new English teacher? (새로 오신 영어 선생님은 어떤 분이니?)

　　 B: She is so kind and humorous. (그 선생님은 매우 친절하고 유머가 풍부하셔.)

② 둘 중에 더 좋아하는 것 말하기

A There are two kinds of *Mona Lisas*. Which do you prefer?

두 종류의 모나리자가 있어. 어느 것을 더 좋아하니?

B I prefer Botero's *Mona Lisa* to da Vinci's. 나는 다 빈치의 모나리자보다 보테로의 모나리자를 더 좋아해.

■ "I prefer A to B."는 두 가지 비교되는 사람이나 사물 등에 대하여 자신이 어떤 것을 더 좋아하는지를 표현할 때 사용된다. 예를 들어, 책을 읽는 것보다 영화 보는 것을 더 좋아한다는 것을 표현하고자 할 때는 "I prefer watching movies to reading books."와 같이 말할 수 있다.

둘 중에 더 좋아하는 것 말하기

- I like watching music videos better than listening to music.
  나는 음악을 듣는 것보다 음악 비디오를 보는 것을 더 좋아한다.

- I prefer taking a taxi to the station if possible. 나는 가능하면 역에 택시 타고 가는 것을 더 좋아한다.

- I think sending text messages is better than talking on the phone.
  나는 문자 메시지를 보내는 것이 전화로 이야기하는 것보다 더 낫다고 생각한다.

핵심 Check

2. 다음 우리말과 일치하도록 빈칸에 알맞은 말을 쓰시오.

(1) **A:** _____ _____ _____ _____, listening to music or reading books?

(음악 듣는 것과 책을 읽는 것 중에 어느 것을 더 좋아하니?)

B: I prefer listening to music to reading books. (나는 책을 읽는 것보다 음악 듣는 것을 더 좋아해.)

(2) **A:** Which do you prefer, taking photos or drawing pictures?

(사진 찍는 것과 그림 그리는 것 중에 어느 것을 더 좋아하니?)

B: I prefer _____ _____ to _____ _____.

(나는 그림을 그리는 것보다 사진 찍는 것을 더 좋아해.)

(3) **A:** Which do you prefer, dogs or cats? (개와 고양이 중에 어느 것을 더 좋아하니?)

B: _____ _____ _____ _____ _____. (나는 고양이보다 개를 더 좋아해.)

Listen & Talk 1-B

W: (*ringing*) Hello, Steve.

M: Hi, Anna. We're meeting at the arts festival tomorrow at 1:30, right?

W: Right. ❶What kind of performance do you want to watch first?

M: I want to watch the hip-hop dance performance first.

W: ❷Sounds good. It's at 2 p.m. at the ❸gym, right?

M: Yeah, and ❹how about watching the play, *Romeo and Juliet*, at 4 p.m.?

W: Oh, the ❺one at the Main Hall near the gym? Sure!

W: (전화벨 소리) 안녕, Steve.

M: 안녕, Anna. 우리 내일 1시 30분에 예술 축제에서 만나는 거 맞지?

W: 맞아. 먼저 어떤 종류의 공연을 보고 싶어?

M: 난 힙합 댄스 공연을 먼저 보고 싶어.

W: 좋은 생각이야. 체육관에서 오후 2시에 하는 거 맞지?

M: 응, 그리고 오후 4시에 '로미오와 줄리엣' 연극을 보는 건 어때?

W: 아, 체육관 근처 대강당에서 하는 연극 말이지? 좋아!

❶ 구체적인 종류를 묻는 질문으로 'What sort of performance do you want to watch first?'로 바꾸어 쓸 수 있다.

❷ (That) sounds good. = Good idea.

❸ gym: 체육관

❹ 제안하는 표현으로 What about ~? = Why don't we ~? = Let's ~ 구문으로 바꾸어 쓸 수 있다.

❺ one은 play를 가리킨다.

Check(√) True or False

(1) Anna and Steve are going to visit the arts festival tomorrow.　　　T ☐　F ☐

(2) Anna prefers watching the play to the hip-hop dance performance.　　T ☐　F ☐

Communication

M: Hi, we are planning a school festival, so we want to ❶find out students' favorite types of performances. ❷May I ask you a few questions?

W: Sure.

M: What kind of performance do you like best?

W: I like music performances best.

M: Okay. Then, which do you prefer, rock or hip-hop?

W: I ❸prefer rock to hip-hop.

M: Who's your favorite musician?

W: ❹My favorite musician is TJ.

M: Great. Thank you for your answers.

M: 안녕하세요, 저희는 학교 축제를 계획 중이고, 그래서 학생들이 어떤 종류의 공연을 좋아하는지 알고 싶습니다. 몇 가지 질문을 해도 될까요?

W: 물론이죠.

M: 어떤 종류의 공연을 가장 좋아하나요?

W: 저는 음악 공연을 가장 좋아해요.

M: 알겠습니다. 그러면 록과 힙합 중 어느 것을 더 좋아하나요?

W: 저는 힙합보다 록을 더 좋아해요.

M: 가장 좋아하는 뮤지션은 누구인가요?

W: 제가 가장 좋아하는 뮤지션은 TJ입니다.

M: 좋습니다. 답변해 주셔서 감사합니다.

❶ find out: ~을 알아내다

❷ 부탁을 나타내는 표현으로 'Can I ask you a few questions?'로 바꾸어 쓸 수 있다.

❸ prefer A to B: A를 B보다 더 좋아하다.

❹ I love TJ. 또는 I like TJ best.로 바꾸어 쓸 수 있다.

Check(√) True or False

(3) The boy is asking some questions to prepare a school festival.　　T ☐　F ☐

(4) The girl likes rock more than hip-hop.　　T ☐　F ☐

Listen & Talk 1 A-1

W: Brian, is your band going to play at the Teen Music Festival?

M: Yes, we're practicing ❶almost every day.

W: ❷What kind of music are you going to play ❸this year?

M: Rock music. We'll play songs from the nineties.

❶ almost: 거의
❷ 'What sort of music are you going to play this year?'로 바꾸어 쓸 수 있다.
❸ this year: 올해

Listen & Talk 1 A-2

W: ❶Can you help me? I don't know how to paint clean lines.

M: What kind of ❷brush were you using?

W: This round brush.

M: When you paint lines, a ❸flat brush is better. Try this one.

W: Okay, thank you.

❶ 도움을 요청하는 표현으로 'Can you give me your hand?' = 'Would you help me?' 등으로 바꾸어 쓸 수 있다.
❷ brush: 붓
❸ flat: 평평한

Listen & Talk 2 A-1

M: What are you reading, Jina?

W: The ❶novel, *Life of Pi*. ❷It's a story of a boy and a tiger.

M: ❷It's a great book. I've seen the movie of ❷it, too. I prefer the movie to the novel.

W: Why do you like ❷it better?

M: The ❸scenes are very beautiful. And the tiger ❹looks so ❺real.

❶ novel: 소설
❷ It[it]은 모두 *Life of Pi*를 가리킨다.
❸ scene: 장면
❹ look+형용사: ~처럼 보이다
❺ real: 진짜의 (↔ fake: 가짜의)

Listen & Talk 2 A-2

W: ❶Have you listened to Jane's new song, *Girl Friend*?

M: Yeah, ❷it's really cool. The guitar part is great.

W: ❸There is also a dance version of the song on the album.

M: I've listened to ❹it, but I prefer the guitar version to the dance version. ❺It matches her voice better.

❶ 현재완료(have+p.p) 구문으로 경험을 묻고 있다.
❷ it은 Jane's new song, *Girl Friend*를 가리킨다.
❸ There is+단수 명사: ~가 있다
❹ it은 a dance version을 가리킨다.
❺ It은 the guitar version을 가리킨다.

Listen & Talk 2 B

W: I saw an interesting painting in an art book. ❶Look at this.

M: Wow, it looks like da Vinci's *Mona Lisa*.

W: ❷Actually, it's *Mona Lisa* by Fernando Botero. Which do you prefer?

M: I prefer da Vinci's to Botero's. Da Vinci's *Mona Lisa* has an interesting smile. ❸How about you?

W: Well, I prefer Botero's to da Vinci's. His *Mona Lisa* is cute, and ❹it looks ❺modern.

❶ look at: ~을 보다
❷ actually: 사실은, 실제로
❸ How about you? = What about you?: 너는 어때?
❹ Botero's *Mona Lisa*를 가리킨다.
❺ modern: 현대적인

Wrap Up 1

M: Can you help me? I want to buy a guitar.

W: ❶There are various kinds of guitars. What kind of music do you want to play?

M: I want to play pop songs.

W: Then you should get a classical guitar.

M: Okay, I will take a classical guitar.

❶ There are+복수 명사

● 다음 우리말과 일치하도록 빈칸에 알맞은 말을 쓰시오.

> **Listen & Talk 1 A-1**

W: Brian, is your band _____ _____ _____ at the Teen Music Festival?

M: Yes, we're practicing _____ _____ _____.

W: _____ _____ _____ are you going to play this year?

M: Rock music. We'll _____ _____ from the nineties.

> **Listen & Talk 1 A-2**

W: Can you help me? I don't know _____ _____ _____ _____ _____.

M: _____ _____ _____ were you using?

W: This round brush.

M: When you paint lines, a _____ brush is _____. _____ this one.

W: Okay, thank you.

> **Listen & Talk 1 B**

W: (*ringing*) Hello, Steve.

M: Hi, Anna. We're _____ at the arts festival tomorrow at 1:30, _____?

W: Right. What kind of performance _____ _____ _____ _____ _____?

M: I _____ _____ watch the hip-hop dance performance first.

W: _____ good. It's at 2 p.m. at the gym, _____?

M: Yeah, and how about _____ _____ _____, *Romeo and Juliet*, at 4 p.m.?

W: Oh, _____ _____ at the Main Hall near the gym? Sure!

> **Listen & Talk 2 A-1**

M: What are you reading, Jina?

W: The novel, *Life of Pi*. It's _____ _____ of a boy and a tiger.

M: It's a great book. I've seen the movie _____ _____, too. I _____ the movie _____ the novel.

W: Why do you _____ it _____?

M: The _____ are very beautiful. And the tiger looks so _____.

해석

W: Brian, 너희 밴드는 '십 대 음악 축제'에서 연주할 거야?

M: 응, 우리는 거의 매일 연습하고 있어.

W: 너희는 올해 어떤 종류의 음악을 연주하려고 해?

M: 록 음악. 우리는 90년대 곡들을 연주할 거야.

W: 나 좀 도와줄래? 나는 선을 깔끔하게 그리는 방법을 모르겠어.

M: 어떤 종류의 붓을 사용하고 있었니?

W: 이 둥근 붓이야.

M: 선을 그릴 때는 납작한 붓이 더 나아. 이것을 써 봐.

W: 알았어, 고마워.

W: (전화벨 소리) 안녕, Steve.

M: 안녕, Anna. 우리 내일 1시 30분에 예술 축제에서 만나는 거 맞지?

W: 맞아. 먼저 어떤 종류의 공연을 보고 싶어?

M: 난 힙합 댄스 공연을 먼저 보고 싶어.

W: 좋은 생각이야. 체육관에서 오후 2시에 하는 거 맞지?

M: 응, 그리고 오후 4시에 '로미오와 줄리엣' 연극을 보는 건 어때?

W: 아, 체육관 근처 대강당에서 하는 연극 말이지? 좋아!

M: 지나야, 너 무엇을 읽고 있니?

W: '파이 이야기'라는 소설이야. 한 소년과 호랑이에 대한 이야기이지.

M: 훌륭한 책이야. 나는 그것을 영화로도 봤어. 나는 소설보다는 영화가 더 좋아.

W: 왜 영화가 더 좋은데?

M: 장면이 매우 아름다워. 그리고 호랑이가 매우 진짜같이 보이거든.

Listen & Talk 2 A-2

W: _____ you _____ to Jane's new song, *Girl Friend*?

M: Yeah, it's really _____. The guitar _____ is great.

W: There is also a _____ _____ of the song on the album.

M: I've listened to it, but _____ _____ _____ _____ to the dance version. It _____ her voice better.

Listen & Talk 2 B

W: I saw an _____ _____ in an art book. Look at this.

M: Wow, it _____ _____ da Vinci's *Mona Lisa*.

W: Actually, it's *Mona Lisa* by Fernando Botero. _____ _____ _____ _____?

M: I _____ da Vinci's _____ Botero's. Da Vinci's *Mona Lisa* has an interesting smile. _____ _____ _____?

W: Well, I _____ Botero's _____ da Vinci's. His *Mona Lisa* is cute, and it looks _____.

Communication

M: Hi, we are planning a school festival, _____ we want to _____ _____ students' favorite types of performances. _____ I _____ you a few questions?

W: Sure.

M: _____ _____ _____ _____ do you like best?

W: I like music performances best.

M: Okay. Then, which _____ you _____, rock or hip-hop?

W: I _____ _____ _____ _____.

M: Who's your _____ _____?

W: My favorite musician is TJ.

M: Great. _____ you _____ your answers.

Wrap Up 1

M: _____ you _____ me? I want to buy a guitar.

W: There are _____ _____ of guitars. _____ _____ _____ _____ do you want to play?

M: I _____ _____ play pop songs.

W: Then you _____ _____ a classical guitar.

M: Okay, I will take a classical guitar.

해석

W: 너는 Jane의 새 노래인 '여자 친구'를 들어 봤니?
M: 응, 정말 멋져. 기타 부분이 굉장하지.
W: 앨범에는 그 노래의 댄스 버전도 있어.
M: 나는 그것을 들었는데 댄스 버전보다는 기타 버전이 더 좋아. 그 버전이 그녀의 목소리와 더 잘 어울리거든.

W: 나 미술 책에서 흥미로운 그림을 봤어. 이것 봐.
M: 와, 그것은 다빈치의 '모나리자'처럼 보이는데.
W: 사실 이 그림은 페르난도 보테로의 '모나리자'야. 넌 어느 것이 더 마음에 드니?
M: 나는 보테로의 그림보다 다빈치의 모나리자가 더 좋아. 다빈치의 '모나리자'에는 흥미로운 미소가 있어. 너는 어때?
W: 음, 나는 다빈치의 모나리자보다는 보테로의 모나리자가 더 좋아. 그의 '모나리자'는 귀엽고 현대적으로 보여.

M: 안녕하세요, 저희는 학교 축제를 계획 중이고, 그래서 학생들이 어떤 종류의 공연을 좋아하는지 알고 싶습니다. 몇 가지 질문을 해도 될까요?
W: 물론이죠.
M: 어떤 종류의 공연을 가장 좋아하나요?
W: 저는 음악 공연을 가장 좋아해요.
M: 알겠습니다. 그러면 록과 힙합 중 어떤 것을 더 좋아하나요?
W: 저는 힙합보다 록을 더 좋아해요.
M: 가장 좋아하는 뮤지션은 누구인가요?
W: 제가 가장 좋아하는 뮤지션은 TJ입니다.
M: 좋습니다. 답변해 주셔서 감사합니다.

M: 저 좀 도와주시겠어요? 저는 기타를 하나 사고 싶어요.
W: 다양한 종류의 기타가 있어요. 어떤 종류의 음악을 연주하고 싶으신가요?
M: 저는 팝송을 연주하려고 해요.
W: 그럼 클래식 기타를 사셔야 해요.
M: 알겠습니다, 클래식 기타로 살게요.

[01~02] 다음 대화를 읽고 물음에 답하시오.

Sora: (A)Can you help me? I don't know how to paint clean lines.

Mike: _____ (B)

Sora: This round brush.

Mike: When you paint lines, a flat brush is better. Try this one.

Sora: Okay, thank you.

01 위 대화의 밑줄 친 (A)와 바꾸어 쓸 수 있는 것을 모두 고르시오.

① Can you give me a hand? ② Do you need any help?

③ What can I do for you?   ④ Would you do me a favor?

⑤ Can I give you a hand?

02 위 대화의 빈칸 (B)에 들어갈 말을 〈보기〉에 주어진 단어를 배열하여 완성하시오.

┌─ 보기 ├
of / brush / you / what / using / were / kind

➡ _____

[03~04] 다음 대화를 읽고 물음에 답하시오.

Minsu: What are you reading, Jina?

Jina: The novel, *Life of Pi*. It's a story of a boy and a tiger.

Minsu: It's a great book. I've seen the movie of (A)it, too. I prefer the movie to the novel.

Jina: Why do you like (B)it better?

Minsu: The scenes are very beautiful. And the tiger looks so real.

03 위 대화의 밑줄 친 (A)와 (B)의 it이 각각 가리키는 것을 찾아 쓰시오.

(A) _____   (B) _____

04 위 대화의 내용과 일치하지 않는 것은?

① Jina is reading *Life of Pi*.

② *Life of Pi* is the novel about a boy and a tiger.

③ Minsu has seen the movie of *Life of Pi*.

④ Minsu likes the novel more than the movie.

⑤ The scenes are very beautiful in the movie.

01 다음 대화의 내용과 일치하지 <u>않는</u> 것은?

> Susan: Brian, is your band going to play at the Teen Music Festival?
> Brian: Yes, we're practicing almost every day.
> Susan: What kind of music are you going to play this year?
> Brian: Rock music. We'll play songs from the nineties.

① Brian의 밴드는 '십 대 음악 축제'에서 연주할 것이다.
② Brian의 밴드는 거의 매일 연습하고 있다.
③ Brian의 밴드는 올해 록 음악을 연주할 것이다.
④ Brian의 밴드는 90년대 곡들을 연주할 것이다.
⑤ Brian의 밴드는 90분 동안 연주할 것이다.

[02~03] 다음 대화를 읽고 물음에 답하시오.

> Sue: Have you listened to Jane's new song, *Girl Friend*?
> Tony: Yeah, (A)<u>it</u>'s really cool. The guitar part is great.
> Sue: There is also a dance version of the song on the album.
> Tony: I've listened to (B)<u>it</u>, but I prefer the guitar version to the dance version. (C) <u>It</u> matches her voice better.

서답형

02 위 대화의 밑줄 친 (A)~(C)의 it이 가리키는 것을 각각 찾아 쓰시오.

(A) _____
(B) _____
(C) _____

03 위 대화의 내용과 일치하지 <u>않는</u> 것은?

① Jane released her new song, *Girl Friend*.
② Tony likes the guitar part of *Girl Friend*.
③ There are both a dance version and the guitar version of *Girl Friend* on the album.
④ Tony thought that Jane's voice matches the dance version.
⑤ Tony likes the guitar version more than the dance version.

04 다음 대화를 읽고 대답할 수 <u>없는</u> 질문은?

> Anna: (*ringing*) Hello, Steve.
> Steve: Hi, Anna. We're meeting at the arts festival tomorrow at 1:30, right?
> Anna: Right. What kind of performance do you want to watch first?
> Steve: I want to watch the hip-hop dance performance first.
> Anna: Sounds good. It's at 2 p.m. at the gym, right?
> Steve: Yeah, and how about watching the play, *Romeo and Juliet*, at 4 p.m.?
> Anna: Oh, the one at the Main Hall near the gym? Sure!

① What is Anna going to do with Steve tomorrow?
② What kind of performance does Steve want to watch first?
③ When is the hip-hop dance performance?
④ Where can Anna and Steve watch the play, *Romeo and Juliet*?
⑤ Why does Steve suggest watching the play, *Romeo and Juliet*?

서답형

05 다음 대화의 내용과 일치하도록 주어진 표를 완성하시오.

> Mina: I saw an interesting painting in an art book. Look at this.
>
> Jack: Wow, it looks like da Vinci's *Mona Lisa*.
>
> Mina: Actually, it's *Mona Lisa* by Fernando Botero. Which do you prefer?
>
> Jack: I prefer da Vinci's to Botero's. Da Vinci's *Mona Lisa* has an interesting smile. How about you?
>
> Mina: Well, I prefer Botero's to da Vinci's. His *Mona Lisa* is cute, and it looks modern.

Title	*Mona Lisa*	
Painter	Leonardo da Vinci	Fernando Botero
Who prefers	(A)	(B)
opinion	(C)	(D)

(A) _____ (B) _____

(C) _____

(D) _____

[06~08] 다음 대화를 읽고 물음에 답하시오.

> Jason: Hi, we are planning a school festival, so we want to find out students' favorite types of performances. (A) May I ask you a few questions?
>
> Emily: Sure.
>
> Jason: What kind of performance do you like best?
>
> Emily: I like music performances best.

> Jason: Okay. Then, (B)어느 것을 더 좋아하나요, rock or hip-hop?
>
> Emily: I prefer rock to hip-hop.
>
> Jason: Who's your favorite musician?
>
> Emily: My favorite musician is TJ.
>
> Jason: Great. Thank you for your answers.

06 위 대화의 밑줄 친 (A)와 바꾸어 쓸 수 있는 것은?

① Do you have any questions?
② Do you want to ask any questions?
③ Would you answer a few questions?
④ How can I ask a few questions of you?
⑤ Did you answer a few questions?

서답형

07 위 대화의 밑줄 친 (B)의 우리말을 4단어를 사용하여 영작하시오.

➡ _____

서답형

08 What kind of music does Emily like better?

➡ _____

서답형

09 다음 주어진 문장 뒤에 이어지는 대화가 자연스럽게 이어지도록 순서대로 배열하시오.

> Can you help me? I want to buy a guitar.

> (A) Okay, I will take a classical guitar.
> (B) I want to play pop songs.
> (C) There are various kinds of guitars. What kind of music do you want to play?
> (D) Then you should get a classical guitar.

➡ _____

01 다음 대화의 빈칸 (A)~(C)에 들어갈 알맞은 대답을 〈보기〉에서 찾아 쓰시오.

> Jason: Hi, we are planning a school festival, so we want to find out students' favorite types of performances. May I ask you a few questions?
>
> Emily: Sure.
>
> Jason: What kind of performance do you like best?
>
> Emily: (A) _____
>
> Jason: Okay. Then, which do you prefer, rock or hip-hop?
>
> Emily: (B) _____
>
> Jason: Who's your favorite musician?
>
> Emily: (C) _____
>
> Jason: Great. Thank you for your answers.

┌─ 보기 ─
ⓐ My favorite musician is TJ.
ⓑ I like music performances best.
ⓒ I prefer rock to hip-hop.
└

(A) _____ (B) _____ (C) _____

[02~03] 다음 대화를 읽고 물음에 답하시오.

Sue: Have you listened to Jane's new song, *Girl Friend*?

Tony: Yeah, it's really cool. The guitar part is great.

Sue: There is also a dance version of the song on the album.

Tony: I've listened to it, but I prefer the guitar version to the dance version. It matches her voice better.

02 What song have Tony and Sue listened to in Jane's album?

➡ _____

03 Why does Tony prefer the guitar version to the dance version?

➡ _____
_____

[04~06] 다음 대화를 읽고 물음에 답하시오.

Minsu: What are you reading, Jina?

Jina: The novel, *Life of Pi*. It's a story of a boy and a tiger.

Minsu: It's a great book. I've seen the movie of it, too. (A)나는 소설보다는 영화가 더 좋아. (prefer)

Jina: Why do you like it better?

Minsu: The scenes are very beautiful. And the tiger looks so real.

04 위 대화의 밑줄 친 (A)의 우리말을 주어진 단어를 사용하여 영작하시오.

➡ _____

05 What is the novel, *Life of Pi*, about?

➡ _____

06 Why does Minsu prefer the movie to the novel?

➡ _____
_____

Grammar

① 사역동사

> • He **made** me **do** the laundry. 그는 내가 빨래를 하도록 시켰다.
> • Alicia **had** her son **park** her car. Alicia는 그녀의 아들이 그녀의 차를 주차하게 했다.

■ 사역동사는 문장의 주어가 목적어에게 어떠한 행동을 하도록 시키는 동사로 make, have, let 등이 이에 속한다.

- Gloria **let** me **go** home early. Gloria는 내가 집에 일찍 가도록 허락해 주었다.
- Paul **had** my sister **sing** in front of many people. Paul은 내 여동생이 많은 사람들 앞에서 노래하게 했다.
- They **make** us **do** our best. 그들은 우리가 최선을 다하게 만든다.

■ 사역동사는 5형식에 속하여 목적격 보어를 갖는데, 사역동사의 목적격 보어는 동사원형의 형태를 취하며, '~에게 …하게 하다'라고 해석하는 것에 유의한다.

- The teacher **made** us **find** the dog. 선생님은 우리가 그 개를 찾도록 시키셨다.
- She **had** me **do** the job instead of her. 그녀는 그녀 대신에 내가 그 일을 하도록 시켰다.
- The sisters **made** me buy the car. 그 자매들은 내가 그 차를 사게 했다.
- I **had** my sister **fix** dinner. 나는 내 여동생이 저녁 식사를 차리게 했다.

■ 준사역동사에 해당하는 help는 목적격 보어로 to부정사나 동사원형 형태를 취한다.

- We **helped** the man **stand[to stand]** on his own. 우리는 그 남자가 혼자 힘으로 설 수 있도록 도왔다.

핵심 Check

1. 다음 우리말과 일치하도록 빈칸에 알맞은 말을 쓰시오.
   (1) Mike는 내가 그의 가방을 지켜보게 했다.
      ➡ Mike had _____ _____ his bag.
   (2) 나는 그가 내 스마트폰을 사용하게 한다.
      ➡ I let _____ _____ my smartphone.
   (3) 엄마는 아빠가 일찍 집에 오게 하셨다.
      ➡ My mom made _____ _____ _____ home early.

② 간접의문문

- Do you know **who he is**? 너는 그가 누구인지 아니?
- I wonder **what her name is**. 나는 그녀의 이름이 무엇인지 궁금해.

■ 의문문이 문장 내에서 주어, 목적어, 보어 역할을 할 때 이를 간접의문문이라고 한다. 간접의문문의 어순은 '의문사+주어+동사'임에 유의한다.

- I don't know **how you came here**. 나는 네가 어떻게 이곳에 왔는지 모르겠어.
- He doesn't remember **what her name is**. 그는 그녀의 이름이 무엇인지 기억하지 못한다.
- Jane wants to know **where her mother is**. Jane은 그녀의 엄마가 어디에 있는지 알고 싶다.

■ 의문사가 주어로 쓰인 경우 의문사가 동시에 주어 역할을 하므로 의문사 뒤에 동사가 바로 이어서 나올 수 있다.

- Do you know **who invented the light bulb**? 누가 전구를 발명했는지 아니?
- Can you tell me **what made her upset**? 무엇이 그녀를 화나게 했는지 말해줄 수 있니?

■ think, believe, guess, imagine, suppose 등과 같은 동사가 주절에 있을 경우 간접의문문의 의문사를 문장 맨 앞으로 배치한다.

- Do you think what it is? (✗)

  What do you think **it is**? (○) 너는 그것이 무엇이라고 생각하니?

- Do you guess who he is? (✗)

  Who do you guess **he is**? (○) 너는 그가 누구라고 생각하는 거야?

■ 의문사가 없는 경우 간접의문문의 어순은 'if/whether+주어+동사'로 쓴다.

- Can you tell me? + Is he hungry?
  → Can you tell me **if[whether] he is hungry**? 그가 배가 고픈지 내게 말해줄래?
- I wonder **whether Kevin wants to come**. Kevin이 오기를 원하는지 궁금하다.
- I want to know **whether they will accept the job**. 그들이 그 일을 받아들일지 알고 싶어.

핵심 Check

2. 다음 두 문장을 하나의 문장으로 연결할 때 빈칸에 알맞은 말을 쓰시오.

(1) Do you know? Who is she?

   ➡ Do you know ＿＿＿＿ ＿＿＿＿ ＿＿＿＿?

(2) Can you tell me? Why do you study English?

   ➡ Can you tell me ＿＿＿＿ ＿＿＿＿ ＿＿＿＿ English?

(3) I wonder. Where did you go yesterday?

   ➡ I wonder ＿＿＿＿ ＿＿＿＿ ＿＿＿＿ yesterday.

01 다음 문장에서 어법상 <u>어색한</u> 부분을 바르게 고쳐 쓰시오.

(1) My teacher made me to read this book.

_____ ➡ _____

(2) I wonder how was the weather yesterday.

_____ ➡ _____

(3) My father let me buying the laptop computer.

_____ ➡ _____

(4) I didn't know who were you at first.

_____ ➡ _____

02 다음 두 문장을 간접의문문을 이용하여 하나의 문장으로 쓰시오.

(1) Oliver wanted to ask. Was she satisfied with his service?

➡ _____

(2) Can you tell me? Where are we going?

➡ _____

(3) I'd like to know. What do you do during your free time?

➡ _____

(4) I wonder. How often do you water the plant?

➡ _____

03 주어진 어구를 바르게 배열하여 다음 우리말을 영어로 쓰시오. 필요하다면 어형을 바꾸시오.

(1) 그 상사는 그가 사무실에 머무르게 시켰다.

(the office / make / stay / him / in / the boss)

➡ _____

(2) 너는 네 친구가 네 자전거를 빌려가도록 허락했니?

(bicycle / did / your / you / borrow / let / friend / your)

➡ _____

(3) 우리는 그가 밀짚모자를 쓰게 했어요.

(have / wear / we / him / a straw hat)

➡ _____

(4) 제가 답을 보게 해 주세요.

(the answer / me / please / see / let)

➡ _____

01 다음 빈칸에 들어갈 말로 적절하지 <u>않은</u> 것은?

> Mary _____ us play the computer game.

① made ② saw ③ let
④ had ⑤ wanted

02 다음 우리말을 영어로 바르게 옮긴 것은?

> 나는 그 남자가 내 차를 세차하게 만들었다.

① I wanted the man to wash my car.
② I wondered whether the man washed my car.
③ I made the man wash my car.
④ I asked the man to wash my car.
⑤ I saw the man wash my car.

03 다음 중 빈칸에 들어갈 수 <u>없는</u> 말은?

> Who do you _____ has this car?

① guess ② imagine ③ think
④ wonder ⑤ suppose

04 다음 중 빈칸에 들어갈 단어 'do'의 형태가 <u>다른</u> 하나는?

① Julie made me _____ my best.
② Clara saw me _____ aerobics.
③ They let me _____ the flowers.
④ Paul had me _____ some research.
⑤ June allowed me _____ the cooking with her brother.

05 다음 빈칸에 알맞은 말을 쓰시오.

> 그들은 내가 이곳에 일찍 오게 했습니다.
> ➡ They made me _____ here early.

06 다음 우리말을 영어로 옮길 때 다섯 번째로 오는 단어를 쓰시오.

> 나는 네가 이곳에 언제 도착할 것인지 궁금해.

➡ _____

07 다음 중 어법상 올바른 문장의 개수는?

> ⓐ Susan had them finish the homework until that night.
> ⓑ I want to know when will they call me again.
> ⓒ My brother let me wearing this new T-shirt.
> ⓓ Tell me who told you the secret.
> ⓔ Could you tell me what Jason is doing in his room?

① 1개 ② 2개 ③ 3개
④ 4개 ⑤ 5개

08 다음 중 빈칸에 들어갈 말로 가장 적절한 것은?

> I wonder. Why is he running?
> = I wonder _____.

① why he running
② whether he is running
③ why he is running
④ why is he running
⑤ whether he running

서답형

09 주어진 단어를 활용하여 다음 우리말을 영어로 쓰시오.

너는 그 창문을 누가 깼다고 생각하니?
(suppose / break)

➡ _____

중요

10 다음 중 밑줄 친 부분이 어색한 것은?

① Can you tell me where he is from?
② Do you know who Hanguel made?
③ I wonder how often you visit your grandparents.
④ Tell me when she sent the email to me.
⑤ Do you understand what he is trying to say?

11 다음 중 빈칸에 들어갈 말이 바르게 짝지어진 것은?

• Mr. Davidson made the children _____ their hands before dinner.
• Tell me _____ while your parents are not at home.

① to wash – who do you take care of
② to wash – who you will take care of
③ wash – who will take care of you
④ wash – whom you take care of
⑤ washing – whom you take care of

서답형

12 주어진 어구를 바르게 배열하여 대화를 완성하시오.

A: My teacher made me do my paper again.
B: _____
(do you think / you / why / made / she / it / again / do)

서답형

13 주어진 단어를 활용하여 다음 우리말을 영어로 쓰시오.

나는 그가 내 시계를 고치게 했어.
(make / repair)

➡ _____

중요

14 다음 우리말을 영어로 옮길 때 다섯 번째로 오는 단어는?

지금 몇 시라고 생각하세요?

① time   ② you   ③ it
④ think   ⑤ is

15 다음 빈칸에 들어갈 말로 적절하지 <u>않은</u> 것은?

Did you _____ them study together for the exam?

① have   ② make   ③ let
④ allow   ⑤ help

중요

16 다음 빈칸에 들어갈 말로 가장 적절한 것은?

A: Do you know _____ now?
B: Oh, she is making some cookies in the kitchen.

① what is Molly doing
② what Molly doing
③ what Molly is doing
④ Molly is doing what
⑤ Molly is doing

17 다음 빈칸에 들어갈 말로 가장 적절한 것은?

Lily always makes him _____.

① laughing   ② to laugh   ③ laugh
④ laughs   ⑤ to laughing

18 다음 빈칸에 공통으로 들어갈 말로 가장 적절한 것은?

> • Karl _____ her son a tennis player.
> • Jina _____ me some delicious cookies.
> • He _____ us jump the rope.
> • June _____ the paper robot very well.

① had   ② let   ③ went

④ made   ⑤ want

19 다음 중 영어로 옮긴 것이 바르지 <u>않은</u> 것은?

① 나는 그 아이들이 벽에 페인트칠을 하도록 허락했다.
> → I let the children paint on the wall.

② 누가 올 것이라고 생각해?
> → Who do you think will come?

③ 우리 선생님은 가끔 우리에게 무엇을 하라고 시키시니?
> → What does our teacher sometimes make us do?

④ 나는 그가 그녀에게서 무엇을 빌렸는지 몰라요.
> → I don't know what he borrowed from her.

⑤ 누가 그 건물을 지었다고 생각하니?
> → Who do you guess the building built?

20 다음 빈칸에 들어갈 말로 가장 적절한 것은?

> A: I'd like to know _____.
> B: I'm in the 8th grade.

① where you are now

② which grade are you

③ which grade you are in

④ who you are

⑤ which you are in the grade

21 빈칸에 들어갈 말로 가장 적절한 것은?

> Did you _____ the students ride the bikes?

① want   ② force   ③ allow

④ have   ⑤ enable

22 주어진 단어를 활용하여 빈칸에 알맞은 말을 쓰시오. (7단어)

> Jason: I would like to know _____.
> (what / do / when / free)
> Kelly: I write songs when I am free.

➡ _____

23 다음 중 어법상 <u>어색한</u> 것은?

① He made me stand on the street for an hour.

② They helped me to finish the project very well.

③ Do you think who you are?

④ Tell me when your birthday is.

⑤ Julian had her say sorry again.

24 주어진 문장과 같은 의미의 문장은?

> Mom tells me to do something.

① Mom enables me to do something.

② Mom makes me do something.

③ Mom sees me do something.

④ Mom thinks I do something.

⑤ Mom wants to know when I do something.

25 다음 두 문장을 하나의 문장으로 쓰시오.

> I want to know. Did she like the present?

➡ _____

01 주어진 단어를 활용하여 다음 우리말을 영어로 바르게 옮기시오.

> 엄마는 나와 내 여동생이 집을 청소하게 시키셨다.
> (make, clean)

➡ _____

02 주어진 단어를 활용하여 다음 우리말을 영어로 쓰시오.

> 누가 그 돈을 훔쳤다고 생각하니?
> (think / steal)

➡ _____

03 주어진 단어를 바르게 배열하여 다음 우리말을 영어로 쓰시오.

> 그들이 언제 너를 집에 가게 했는지 말해 줄 수 있니? (home / can / go / tell / when / you / me / they / you / let)

➡ _____

04 다음 빈칸에 알맞은 말을 쓰시오.

(1) 아빠는 내가 그의 차를 운전하게 허락하신다.
➡ My father lets _____ _____
_____ _____.

(2) Jane은 그가 자기에게 물 한 잔을 가져오게 했다.
➡ Jane had _____ _____ _____
a glass of water.

(3) 그녀는 내가 그녀를 쳐다보게 만들었다.
➡ She made _____ _____ _____
her.

05 주어진 단어를 활용하여 다음 문장과 같은 의미의 문장을 쓰시오.

> Brad forced me to accept the job.
> (make)

➡ _____

06 〈보기〉와 같이 다음 두 문장을 하나의 문장으로 쓰시오.

> ┤ 보기 ├
> Can you tell me? Who is she?
> ➡ Can you tell me who she is?

(1) I don't know. Where does he live?
➡ _____

(2) Do you guess? How old is he?
➡ _____

(3) Can you tell me? Why were you absent from school?
➡ _____

(4) I want to know. When did you meet him for the first time?
➡ _____
_____

(5) Do you think? When does the concert start?
➡ _____

(6) Do you imagine? Why is the baby crying?
➡ _____

(7) Do you know? Was Charley sleeping at that time?
➡ _____
_____

07 주어진 단어를 활용하여 다음 우리말을 영어로 쓰시오.

> 나는 나의 사촌이 숙제하는 것을 도와줬습니다.
> (help / his)

➡ _____

⭐ 중요

08 주어진 단어를 어법이나 내용에 맞게 빈칸에 쓰시오.

> ┌─ 보기 ─┐
> take / publish / report / work / play

(1) Don't let the children _____ with matches.

(2) Do you know who _____ these books last year?

(3) Julia made the professional photographer _____ pictures of her.

(4) The boss had the employees _____ harder.

(5) What do you think the scientist _____ _____ tomorrow?

09 다음 상황을 읽고 빈칸에 알맞은 말을 쓰시오.

> Andy: How much are the oranges?
> Paul: How many oranges do you want to buy?

➡ Andy wants to know how much _____ _____. So Paul asks Andy _____.

⭐ 중요

10 주어진 단어를 활용하여 다음 우리말을 영어로 쓰시오.

> 여자는 남자가 물을 마시게 한다.
> (the woman / the man / let)

➡ _____

11 주어진 단어를 바르게 배열하여 다음 우리말을 영어로 쓰시오. 필요하다면 어형을 변환하시오.

> 그 정장은 나를 멋지게 보이도록 만들어.
> (fancy / the suit / look / make / me)

➡ _____

🏠 고난이도

12 주어진 단어를 활용하여 다음 대화를 영어로 쓰시오.

> A: 그 영화가 어땠다고 생각하니? (how / think / be)
> B: It was so boring. 그것은 나를 졸리게 만들었어. (make / feel)

A: _____

B: _____

13 다음 우리말을 영어로 쓰시오.

> 어제 그 차를 누가 운전했는지 아니?

➡ _____

14 다음 중 어법상 틀린 것을 바르게 고쳐 올바른 문장으로 다시 쓰시오.

(1) Can you tell me when did she write this book?

➡ _____

(2) You can lead a horse to water, but you can't make him to drink.

➡ _____
_____

(3) I wonder that he is full or not.

➡ _____

Reading

교과서

The More You See, The More You Know

Welcome to the World Art Museum tour. When you go to an art
museum, how much time do you spend looking at each painting?
Many visitors glance at one painting for only a few seconds
before they move on. But you might miss the important details of
paintings since it is hard to notice them right away.

Today, we'll look at two paintings closely and I'll help you see
interesting details.

Look at this painting first. The seaside landscape is so peaceful and
beautiful, isn't it? The title of this painting is *Landscape with the Fall
of Icarus*. So, can you see where Icarus is? Do you see two legs that
are sticking out of the water near the ship? This is Icarus in the famous
myth in Greece. In the myth, Icarus' father made wings for him with
feathers and wax and told him to stay away from the sun.

detail 세부 사항
since ～ 때문에
notice ～을 알아차리다
glance at ～을 힐끗 보다
right away 즉시, 바로
seaside 해변, 바닷가
landscape 풍경
stick 내밀다
myth 신화
wing 날개
feather 깃털
wax 밀랍
stay away from ～을 가까이 하지 않다

📎 **확인문제**

● 다음 문장이 본문의 내용과 일치하면 T, 일치하지 <u>않으면</u> F를 쓰시오.

1 It is enough to spend a few minutes looking at a painting. ☐

2 It is hard to notice the important details of paintings right away. ☐

3 We can see peaceful and beautiful landscape in the first painting. ☐

4 Icarus is waving his hands in the painting. ☐

5 Icarus made his wings without any help. ☐

However, Icarus didn't listen. He <u>flew</u> too close to the sun. So, the
fly–flew–flown
wax melted and he fell into the water. Now, look at the entire painting

again. <u>Despite</u> the tragedy of Icarus, people are going on with their
전치사(~에도 불구하고)
<u>everyday</u> activities. Does the painting still <u>look peaceful</u>?
일상의　　　　　　　　　　　　　　　감각동사+형용사: 평화스럽게 보이다

<u>What do you think the artist is trying to tell us?</u>
간접의문문: think, imagine, guess 등이 동사로 쓰인 문장에서 간접의문문의 의문사를 문장 맨 앞으로 보냄

Now, let's <u>move on to</u> the next painting. Do you see the artist <u>behind</u>
~으로 옮겨가다　　　　　　　　　　　　　　　　　　　　~ 뒤에
the large canvas? He is Diego Velázquez, and he actually painted this

picture. <u>Who do you think he is painting?</u> Take a quick look. The
Do you think? + Who is he painting?
young princess <u>seems to</u> be the main person because she is in the center
~인 것처럼 보이다
of the painting. But the title of the painting is *The Maids of Honour.*

Then, is the artist drawing the two women <u>beside</u> the princess? Take
~ 옆에 있는
a close look. It will <u>make you wonder</u> about the painting more. <u>Try to</u>
앞 문장 'Take a close look.'을 가리킴　사역동사+목적어+동사원형: 목적어가 ~하게 하다　　　　　~하려고 애쓰다
see <u>which direction the artist is looking at</u>. Can you see the king and
Try to see. + Which direction is the artist looking at?
the queen <u>in the mirror</u> <u>in the background of the painting</u>? <u>Who do you</u>
형용사구　　　　　　the mirror를 수식하는 형용사구　　　　　= Do you think? +
think he is painting now?
Who is he painting now?

melt 녹다
despite ~에도 불구하고
tragedy 비극
artist 예술가, 미술가
canvas 화폭, 캔버스
wonder 궁금해 하다
direction 방향
take a look 보다
beside ~옆에
background 배경

📎 확인문제

● 다음 문장이 본문의 내용과 일치하면 T, 일치하지 <u>않으면</u> F를 쓰시오.

1　Icarus followed what his father had said. ☐

2　Icarus fell into the water because the wax melted. ☐

3　Diego Velázquez is in the painting. ☐

4　There are two women beside the princess. ☐

5　There is a mirror in the background of the painting. ☐

6　Diego Velázquez drew himself in the mirror of the painting. ☐

● 우리말을 참고하여 빈칸에 알맞은 말을 쓰시오.

1 _____ _____ the World Art Museum tour.

2 _____ you _____ _____ an art museum, _____ _____ _____ do you spend _____ at each painting?

3 Many visitors _____ _____ one painting _____ only _____ _____ seconds before they move _____.

4 But you _____ _____ the important details of paintings _____ it is hard _____ _____ _____ right away.

5 Today, we'll _____ _____ two paintings _____ and I'll _____ _____ _____ interesting details.

6 Look _____ this painting _____.

7 The _____ _____ is so _____ and beautiful, _____ _____?

8 The _____ of this painting _____ *Landscape with the Fall of Icarus*.

9 So, can you see _____ _____ _____?

10 Do you see two legs that _____ _____ _____ _____ near the ship?

11 This is Icarus _____ _____ _____ in Greece.

12 In the myth, Icarus' father _____ _____ _____ _____ with feathers and wax and told him _____ _____ _____ the sun.

13 _____, Icarus didn't _____.

14 He _____ _____ _____ to the sun.

15 So, the wax _____ and he _____ _____ the water.

1 세계 미술관(the World Art Museum)에 오신 것을 환영합니다.

2 미술관에 갈 때 여러분은 각각의 그림을 보는 데 얼마나 많은 시간을 보내나요?

3 많은 방문객들은 이동하기 전에 하나의 그림을 몇 초간만 힐끗 봅니다.

4 하지만 그림의 중요한 세부 사항들을 즉시 알아채는 것은 어렵기 때문에 여러분은 그것들을 놓칠 수 있습니다.

5 오늘 우리는 두 개의 그림을 자세히 살펴볼 것이고, 여러분이 흥미로운 세부 사항들을 볼 수 있도록 제가 도와드리겠습니다.

6 먼저 이 그림을 보세요.

7 바닷가 풍경이 매우 평화롭고 아름답죠. 그렇지 않나요?

8 이 그림의 제목은 '추락하는 이카루스가 있는 풍경'입니다.

9 그러면 이카루스가 어디에 있는지 보이나요?

10 배 근처에 물 밖으로 나와 있는 두 다리가 보이죠?

11 이것이 그리스의 유명한 신화에 나오는 이카루스입니다.

12 신화에서 이카루스의 아버지는 그를 위해 깃털과 밀랍으로 날개를 만들어 주었고 그에게 태양을 가까이 하지 말라고 말했습니다.

13 하지만 이카루스는 듣지 않았습니다.

14 그는 태양에 너무 가깝게 날았습니다.

15 그래서 밀랍이 녹았고 그는 물에 빠졌습니다.

16 Now, look _____ the _____ painting again.

17 _____ the tragedy of Icarus, people are _____ _____ _____ their everyday activities.

18 Does the painting _____ _____ _____?

19 _____ _____ _____ _____ the artist is trying to tell us?

20 Now, let's _____ _____ _____ the next painting.

21 Do you _____ the artist _____ the large canvas?

22 He is Diego Velázquez, and he _____ _____ this picture.

23 _____ _____ _____ _____ _____ _____ painting?

24 _____ a quick look.

25 The young princess _____ _____ _____ the main person _____ she is in the center of the painting.

26 But the _____ of the _____ is *The Maids of Honour*.

27 Then, is the artist _____ the two women _____ the princess?

28 _____ a close look.

29 It will _____ _____ _____ about the painting more.

30 Try to see _____ _____ _____ _____ _____ looking at.

31 Can you _____ the king and the queen _____ _____ in the _____ of the painting?

32 _____ _____ _____ _____ _____ _____ painting now?

16 이제. 그림 전체를 다시 보세요.

17 이카루스의 비극에도 불구하고 사람들은 일상의 활동을 계속하고 있습니다.

18 그림이 여전히 평화로워 보이나요?

19 화가가 우리에게 무엇을 말하려 한다고 생각하나요?

20 이제. 다음 그림으로 넘어갑시다.

21 커다란 캔버스 뒤에 있는 화가가 보이나요?

22 그는 Diego Velázquez이고, 그가 실제로 이 그림을 그렸습니다.

23 그가 누구를 그리고 있다고 생각하나요?

24 재빨리 봅시다.

25 어린 공주가 그림의 중앙에 있기 때문에 주인공처럼 보입니다.

26 하지만 그림의 제목은 '시녀들' 입니다.

27 그렇다면 화가는 공주 옆에 있는 두 여인을 그리고 있나요?

28 자세히 보세요.

29 그림에 대해 더 궁금해하게 될 겁니다.

30 화가가 바라보고 있는 방향을 보려고 노력해 보세요.

31 그림의 배경에 있는 거울 속 왕과 왕비가 보이나요?

32 이제 여러분은 그가 누구를 그리고 있다고 생각하나요?

● 우리말을 참고하여 본문을 영작하시오.

1 세계 미술관(the World Art Museum)에 오신 것을 환영합니다.

➡ _____

2 미술관에 갈 때 여러분은 각각의 그림을 보는 데 얼마나 많은 시간을 보내나요?

➡ _____

3 많은 방문객들은 이동하기 전에 하나의 그림을 몇 초간만 힐끗 봅니다.

➡ _____

4 하지만 그림의 중요한 세부 사항들을 즉시 알아채는 것은 어렵기 때문에 여러분들은 그것들을 놓칠 수 있습니다.

➡ _____

5 오늘 우리는 두 개의 그림을 자세히 살펴볼 것이고, 여러분이 흥미로운 세부 사항들을 볼 수 있도록 제가 도와드리겠습니다.

➡ _____

6 먼저 이 그림을 보세요.

➡ _____

7 바닷가 풍경이 매우 평화롭고 아름답죠. 그렇지 않나요?

➡ _____

8 이 그림의 제목은 '추락하는 이카루스가 있는 풍경'입니다.

➡ _____

9 그러면 이카루스가 어디에 있는지 보이나요?

➡ _____

10 배 근처에 물 밖으로 나와 있는 두 다리가 보이죠?

➡ _____

11 이것이 그리스의 유명한 신화에 나오는 이카루스입니다.

➡ _____

12 신화에서 이카루스의 아버지는 그를 위해 깃털과 밀랍으로 날개를 만들어 주었고 그에게 태양을 가까이 하지 말라고 말했습니다.

➡ _____

_____

13 하지만 이카루스는 듣지 않았습니다.

➡ _____

14 그는 태양에 너무 가깝게 날았습니다.

➡ _____

15 그래서 밀랍이 녹았고 그는 물에 빠졌습니다.

➡ _____

16 이제, 그림 전체를 다시 보세요.

➡ _____

17 이카루스의 비극에도 불구하고 사람들은 일상의 활동을 계속하고 있습니다.

➡ _____

18 그림이 여전히 평화로워 보이나요?

➡ _____

19 화가가 우리에게 무엇을 말하려 한다고 생각하나요?

➡ _____

20 이제, 다음 그림으로 넘어갑시다.

➡ _____

21 커다란 캔버스 뒤에 있는 화가가 보이나요?

➡ _____

22 그는 Diego Velázquez이고, 그가 실제로 이 그림을 그렸습니다.

➡ _____

23 그가 누구를 그리고 있다고 생각하나요?

➡ _____

24 재빨리 봅시다.

➡ _____

25 어린 공주가 그림의 중앙에 있기 때문에 주인공처럼 보입니다.

➡ _____

26 하지만 그림의 제목은 '시녀들'입니다.

➡ _____

27 그렇다면 화가는 공주 옆에 있는 두 여인을 그리고 있나요?

➡ _____

28 자세히 보세요.

➡ _____

29 그림에 대해 더 궁금해하게 될 겁니다.

➡ _____

30 화가가 바라보고 있는 방향을 보려고 노력해 보세요.

➡ _____

31 그림의 배경에 있는 거울 속 왕과 왕비가 보이나요?

➡ _____

32 이제 여러분은 그가 누구를 그리고 있다고 생각하나요?

➡ _____

[01~04] 다음 글을 읽고 물음에 답하시오.

Welcome to the World Art Museum tour. When you go to an art museum, how much time do you spend looking at each painting? Many visitors glance at one painting for only a few seconds before they move on. But you might miss the important details of paintings (A)since it is hard (B)to notice them right away. Today, we'll look at two paintings closely and I'll help you see interesting details.

01 다음 중 밑줄 친 (A)를 대신하여 쓰일 수 있는 것은?

① because   ② when   ③ if
④ because of   ⑤ while

서답형

02 다음과 같이 풀이되는 단어를 위 글에서 찾아 쓰시오.

> to see or become conscious of something or someone

➡ _____

중요

03 다음 중 밑줄 친 (B)와 쓰임이 같은 것은?

① They hoped to meet again someday.
② Are you happy to see me again?
③ It is necessary to keep your promise.
④ Is there anything to drink?
⑤ His hobby is to make something.

서답형

04 According to the writer, how many paintings will we look at closely? Answer in English with a full sentence.

➡ _____

[05~10] 다음 글을 읽고 물음에 답하시오.

Look at this painting first. The seaside landscape is so peaceful and beautiful, isn't it? The title of this painting is *Landscape with the Fall of Icarus*. So, _____(A)_____? Do you see two legs that are sticking out of the water near the ship? This is Icarus in the famous myth in Greece. ① In the myth, Icarus' father made wings for him with feathers and wax and told him to stay away from the sun. ② He flew too close to the sun. ③ So, the wax melted and he fell into the water. ④ Now, look at the entire painting again. ⑤ _____(B)_____ the tragedy of Icarus, people are going on with their everyday activities. Does the painting still look peaceful? What do you think the artist is trying to tell us?

서답형

05 다음 두 문장을 하나의 문장으로 연결하여 빈칸 (A)에 알맞게 쓰시오.

> • Can you see?
> • Where is Icarus?

➡ _____

06 다음 중 빈칸 (B)에 들어갈 말로 가장 적절한 것은?

① In spite of   ② Due to
③ In addition to   ④ Thanks to
⑤ Along with

서답형

07 다음 중 주어진 문장이 들어가기에 가장 적절한 곳은?

> However, Icarus didn't listen.

①   ②   ③   ④   ⑤

서답형

08 위 글을 읽고 다음 질문에 완전한 문장의 영어로 답하시오.

Q: What is the title of the painting?

➡ _____

09 첫 번째 그림에서 찾아볼 수 없는 것은?

① peaceful landscape
② people doing their everyday activities
③ Icarus flying to the sun
④ a ship on the water
⑤ two legs sticking out of the water

10 위 글의 내용과 일치하지 않는 것은?

① The landscape of the first painting looks peaceful and beautiful.
② We can see only two legs of Icarus in the painting.
③ Icarus can be seen near the ship in the painting.
④ Icarus made his wings by himself.
⑤ Icarus flew close to the sun and fell into water.

[11~15] 다음 글을 읽고 물음에 답하시오.

Now, let's move on to the next painting. Do you see the artist behind the large canvas? He is Diego Velázquez, and he actually painted this picture. Who do you think he is painting? Take a quick look. ⓐ어린 공주가 그림의 중앙에 있기 때문에 주인공처럼 보입니다. But the title of the painting is *The Maids of Honour*. Then, is the artist drawing the two women beside the princess? Take a close look. It will make you __(A)__ about the painting more. Try to see which direction the artist is looking at. Can you see the king and the queen in the mirror in the background of the painting? Who do you think he is (B)painting now?

서답형

11 단어 'wonder'를 어법에 맞게 빈칸 (A)에 쓰시오.

➡ _____

12 다음 중 밑줄 친 (B)와 쓰임이 같은 것은?

① Are you interested in writing a poem?
② His job is delivering mails.
③ Jason was doing his laundry.
④ Mina enjoyed watching movies with me.
⑤ David didn't mind asking about it.

서답형

13 위 글의 밑줄 친 우리말 ⓐ를 주어진 어휘를 이용하여 18 단어로 영작하시오. (the young princess로 시작할 것.)

the young princess, the painting, the main person, the center, because, be

➡ _____

_____

서답형

14 Where can we find the artist of the next painting? Answer in English with a full sentence. Use the word 'him,'

➡ _____

15 다음 중 위 글을 읽고 답할 수 없는 질문은?

① What is the name of the artist of the second painting?
② What makes the young princess seem to be the main person?
③ What is the title of the painting?
④ How many women are there beside the princess?
⑤ How large is the painting?

[16~18] 다음 글을 읽고 물음에 답하시오.

Welcome to the World Art Museum tour. When you go to an art museum, (A)[how many / how much] time do you spend looking at each painting? Many visitors glance at one painting for only a few seconds before they move on. But you might miss the important details of paintings since it is hard to notice (B)[it / them] right away. Today, we'll look at two paintings closely and I'll help you (C)[seeing / to see] interesting details.

16 (A)~(C)에서 어법상 옳은 것끼리 바르게 짝지어진 것은?

① how much – them – seeing
② how much – them – to see
③ how many – it – to see
④ how many – it – seeing
⑤ how many – them – to see

서답형

17 According to the writer, how long does it take many visitors to see one painting? Answer in English with a full sentence. Use the words 'it', 'them' and 'to.'

➡ _____

18 다음 중 위 글 다음에 이어질 내용으로 가장 적절한 것은?

① the problem of the museum tour
② a request for donating good paintings
③ how to see the details of paintings
④ bad behaviors of people in the museum
⑤ how to be friendly with the curator

[19~23] 다음 글을 읽고 물음에 답하시오.

Look at this painting first. The seaside landscape is so peaceful and beautiful, ①isn't it? The title of this painting is *Landscape with the Fall of Icarus*. So, can you see ②where is Icarus?

(A) So, the wax melted and he fell into the water. Now, look at the entire painting again. Despite the tragedy of Icarus, people are going on with their everyday activities.

(B) In the myth, Icarus' father made wings ③ for him with feathers and wax and told him ④to stay away from the sun. ___ⓐ___, Icarus didn't listen. He flew too close to the sun.

(C) Do you see two legs that ⑤are sticking out of the water near the ship? This is Icarus in the famous myth in Greece.

Does the painting still look peaceful? What do you think the artist is trying to tell us?

19 다음 중 빈칸 ⓐ에 들어갈 말로 가장 적절한 것은?

① Moreover   ② Therefore
③ However   ④ For example
⑤ Thus

20 자연스러운 내용이 되도록 (A)~(C)를 바르게 나열한 것은?

① (A) – (B) – (C)   ② (B) – (A) – (C)
③ (B) – (C) – (A)   ④ (C) – (A) – (B)
⑤ (C) – (B) – (A)

21 ①~⑤ 중 어법상 바르지 않은 것은?

①   ②   ③   ④   ⑤

22 Which is NOT true about Icarus?

① He is in the famous myth in Greece.

② His father made wings for him.

③ He had wings made of feathers and wax.

④ He flew close to the sun.

⑤ He listened to his father very well.

서답형

23 According to the passage, what did Icarus' father tell Icarus? Answer in English with a full sentence.

➡ _____

[24~25] 다음 글을 읽고 물음에 답하시오.

Today, I went to the Amazing Art exhibition. At the exhibition, I saw many interesting pieces of art. Among them, I liked the piece called *Moon Tree*. It was made by French artist, David Myriam. Interestingly, sand was used in this painting. I like it because a tree in the moon makes me ____(A)____. Now I know that anything can be used to make art. Anything is possible!

24 다음 중 빈칸 (A)에 들어갈 말로 적절한 것은?

① feels calm ② feel calmly

③ feel calm ④ feeling calm

⑤ feeling calmly

25 Which is NOT true about the passage?

① There were many interesting pieces of art at the Amazing Art exhibition.

② What the writer liked was *Moon Tree*.

③ *Moon Tree* was made by David Myriam.

④ David Myriam used a tree in his painting.

⑤ David Myriam is French.

[26~28] 다음 글을 읽고 물음에 답하시오.

Now, let's move on to the next painting. Do you see the artist behind the large canvas? He is Diego Velázquez, and he actually painted this picture. Who do you ____(A)____ he is painting? Take a quick look. The young princess seems to be the main person because she is in the center of the painting. But the title of the painting is *The Maids of Honour*. Then, is the artist drawing the two women beside the princess? Take a close look. It will make you wonder about the painting more. Try to see which direction the artist is looking at. Can you see the king and the queen in the mirror in the background of the painting? Who do you think he is painting now?

26 다음 중 빈칸 (A)에 들어갈 말로 적절하지 않은 것은?

① think ② guess ③ believe

④ know ⑤ imagine

서답형

27 According to the passage, who is in the middle of the painting? Answer in English with a full sentence.

➡ _____

28 위 글의 내용과 일치하지 않는 것은?

① Diego Velázquez drew *The Maids of Hornour*.

② Diego Velázquez doesn't appear in the painting.

③ Both the king and the queen can be found in the painting.

④ There are two women beside the princess in the painting.

⑤ A mirror was drawn in the background of the painting.

[01~03] 다음 글을 읽고 물음에 답하시오.

Welcome to the World Art Museum tour. (A)When you go to an art museum, how much time do you spend looking at each painting? Many visitors glance at one painting for only a few seconds before they move on. But you might miss the important details of paintings since it is hard to notice (B)them right away. Today, we'll look at two paintings closely and (C)여러분이 흥미로운 세부 사항들을 볼 수 있도록 제가 도와드리겠습니다.

01 다음은 밑줄 친 (A)와 같은 의미의 문장이다. 빈칸을 알맞게 채우시오.

I wonder _____ when you go to an art museum.

➡ _____

02 위 글의 밑줄 친 (B)가 의미하는 것을 위 글에서 찾아 쓰시오.

➡ _____

03 주어진 단어를 활용하여 밑줄 친 우리말 (C)를 영어로 쓰시오.

(help / see)

➡ _____

[04~08] 다음 글을 읽고 물음에 답하시오.

Look at this painting first. The seaside landscape is so peaceful and beautiful, isn't it? The title of this painting is *Landscape with the Fall of Icarus*. So, can you see where Icarus is? Do you see two legs that are sticking out of the water near the ship? This is Icarus in the famous myth in Greece.

In the myth, Icarus' father made wings for him with feathers and wax and told him to stay away from the sun. However, Icarus didn't listen. He flew too close to the sun. So, the wax melted and he fell into the water. Now, look at the entire painting again. Despite the tragedy of Icarus, people are going on with their everyday activities. Does the painting still look peaceful? _____(A)_____

04 다음 두 문장을 하나의 문장으로 만들어 빈칸 (A)에 쓰시오.

• Do you think?
• What is the artist trying to tell us?

➡ _____

05 다음은 화가가 위 그림을 통해 말하려는 것이다. 빈칸에 적절한 말을 위 글에서 찾아 쓰시오.

The artist is trying to tell us that we do not know other people's _____.

➡ _____

06 What did Icarus' father make for Icarus? Answer in English with five words.

➡ _____

07 위 글의 내용에 맞게 빈칸에 알맞은 말을 쓰시오.

A: What made the wax _____?
B: Flying too close to the sun made it so.

➡ _____

08 다음은 '추락하는 이카루스가 있는 풍경'을 감상하고 있는 두 학생의 대화이다. 빈칸에 알맞은 말을 쓰시오.

> A: Can you tell me _____? I can't find him.
> B: Oh, he is near the ship.
> A: The two legs that _____? Is that him?
> B: Yes, he is.

➡ _____ , _____

[09~13] 다음 글을 읽고 물음에 답하시오.

　Now, let's move on to the next painting. Do you see the artist behind the large canvas? He is Diego Velázquez, and he (A)actual painted this picture. Who do you think he is painting? Take a quick look. The young princess seems to be the main person because she is in the center of the painting. But the title of the painting is *The Maids of Honour*. Then, is the artist drawing the two women beside the princess? Take a close look. (B)It will make you wonder about the painting more. Try to see which direction the artist is looking at. Can you see the king and the queen in the mirror in the background of the painting? Who do you think he is painting now?

09 밑줄 친 (A)를 알맞은 형으로 고치시오.

➡ _____

10 Who painted the picture, *The Maids of Honour*? Answer in English with a full sentence.

➡ _____

11 밑줄 친 (B)가 의미하는 것을 우리말로 쓰시오.

➡ _____

12 Who are the people in the mirror in the background of the painting? Answer in English with a full sentence.

➡ _____

13 위 글의 표현을 이용하여 다음 우리말을 영어로 쓰시오.

> 나는 누가 실제로 이 그림을 그렸는지 궁금해.

➡ _____

[14~15] 다음 글을 읽고 물음에 답하시오.

　Today, I went to the Amazing Art exhibition. At the exhibition, I saw many interesting pieces of art. Among them, I liked the piece called *Moon Tree*. It was made by French artist, David Myriam. Interestingly, sand was used in this painting. I like it because a tree in the moon makes me feel calm. Now I know that anything can be used to make art. Anything is possible!

14 위 글의 내용에 맞게 빈칸에 알맞은 말을 쓰시오.

> A: Do you know _____ in this painting?
> B: Yes, I do. He used sand.

15 Write the reason why the writer likes *Moon Tree*. Use the word 'because.'

➡ _____

Listen & Talk

M: What are you reading, Sally?

W: I'm reading *The Maze Runner*. It's about boys who are put in a maze.

= The Maze Runner 주격 관계대명사

M: It's a great story. I've seen the movie of it, too. I prefer the novel to the

현재완료   prefer A to B: B보다 더 A가 좋다

movie.

W: Why do you like it better?

= the novel

M: The novel has various stories. But the movie didn't show some important

parts of the story.

구문해설 • maze: 미로 • novel: 소설

Grammar in Real Life

1. Princess, please let me in.

let A in: A를 들어가게 하다

2. Who are you?

3. The princess promised me, "If you help me, I'll let you enter the palace and

사역동사+목적어+동사원형: 목적어가 ~하게 하다

 be my friend."

(let you) be my friend

4. Come here. I'll have people serve you some cookies and tea.

사역동사   4형식 동사(~에게 …을 내어주다)

5. No! Never let him in. I don't like him.

부정 명령문

6. Don't worry, Frog. I'll make the princess keep her promise.

사역동사+목적어+동사원형: 목적어가 ~하게 하다

구문해설 • promise: 약속하다 • enter: ~로 들어가다 • serve: ~을 내어주다

     • keep one's promise: ~의 약속을 지키다

Think and Write C

Today, I went to the Amazing Art exhibition. At the exhibition, I saw many

interesting pieces of art. Among them, I liked the piece called *Moon Tree*. It

흥미를 유발하는   many interesting pieces of art = which was called

was made by French artist, David Myriam. Interestingly, sand was used in this

수동태

painting. I like it because a tree in the moon makes me feel calm. Now I know

이유를 나타내는 접속사   사역동사+목적어+동사원형

that anything can be used to make art. Anything is possible!

명사절을 이끄는 접속사 부사적 용법

구문해설 • exhibition: 전시회 • interesting: 흥미로운 • called: ~라고 불리는

     • be made by: ~에 의해 만들어지다 • calm: 고요한

해석

M: Sally, 너는 무엇을 읽고 있니?

W: 나는 '미로를 달리는 사람'을 읽고 있어. 미로에 갇힌 소년들에 관한 내용 이야.

M: 그건 대단한 이야기이지. 나는 그것을 영화로도 봤어. 나는 영화보다는 소설이 더 좋아.

W: 왜 소설이 더 좋은데?

M: 소설에는 다양한 이야기가 담겨 있어. 하지만 영화에서는 이야기의 중요한 몇 부분이 나오지 않았어.

1. 공주님, 저를 들어가게 해 주세요.
2. 그대는 누군가?
3. 공주님은 제게 "네가 날 도와준다면, 나는 너를 궁전에 들어오게 하고 내 친구가 되게 해 주겠어."라고 약속하셨어요.
4. 이쪽으로 오게. 내가 사람들을 시켜 자네에게 과자와 차를 가져다 주게 하겠네.
5. 안 돼요! 그를 들어오게 하지 마세요. 저는 그를 좋아하지 않아요.
6. 걱정 말게, 개구리. 나는 공주가 그녀의 약속을 지키게 하겠네.

오늘 나는 놀라운 미술 전시회에 갔다. 전시회에서, 나는 많은 흥미로운 미술 작품들을 보았다. 그 중에서, 나는 *Moon Tree*라고 불리는 작품이 좋았다. 그것은 프랑스 미술가 David Myriam에 의해 만들어졌다. 흥미롭게도, 모래가 이 미술품에 사용되었다. 달 속에 있는 나무 한 그루가 내 마음을 고요하게 만들기 때문에 나는 그것이 좋다. 이제 나는 어떠한 것이든 미술을 만들기 위해 사용될 수 있다는 사실을 안다. 무엇이든 가능하다!

Words & Expressions

01 다음 짝지어진 단어의 관계가 같도록 빈칸에 알맞은 말을 쓰시오.

> prince: princess = comedy : _____

02 다음 영영풀이가 가리키는 것을 고르시오.

> a very sad event, especially one involving death

① comedy   ② artwork   ③ detail

④ tear   ⑤ tragedy

03 다음 중 밑줄 친 부분의 뜻풀이가 바르지 않은 것은?

① Some birds have colorful <u>feathers</u>. 깃털

② I will <u>exhibit</u> my pictures someday. 전시하다

③ <u>Frogs</u> sleep during winter. 개구리

④ We need <u>flat</u> ground to build a house. 울퉁불퉁한

⑤ I looked down on the peaceful <u>landscape</u> from the hill. 풍경

04 다음 우리말에 맞게 빈칸에 알맞은 말을 쓰시오.

(1) 이탈리아에는 항상 많은 관광객들이 있다.

➡ There are always many _____ in Italy.

(2) 네 친구에게 혀를 내밀지 마라.

➡ Don't _____ your tongue at your friend.

(3) Tom은 정말 소설가를 만나고 싶어 한다.

➡ Tom really wants to meet the _____.

05 다음 우리말에 맞게 주어진 단어를 사용하여 영작하시오.

(1) 나는 시보다 소설을 더 좋아한다. (prefer)

➡ _____

(2) 우리 가족은 해변으로 여행갈 것이다.

(trip, take, seaside)

➡ _____

(3) 그 전쟁은 전 세계에 비극이었다. (whole)

➡ _____

06 다음 주어진 문장의 밑줄 친 stick과 같은 의미로 쓰인 것은?

> Don't <u>stick</u> your head out of the window.

① Did your brother <u>stick</u> a stamp on the letter?

② Would you <u>stick</u> your arms out of your sleeves?

③ Brian is using a <u>stick</u> to find something.

④ Will you <u>stick</u> a note on the door?

⑤ He is striking the tree with a <u>stick</u>.

07 다음 문장에 공통으로 들어갈 말을 고르시오.

> • We need to _____ our attention to our mistakes.
>
> • Can you _____ me to Seoul Station?
>
> • Is there a _____ flight to San Francisco?

① direct   ② prefer

③ melt   ④ notice

⑤ promise

Conversation

[08~09] 다음 대화를 읽고 물음에 답하시오.

Jean: (A) What are you reading, Sally?

Sally: (B) I'm reading *The Maze Runner*. It's about boys who are put in a maze.

Jean: (C) It's a great story. I've seen the movie of it, too. I prefer the novel to the movie.

Sally: (D) Why do you like it better?

Jean: (E) But the movie didn't show some important parts of the story.

08 위 대화의 (A)~(E) 중 주어진 문장이 들어가기에 적절한 곳은?

> The novel has various stories.

① (A)　② (B)　③ (C)　④ (D)　⑤ (E)

09 위 대화의 내용과 일치하지 <u>않는</u> 것은?

① Sally is reading *The Maze Runner*.

② *The Maze Runner* is about boys who are put in a maze.

③ Jean saw the movie of *The Maze Runner* with Sally.

④ Jean prefers the novel to the movie because the novel has various stories.

⑤ Jean thinks that the movie missed some important parts of the story.

[10~11] 다음 대화를 읽고 물음에 답하시오.

Anna: (*ringing*) Hello, Steve.

Steve: Hi, Anna. We're meeting at the arts festival tomorrow at 1:30, right?

Anna: Right. _____ (A)

Steve: I want to watch the hip-hop dance performance first.

Anna: Sounds good. It's at 2 p.m. at the gym, right?

Steve: Yeah, and how about watching the play, *Romeo and Juliet*, at 4 p.m.?

Anna: Oh, the one at the Main Hall near the gym? Sure!

10 위 대화의 빈칸 (A)에 들어갈 말을 〈보기〉에 주어진 단어를 모두 배열하여 완성하시오.

> ┤ 보기 ├
>
> kind / do / to / of / watch / you / what / performance/ want / first

➡ _____

11 위 대화의 내용과 일치하지 <u>않는</u> 것은?

① Anna와 Steve는 내일 1시 30분에 예술 축제에서 만나기로 했다.

② Steve는 먼저 힙합 댄스 공연을 보고 싶어 한다.

③ 힙합 댄스 공연은 체육관에서 2시에 열린다.

④ '로미오와 줄리엣' 연극이 오후 4시에 공연된다.

⑤ Anna와 Steve는 연극을 보기 위해 대강당에서 체육관으로 이동할 것이다.

12 다음 짝지어진 대화가 <u>어색한</u> 것은?

① A: What kind of music do you like most?
　 B: I love hip-hop.

② A: There are two kinds of guitars. Which do you prefer?
　 B: I prefer the classic guitar.

③ A: What kind of brush were you using?
　 B: I don't know how to paint clean lines.

④ A: I prefer the movie to the novel.
　 B: Why do you like it better?

⑤ A: What kind of movie do you like?
　 B: I like horror movies.

[13~14] 다음 대화를 읽고 물음에 답하시오.

Minsu: What are you reading, Jina? (A)
Jina: The novel, *Life of Pi*. It's a story of a boy and a tiger. (B)
Minsu: It's a great book. I've seen the movie of it, too. (C)
Jina: Why do you like it better? (D)
Minsu: The scenes are very beautiful. And the tiger looks so real. (E)

13 위 대화의 (A)~(E) 중 주어진 문장이 들어가기에 적절한 곳은?

I prefer the movie to the novel.

① (A) ② (B) ③ (C) ④ (D) ⑤ (E)

14 위 대화를 읽고 대답할 수 <u>없는</u> 것은?

① What is Jina doing now?
② What is *Life of Pi* about?
③ Which one does Minsu prefer, the novel or the movie?
④ How does the tiger look in the movie?
⑤ When did Minsu see the movie?

[15~16] 다음 대화를 읽고 물음에 답하시오.

Sora: Can you help me? I don't know how to paint clean lines.
Mike: What kind of brush were you using?
Sora: This round brush.
Mike: When you paint lines, a flat brush is better. Try this one.
Sora: Okay, thank you.

15 What's the matter with Sora?

➡ _____

16 After talking with Mike, what will Sora use to paint lines?

➡ _____

Grammar

17 다음 우리말을 영어로 바르게 옮긴 것은?

누가 너를 이 파티에 초대했는지 말해 줘.

① Tell me who you invited to this party.
② Tell me whom you will invite to this party.
③ Tell me who invited you to this party.
④ I wonder how you were invited to this party.
⑤ I wonder whom you came with.

18 다음 빈칸에 공통으로 들어갈 말로 적절한 것은?

• _____ he comes late, there will be no food.
• Do you want to know _____ Jane swims every Sunday?

① that ② who ③ what
④ whether ⑤ if

19 다음 중 어법상 <u>틀린</u> 것은?

① Kelly made me do her homework.
② Julia wondered who brought the book.
③ Jerry asked me what I ate for lunch.
④ Olivia let him to use her computer.
⑤ Tell me whether Tom is tired now.

20 주어진 단어를 활용하여 다음 우리말을 영어로 쓰시오.

그녀가 지금 어디에 있다고 생각하시나요?
(think / where)

➡ _____

21 다음 우리말을 영어로 쓸 때 세 번째 오는 단어와 일곱 번째 오는 단어를 바르게 묶은 것은?

> 당신이 내게 이 꽃을 보내도록 누가 시켰는지 궁금해요.

① wonder – made ② who – me
③ who – send ④ made – this
⑤ made – flower

22 다음 두 문장을 하나의 문장으로 바르게 쓴 것은?

> Can you tell me? Who kicked the ball?

① Can you tell me who the ball kicked?
② Can you tell me if who kicked the ball?
③ Can you tell me who kicked the ball?
④ Can you tell me who is kicking the ball?
⑤ Can you tell me who the ball is kicking?

23 다음 중 빈칸에 들어갈 말로 적절하지 <u>않은</u> 것은?

> Thomson _____ us carry the boxes.

① had ② made ③ helped
④ let ⑤ told

24 다음 빈칸에 알맞은 말을 쓰시오. 한 칸에 하나의 단어만 쓰시오.

> 나는 그들이 집안일을 하는 것을 돕습니다.
> ➡ I _____ them _____ the chores.
>
> * chore: 집안일

25 다음 중 어법상 올바른 문장의 개수는?

> ⓐ Can you tell me who are you talking with?
> ⓑ Their parents always have them to go to school early in the morning.
> ⓒ I want to know what they are doing now.
> ⓓ Can you tell me what does Jason do for a living?
> ⓔ May I ask that you have brothers or sisters?

① 1개 ② 2개 ③ 3개 ④ 4개 ⑤ 5개

26 주어진 단어를 활용하여 다음 우리말을 영어로 쓰시오.

> 그 괴물은 아이들이 비명을 지르게 했다.
> (monster, make, scream)

➡ _____

27 간접의문문을 이용하여 다음 두 문장을 하나의 문장으로 쓰시오.

(1) I didn't hear. What did you say?
   ➡ _____
(2) I'd like to know. Are you friends with Jina?
   ➡ _____

28 다음 중 빈칸에 들어갈 말로 적절한 것을 <u>모두</u> 고르시오.

> May I ask _____ Brady is here?

① whether ② if ③ where
④ what ⑤ who

Reading

[29~33] 다음 글을 읽고 물음에 답하시오.

Look at this painting first. The seaside landscape is so peaceful and beautiful, isn't it? The title of this painting is *Landscape with the Fall of Icarus*. So, can you see where Icarus is? Do you see two legs that are sticking out of the water near the ship? This is Icarus in the famous myth in Greece. In the myth, Icarus' father made wings for ①him with feathers and wax and told ②him to stay away from the sun. However, Icarus didn't listen to ③him. ④He flew too close to the sun. So, the wax melted and ⑤he fell into the water. Now, look at the entire painting again. Despite the tragedy of Icarus, people are going on with their everyday activities. (A)Does the painting still look peaceful? What do you think the artist is trying to tell us?

29 위 글의 밑줄 친 ①~⑤ 중 지칭하는 바가 다른 하나는?

①　　②　　③　　④　　⑤

30 What were Icarus' wings made of? Use the word 'they.'

➡ _____

31 다음 중 위 글의 내용과 일치하지 <u>않는</u> 것은?

① You can see the seaside landscape in the painting.
② There is a story behind the painting.
③ Icarus' father made Icarus wings.
④ Icarus didn't listen to what his father said.
⑤ Icarus flew close to the sun without wings.

32 위 글의 밑줄 친 (A)를 어법에 맞게 다음 빈칸에 쓰시오.

I wonder _____ .

➡ _____

33 다음과 같이 풀이되는 단어를 위 글에서 찾아 쓰시오.

a very sad event, especially one involving death

➡ _____

[34~36] 다음 글을 읽고 물음에 답하시오.

Welcome to the World Art Museum tour. When you go to an art museum, how much time do you spend (A)[looking / to look] at each painting? Many visitors glance at one painting for only (B)[a few / a little] seconds before they move on. But you might miss the important details of paintings since ⓐit is hard to notice them right away. Today, we'll look at two paintings (C)[close / closely] and I'll help you see interesting details.

34 (A)~(C)에서 어법상 옳은 것을 고르시오.

(A) _____ (B) _____ (C) _____

35 What is the problem with taking only several seconds to look at a painting? Answer in English with a full sentence.

➡ _____

36 다음 중 밑줄 친 ⓐ와 쓰임이 같은 것은?

① It was cold yesterday morning.
② It is still bright outside.
③ It was difficult to tell you all of my secrets.
④ It hurt my feeling.
⑤ It is going up the tree.

[01~02] 다음 대화를 읽고 물음에 답하시오.

Sue: Have you (A)listened to Jane's new song, *Girl Friend*?

Tony: Yeah, it's really cool. The guitar part is great.

Sue: There is also a dance version (B)of the song (C)on the album.

Tony: I've listened to it, but I prefer the guitar version (D)than the dance version. It matches her voice (E)better.

출제율 90%

01 위 대화의 (A)~(E) 중 어법상 어색한 것을 찾아 바르게 고치시오.

➡ _____

출제율 95%

02 위 대화를 읽고 대답할 수 없는 것은?

① What are Sue and Tony talking about?

② What does Tony think about Jane's new song, *Girl Friend*?

③ How many versions of *Girl Friend* are there on the album?

④ Why does Tony like the guitar version more than the dance version?

⑤ What does Tony think about the dance version of *Girl Friend*?

[03~05] 다음 대화를 읽고 물음에 답하시오.

Jason: Hi, we are planning a school festival, so we want to find out students' favorite types of performances. May I ask you a few questions?

Emily: Sure.

Jason: _____(A)

Emily: I like music performances best.

Jason: Okay. Then, which do you prefer, rock or hip-hop?

Emily: I prefer rock to hip-hop.

Jason: (B)Who's your favorite musician? (which, like)

Emily: My favorite musician is TJ.

Jason: Great. Thank you for your answers.

출제율 95%

03 위 대화의 빈칸 (A)에 들어갈 말을 <보기>에 주어진 단어를 모두 배열하여 완성하시오.

┌─── 보기 ────┐
of / you / what / best / like / do / kind / performance
└─────────────┘

➡ _____

출제율 85%

04 위 대화의 밑줄 친 (B)를 주어진 단어를 사용하여 의미가 같도록 다시 쓰시오.

➡ _____

출제율 100%

05 위 대화의 내용과 일치하지 않는 것을 고르시오.

① Jason은 학교 축제를 계획하고 있다.

② Jason은 학생들이 가장 선호하는 공연의 종류에 대해 알아보고 있다.

③ Emily는 음악 공연을 가장 좋아한다.

④ Emily는 힙합 공연을 록 공연보다 더 좋아한다.

⑤ Emily가 가장 좋아하는 음악가는 TJ이다.

[06~07] 다음 대화를 읽고 물음에 답하시오.

Anna: (*ringing*) Hello, Steve.

Steve: Hi, Anna. We're meeting at the arts festival tomorrow at 1:30, right?

Anna: Right. What kind of ____ⓐ____ do you want to watch first?

Steve: I want to watch the hip-hop dance performance first.

Anna: Sounds good. It's at 2 p.m. at the gym, right?

Steve: Yeah, and how about watching the play, *Romeo and Juliet*, at 4 p.m.?

Anna: Oh, the one at the Main Hall near the gym? Sure!

출제율 95%

06 위 대화의 빈칸 ⓐ에 들어갈 적절한 말을 대화에서 찾아 쓰시오.

➡ _____

출제율 95%

07 다음 대화의 내용과 일치하도록 빈칸을 완성하시오.

<Arts Festival Schedule>		
Performance	Time	Place
Dance: hip-hop	(A)	(B)
(C) : *Romeo and Juliet*	4:00 p.m	(D)

(A) _____ (B) _____

(C) _____ (D) _____

[08~09] 다음 대화를 읽고 물음에 답하시오.

Mina: I saw an interesting painting in an art book. Look at this. (A)

Jack: Wow, it looks like da Vinci's *Mona Lisa*. (B)

Mina: Actually, it's *Mona Lisa* by Fernando Botero. Which do you prefer? (C)

Jack: I prefer da Vinci's to Botero's. Da Vinci's *Mona Lisa* has an interesting smile. (D)

Mina: Well, I prefer Botero's to da Vinci's. His *Mona Lisa* is cute, and it looks modern. (E)

출제율 85%

08 위 대화의 (A)~(E) 중 다음 주어진 문장이 들어가기에 적절한 곳은?

How about you?

① (A) ② (B) ③ (C) ④ (D) ⑤ (E)

출제율 100%

09 위 대화를 읽고 대답할 수 없는 것은?

① What did Mina see in the art book?

② Which *Mona Lisa* does Jack prefer?

③ What does Jack think about da Vinci's *Mona Lisa*?

④ Why does Mina like Botero's *Mona Lisa*?

⑤ Why does Botero's *Mona Lisa* look modern?

출제율 95%

10 다음 대화가 자연스럽게 이어지도록 순서대로 배열하시오.

(A) The scenes are very beautiful. And the tiger looks so real.

(B) The novel, *Life of Pi*. It's a story of a boy and a tiger.

(C) What are you reading, Jina?

(D) Why do you like it better?

(E) It's a great book. I've seen the movie of it, too. I prefer the movie to the novel.

➡ _____

출제율 90%

11 다음 우리말을 영어로 바르게 옮긴 것은?

누가 너에게 그 비밀을 말해 줬는지 궁금해.

① I wonder who the secret you told.

② I wonder whom did you tell the secret.

③ I wonder who told you the secret.

④ I want to know who you told the secret.

⑤ Tell me who you want to tell the secret.

12 다음 빈칸에 들어갈 말이 바르게 짝지어진 것은? 출제율 95%

• They made us _____ by their house.
• The teacher had students _____ softball.

① to drop – to play
② dropped – playing
③ dropped – played
④ drop – play
⑤ dropping – playing

13 다음 빈칸에 알맞은 말을 쓰시오. 출제율 95%

I don't know. What did you wear for the Halloween party?
= I don't know _____
for the Halloween party.

14 다음 빈칸에 들어갈 말로 적절하지 <u>않은</u> 것은? 출제율 90%

I _____ my sister set the table.

① had   ② made   ③ let
④ helped   ⑤ wanted

15 다음 중 어법상 바르지 <u>않은</u> 것은? 출제율 100%

① Do you know what the teacher made us do?
② I wonder whether Jessy is sad or happy.
③ Please let her knows what he likes.
④ Can you tell me who let you go out at night?
⑤ Terry asks me if there was something to drink.

16 다음 빈칸에 들어갈 말이 바르게 짝지어진 것은? 출제율 90%

A: Can you tell me what kind of fruit _____?
B: I like tomato most.

① you like least   ② you like most
③ you used to like   ④ do you like most
⑤ did you like

17 주어진 단어를 활용하여 다음 우리말을 영어로 쓰시오. 출제율 85%

나의 부모님은 주말마다 내가 늦잠을 자도록 허락하신다. (let / late / on weekends)

➡ _____

[18~20] 다음 글을 읽고 물음에 답하시오.

Now, let's move on to the next painting. Do you see the artist behind the large canvas? ① He is Diego Velázquez, and he actually painted this picture. ② Who do you think he is painting? Take a quick look. ③ The young princess seems to be the main person because she is in the center of the painting. ④ Then, is the artist drawing the two women beside the princess? Take a close look. ⑤ It will make you wonder about the painting more. Try to see which direction the artist is looking at. Can you see the king and the queen in the mirror in the background of the painting? Who do you think he is painting now?

18 ①~⑤ 중 다음 주어진 문장이 들어가기에 가장 적절한 곳은? 출제율 95%

But the title of the painting is *The Maids of Honour.*

①   ②   ③   ④   ⑤

19 다음 중 위 글을 읽고 답할 수 있는 것은?

① Why did Diego Velázquez paint the picture?

② When did Diego Velázquez paint the picture?

③ How many maids are there in the picture?

④ Where did Diego Velázquez paint the picture?

⑤ How often did Diego Velázquez meet the king to paint the picture?

20 다음 중 위 그림에서 찾을 수 없는 것은?

① an artist who painted the picture

② a young prince between two women

③ the young princess in the middle of the painting

④ the mirror in the background

⑤ the king and the queen

[21~22] 다음 글을 읽고 물음에 답하시오.

This is Icarus in the famous myth in Greece. In the myth, Icarus' father made wings for him with feathers and wax and told him to stay away from the sun. However, Icarus didn't listen. He flew too close to the sun. ___(A)___, the wax melted and he fell into the water. Now, look at the entire painting again. Despite the tragedy of Icarus, people are going on with their everyday activities. Does the painting still look peaceful? What do you think the artist is trying to tell us?

21 다음 중 빈칸 (A)에 들어갈 말로 알맞은 것은?

① So   ② But

③ Though   ④ Still

⑤ Instead

22 위 글에 대한 다음 질문을 완성하시오.

A: Can you tell me _____?
(이카루스에게 무슨 일이 생겼는지 말해 줄래?)

B: He flew too close to the sun and the wax of his wings melted.

[23~24] 다음 글을 읽고 물음에 답하시오.

Amazing Sand Art
Today, I went to the Amazing Art exhibition. At the exhibition, I saw many interesting pieces of art. Among them, I liked the piece called *Moon Tree*. It was made by French artist, David Myriam. Interestingly, sand was used in this painting. I like it because a tree in the moon makes me feel calm. Now I know that anything can be used to make art. Anything is possible!

23 위 글의 표현을 활용하여 다음 우리말을 영어로 쓰시오.

나는 네가 많은 흥미로운 예술 작품들을 보았는지 궁금해.

➡ _____

24 Which is NOT true about the passage?

① The writer went to an art exhibition.

② There were many interesting pieces of art at the Amazing Art exhibition.

③ *Moon Tree* was made by David Myriam.

④ David Myriam made *Moon Tree* by using paint.

⑤ The writer realized anything can be used to make art.

[01~03] 다음 대화를 읽고 물음에 답하시오.

> Anna: (ringing) Hello, Steve.
>
> Steve: Hi, Anna. We're meeting at the arts festival tomorrow at 1:30, right?
>
> Anna: Right. What kind of performance do you want to watch first?
>
> Steve: I want to watch the hip-hop dance performance first.
>
> Anna: Sounds good. It's at 2 p.m. at the gym, right?
>
> Steve: Yeah, and how about watching the play, *Romeo and Juliet*, at 4 p.m.?
>
> Anna: Oh, the one at the Main Hall near the gym? Sure!

01 What festival will Anna and Steve go to?

➡ _____

02 ⭐중요 Where will Anna and Steve watch the hip-hop dance performance?

➡ _____

03 What time and where is *Romeo and Juliet*?

➡ _____

04 ⭐중요 간접의문문을 이용하여 다음 두 문장을 하나의 문장으로 쓰시오.

(1) Tell me. Where does Maria live?

➡ _____

(2) I wonder. Are you married?

➡ _____

(3) May I ask? Is he alone?

➡ _____

(4) Can you tell me? Who drove your car?

➡ _____

05 주어진 단어를 바르게 배열하여 다음 우리말을 영어로 쓰시오.

> 어떤 것도 내가 나의 마음을 바꾸도록 하지는 못할 거야.
> (my mind / change / make / nothing / me / will)

➡ _____

06 다음 빈칸에 알맞은 말을 쓰시오.

> 누가 그 문을 열었는지 궁금해.
> ➡ I wonder _____ .

07 ⭐중요 괄호 안의 말을 바르게 배열하여 대화를 완성하시오.

> A: I want (how many / read / last year / know / to / books / you).
> B: I read about 10 books.

➡ _____

Look at this painting first. The seaside landscape is so peaceful and beautiful, isn't it? The title of this painting is *Landscape with the Fall of Icarus*. So, can you see where Icarus is? Do you see two legs that are sticking out of the water near the ship? This is Icarus in the famous myth in Greece. In the myth, Icarus' father made wings for him with feathers and wax and told him to stay away from the sun. However, Icarus didn't listen. He flew too close to the sun. So, the wax ___(A)___ and he ___(B)___ the water. Now, look at the entire painting again. Despite the tragedy of Icarus, people are going on with their everyday activities. Does the painting still look peaceful? ⓐ화가가 우리에게 무엇을 말하려 한다고 생각하나요?(think, try)

08 위 글의 빈칸 (A)와 (B)에 알맞은 말을 쓰시오.

(A) _____ (B) _____

중요

09 주어진 단어를 활용하여 밑줄 친 우리말 ⓐ를 영어로 쓰시오.

➡ _____

10 위 글의 내용에 맞게 빈칸에 알맞은 말을 쓰시오.

A: Where is Icarus?
B: He is _____ _____ _____. You can see his legs _____ _____ _____ _____ _____.

11 주어진 단어를 활용하여 다음 우리말을 영어로 쓰시오.

그는 그의 아들이 태양에서 멀리 떨어지게 하지 못했다. (make / stay)

➡ _____

중요

12 위 글의 내용에 맞게 빈칸에 알맞은 말을 쓰시오.

Q: What happened to Icarus?
A: He _____ too _____ to the sun and the _____ of his wings _____.

Now, let's move ___ⓐ___ to the next painting. Do you see the artist behind the large canvas?

(A) The young princess seems to be the main person because she is in the center of the painting.

(B) It will make you wonder about the painting more. Try to see which direction the artist is looking at.

(C) But the title of the painting is *The Maids of Honour*. Then, is the artist drawing the two women beside the princess? Take a close look.

(D) He is Diego Velázquez, and he actually painted this picture. Who do you think he is painting? Take a quick look.

Can you see the king and the queen in the mirror ___ⓑ___ the background of the painting? Who do you think he is painting now?

13 자연스러운 글이 되도록 (A)~(D)를 바르게 나열하시오.

➡ _____

14 위 글의 빈칸 ⓐ와 ⓑ에 알맞은 말을 쓰시오.

ⓐ _____ ⓑ _____

01 다음 대화의 내용과 일치하도록 Mina의 일기를 완성하시오.

Mina: I saw an interesting painting in an art book. Look at this.
Jack: Wow, it looks like da Vinci's *Mona Lisa*.
Mina: Actually, it's *Mona Lisa* by Fernando Botero. Which do you prefer?
Jack: I prefer da Vinci's to Botero's. Da Vinci's *Mona Lisa* has an interesting smile. How about you?
Mina: Well, I prefer Botero's to da Vinci's. His *Mona Lisa* is cute, and it looks modern.

Mon, Oct 14th, 2019
Today, I saw an interesting painting in an art book. It looked like da Vinci's *Mona Lisa*, but it was *Mona Lisa* by Fernando Botero. Between them, Jack preferred (A) _____ _____ to (B)_____, because of (C)_____ on da Vinci's *Mona Lisa*. However, I like (D)_____ much more because his *Mona Lisa* is cute and it looks modern.

02 다음 설문 조사표를 보고 대화를 완성하시오.

Museum Survey   Name: Clark
01 What grade are you in?   □ 7th grade   ☑ 8th grade   □ 9th grade
02 How often do you go to a museum?
□ once a month   ☑ twice a month   □ once a year   □ others: _____
03 What kind of museum do you like to go to?
☑ art museum   □ history museum   □ others: _____
04 How long do you usually spend time in the museum?
□ about an hour   ☑ about two hours   □ about three hours   □ about four hours

Q: I would like to know _____.
A: I am in the 8th grade.
Q: May I ask _____?
A: I go to a museum twice a month.
Q: I wonder _____.
A: I like to go to the art museum.
Q: Would you mind telling me _____?
A: Certainly not. I usually spend about two hours in the museum.

단원별 모의고사

01 다음 문장에 공통으로 들어갈 말을 고르시오.

> • Tom, _____ your teeth clean.
> • I didn't need the _____ anymore.
> • This _____ was worn out.

① produce   ② stick

③ wax   ④ flat

⑤ brush

02 다음 문장의 빈칸에 들어갈 말을 〈보기〉에서 골라 쓰시오.

> ┌─ 보기 ─┐
> tourist / wonder / direction / melt / despite

(1) _____ the butter over low heat.

(2) _____ the bad weather, we went on a picnic at a beach.

(3) A foreign _____ asked me to take her picture.

(4) Everyone in the photo is looking in the same _____.

(5) I _____ why she did that.

[03~05] 다음 대화를 읽고 물음에 답하시오.

M: (A)Can you help me? (hand) I want to buy a guitar.

W: There are various kinds of guitars. (B)어떤 종류의 음악을 연주하고 싶으신가요?

M: I want to play pop songs.

W: Then you should get a classical guitar.

M: Okay, I will take a classical guitar.

03 위 대화에서 밑줄 친 (A)와 의미가 같도록 주어진 단어를 사용하여 다시 쓰시오.

➡ _____

04 위 대화의 밑줄 친 우리말 (B)를 영작하시오.

➡ _____

05 위 대화에서 나타난 두 사람의 관계로 적절한 것은?

① student – teacher

② tourist – guide

③ customer – clerk

④ patient – doctor

⑤ interviewee – interviewer

[06~07] 다음 대화를 읽고 물음에 답하시오.

Jason: Hi, we are planning a school festival, so we want to find out students' favorite types of performances. May I ask you (A)[a few / few] questions?

Emily: Sure.

Jason: What kind of performance do you like (B)[more / most]?

Emily: I like music performances best.

Jason: Okay. Then, which do you prefer, rock (C)[and / or] hip-hop?

Emily: I prefer rock to hip-hop.

Jason: Who's your favorite musician?

Emily: My favorite musician is TJ.

Jason: Great. Thank you for your answers.

06 위 대화의 (A)~(C)에 들어갈 말로 바르게 짝지어진 것은?

① a few – more – and

② a few – most – or

③ a few – most – and

④ few – most – or

⑤ few – more – and

07 위 대화를 읽고 대답할 수 없는 것은?

① What does Jason want Emily to do?

② What kind of performance does Emily like best?

③ What kind of music does Emily like?

④ Who is Emily's favorite musician?

⑤ Why does Emily like TJ most?

[08~09] 다음 대화를 읽고 물음에 답하시오.

Mina: I saw an (A)interesting painting in an art book. Look (B)at this.

Jack: Wow, it looks like da Vinci's *Mona Lisa*.

Mina: Actually, it's *Mona Lisa* by Fernando Botero. (C)How do you prefer?

Jack: I prefer da Vinci's (D)to Botero's. Da Vinci's *Mona Lisa* has an interesting smile. How (E)about you?

Mina: Well, I prefer Botero's to da Vinci's. His *Mona Lisa* is cute, and it looks modern.

08 위 대화의 밑줄 친 (A)~(E) 중 어색한 것을 찾아 바르게 고치시오.

➡ _____

09 위 대화의 내용과 일치하지 않는 것은?

① Mina는 미술책에서 페르난도 보테로의 '모나리자'를 보았다.

② Jack은 보테로의 '모나리자'보다 다빈치의 '모나리자'를 더 좋아한다.

③ Jack은 다빈치의 '모나리자'에 흥미로운 미소가 있다고 생각한다.

④ Mina는 다빈치의 '모나리자'보다는 보테로의 '모나리자'를 더 좋아한다.

⑤ Mina는 다빈치의 '모나리자'가 귀엽고 현대적이라고 생각한다.

[10~12] 다음 대화를 읽고 물음에 답하시오.

Susan: Brian, is your band going to play at the Teen Music Festival?

Brian: Yes, we're practicing (A)almost every day.

Susan: (B)너희는 올해 어떤 종류의 음악을 연주하려고 하니?

Brian: Rock music. We'll play songs from the (C)ninety.

10 위 대화의 밑줄 친 (A)와 같은 뜻의 단어를 쓰시오.

➡ _____

11 위 대화의 밑줄 친 (A)의 우리말을 영작하시오.

➡ _____

12 위 대화의 밑줄 친 (C)를 알맞은 형으로 고치시오.

➡ _____

13 다음 빈칸에 들어갈 말로 가장 적절한 것은?

Rapunzel's mom _____ in the tower.

① makes Rapunzel staying

② made herself to stay

③ made Rapunzel stayed

④ made herself staying

⑤ made Rapunzel stay

14 주어진 단어를 활용하여 다음 우리말을 7 단어로 이루어진 한 문장으로 쓰시오.

좋은 음악은 네가 기분이 더 좋아지도록 만들 것이다. (make / feel)

➡ _____

15 다음 빈칸에 들어갈 말로 적절하지 <u>않은</u> 것은?

Do you know _____?

① who called you last night
② when the Morisons will arrive
③ where they are going to meet
④ how the word is spelled
⑤ what Tom made upset

16 간접의문문을 이용하여 다음 두 문장을 하나의 문장으로 쓰시오.

(1) Do you remember? Where did you find this bag?

➡ _____

(2) Can you tell me? Why does Kelly want to become a dancer?

➡ _____

17 다음 중 어법상 바르지 <u>않은</u> 것은?

① She made their dreams come true.
② Would you mind telling me who pushed you?
③ I want you to tell me when you will start the project.
④ Do you know who the lights turned off?
⑤ I had the man fix my chair.

[18~21] 다음 글을 읽고 물음에 답하시오.

Look at this painting first. The seaside landscape is so peaceful and beautiful, isn't it? The title of this painting is *Landscape with the Fall of Icarus*. So, can you see where Icarus is? Do you see two legs that are sticking out of the water near the ship? This is Icarus in the famous myth in Greece. In the myth, Icarus' father made wings for him with feathers and wax and told him to stay away ___(A)___ the sun. However, Icarus didn't listen. He flew too close to the sun. So, the wax melted and he fell into the water. Now, look at the entire painting again. Despite the tragedy of Icarus, people are going on with their everyday activities. Does the painting still look peaceful? What do you think the artist is trying to tell us?

18 다음 중 빈칸 (A)에 들어갈 말과 같은 말이 들어가는 것은?

① I want you to listen _____ my words.
② Do you take good care _____ your plants?
③ Many people suffer _____ headache.
④ Turn _____ the lights when you go out.
⑤ She will be satisfied _____ your presents.

19 When Icarus fell into the water, what were the other people in the painting doing? Answer in English with a full sentence.

➡ _____

20 다음 중 위 글의 내용과 일치하지 <u>않는</u> 것은?

① Icarus flew too close to the sun.
② Icarus' legs are sticking out of the ship.
③ Icarus' father wanted his son not to fly close to the sun.
④ Icarus' wings were made by his father.
⑤ People in the painting didn't care about the tragedy of Icarus.

21 위 글의 내용에 맞게 다음 대화의 빈칸을 채우시오.

> A: I would like to know _____.
> B: Oh, that's because he flew too close to the sun.

➡ _____

23 위 글의 ①~⑤ 중 어법상 바르지 않은 것은?

①   ②   ③   ④   ⑤

24 다음과 같이 풀이되는 단어를 위 글에서 찾아 쓰시오.

> a piece of thick cloth used by artists for painting on

➡ _____

[22~25] 다음 글을 읽고 물음에 답하시오.

Now, let's move on to the next painting. Do you see the artist behind the large canvas? He is Diego Velázquez, and he actually painted this picture. _____(A)_____ Take a quick look. The young princess seems to be the main person ①because she is in the center of the painting. But the title of the painting is *The Maids of Honour*. Then, is the artist ②drawing the two women ③beside the princess? Take a close look. It will make you ④wonder about the painting more. Try to see which direction ⑤is the artist looking at. Can you see the king and the queen in the mirror in the background of the painting? _____(B)_____

22 (A)와 (B)에 공통으로 들어갈 말로 가장 적절한 것은?

① When do you think he drew this painting?
② Who do you imagine he is painting?
③ How do you guess he is painting?
④ Do you know where he is painting?
⑤ What made him paint?

25 Which is NOT true about the artist who painted *The Maids of Honour*?

① His name is Diego Velázquez.
② He drew the young princess in the painting.
③ The king and the queen appear in the painting.
④ He drew himself behind the large canvas.
⑤ He drew the king and the queen in front of the princess.

INSIGHT
on the textbook

교과서 파헤치기

※ 다음 영어를 우리말로 쓰시오.

01 avoid	22 stand
02 suggestion	23 limit
03 upset	24 explain
04 worry	25 advise
05 contact	26 yet
06 advice	27 pack
07 fight	28 difficult
08 haircut	29 forgive
09 alone	30 elementary
10 stuff	31 fear
11 hurt	32 reason
12 messy	33 solve
13 wise	34 line
14 share	35 focus on
15 lunch break	36 wake up
16 repeat	37 stay up late
17 matter	38 gain weight
18 yell	39 on purpose
19 since	40 shut down
20 mean	41 work out
21 hate	42 in the end
	43 point out

※ 다음 우리말을 영어로 쓰시오.

01 거울 _____

02 초보의, 초급의 _____

03 공유하다, 나누다 _____

04 어려운 _____

05 반복하다 _____

06 소리치다 _____

07 접촉, 닿음 _____

08 조언하다, 충고하다 _____

09 문제 _____

10 싸다, 꾸리다 _____

11 싸우다 _____

12 점심시간 _____

13 이발, 머리 깎기 _____

14 물건 _____

15 다치게 하다 _____

16 참다, 견디다 _____

17 피하다 _____

18 한계, 제한 _____

19 아직 _____

20 치통 _____

21 제안 _____

22 홀로, 혼자 _____

23 걱정하다; 걱정 _____

24 어질러진, 더러운 _____

25 속상한, 마음이 상한 _____

26 이유, 까닭 _____

27 싫어하다 _____

28 (연극, 영화의) 대사 _____

29 조언 _____

30 용서하다 _____

31 설명하다 _____

32 두려움, 공포 _____

33 현명한 _____

34 풀다, 해결하다 _____

35 결국, 마침내 _____

36 ~에 집중하다 _____

37 (기계가) 멈추다 _____

38 체중이 늘다 _____

39 좋다가 나쁘다가 하는 _____

40 늦게까지 자지 않고 있다 _____

41 고의로 _____

42 자명종을 맞추다 _____

43 잠에서 깨다 _____

※ 다음 영영풀이에 알맞은 단어를 <보기>에서 골라 쓴 후, 우리말 뜻을 쓰시오.

1 _____ : dirty and/or untidy: _____

2 _____ : to dislike something very much: _____

3 _____ : a pain in one of your teeth: _____

4 _____ : the state of touching something: _____

5 _____ : the act of someone cutting your hair: _____

6 _____ : the words spoken by an actor in a play or film/movie: _____

7 _____ : to say or write something again or more than once: _____

8 _____ : to have or use something at the same time as somebody else: _____

9 _____ : an idea or a plan that you mention for somebody else to think about:

_____

10 _____ : the bad feeling that you have when you are in danger: _____

11 _____ : to keep away from somebody/something; to try not to do something:

_____

12 _____ : in or connected with the first stages of a course of study: _____

13 _____ : to cause physical pain to somebody/yourself; to injure somebody/

yourself: _____

14 _____ : to shout loudly, for example because you are angry, excited, frightened

or in pain: _____

15 _____ : an opinion or a suggestion about what somebody should do in a particular

situation: _____

16 _____ : to stop feeling angry with somebody who has done something to harm,

annoy or upset you: _____

보기			
forgive	advice	toothache	contact
line	messy	hurt	elementary
hate	yell	repeat	share
fear	suggestion	avoid	haircut

※ 다음 우리말과 일치하도록 빈칸에 알맞은 말을 쓰시오.

Listen & Talk 1-A-1

M: You don't _____ so _____ today. What's the _____?

W: I _____ my _____ _____ T-shirt. But I _____ grape juice on it.

M: Oh, no. _____ you _____ your sister?

W: No, _____ _____. I don't know _____ _____ _____.

M: 너 오늘은 별로 행복해 보이지가 않네. 무슨 일 있어?
W: 언니가 가장 좋아하는 티셔츠를 입었어. 그런데 거기에 포도 주스를 쏟았지 뭐야.
M: 오, 저런. 너희 언니에게 말했어?
W: 아니, 아직. 내가 뭘 해야 할지 모르겠어.

Listen & Talk 1-A-2

Sora: David, you _____ _____ today. _____ _____ _____ _____?

David: I _____ _____ _____ but it's too short. I look _____.

Sora: _____ _____ your hat and _____ _____ _____.
(pause) Oh, it _____ _____.

David: Really? I guess I'm just _____ _____ _____ it yet.

Sora: David, 너 오늘 침울해 보여. 무슨 일 있어?
David: 머리를 잘랐는데 너무 짧아. 우스꽝스럽게 보여.
Sora: 모자를 벗으면 내가 한 번 볼게. 오, 괜찮아 보이는데.
David: 정말? 난 아직 익숙해지지 않은 것 같아.

Listen & Talk 1-B

Jane: You _____ _____. What's _____ _____?

Mike: _____ _____ _____ _____ _____ _____ _____ _____ _____. I'm so hungry.

Jane: Oh, that's _____ _____. We still have two more hours _____ _____ _____.

Mike: Our school should have a _____ _____. Then, we _____ _____ a quick breakfast or snacks.

Jane: I _____ _____, _____. _____ can we _____ that _____?

Mike: We _____ _____ it on the _____ board.

Jane: 너 피곤해 보인다. 무슨 일 있어?
Mike: 오늘 아침에 밥을 못 먹었어. 너무 배가 고파.
Jane: 오, 안됐다. 점심시간까지 아직 두 시간도 더 남았는데.
Mike: 우리 학교도 매점이 있어야 돼. 그러면 간단히 아침이나 간식을 먹을 수 있잖아.
Jane: 내 생각도 그래. 어떻게 하면 우리가 그 제안을 할 수 있을까?
Mike: 우리는 이걸 제안 게시판에 올릴 수 있어.

Listen & Talk 2 A-1

Sujin: I don't know _____ _____ _____ _____ in math. Can you _____ _____ _____ _____?

Jake: _____ do you _____ for tests?

Sujin: I just _____ _____ _____ problems.

Jake: Well, don't _____ everything. I think you _____ _____ _____ the _____ you _____ _____.

Sujin: 수학을 더 잘하는 방법을 모르겠어. 나에게 조언을 좀 해 줄래?
Jake: 시험을 목표로 어떻게 공부해?
Sujin: 난 그냥 많은 문제를 풀어 봐.
Jake: 글쎄, 전부 풀지 마. 내 생각엔 네가 틀린 문제들에 집중해야 할 것 같아.

Listen & Talk 2 A-2

Emily: I _____ _____ _____ again. I just can't _____ _____ in the morning.

Tom: Do you _____ _____ _____?

Emily: Yeah, but I _____ _____ _____ and go back to sleep.

Tom: I _____ _____ _____ put it _____ _____ your bed. _____ _____, you'll have to _____ _____ _____ _____.

Emily: 나 또 수업에 늦었어. 난 정말 아침에 못 일어나겠어.
Tom: 자명종은 맞춰 두는 거야?
Emily: 응, 그렇지만 자명종을 끄고 다시 잠들게 돼.
Tom: 내 생각엔 자명종을 침대에서 멀리 떨어진 곳에 두어야 할 것 같아. 그러면 침대에서 일어날 수밖에 없을 거야.

Review 1

Eric: Ms. Morris, I just can't _____ _____ _____ _____. _____ _____ _____ _____?

Ms. Morris: Well, _____ _____ _____ _____ a special program? When you _____ a time _____, the computer _____ _____ at that time.

Eric: Oh, that's _____ _____ _____.

Ms. Morris: And _____ _____ _____ _____ _____ the computer _____ _____ your room and _____ the living room.

Eric: _____ _____ I _____. Thank you _____ _____ _____, Ms. Morris.

Eric: Morris 선생님, 저 컴퓨터 게임하는 것을 멈출 수가 없어요. 제가 어떻게 해야 할까요?
Mr. Morris: 음, 특별한 프로그램을 써 보는 게 어떨까? 네가 시간 제한을 정해 두면 컴퓨터가 그 시간에 맞춰 종료돼.
Eric: 오, 좋은 생각이네요.
Mr. Morris: 그리고 내 생각엔 컴퓨터를 네 방에서 거실로 옮겨 두어야 할 것 같아.
Eric: 제 생각에도 그래야 할 것 같아요. Morris 선생님, 조언해 주셔서 감사합니다.

Communication

Solomon: Hello, you're _____ _____ _____.

Amy: Hi, Solomon. I'm Amy.

Solomon: Hi, Amy. _____ _____ _____?

Amy: I hate _____ my room _____ my little sister. She uses my _____ _____ _____ me first. _____ _____ I _____?

Solomon: Hmm.... I think you should _____ _____ _____ _____. And you should also _____ _____ with your sister.

Amy: Oh, _____ _____ _____. _____ _____ the advice.

Solomon: 안녕하세요. (방송에) 연결되었습니다.
Amy: 안녕하세요, Solomon. 전 Amy라고 해요.
Solomon: 안녕하세요, Amy. 무슨 일 있어요?
Amy: 전 여동생이랑 제 방을 같이 쓰는 게 싫어요. 그 애는 제게 먼저 물어보지도 않고 제 물건을 쓰거든요. 제가 어떻게 해야 할까요?
Solomon: 흠.... 제 생각엔 당신의 기분을 여동생에게 말해야 할 것 같아요. 그리고 여동생과 몇 가지 규칙을 만들어 봐요.
Amy: 오, 그렇게 할게요. 조언 감사해요.

※ 다음 우리말에 맞도록 대화를 영어로 쓰시오.

Listen & Talk 1-A-1

M: _____

W: _____

M: _____

W: _____

Listen & Talk 1-A-2

Sora: _____

David: _____

Sora: _____

David: _____

Listen & Talk 1-B

Jane: _____

Mike: _____

Jane: _____

Mike: _____

_____

Jane: _____

Mike: _____

Listen & Talk 2 A-1

Sujin: _____

Jake: _____

Sujin: _____

Jake: _____

해석

M: 너 오늘은 별로 행복해 보이지가 않네. 무슨 일 있어?
W: 언니가 가장 좋아하는 티셔츠를 입었어. 그런데 거기에 포도 주스를 쏟았지 뭐야.
M: 오, 저런. 너희 언니에게 말했어?
W: 아니, 아직. 내가 뭘 해야 할지 모르겠어.

Sora: David, 너 오늘 침울해 보여. 무슨 일 있어?
David: 머리를 잘랐는데 너무 짧아. 우스꽝스럽게 보여.
Sora: 모자를 벗으면 내가 한 번 볼게. 오, 괜찮아 보이는데.
David: 정말? 난 아직 익숙해지지 않은 것 같아.

Jane: 너 피곤해 보인다. 무슨 일 있어?
Mike: 오늘 아침에 밥을 못 먹었어. 너무 배가 고파.
Jane: 오, 안됐다. 점심시간까지 아직 두 시간도 더 남았는데.
Mike: 우리 학교도 매점이 있어야 돼. 그러면 간단히 아침이나 간식을 먹을 수 있잖아.
Jane: 내 생각도 그래. 어떻게 하면 우리가 그 제안을 할 수 있을까?
Mike: 우리는 이걸 제안 게시판에 올릴 수 있어.

Sujin: 수학을 더 잘하는 방법을 모르겠어. 나에게 조언을 좀 해 줄래?
Jake: 시험을 목표로 어떻게 공부해?
Sujin: 난 그냥 많은 문제를 풀어 봐.
Jake: 글쎄, 전부 풀지 마. 내 생각엔 네가 틀린 문제들에 집중해야 할 것 같아.

Listen & Talk 2 A-2

Emily: _____

Tom: _____

Emily: _____

Tom: _____

Emily: 나 또 수업에 늦었어. 난 정말 아침에 못 일어나겠어.
Tom: 자명종은 맞춰 두는 거야?
Emily: 응, 그렇지만 자명종을 끄고 다시 잠들게 돼.
Tom: 내 생각엔 자명종을 침대에서 멀리 떨어진 곳에 두어야 할 것 같아. 그러면 침대에서 일어날 수밖에 없을 거야.

Review 1

Eric: _____

Ms. Morris: _____

_____

Eric: _____

Ms. Morris: _____

_____

Eric: _____

Eric: Morris 선생님, 저 컴퓨터 게임하는 것을 멈출 수가 없어요. 제가 어떻게 해야 할까요?
Mr. Morris: 음, 특별한 프로그램을 써 보는 게 어떨까? 네가 시간 제한을 정해 두면 컴퓨터가 그 시간에 맞춰 종료돼.
Eric: 오, 좋은 생각이네요.
Mr. Morris: 그리고 내 생각엔 컴퓨터를 네 방에서 거실로 옮겨 두어야 할 것 같아.
Eric: 제 생각에도 그래야 할 것 같아요. Morris 선생님, 조언해 주셔서 감사합니다.

Communication

Solomon: _____

Amy: _____

Solomon: _____

Amy: _____

_____

Solomon: _____

_____

Amy: _____

Solomon: 안녕하세요, (방송에) 연결되었습니다.
Amy: 안녕하세요, Solomon. 전 Amy라고 해요.
Solomon: 안녕하세요, Amy. 무슨 일 있어요?
Amy: 전 여동생이랑 제 방을 같이 쓰는 게 싫어요. 그 애는 제게 먼저 물어보지도 않고 제 물건을 쓰거든요. 제가 어떻게 해야 할까요?
Solomon: 흠.... 제 생각엔 당신의 기분을 여동생에게 말해야 할 것 같아요. 그리고 여동생과 몇 가지 규칙을 만들어 봐요.
Amy: 오, 그렇게 할게요. 조언 감사해요.

※ 다음 우리말과 일치하도록 빈칸에 알맞은 것을 골라 쓰시오.

1 Bella is 15 years _____ this year and _____ days her feelings are _____ up and _____.

    A. these   B. down   C. old   D. going

2 Today, she _____ _____.

    A. down   B. looks

3 _____ listen to Bella's _____ and _____ out why.

    A. find   B. let's   C. feelings

Day 1

4 Anger: _____ a day! I can't believe Jenny _____ Bella _____ the school play.

    A. at   B. what   C. after   D. yelled

5 Sadness: Well, that's _____ Bella _____ her _____ on stage.

    A. forgot   B. because   C. lines

6 Anger: Jenny pointed _____ the mistake _____ Bella _____.

    A. made   B. out   C. that

7 How _____ she do that _____ _____ of everyone?

    A. front   B. could   C. in

8 Joy: But I'm _____ Jenny did not _____ to _____ Bella.

    A. hurt   B. mean   C. sure

9 They _____ _____ best friends _____ elementary school. Remember?

    A. since   B. been   C. have

10 Anger: That's _____ I'm _____.

    A. saying   B. what

11 A true friend would _____ _____ Bella _____ like that.

    A. put   B. never   C. down

12 Fear: I'm worried _____ they are not _____ to _____ friends anymore.

    A. going   B. that   C. be

13 Joy: Come on, Fear. _____ go too _____. We'll _____.

    A. don't   B. far   C. see

Day 2

14 Anger: I can't _____ Jenny. She didn't _____ a _____ to Bella.

    A. word   B. forgive   C. say

15 Fear: Jenny didn't _____ _____ _____ her.

    A. at   B. even   C. look

1 Bella는 올해 15세이고 요즘 그 애의 기분은 좋다가 안 좋다가 한다.

2 오늘 그 애는 우울해 보인다.

3 Bella의 감정에 귀 기울여 보고 그 이유를 알아보자.

Day 1

4 Anger: 정말 끔찍한 하루야! 학교 연극이 끝난 후 Jenny가 Bella에게 소리를 지르다니 믿을 수가 없어.

5 Sadness: 글쎄, 그건 Bella가 무대에서 그녀의 대사를 잊어버렸기 때문이잖아.

6 Anger: Jenny는 Bella가 저지른 실수를 지적했잖아.

7 어떻게 모든 사람 앞에서 그렇게 할 수가 있니?

8 Joy: 하지만 난 Jenny가 Bella에게 상처를 주려고 했던 건 아니었다고 확신해.

9 그들은 초등학교 때부터 가장 친한 친구였잖아. 기억하지?

10 Anger: 내 말이 바로 그거야.

11 진정한 친구라면 절대로 그런 식으로 Bella를 깎아내리지 않을 거야.

12 Fear: 나는 그들이 더 이상 친구로 지내지 않을까봐 걱정돼.

13 Joy: 자, Fear. 너무 극단적으로 생각하지 마. 곧 알게 되겠지.

Day 2

14 Anger: 난 Jenny를 용서할 수 없어. 그 애는 Bella에게 한마디도 말을 안 했어.

15 Fear: Jenny는 심지어 Bella를 쳐다 보지도 않았어.

16 Jenny _____ _____ _____ this cold before.

A. never   B. has   C. been

17 Sadness: Bella ate _____ _____ lunch today. Poor Bella!

A. during   B. alone

18 Joy: Jenny is Bella's _____ _____.

A. friend   B. best

19 I'm sure there is a _____ that we don't _____ _____.

A. about   B. reason   C. know

20 Anger: I can't _____ this _____ _____.

A. any   B. stand   C. longer

21 Bella should just _____ and _____ her _____ her feelings.

A. about   B. tell   C. go

22 Fear: I don't _____ Bella _____ be _____ again.

A. to   B. hurt   C. want

23 She should _____ it _____.

A. go   B. let

24 Joy: They are good friends. They will _____ it _____.

A. out   B. work

Day 3

25 Joy: Whew! I'm _____ happy _____ they are _____ again.

A. that   B. talking   C. so

26 Anger: Yeah, Bella _____ to Jenny and _____ to _____ first.

A. talked   B. went   C. her

27 Joy: Jenny didn't _____ Bella _____ _____.

A. on   B. avoid   C. purpose

28 Sadness: Yeah, Jenny _____ know a _____ to _____ sorry.

A. say   B. way   C. didn't

29 Fear: I hope Bella _____ have _____ _____ problems like this.

A. any   B. doesn't   C. more

30 Joy: Me, _____. But problems are _____ of growing _____.

A. part   B. too   C. up

31 Just _____ this time, Bella will _____ the problems, solve them, and become _____ in the _____.

A. face   B. like   C. end   D. wiser

16 Jenny가 전에 이렇게 차가웠던 적이 없었어.

17 Sadness: Bella는 오늘 점심시간에 혼자 밥을 먹었잖아. 가엾은 Bella!

18 Joy: Jenny는 Bella의 가장 친한 친구야.

19 나는 우리가 모르는 어떤 이유가 있다고 확신해.

20 Anger: 나는 더 이상 이 상황을 못 참아.

21 Bella는 일단 가서 Jenny에게 자신의 감정을 말해야 해.

22 Fear: 나는 Bella가 또다시 상처 받는 걸 원하지 않아.

23 그 애는 그냥 내버려 두어야 해.

24 Joy: 그 애들은 좋은 친구야. 그 애들이 잘 해낼 거야.

Day 3

25 Joy: 휴! 나는 그 애들이 다시 이야기하게 되어 무척 기뻐.

26 Anger: 그래, Bella가 Jenny에게 가서 그 애에게 먼저 말을 걸었지.

27 Joy: Jenny는 일부러 Bella를 피한 게 아니었어.

28 Sadness: 맞아, Jenny는 사과하는 방법을 몰랐던 거야.

29 Fear: 나는 Bella에게 이번과 같은 문제가 더 이상 없기를 바라.

30 Joy: 나도 그래. 하지만 문제들은 성장의 일부야.

31 이번과 꼭 마찬가지로 Bella는 문제들에 직면하게 될 거고, 그것들을 해결할 거고, 그리고 결국 더 현명해질 거야.

※ 다음 우리말과 일치하도록 빈칸에 알맞은 말을 쓰시오.

1 Bella is 15 _____ _____ this year and _____ her feelings are _____ _____ _____ _____.

2 Today, she _____ _____.

3 _____ _____ _____ Bella's _____ and _____ _____.

Day 1

4 Anger: _____ _____ _____ ! I can't believe Jenny _____ _____ Bella _____ the school play.

5 Sadness: Well, that's _____ Bella _____ her _____ _____ _____.

6 Anger: Jenny _____ _____ the mistake _____.

7 How _____ she do that _____ _____ _____ everyone?

8 Joy: But I'm _____ Jenny _____ _____ _____ _____ Bella.

9 They _____ _____ best friends _____ _____. Remember?

10 Anger: That's _____ I'm _____.

11 A true friend _____ _____ _____ Bella _____ like that.

12 Fear: I'm worried _____ they are _____ _____ _____.

13 Joy: Come on, Fear. _____ _____ _____ _____ _____. We'll _____.

Day 2

14 Anger: I _____ _____ Jenny. She _____ _____ _____ to Bella.

15 Fear: Jenny _____ _____ _____ _____ her.

1 Bella는 올해 15세이고 요즘 그 애의 기분은 좋다가 안 좋다가 한다.

2 오늘 그 애는 우울해 보인다.

3 Bella의 감정에 귀 기울여 보고 그 이유를 알아보자.

Day 1

4 Anger: 정말 끔찍한 하루야! 학교 연극이 끝난 후 Jenny 가 Bella에게 소리를 지르다 니 믿을 수가 없어.

5 Sadness: 글쎄, 그건 Bella가 무대에서 그녀의 대사를 잊 어버렸기 때문이잖아.

6 Anger: Jenny는 Bella가 저지 른 실수를 지적했잖아.

7 어떻게 모든 사람 앞에서 그렇 게 할 수가 있니?

8 Joy: 하지만 난 Jenny가 Bella 에게 상처를 주려고 했던 건 아니었다고 확신해.

9 그들은 초등학교 때부터 가장 친한 친구였잖아. 기억하지?

10 Anger: 내 말이 바로 그거야.

11 진정한 친구라면 절대로 그런 식으로 Bella를 깎아내리지 않 을 거야.

12 Fear: 나는 그들이 더 이상 친구 로 지내지 않을까봐 걱정돼.

13 Joy: 자, Fear. 너무 극단적으로 생각하지 마. 곧 알게 되겠지.

Day 2

14 Anger: 난 Jenny를 용서할 수 없어. 그 애는 Bella에게 한마디도 말을 안 했어.

15 Fear: Jenny는 심지어 Bella를 쳐 다 보지도 않았어.

16 Jenny _____ _____ _____ this cold before.

17 Sadness: Bella _____ _____ _____ lunch today. Poor Bella!

18 Joy: Jenny is _____ _____ _____.

19 I'm sure there is a _____ _____ _____ _____ _____ _____.

20 Anger: I _____ _____ this _____ _____.

21 Bella should just _____ and _____ her _____ her feelings.

22 Fear: I don't _____ Bella _____ _____ again.

23 She _____ _____ _____ _____.

24 Joy: They are good friends. They will _____ _____.

Day 3

25 Joy: Whew! I'm so happy _____ they _____ _____ again.

26 Anger: Yeah, Bella _____ _____ Jenny and _____ _____ _____ first.

27 Joy: Jenny _____ _____ Bella _____ _____.

28 Sadness: Yeah, Jenny didn't know _____ _____ _____ _____ _____.

29 Fear: I hope Bella doesn't have _____ _____ _____ _____ this.

30 Joy: _____, _____. But problems are _____ _____ _____ _____.

31 _____ _____ this time, Bella will _____ the problems, _____ _____ _____, and become _____ in the _____.

---

16 Jenny가 전에 이렇게 차가웠던 적이 없었어.

17 Sadness: Bella는 오늘 점심시간에 혼자 밥을 먹었잖아. 가엾은 Bella!

18 Joy: Jenny는 Bella의 가장 친한 친구야.

19 나는 우리가 모르는 어떤 이유가 있다고 확신해.

20 Anger: 나는 더 이상 이 상황을 못 참아.

21 Bella는 일단 가서 Jenny에게 자신의 감정을 말해야 해.

22 Fear: 나는 Bella가 또다시 상처받는 걸 원하지 않아.

23 그 애는 그냥 내버려 두어야 해.

24 Joy: 그 애들은 좋은 친구야. 그 애들이 잘 해낼 거야.

Day 3

25 Joy: 휴! 나는 그 애들이 다시 이야기하게 되어 무척 기뻐.

26 Anger: 그래, Bella가 Jenny에게 가서 그 애에게 먼저 말을 걸었지.

27 Joy: Jenny는 일부러 Bella를 피한 게 아니었어.

28 Sadness: 맞아, Jenny는 사과하는 방법을 몰랐던 거야.

29 Fear: 나는 Bella에게 이번과 같은 문제가 더 이상 없기를 바라.

30 Joy: 나도 그래. 하지만 문제들은 성장의 일부야.

31 이번과 꼭 마찬가지로 Bella는 문제들에 직면하게 될 거고, 그것들을 해결할 거고, 그리고 결국 더 현명해질 거야.

※ 다음 문장을 우리말로 쓰시오.

1 Bella is 15 years old this year and these days her feelings are going up and down.

➡ _____

2 Today, she looks down.

➡ _____

3 Let's listen to Bella's feelings and find out why.

➡ _____

4 Anger: What a day! I can't believe Jenny yelled at Bella after the school play.

➡ _____

5 Sadness: Well, that's because Bella forgot her lines on stage.

➡ _____

6 Anger: Jenny pointed out the mistake that Bella made.

➡ _____

7 How could she do that in front of everyone?

➡ _____

8 Joy: But I'm sure Jenny did not mean to hurt Bella.

➡ _____

9 They have been best friends since elementary school. Remember?

➡ _____

10 Anger: That's what I'm saying.

➡ _____

11 A true friend would never put Bella down like that.

➡ _____

12 Fear: I'm worried that they are not going to be friends anymore.

➡ _____

13 Joy: Come on, Fear. Don't go too far. We'll see.

➡ _____

14 Anger: I can't forgive Jenny. She didn't say a word to Bella.

➡ _____

15 Fear: Jenny didn't even look at her.

➡ _____

16 Jenny has never been this cold before.

➡ _____

17 Sadness: Bella ate alone during lunch today. Poor Bella!

➡ _____

18 Joy: Jenny is Bella's best friend.

➡ _____

19 I'm sure there is a reason that we don't know about.

➡ _____

20 Anger: I can't stand this any longer.

➡ _____

21 Bella should just go and tell her about her feelings.

➡ _____

22 Fear: I don't want Bella to be hurt again.

➡ _____

23 She should let it go.

➡ _____

24 Joy: They are good friends. They will work it out.

➡ _____

25 Joy: Whew! I'm so happy that they are talking again.

➡ _____

26 Anger: Yeah, Bella went to Jenny and talked to her first.

➡ _____

27 Joy: Jenny didn't avoid Bella on purpose.

➡ _____

28 Sadness: Yeah, Jenny didn't know a way to say sorry.

➡ _____

29 Fear: I hope Bella doesn't have any more problems like this.

➡ _____

30 Joy: Me, too. But problems are part of growing up.

➡ _____

31 Just like this time, Bella will face the problems, solve them, and become wiser in the end.

➡ _____

※ 다음 괄호 안의 단어들을 우리말에 맞도록 바르게 배열하시오.

1 (is / Bella / years / 15 / old / year / this / and / days / these / feelings / her / going / are / down. / and / up)

➡ _____

_____

2 (she / today, / down. / looks)

➡ _____

3 (listen / let's / Bella's / to / and / feelings / why. / out / find)

➡ _____

4 (a / what / day! // can't / I / Jenny / believe / at / yelled / Bella / the / play. / school / after)

➡ Anger: _____

_____

5 (that's / well, / Bella / because / forgot / lines / her / stage. / on)

➡ Sadness: _____

6 (pointed / Jenny / the / out / that / mistake / made. / Bella)

➡ Anger: _____

7 (could / how / do / she / that / front / in / everyone? / of)

➡ _____

8 (I'm / but / Jenny / sure / not / did / to / mean / Bella. / hurt)

➡ Joy: _____

9 (have / they / been / friends / best / school. / elementary / since // remember?)

➡ _____

10 (what / that's / saying. / I'm)

➡ Anger: _____

11 (true / a / would / friend / put / never / Bella / that. / like / down)

➡ _____

12 (worried / I'm / they / that / not / are / to / going / anymore. / friends / be)

➡ Fear: _____

13 (on, / come / Fear. // go / don't / far. / too // see. / we'll)

➡ Joy: _____

14 (can't / I / Jenny. / forgive // didn't / she / word / a / say / Bella. / to)

➡ Anger: _____

15 (didn't / Jenny / look / even / her. / at)

➡ Fear: _____

1 Bella는 올해 15세이고 요즘 그 애의 기분은 좋다가 안 좋다가 한다.

2 오늘 그 애는 우울해 보인다.

3 Bella의 감정에 귀 기울여 보고 그 이유를 알아보자.

Day **1**

4 Anger: 정말 끔찍한 하루야! 학교 연극이 끝난 후 Jenny 가 Bella에게 소리를 지르다 니 믿을 수가 없어.

5 Sadness: 글쎄, 그건 Bella가 무대에서 그녀의 대사를 잊 어버렸기 때문이잖아.

6 Anger: Jenny는 Bella가 저지 른 실수를 지적했잖아.

7 어떻게 모든 사람 앞에서 그렇 게 할 수가 있니?

8 Joy: 하지만 난 Jenny가 Bella 에게 상처를 주려고 했던 건 아니었다고 확신해.

9 그들은 초등학교 때부터 가장 친한 친구였잖아. 기억하지?

10 Anger: 내 말이 바로 그거야.

11 진정한 친구라면 절대로 그런 식으로 Bella를 깎아내리지 않 을 거야.

12 Fear: 나는 그들이 더 이상 친구 로 지내지 않을까봐 걱정돼.

13 Joy: 자, Fear. 너무 극단적으로 생각하지 마. 곧 알게 되겠지.

Day **2**

14 Anger: 난 Jenny를 용서할 수 없어. 그 애는 Bella에게 한마디도 말을 안 했어.

15 Fear: Jenny는 심지어 Bella를 쳐 다 보지도 않았어.

16 (has / Jenny / been / never / before. / cold / this)

➡ _____

17 (ate / Bella / during / alone / today. / lunch // Bella! / poor)

➡ Sadness: _____

18 (is / Jenny / friend. / best / Bella's)

➡ Joy: _____

19 (sure / I'm / is / there / reason / a / that / don't / we / about. / know)

➡ _____

20 (can't / I / this / stand / longer. / any)

➡ Anger: _____

21 (should / Bella / go / just / and / her / tell / about / feelings. / her)

➡ _____

22 (don't / I / want / to / Bella / again. / hurt / be)

➡ Fear: _____

23 (should / she / go. / it / let)

➡ _____

24 (are / they / friends. / good // will / they / out. / it / work)

➡ Joy: _____

25 (I'm / whew! / so / that / happy / they / again. / talking / are)

➡ Joy: _____

26 (Bella / yeah, / to / went / Jenny / and / first. / her / to / talked)

➡ Anger: _____

27 (didn't / Jenny / avoid / purpose. / on / Bella)

➡ Joy: _____

28 (Jenny / yeah, / know / didn't / way / a / sorry. / say / to)

➡ Sadness: _____

29 (hope / I / doesn't / Bella / any / have / problems / this. / like / more)

➡ Fear: _____

30 (too. / me, // problems / but / part / are / up. / growing / of)

➡ Joy: _____

31 (like / just / time, / this / Bella / face / will / problems, / the / them, / solve / become / and / wiser / end. / the / in)

➡ _____

_____

16 Jenny가 전에 이렇게 차가웠던 적이 없었어.

17 Sadness: Bella는 오늘 점심시간에 혼자 밥을 먹었잖아. 가엾은 Bella!

18 Joy: Jenny는 Bella의 가장 친한 친구야.

19 나는 우리가 모르는 어떤 이유가 있다고 확신해.

20 Anger: 나는 더 이상 이 상황을 못 참아.

21 Bella는 일단 가서 Jenny에게 자신의 감정을 말해야 해.

22 Fear: 나는 Bella가 또다시 상처 받는 걸 원하지 않아.

23 그 애는 그냥 내버려 두어야 해.

24 Joy: 그 애들은 좋은 친구야. 그 애들이 잘 해낼 거야.

Day 3

25 Joy: 휴! 나는 그 애들이 다시 이야기하게 되어 무척 기뻐.

26 Anger: 그래, Bella가 Jenny에게 가서 그 애에게 먼저 말을 걸었지.

27 Joy: Jenny는 일부러 Bella를 피한 게 아니었어.

28 Sadness: 맞아, Jenny는 사과하는 방법을 몰랐던 거야.

29 Fear: 나는 Bella에게 이번과 같은 문제가 더 이상 없기를 바라.

30 Joy: 나도 그래. 하지만 문제들은 성장의 일부야.

31 이번과 꼭 마찬가지로 Bella는 문제들에 직면하게 될 거고, 그것들을 해결할 거고, 그리고 결국 더 현명해질 거야.

※ 다음 우리말을 영어로 쓰시오.

1 ▶ Bella는 올해 15세이고 요즘 그 애의 기분은 좋다가 안 좋다가 한다.

➡ _____

2 ▶ 오늘 그 애는 우울해 보인다.

➡ _____

3 ▶ Bella의 감정에 귀 기울여 보고 그 이유를 알아보자.

➡ _____

4 ▶ Anger: 정말 끔찍한 하루야! 학교 연극이 끝난 후 Jenny가 Bella에게 소리를 지르다니 믿을 수가 없어.

➡ _____

5 ▶ Sadness: 글쎄, 그건 Bella가 무대에서 그녀의 대사를 잊어버렸기 때문이잖아.

➡ _____

6 ▶ Anger: Jenny는 Bella가 저지른 실수를 지적했잖아.

➡ _____

7 ▶ 어떻게 모든 사람 앞에서 그렇게 할 수가 있니?

➡ _____

8 ▶ Joy: 하지만 난 Jenny가 Bella에게 상처를 주려고 했던 건 아니었다고 확신해.

➡ _____

9 ▶ 그들은 초등학교 때부터 가장 친한 친구였잖아. 기억하지?

➡ _____

10 ▶ Anger: 내 말이 바로 그거야.

➡ _____

11 ▶ 진정한 친구라면 절대로 그런 식으로 Bella를 깎아내리지 않을 거야.

➡ _____

12 ▶ Fear: 나는 그들이 더 이상 친구로 지내지 않을까봐 걱정돼.

➡ _____

13 ▶ Joy: 자, Fear. 너무 극단적으로 생각하지 마. 곧 알게 되겠지.

➡ _____

14 ▶ Anger: 난 Jenny를 용서할 수 없어. 그 애는 Bella에게 한마디도 말을 안 했어.

➡ _____

15 ▶ Fear: Jenny는 심지어 Bella를 쳐다보지도 않았어.

➡ _____

16 Jenny가 전에 이렇게 차가웠던 적이 없었어.

➡ _____

17 Sadness: Bella는 오늘 점심시간에 혼자 밥을 먹었잖아. 가엾은 Bella!

➡ _____

18 Joy: Jenny는 Bella의 가장 친한 친구야.

➡ _____

19 나는 우리가 모르는 어떤 이유가 있다고 확신해.

➡ _____

20 Anger: 나는 더 이상 이 상황을 못 참아.

➡ _____

21 Bella는 일단 가서 Jenny에게 자신의 감정을 말해야 해.

➡ _____

22 Fear: 나는 Bella가 또다시 상처받는 걸 원하지 않아.

➡ _____

23 그 애는 그냥 내버려 두어야 해.

➡ _____

24 Joy: 그 애들은 좋은 친구야. 그 애들이 잘 해낼 거야.

➡ _____

25 Joy: 휴! 나는 그 애들이 다시 이야기하게 되어 무척 기뻐.

➡ _____

26 Anger: 그래, Bella가 Jenny에게 가서 그 애에게 먼저 말을 걸었지.

➡ _____

27 Joy: Jenny는 일부러 Bella를 피한 게 아니었어.

➡ _____

28 Sadness: 맞아, Jenny는 사과하는 방법을 몰랐던 거야.

➡ _____

29 Fear: 나는 Bella에게 이번과 같은 문제가 더 이상 없기를 바라.

➡ _____

30 Joy: 나도 그래. 하지만 문제들은 성장의 일부야.

➡ _____

31 이번과 꼭 마찬가지로 Bella는 문제들에 직면하게 될 거고, 그것들을 해결할 거고, 그리고 결국 더 현명해질 거야.

➡ _____

※ 다음 우리말과 일치하도록 빈칸에 알맞은 말을 쓰시오.

Wrap up 1

1. Mr. Jones: Daisy, you're _____ _____.

2. Daisy: I'm really sorry, Mr. Jones. I _____ _____ _____ again _____ _____.

3. Mr. Jones: Well, I think you _____ _____ _____ go to bed _____.

4. You _____ _____ _____ your bag the night before, so you can _____ _____ in the morning.

5. Daisy: Okay, Mr. Jones. I'll _____ _____ _____.

1. Mr. Jones: Daisy, 너 또 지각이구나.
2. Daisy: Jones 선생님, 정말 죄송해요. 어 젯밤에 또 늦게까지 자지 않고 깨어 있 었어요.
3. Mr. Jones: 음, 내 생각엔 넌 더 일찍 잠 자리에 들려고 노력해야 할 것 같구나.
4. 또 전날 밤에 가방을 싸 둔다면 아침에 시간을 절약할 수 있어.
5. Daisy: 알겠어요, Jones 선생님. 조언해 주신 것을 해 볼게요.

Read & Think

1. Bella: Jenny, I was _____ _____ you _____ _____ my mistake _____ _____ _____ _____.

2. But I'm sure you didn't _____ _____ _____ my feelings.

3. Jenny: I'm so sorry, Bella. _____ _____ _____ _____ to me first.

1. Bella: Jenny야, 네가 다른 사람들 앞 에서 내 잘못을 지적했을 때 화가 났어.
2. 그렇지만 난 네가 내게 상처를 주려고 일부러 그런 게 아니라고 믿어.
3. Jenny: Bella야, 미안해. 먼저 내게 와 줘서 고마워.

Think & Write

1. Dear _____ _____,

2. I _____ _____ _____ you a problem that I _____.

3. I'm _____ _____ my terrible _____ _____.

4. I _____ _____ this problem _____ _____ _____ _____.

5. I want to _____ _____ in math.

6. But when I _____ _____ _____ math, I just _____ _____ _____ it.

7. I don't know _____ _____ _____.

8. I _____ _____ _____ a good night's sleep _____ _____ this worry.

9. Can you _____ my worries _____?

1. 걱정 인형에게.
2. 나는 너에게 내가 가진 문제를 말하고 싶어.
3. 나는 나의 끔찍한 수학 성적이 걱정 돼.
4. 나는 작년부터 이 문제를 가지고 있어.
5. 나는 수학을 더 잘하고 싶어.
6. 하지만 내가 수학을 공부하려고 하면, 나는 단지 그것에 집중할 수 없어.
7. 나는 무엇을 해야 할지 모르겠어.
8. 이 걱정 때문에 밤에 잠도 잘 못자.
9. 내 걱정을 없애 줄 수 있겠니?

※ 다음 우리말을 영어로 쓰시오.

Wrap up 1

1. Mr. Jones: Daisy, 너 또 지각이구나.
   ➡ _____

2. Daisy: Jones 선생님, 정말 죄송해요. 어젯밤에 또 늦게까지 자지 않고 깨어 있었어요.
   ➡ _____

3. Mr. Jones: 음, 내 생각엔 넌 더 일찍 잠자리에 들려고 노력해야 할 것 같구나.
   ➡ _____

4. 또 전날 밤에 가방을 싸 둔다면 아침에 시간을 절약할 수 있어.
   ➡ _____

5. Daisy: 알겠어요, Jones 선생님. 조언해 주신 것을 해 볼게요.
   ➡ _____

Read & Think

1. Bella: Jenny야, 네가 다른 사람들 앞에서 내 잘못을 지적했을 때 화가 났었어.
   ➡ _____

2. 그렇지만 난 네가 내게 상처를 주려고 일부러 그런 게 아니라고 믿어.
   ➡ _____

3. Jenny: Bella야, 미안해. 먼저 내게 와 줘서 고마워.
   ➡ _____

Think & Write

1. 걱정 인형에게,
   ➡ _____

2. 나는 너에게 내가 가진 문제를 말하고 싶어.
   ➡ _____

3. 나는 나의 끔찍한 수학 성적이 걱정 돼.
   ➡ _____

4. 나는 작년부터 이 문제를 가지고 있어.
   ➡ _____

5. 나는 수학을 더 잘하고 싶어.
   ➡ _____

6. 하지만 내가 수학을 공부하려고 하면, 나는 단지 그것에 집중할 수 없어.
   ➡ _____

7. 나는 무엇을 해야 할지 모르겠어.
   ➡ _____

8. 이 걱정 때문에 밤에 잠도 잘 못자.
   ➡ _____

9. 내 걱정을 없애 줄 수 있겠니?
   ➡ _____

※ 다음 영어를 우리말로 쓰시오.

01 blind _____

02 dead _____

03 seem _____

04 attract _____

05 careless _____

06 throughout _____

07 curious _____

08 sense _____

09 dangerous _____

10 huge _____

11 thick _____

12 appear _____

13 ginger _____

14 feed _____

15 attack _____

16 shelter _____

17 rescue _____

18 giant _____

19 restless _____

20 tongue _____

21 friendship _____

22 trunk _____

23 strength _____

24 tail _____

25 humorous _____

26 insect _____

27 allow _____

28 unbelievably _____

29 whale _____

30 lifeless _____

31 approach _____

32 probably _____

33 female _____

34 adventurous _____

35 thanks to _____

36 keep one's eyes on _____

37 be born _____

38 care for _____

39 tell the difference _____

40 millions of _____

41 become part of _____

42 give a presentation _____

43 next to _____

※ 다음 우리말을 영어로 쓰시오.

01	거대한	22	혀
02	나타나다	23	(종이) 한 장
03	구조	24	곤충
04	궁금한, 호기심이 많은	25	언어
05	죽은	26	가만히 못 있는
06	모험심이 강한	27	믿을 수 없을 정도로
07	허락하다	28	힘
08	돌고래	29	눈 먼, 맹인인
09	우정	30	먹이를 주다
10	뱀	31	보호소
11	위험한	32	끌다, ~을 끌어당기다
12	다가가다, 다가오다	33	두꺼운
13	생강	34	(코끼리의) 코
14	죽은, 생명이 없는	35	~ 덕분에
15	공격하다	36	~ 옆에
16	구멍	37	~을 돌보다
17	부주의한	38	~의 일원이 되다
18	감각	39	수백만의
19	재미있는, 유머러스한	40	발표하다
20	~ 동안, ~ 내내	41	태어나다
21	암컷의	42	~에서 눈을 떼지 않다
		43	차이를 구별하다

※ 다음 영영풀이에 알맞은 단어를 <보기>에서 골라 쓴 후, 우리말 뜻을 쓰시오.

1 _____ : no longer alive: _____

2 _____ : the long nose of an elephant: _____

3 _____ : not able to see: _____

4 _____ : having a strong desire to know about something: _____

5 _____ : to give food to a person or an animal: _____

6 _____ : not afraid to do new and dangerous or exciting things: _____

7 _____ : to come near to somebody/something in distance or time: _____

8 _____ : the feeling or relationship that friends have; the state of being friends:

_____

9 _____ : any small creature with six legs and a body divided into three parts:

_____

10 _____ : a very large animal that lives in the ocean and looks like a very large

fish: _____

11 _____ : to save somebody/something from a dangerous or harmful situation:

_____

12 _____ : a structure built to give protection, especially from the weather or from

attack: _____

13 _____ : the soft part in the mouth that moves around, used for tasting, swallowing,

speaking, etc.: _____

14 _____ : to let somebody/something do something; to let something happen or be

done: _____

15 _____ : not giving enough attention and thought to what you are doing, so that

you make mistakes: _____

16 _____ : the part that sticks out and can be moved at the back of the body of a

bird, an animal or a fish: _____

보기			
allow	feed	tongue	approach
blind	careless	trunk	friendship
tail	shelter	rescue	whale
curious	dead	insect	adventurous

※ 다음 우리말과 일치하도록 빈칸에 알맞은 말을 쓰시오.

Listen & Talk 1 A-1

Ryan: Judy, did you _____ a _____ for your science project?

Judy: Not yet. _____ _____ you, Ryan?

Ryan: _____ _____ _____ _____ _____. So I'm _____ _____ _____ the project on that.

Judy: That's an _____ _____!

Listen & Talk 1 A-2

Jane: _____ _____ this picture of a _____ flower.

Tom: Wow, it is _____ _____ a person.

Jane: Yeah. I'm really _____ _____ this flower. It also _____ here that the flower _____ very _____, but _____ love the smell.

Tom: Hmm, I _____ _____.

Listen & Talk 1 B

Clare: Do you think we can _____ _____ with lions, Todd?

Todd: No, Clare. I _____ _____ _____.

Clare: Well, I _____ a video clip about _____ _____ two men _____ a lion.

Todd: Really? I'm _____ _____ the story. Can you tell me more?

Clare: The two men _____ a baby lion and _____ her _____ into the _____. When the men and the lion met _____ _____ _____, she remembered them.

Todd: Wow, that's so _____.

Listen & Talk 2 A-1

Dylan: _____ _____ this picture, Mina. We got a new _____ yesterday. He's only _____ _____ old.

Mina: Oh, Dylan, he's _____ _____!

Dylan: Yeah. He's _____ _____ _____ my hand now, but he'll get _____ _____ in a _____ _____.

Mina: Wow, puppies _____ very quickly.

Listen & Talk 2 A-2

Kelly: George, that red house _____ _____ is my _____ house.

George: Wow, the tree _____ the house is _____ _____.

Kelly: Actually, that tree is _____ _____ _____ _____, thirteen years old.

George: _____ do you _____ that, Kelly?

Kelly: My grandfather _____ the tree in 2004 when I _____ _____.

Kelly: George, 저기에 있는 빨간 집이 우리 할아버지와 할머니 댁이야.

George: 와, 집 옆에 있는 나무가 굉장히 크네.

Kelly: 사실, 저 나무의 나이는 나랑 같아서 수령이 13년 되었어.

George: 그걸 어떻게 알아, Kelly?

Kelly: 할아버지께서 내가 태어난 해인 2004년에 그 나무를 심으셨거든.

Listen & Talk 2 B

Toby: Hi, I'm Toby. I'm _____ to _____ _____ _____ about the blue whale. It's _____ _____ sea animal in the world. _____ _____ is it? Well, it's about 30m long. That means it's _____ _____ a basketball court. _____ _____ _____ is that its tongue is _____ _____ _____ an elephant! Surprising, _____ _____?

Toby: 안녕하세요, 저는 Toby입니다. 저는 흰긴수염고래에 대해서 발표를 하려고 해요. 그 고래는 세상에서 가장 큰 바다 동물이에요. 얼마나 크냐고요? 음, 길이가 30미터 정도 돼요. 그 말은 그 고래가 농구 경기장보다 길다는 뜻이에요. 또 다른 흥미로운 점은 그 고래의 혀가 코끼리만큼 무겁다는 거예요! 놀랍죠, 그렇지 않나요?

Communication

Emily: Hello, Dr. Watson. Can you _____ _____ about your study?

Dr. Watson: I study animals that lived _____ _____ _____ _____.

Emily: Oh, I'm _____ _____ those animals. Were there _____ interesting ones?

Dr. Watson: Yes, there were _____. This is the _____ kangaroo. It lived in Australia. It was _____ _____ _____ three men and it _____ _____ well.

Emily: That's _____!

Emily: 안녕하세요, Watson 박사님. 박사님의 연구에 대해 이야기해 주시겠어요?

Dr Watson: 전 수백만 년 전에 살았던 동물들을 연구합니다.

Emily: 오, 전 그 동물들이 궁금해요. 흥미로운 동물들이 있었나요?

Dr Watson: 네, 많이 있었죠. 이 동물은 '자이언트 캥거루'입니다. 호주에서 살았어요. 사람 세 명만큼 무거웠고, 잘 뛰지 못했어요.

Emily: 그거 정말 놀랍군요!

※ 다음 우리말에 맞도록 대화를 영어로 쓰시오.

 해석

Listen & Talk 1 A-1

Ryan: _____

Judy: _____

Ryan: _____

_____

Judy: _____

Ryan: Judy, 너 과학 과제로 할 주제 골랐어?
Judy: 아직. 너는 어때, Ryan?
Ryan: 나는 날씨 변화가 궁금하거든. 그래서 난 그것에 관한 과제를 하려고 생각 중이야.
Judy: 주제가 흥미로운걸!

Listen & Talk 1 A-2

Jane: _____

Tom: _____

Jane: _____

Tom: _____

Jane: 이 커다란 꽃 사진을 봐.
Tom: 와, 사람보다 더 크네.
Jane: 그래. 나는 이 꽃이 정말 궁금해. 또 여기에 나와 있는데 그 꽃은 냄새가 매우 고약하지만 벌레들은 그 냄새를 좋아한대.
Tom: 흠, 이유가 궁금하다.

Listen & Talk 1 B

Clare: _____

Todd: _____

Clare: _____

Todd: _____

Clare: _____

Todd: _____

Clare: 우리가 사자와 친구가 될 수 있을 거라고 생각해, Todd?
Todd: 아니, Clare. 난 그렇게 생각하지 않아.
Clare: 음, 나 두 남자와 사자 사이의 우정에 대한 동영상을 봤어.
Todd: 정말? 그 이야기가 궁금해. 더 얘기해 줄 수 있어?
Clare: 두 남자가 아기 사자를 길러서 야생으로 돌려보냈어. 일 년 후에 그 남자들과 사자가 만났을 때, 그 사자는 그들을 기억했다는 거야.
Todd: 와, 정말 감동적이구나.

Listen & Talk 2 A-1

Dylan: _____

_____

Mina: _____

Dylan: _____

Mina: _____

Dylan: 이 사진 좀 봐, 미나야. 우리 어제 새 강아지를 데리고 왔어. 그 강아지는 2주밖에 안 됐어.
Mina: 오, Dylan, 걔 너무 조그맣다!
Dylan: 맞아. 그 애는 지금 내 손만큼 작지만, 몇 달 뒤에는 훨씬 더 커질 거야.
Mina: 와, 강아지들은 정말 빨리 크네.

Listen & Talk 2 A-2

Kelly: _____

George: _____

Kelly: _____

George: _____

Kelly: _____

Kelly: George, 저기에 있는 빨간 집이 우리 할아버지와 할머니 댁이야.

George: 와, 집 옆에 있는 나무가 굉장히 크네.

Kelly: 사실, 저 나무의 나이는 나랑 같아서 수령이 13년 되었어.

George: 그걸 어떻게 알아, Kelly?

Kelly: 할아버지께서 내가 태어난 해인 2004년에 그 나무를 심으셨거든.

Listen & Talk 2 B

Toby: _____
_____
_____
_____

Toby: 안녕하세요, 저는 Toby입니다. 저는 흰긴수염고래에 대해서 발표를 하려고 해요. 그 고래는 세상에서 가장 큰 바다 동물이에요. 얼마나 크냐고요? 음, 길이가 30미터 정도 돼요. 그 말은 그 고래가 농구 경기장보다 길다는 뜻이에요. 또 다른 흥미로운 점은 그 고래의 혀가 코끼리만큼 무겁다는 거예요! 놀랍죠, 그렇지 않나요?

Communication

Emily: _____

Dr. Watson: _____

Emily: _____

Dr. Watson: _____
_____

Emily: _____

Emily: 안녕하세요, Watson 박사님. 박사님의 연구에 대해 이야기해 주시겠어요?

Dr Watson: 전 수백만 년 전에 살았던 동물들을 연구합니다.

Emily: 오, 전 그 동물들이 궁금해요. 흥미로운 동물들이 있었나요?

Dr Watson: 네, 많이 있었죠. 이 동물은 '자이언트 캥거루'입니다. 호주에서 살았어요. 사람 세 명만큼 무거웠고, 잘 뛰지 못했어요.

Emily: 그거 정말 놀랍군요!

※ 다음 우리말과 일치하도록 빈칸에 알맞은 것을 골라 쓰시오.

Date/Time: July 8th / 2:35 p.m.

1 Notes: Today was _____ _____ day _____ Africa.

    A. in   B. first   C. my

2 I _____ lots of _____ _____ elephants.

    A. took   B. of   C. pictures

3 This morning, I _____ an elephant group _____ a small water _____.

    A. by   B. found   C. hole

4 I _____ a baby elephant _____ water _____ her mother.

    A. drinking   B. saw   C. beside

5 Her eyes _____ as _____ _____ stars.

    A. as   B. were   C. bright

6 I _____ _____ a _____, Stella.

    A. her   B. name   C. gave

7 _____ noon, I _____ a group of lions _____ Stella.

    A. saw   B. around   C. approaching

8 The elephants _____ _____ Stella and made a _____ wall.

    A. thick   B. around   C. stood

9 _____ _____ them, Stella was _____.

    A. safe   B. to   C. thanks

Date/Time: July 12th / 7:20 p.m.

10 Notes: _____ sunset, I _____ a strange _____.

    A. heard   B. around   C. sound

11 I _____ the sound and _____ Stella _____ next to her mom.

    A. crying   B. followed   C. found

12 She was _____ _____ and Stella was _____.

    A. dead   B. alone   C. lying

13 _____ is dangerous _____ _____ alone in _____ a wild area.

    A. such   B. it   C. stay   D. to

14 _____, it was _____ to be dark soon.

    A. more   B. what's   C. going

15 Elephants _____ _____ _____ at night.

    A. well   B. can't   C. see

날짜/시간: 7월 8일, 오후 2시 35분

1 기록: 오늘은 내가 아프리카에 온 첫날이었다.

2 나는 코끼리 사진을 많이 찍었다.

3 오늘 아침에 나는 작은 물웅덩이 옆에 있는 한 코끼리 무리를 발견했다.

4 나는 아기 코끼리 한 마리가 엄마 옆에서 물을 마시고 있는 것을 보았다.

5 그 코끼리의 눈이 별처럼 밝았다.

6 나는 그 코끼리에게 Stella란 이름을 붙여 주었다.

7 정오 즈음에 나는 사자 한 무리가 Stella에게 다가가는 것을 보았다.

8 코끼리들은 Stella 주위에 둘러서서 두꺼운 벽을 만들었다.

9 그 코끼리들 덕분에 Stella는 안전했다.

날짜/시간: 7월 12일, 오후 7시 20분

10 기록: 해질녘에 나는 이상한 소리를 들었다.

11 나는 그 소리를 따라갔고 Stella가 자신의 엄마 옆에서 울고 있는 것을 발견했다.

12 엄마는 죽어서 누워 있었고, Stella는 혼자였다.

13 이러한 야생 지역에서 혼자 있는 것은 위험하다.

14 더욱이 곧 어두워질 것이었다.

15 코끼리들은 밤에 잘 볼 수 없다.

16 So Stella could _____ _____.

    A. attacked   B. be   C. easily

17 I _____ the elephant _____ and _____ help.

    A. for   B. shelter   C. asked   D. called

18 I decided to _____ _____ her _____ the rescue team came.

    A. until   B. by   C. stay

Date/Time: July 12th / 10:40 p.m.

19 Notes: The night was _____ and _____.

    A. quiet   B. dark

20 I _____ my eyes _____ Stella _____ my night camera.

    A. with   B. kept   C. on

21 Stella was _____ _____ _____ her mom.

    A. next   B. to   C. still

22 She was _____ her mom's _____ body _____ her nose.

    A. lifeless   B. with   C. touching

23 It was sad _____ Stella _____ close to her mom.

    A. see   B. staying   C. to

24 I hope Stella _____ _____ the night.

    A. throughout   B. safe   C. stays

Date/Time: July 13th / 6:00 a.m.

25 Notes: A _____ elephant group _____ and Stella _____ them.

    A. new   B. approached   C. appeared

26 At first, I _____ _____ they would not _____ Stella _____ their group.

    A. in   B. let   C. thought   D. that

27 _____ I was _____.

    A. wrong   B. but

28 An elephant, probably the _____ _____ allowed Stella to _____ _____ of the group.

    A. part   B. oldest   C. become   D. female

29 The _____ elephants also _____ to _____ Stella.

    A. seemed   B. other   C. welcome

30 _____, _____ of the _____ elephants _____ Stella.

    A. one   B. fed   C. female   D. unbelievably

31 She _____ Stella as _____ as Stella's mom _____.

    A. did   B. for   C. warmly   D. cared

32 This was _____ an _____ !

    A. moment   B. amazing   C. such

---

16 그래서 Stella는 쉽게 공격을 받을 수 있었다.

17 나는 코끼리 보호소에 전화를 해서 도움을 요청했다.

18 나는 구조대가 올 때까지 Stella 곁에 머물기로 결정했다.

날짜/시간: 7월 12일, 오후 10시 40분

19 기록: 밤은 어둡고 조용했다.

20 나는 야간용 카메라를 이용해서 Stella를 계속 지켜보았다.

21 Stella는 여전히 엄마 곁에 있었다.

22 Stella는 코로 엄마의 죽은 몸을 어루만지고 있었다.

23 Stella가 엄마 가까이에 머물고 있는 것을 보는 것은 슬픈 일이었다.

24 나는 Stella가 밤새도록 안전하게 있기를 바란다.

날짜/시간: 7월 13일, 오전 6시

25 기록: 새로운 코끼리 무리가 나타났고, Stella는 그 무리에 다가갔다.

26 처음에 나는 그 코끼리들이 Stella를 자신의 무리로 받아들이지 않을 것이라고 생각했다.

27 그러나 내 생각이 틀렸다.

28 아마도 가장 나이가 많은 암컷인 듯한 코끼리 한 마리가 Stella가 그 무리의 일원이 되도록 허락했다.

29 다른 코끼리들도 Stella를 반기는 것처럼 보였다.

30 믿을 수 없게도, 암컷 코끼리 중의 한 마리가 Stella에게 젖을 먹였다.

31 그 코끼리는 Stella의 엄마만큼 따뜻하게 Stella를 보살폈다.

32 이것은 너무나 놀라운 순간이었다.

※ 다음 우리말과 일치하도록 빈칸에 알맞은 말을 쓰시오.

Date/Time: July 8th / 2:35 p.m.

1 Notes: Today _____ _____ _____ day _____ Africa.

2 I _____ _____ of _____ _____ elephants.

3 This morning, I _____ an elephant group _____ a small _____ _____.

4 I _____ a baby elephant _____ water _____ her mother.

5 Her eyes _____ _____ _____ _____ stars.

6 I _____ _____ _____ _____, Stella.

7 Around noon, I _____ a group of lions _____ Stella.

8 The elephants _____ _____ Stella and _____ _____ _____ _____.

9 _____ _____ _____, Stella was _____.

Date/Time: July 12th / 7:20 p.m.

10 Notes: _____ _____, I _____ a strange sound.

11 I _____ the sound and _____ Stella _____ _____ _____ her mom.

12 She was _____ _____ and Stella was _____.

13 _____ is dangerous _____ alone _____ _____ _____.

14 _____ _____, _____ was going to _____ soon.

15 Elephants can't _____ _____ _____ _____.

16 So Stella could _____ _____ _____.

17 I called _____ and _____ help.

18 I decided _____ _____ by her _____ the rescue team came.

Date/Time: July 12th / 10:40 p.m.

19 Notes: The night _____ _____ and _____.

20 I _____ my eyes _____ Stella _____ my night camera.

21 Stella was _____ _____ _____ her mom.

22 She _____ _____ her mom's lifeless body _____ her nose.

23 _____ was sad _____ _____ Stella _____ _____ _____ her mom.

24 I hope Stella _____ _____ _____ the night.

Date/Time: July 13th / 6:00 a.m.

25 Notes: A new elephant group _____ and Stella _____ them.

26 At first, I _____ _____ they would not _____ Stella _____ their group.

27 But I _____ _____.

28 An elephant, probably _____ _____ _____ allowed Stella _____ _____ _____ the group.

29 _____ also _____ to welcome Stella.

30 _____, one of the female _____ _____ Stella.

31 She _____ _____ Stella _____ _____ _____ Stella's mom _____.

32 This was _____!

16 그래서 Stella는 쉽게 공격을 받을 수 있었다.

17 나는 코끼리 보호소에 전화를 해서 도움을 요청했다.

18 나는 구조대가 올 때까지 Stella 곁에 머물기로 결정했다.

날짜/시간: 7월 12일, 오후 10시 40분

19 기록: 밤은 어둡고 조용했다.

20 나는 야간용 카메라를 이용해서 Stella를 계속 지켜보았다.

21 Stella는 여전히 엄마 곁에 있었다.

22 Stella는 코로 엄마의 죽은 몸을 어루만지고 있었다.

23 Stella가 엄마 가까이에 머물고 있는 것을 보는 것은 슬픈 일이었다.

24 나는 Stella가 밤새도록 안전하게 있기를 바란다.

날짜/시간: 7월 13일, 오전 6시

25 기록: 새로운 코끼리 무리가 나타났고, Stella는 그 무리에 다가갔다.

26 처음에 나는 그 코끼리들이 Stella를 자신의 무리로 받아들이지 않을 것이라고 생각했다.

27 그러나 내 생각이 틀렸다.

28 아마도 가장 나이가 많은 암컷인 듯한 코끼리 한 마리가 Stella가 그 무리의 일원이 되도록 허락했다.

29 다른 코끼리들도 Stella를 반기는 것처럼 보였다.

30 믿을 수 없게도, 암컷 코끼리 중의 한 마리가 Stella에게 젖을 먹였다.

31 그 코끼리는 Stella의 엄마만큼 따뜻하게 Stella를 보살폈다.

32 이것은 너무나 놀라운 순간이었다.

※ 다음 문장을 우리말로 쓰시오.

Date / Time: July 8th / 2:35 p.m.

1 Notes: Today was my first day in Africa.

➡ _____

2 I took lots of pictures of elephants.

➡ _____

3 This morning, I found an elephant group by a small water hole.

➡ _____

4 I saw a baby elephant drinking water beside her mother.

➡ _____

5 Her eyes were as bright as stars.

➡ _____

6 I gave her a name, Stella.

➡ _____

7 Around noon, I saw a group of lions approaching Stella.

➡ _____

8 The elephants stood around Stella and made a thick wall.

➡ _____

9 Thanks to them, Stella was safe.

➡ _____

Date / Time: July 12th / 7:20 p.m.

10 Notes: Around sunset, I heard a strange sound.

➡ _____

11 I followed the sound and found Stella crying next to her mom.

➡ _____

12 She was lying dead and Stella was alone.

➡ _____

13 It is dangerous to stay alone in such a wild area.

➡ _____

14 What's more, it was going to be dark soon.

➡ _____

15 Elephants can't see well at night.

➡ _____

16 So Stella could easily be attacked.

➡ _____

17 I called the elephant shelter and asked for help.

➡ _____

18 I decided to stay by her until the rescue team came.

➡ _____

Date / Time: July 12th / 10:40 p.m.

19 Notes: The night was dark and quiet.

➡ _____

20 I kept my eyes on Stella with my night camera.

➡ _____

21 Stella was still next to her mom.

➡ _____

22 She was touching her mom's lifeless body with her nose.

➡ _____

23 It was sad to see Stella staying close to her mom.

➡ _____

24 I hope Stella stays safe throughout the night.

➡ _____

Date / Time: July 13th / 6:00 a.m.

25 Notes: A new elephant group appeared and Stella approached them.

➡ _____

26 At first, I thought that they would not let Stella in their group.

➡ _____

27 But I was wrong.

➡ _____

28 An elephant, probably the oldest female allowed Stella to become part of the group.

➡ _____

29 The other elephants also seemed to welcome Stella.

➡ _____

30 Unbelievably, one of the female elephants fed Stella.

➡ _____

31 She cared for Stella as warmly as Stella's mom did.

➡ _____

32 This was such an amazing moment!

➡ _____

※ 다음 괄호 안의 단어들을 우리말에 맞도록 바르게 배열하시오.

Date / Time: July 8th / 2:35 p.m.

1 (Notes: / was / today / first / my / in / Africa. / day)
➡ _____

2 (took / I / of / lots / pictures / elephants. / of)
➡ _____

3 (morning, / this / found / I / elephant / an / by / group / a / water / hole. / small)
➡ _____

4 (saw / I / baby / a / drinking / elephant / beside / water / mother. / her)
➡ _____

5 (eyes / her / as / were / bright / stars. / as)
➡ _____

6 (gave / I / a / her / Stella. / name.)
➡ _____

7 (noon, / around / saw / I / group / a / lions / of / Stella. / approaching)
➡ _____

8 (elephants / the / around / stood / Stella / and / a / made / wall. / thick)
➡ _____

9 (to / thanks / them, / was / safe. / Stella)
➡ _____

Date / Time: July 12th / 7:20 p.m.

10 (Notes: / sunset, / around / heard / I / sound. / strange / a)
➡ _____

11 (followed / I / sound / the / and / Stella / found / next / crying / to / mom. / her)
➡ _____

12 (was / she / dead / lying / and / alone. / was / Stella)
➡ _____

13 (is / it / dangerous / stay / to / alone / such / in / area. / wild / a)
➡ _____

14 (more, / what's / was / it / to / going / be / soon. / dark)
➡ _____

15 (can't / elephants / well / see / night. / at)
➡ _____

날짜/시간: 7월 8일, 오후 2시 35분

1 기록: 오늘은 내가 아프리카에 온 첫날이었다.

2 나는 코끼리 사진을 많이 찍었다.

3 오늘 아침에 나는 작은 물웅덩이 옆에 있는 한 코끼리 무리를 발견했다.

4 나는 아기 코끼리 한 마리가 엄마 옆에서 물을 마시고 있는 것을 보았다.

5 그 코끼리의 눈이 별처럼 밝았다.

6 나는 그 코끼리에게 Stella란 이름을 붙여 주었다.

7 정오 즈음에 나는 사자 한 무리가 Stella에게 다가가는 것을 보았다.

8 코끼리들은 Stella 주위에 둘러서서 두꺼운 벽을 만들었다.

9 그 코끼리들 덕분에 Stella는 안전했다.

날짜/시간: 7월 12일, 오후 7시 20분

10 기록: 해질녘에 나는 이상한 소리를 들었다.

11 나는 그 소리를 따라갔고 Stella가 자신의 엄마 옆에서 울고 있는 것을 발견했다.

12 엄마는 죽어서 누워 있었고, Stella는 혼자였다.

13 이러한 야생 지역에서 혼자 있는 것은 위험하다.

14 더욱이 곧 어두워질 것이었다.

15 코끼리들은 밤에 잘 볼 수 없다.

16 (Stella / so / easily / could / attacked. / be)
➡ _____

17 (called / I / elephant / the / and / shelter / for / help. / asked)
➡ _____

18 (decided / I / stay / to / her / by / the / until / team / came. / rescue)
➡ _____

Date / Time: July 12th / 10:40 p.m.

19 (Notes: / night / the / dark / was / quiet. / and)
➡ _____

20 (kept / I / eyes / my / Stella / on / my / with / camera. / night)
➡ _____

21 (was / Stella / next / still / her / mom. / to)
➡ _____

22 (was / she / her / touching / mom's / lifeless / with / body / nose. / her)
➡ _____

23 (was / it / to / sad / Stella / see / close / staying / to / mom. / her)
➡ _____

24 (hope / I / stays / Stella / safe / the / night. / throughout)
➡ _____

Date / Time: July 13th / 6:00 a.m.

25 (Notes: / new / a / elephant / appeared / group / Stella / and / them. / approached)
➡ _____

26 (first, / at / thought / I / that / would / they / not / Stella / let / their / group. / in)
➡ _____

27 (I / but / wrong. / was)
➡ _____

28 (elephant, / an / the / probably / oldest / the / female / Stella / allowed / to / part / become / the / group. / of)
➡ _____

29 (other / the / elephants / seemed / also / to / Stella. / welcome)
➡ _____

30 (unbelievably, / of / one / female / the / Stella. / fed / elephants)
➡ _____

31 (cared / she / for / as / Stella / warmly / as / mom / did. / Stella's)
➡ _____

32 (was / this / an / such / moment! / amazing)
➡ _____

16 그래서 Stella는 쉽게 공격을 받을 수 있었다.

17 나는 코끼리 보호소에 전화를 해서 도움을 요청했다.

18 나는 구조대가 올 때까지 Stella 곁에 머물기로 결정했다.

날짜/시간: 7월 12일, 오후 10시 40분

19 기록: 밤은 어둡고 조용했다.

20 나는 야간용 카메라를 이용해서 Stella를 계속 지켜보았다.

21 Stella는 여전히 엄마 곁에 있었다.

22 Stella는 코로 엄마의 죽은 몸을 어루만지고 있었다.

23 Stella가 엄마 가까이에 머물고 있는 것을 보는 것은 슬픈 일이었다.

24 나는 Stella가 밤새도록 안전하게 있기를 바란다.

날짜/시간: 7월 13일, 오전 6시

25 기록: 새로운 코끼리 무리가 나타났고, Stella는 그 무리에 다가갔다.

26 처음에 나는 그 코끼리들이 Stella를 자신의 무리로 받아들이지 않을 것이라고 생각했다.

27 그러나 내 생각이 틀렸다.

28 아마도 가장 나이가 많은 암컷인 듯한 코끼리 한 마리가 Stella가 그 무리의 일원이 되도록 허락했다.

29 다른 코끼리들도 Stella를 반기는 것처럼 보였다.

30 믿을 수 없게도, 암컷 코끼리 중의 한 마리가 Stella에게 젖을 먹였다.

31 그 코끼리는 Stella의 엄마만큼 따뜻하게 Stella를 보살폈다.

32 이것은 너무나 놀라운 순간이었다.

※ 다음 우리말을 영어로 쓰시오.

날짜/시간: 7월 8일, 오후 2시 35분

1 기록: 오늘은 내가 아프리카에 온 첫날이었다.

➡ _____

2 나는 코끼리 사진을 많이 찍었다.

➡ _____

3 오늘 아침에 나는 작은 물웅덩이 옆에 있는 한 코끼리 무리를 발견했다.

➡ _____

4 나는 아기 코끼리 한 마리가 엄마 옆에서 물을 마시고 있는 것을 보았다.

➡ _____

5 그 코끼리의 눈이 별처럼 밝았다.

➡ _____

6 나는 그 코끼리에게 Stella란 이름을 붙여 주었다.

➡ _____

7 정오 즈음에 나는 사자 한 무리가 Stella에게 다가가는 것을 보았다.

➡ _____

8 코끼리들은 Stella 주위에 둘러서서 두꺼운 벽을 만들었다.

➡ _____

9 그 코끼리들 덕분에 Stella는 안전했다.

➡ _____

날짜/시간: 7월 12일, 오후 7시 20분

10 기록: 해질녘에 나는 이상한 소리를 들었다.

➡ _____

11 나는 그 소리를 따라갔고 Stella가 자신의 엄마 옆에서 울고 있는 것을 발견했다.

➡ _____

12 엄마는 죽어서 누워 있었고, Stella는 혼자였다.

➡ _____

13 이러한 야생 지역에서 혼자 있는 것은 위험하다.

➡ _____

14 더욱이 곧 어두워질 것이었다.

➡ _____

15 코끼리들은 밤에 잘 볼 수 없다.

➡ _____

16 그래서 Stella는 쉽게 공격을 받을 수 있었다.

➡ _____

17 나는 코끼리 보호소에 전화를 해서 도움을 요청했다.

➡ _____

18 나는 구조대가 올 때까지 Stella 곁에 머물기로 결정했다.

➡ _____

날짜/시간: 7월 12일, 오후 10시 40분

19 기록: 밤은 어둡고 조용했다.

➡ _____

20 나는 야간용 카메라를 이용해서 Stella를 계속 지켜보았다.

➡ _____

21 Stella는 여전히 엄마 곁에 있었다.

➡ _____

22 Stella는 코로 엄마의 죽은 몸을 어루만지고 있었다.

➡ _____

23 Stella가 엄마 가까이에 머물고 있는 것을 보는 것은 슬픈 일이었다.

➡ _____

24 나는 Stella가 밤새도록 안전하게 있기를 바란다.

➡ _____

날짜/시간: 7월 13일, 오전 6시

25 기록: 새로운 코끼리 무리가 나타났고, Stella는 그 무리에 다가갔다.

➡ _____

26 처음에 나는 그 코끼리들이 Stella를 자신의 무리로 받아들이지 않을 것이라고 생각했다.

➡ _____

27 그러나 내 생각이 틀렸다.

➡ _____

28 아마도 가장 나이가 많은 암컷인 듯한 코끼리 한 마리가 Stella가 그 무리의 일원이 되도록 허락했다.

➡ _____

29 다른 코끼리들도 Stella를 반기는 것처럼 보였다.

➡ _____

30 믿을 수 없게도, 암컷 코끼리 중의 한 마리가 Stella에게 젖을 먹였다.

➡ _____

31 그 코끼리는 Stella의 엄마만큼 따뜻하게 Stella를 보살폈다.

➡ _____

32 이것은 너무나 놀라운 순간이었다.

➡ _____

※ 다음 우리말과 일치하도록 빈칸에 알맞은 말을 쓰시오.

Read and Think

1. Some lions _____ _____ _____ Stella.

2. The elephant group made a _____ wall _____ _____ her.

3. Stella _____ _____ _____ _____ her dead mother.

4. I _____ her _____ _____ .

5. The _____ _____ elephant of a new group _____ Stella _____ _____ _____ _____ them.

1. 사자 몇 마리가 Stella를 공격하려고 했다.
2. 코끼리 무리는 Stella를 보호하기 위해 두꺼운 벽을 만들었다.
3. Stella는 그녀의 죽은 엄마 옆에서 울고 있었다.
4. 나는 밤새 그녀를 지켜보았다.
5. 새로운 무리의 가장 나이 많은 암컷 코끼리는 Stella를 그들의 일원이 되도록 허락했다.

Think & Write C

1. _____ _____

2. Date: _____ _____ , 2019

3. Write about _____ _____ _____ :

4. Today, I _____ a plant. It _____ _____ a pitcher plant.

5. It is _____ green and red. It _____ _____ a pitcher.

6. _____ for _____ _____ , it is _____ 15cm long. It is _____ _____ _____ my hand.

7. _____ is interesting _____ the plant _____ _____ and eats them.

1. 식물 일기
2. 날짜: 6월 15일, 2019년
3. 네가 본 것을 써 봐:
4. 오늘, 나는 식물 하나를 봤다. 그것은 벌레잡이 식물이라고 불린다.
5. 그것은 밝은 녹색에 붉은색이다. 그것은 항아리처럼 생겼다.
6. 크기에 대해 말하자면, 그것은 대략 15cm이다. 그것은 내 손만큼 길다.
7. 그 식물이 벌레를 끌어들이고 그것들을 먹는 것은 흥미롭다.

Wrap Up 1

1. Minho: Look! _____ that a _____ _____ ?

2. Sue: _____ , no. It's a _____ _____ .

3. Minho: Oh, really? I'm _____ _____ the difference _____ them.

4. Sue: _____ _____ the tail _____ . A sea dragon has a _____ _____ , but a sea horse _____ _____ .

5. Minho: Oh, I can _____ _____ _____ now!

1. Minho: 봐! 저거 해마 아니야?
2. Sue: 사실은 아니야. 그건 해룡이야.
3. Minho: 아, 정말? 난 그 둘의 차이점이 궁금해.
4. Sue: 꼬리를 주의해서 봐. 해룡은 꼬리가 곧지만, 해마는 그렇지 않아.
5. Minho: 오, 나 이제 구별할 수 있겠다!

※ 다음 우리말을 영어로 쓰시오.

Read and Think

1. 사자 몇 마리가 Stella를 공격하려고 했다.
➡ _____

2. 코끼리 무리는 Stella를 보호하기 위해 두꺼운 벽을 만들었다.
➡ _____

3. Stella는 그녀의 죽은 엄마 옆에서 울고 있었다.
➡ _____

4. 나는 밤새 그녀를 지켜보았다.
➡ _____

5. 새로운 무리의 가장 나이 많은 암컷 코끼리는 Stella를 그들의 일원이 되도록 허락했다.
➡ _____

Think & Write C

1. 식물 일기
➡ _____

2. 날짜: 6월 15일, 2019년
➡ _____

3. 네가 본 것을 써 봐:
➡ _____

4. 오늘, 나는 식물 하나를 봤다. 그것은 벌레잡이 식물이라고 불린다.
➡ _____

5. 그것은 밝은 녹색에 붉은색이다. 그것은 항아리처럼 생겼다.
➡ _____

6. 크기에 대해 말하자면, 그것은 대략 15cm이다. 그것은 내 손만큼 길다.
➡ _____

7. 그 식물이 벌레를 끌어들이고 그것들을 먹는 것은 흥미롭다.
➡ _____

Wrap Up 1

1. Minho: 봐! 저거 해마 아니야?
➡ _____

2. Sue: 사실은 아니야. 그건 해룡이야.
➡ _____

3. Minho: 아, 정말? 난 그 둘의 차이점이 궁금해.
➡ _____

4. Sue: 꼬리를 주의해서 봐. 해룡은 꼬리가 곧지만, 해마는 그렇지 않아.
➡ _____

5. Minho: 오, 나 이제 구별할 수 있겠다!
➡ _____

※ 다음 영어를 우리말로 쓰시오.

01	prince	22	detail
02	classical	23	tragedy
03	melt	24	prefer
04	produce	25	wing
05	direction	26	modern
06	exhibit	27	queen
07	feather	28	rock
08	artist	29	real
09	promise	30	novelist
10	brush	31	since
11	landscape	32	myth
12	novel	33	tourist
13	despite	34	version
14	art work	35	wax
15	teen	36	canvas
16	maze	37	prefer A to B
17	production	38	loot at
18	notice	39	glance at
19	wonder	40	stay away from
20	flat	41	right away
21	seaside	42	take a look
		43	move on

※ 다음 우리말을 영어로 쓰시오.

01	녹다	
02	생산하다	
03	깃털	
04	날개	
05	방향	
06	왕비, 여왕	
07	예술가	
08	붓	
09	왕자	
10	전시하다	
11	개구리	
12	미로	
13	약속하다	
14	소설	
15	~에도 불구하고	
16	현대의	
17	납작한	
18	십 대	
19	~을 알아차리다	
20	풍경	
21	예술 작품	

22	(어떤 것의) 변형	
23	세부 사항	
24	신화	
25	생산	
26	비극	
27	더 좋아하다	
28	궁금해하다	
29	진짜의, 현실적인	
30	화폭, 캔버스	
31	관광객	
32	밀랍, 왁스	
33	록 음악	
34	소설가	
35	희극	
36	~ 때문에, ~이므로	
37	해변, 바닷가	
38	~로 이동하다, 넘어가다	
39	A를 B보다 더 좋아하다	
40	~을 힐끗 보다	
41	~을 보다	
42	~을 가까이하지 않다	
43	즉시, 바로	

※ 다음 영영풀이에 알맞은 단어를 <보기>에서 골라 쓴 후, 우리말 뜻을 쓰시오.

1 _____ : one of the light soft things that cover a bird's body: _____

2 _____ : an area that is close to the sea: _____

3 _____ : to change from a solid to a liquid by applying heat: _____

4 _____ : a very sad event, especially one involving death: _____

5 _____ : the way something or someone moves, faces, or is aimed: _____

6 _____ : to want to know more about something because it interests you:
       _____

7 _____ : an area of countryside, especially in relation to its appearance:
       _____

8 _____ : to see or become conscious of something or someone: _____

9 _____ : to put it in a position where other people can see a part of your body:
       _____

10 _____ : someone who produces art: _____

11 _____ : one of the parts of a bird's or insect's body that it uses for flying:
       _____

12 _____ : a single piece of some information of fact about something: _____

13 _____ : to show something in a public place for people to enjoy or to give them
       information: _____

14 _____ : a kind of popular music with a strong beat that is played on instruments
       that are made louder electronically: _____

15 _____ : a piece of thick cloth used by artists for painting on, usually with oil
       paints, or the painting itself: _____

16 _____ : an ancient story, especially one invented in order to explain natural or
       historical events: _____

※ 다음 우리말과 일치하도록 빈칸에 알맞은 말을 쓰시오.

Listen & Talk 1 A-1

W: Brian, is your band _____ _____ _____ at the Teen Music Festival?

M: Yes, we're _____ _____ _____ _____.

W: _____ _____ _____ _____ are you going to play this year?

M: Rock music. We'll _____ _____ from the _____.

Listen & Talk 1 A-2

W: Can you help me? I don't know _____ _____ _____ _____.

M: _____ _____ _____ _____ were you _____?

W: This _____ _____.

M: _____ you _____ lines, a _____ brush is _____. _____ this one.

W: Okay, thank you.

Listen & Talk 1 B

W: (ringing) Hello, Steve.

M: Hi, Anna. We're _____ at the arts festival tomorrow at 1:30, _____?

W: Right. What kind of _____ _____ _____ _____ _____ _____ _____?

M: I _____ _____ watch the hip-hop dance _____ first.

W: _____ good. It's at 2 p.m. at the gym, _____?

M: Yeah, and how _____ _____ _____ _____, Romeo and Juliet, at 4 p.m.?

W: Oh, _____ _____ at the Main Hall _____ the gym? Sure!

Listen & Talk 2 A-1

M: What _____ you _____, Jina?

W: The novel, Life of Pi. It's _____ _____ of a boy and a tiger.

M: It's a great book. I've _____ the movie _____ _____, _____. I _____ the movie _____ the novel.

W: _____ do you _____ it _____?

M: The _____ are very beautiful. And the tiger _____ so _____.

W: Brian, 너희 밴드는 '십 대 음악 축제'에서 연주할 거야?
M: 응, 우리는 거의 매일 연습하고 있어.
W: 너희는 올해 어떤 종류의 음악을 연주하려고 해?
M: 록 음악. 우리는 90년대 곡들을 연주할 거야.

W: 나 좀 도와줄래? 나는 선을 깔끔하게 그리는 방법을 모르겠어.
M: 어떤 종류의 붓을 사용하고 있었니?
W: 이 둥근 붓이야.
M: 선을 그릴 때는 납작한 붓이 더 나아. 이것을 써 봐.
W: 알았어, 고마워.

W: (전화벨 소리) 안녕, Steve.
M: 안녕, Anna. 우리 내일 1시 30분에 예술 축제에서 만나는 거 맞지?
W: 맞아. 먼저 어떤 종류의 공연을 보고 싶어?
M: 난 힙합 댄스 공연을 먼저 보고 싶어.
W: 좋은 생각이야. 체육관에서 오후 2시에 하는 거 맞지?
M: 응, 그리고 오후 4시에 '로미오와 줄리엣' 연극을 보는 건 어때?
W: 아, 체육관 근처 대강당에서 하는 연극 말이지? 좋아!

M: 지나야, 너 무엇을 읽고 있니?
W: '파이 이야기'라는 소설이야. 한 소년과 호랑이에 대한 이야기이지.
M: 훌륭한 책이야. 나는 그것을 영화로도 봤어. 나는 소설보다는 영화가 더 좋아.
W: 왜 영화가 더 좋은데?
M: 장면이 매우 아름다워. 그리고 호랑이가 매우 진짜같이 보이거든.

Listen & Talk 2 A-2

W: _____ you _____ to Jane's new song, *Girl Friend*?

M: Yeah, it's really _____. The guitar _____ is _____.

W: There is also a _____ _____ of the song on the album.

M: I've _____ _____ it, but _____ _____ _____ _____ _____ to the dance version. It _____ her voice _____.

W: 너는 Jane의 새 노래인 '여자 친구'를 들어 봤니?

M: 응, 정말 멋져. 기타 부분이 굉장하지.

W: 앨범에는 그 노래의 댄스 버전도 있어.

M: 나는 그것을 들었는데 댄스 버전보다는 기타 버전이 더 좋아. 그 버전이 그녀의 목소리와 더 잘 어울리거든.

Listen & Talk 2 B

W: I saw an _____ _____ in an art book. _____ _____ this.

M: Wow, it _____ _____ da Vinci's *Mona Lisa*.

W: Actually, it's *Mona Lisa* by Fernando Botero. _____ _____ _____ _____?

M: I _____ da Vinci's _____ Botero's. Da Vinci's *Mona Lisa* has an interesting _____. _____ _____ _____?

W: Well, I _____ Botero's _____ da Vinci's. His *Mona Lisa* is cute, and it _____ _____.

W: 나 미술 책에서 흥미로운 그림을 봤어. 이것 봐.

M: 와, 그것은 다빈치의 '모나리자'처럼 보이는데.

W: 사실 이 그림은 페르난도 보테로의 '모나리자'야. 넌 어느 것이 더 마음에 드니?

M: 나는 보테로의 그림보다 다빈치의 모나리자가 더 좋아. 다빈치의 '모나리자'에는 흥미로운 미소가 있어. 너는 어때?

W: 음, 나는 다빈치의 모나리자보다는 보테로의 모나리자가 더 좋아. 그의 '모나리자'는 귀엽고 현대적으로 보여.

Communication

M: Hi, we _____ _____ a school festival, _____ we want to _____ _____ students' favorite types of performances. _____ I _____ you _____ _____ _____ _____?

W: Sure.

M: _____ _____ _____ _____ _____ _____ do you like best?

W: I like music _____ _____.

M: Okay. Then, which _____ you _____, rock or hip-hop?

W: I _____ _____ _____ _____ _____.

M: Who's your _____ _____?

W: My _____ _____ is TJ.

M: Great. _____ you _____ your answers.

M: 안녕하세요. 저희는 학교 축제를 계획 중이고, 그래서 학생들이 어떤 종류의 공연을 좋아하는지 알고 싶습니다. 몇 가지 질문을 해도 될까요?

W: 물론이죠.

M: 어떤 종류의 공연을 가장 좋아하나요?

W: 저는 음악 공연을 가장 좋아해요.

M: 알겠습니다. 그러면 록과 힙합 중 어떤 것을 더 좋아하나요?

W: 저는 힙합보다 록을 더 좋아해요.

M: 가장 좋아하는 뮤지션은 누구인가요?

W: 제가 가장 좋아하는 뮤지션은 TJ입니다.

M: 좋습니다. 답변해 주셔서 감사합니다.

Wrap Up 1

M: _____ you _____ me? I want _____ _____ a guitar.

W: There are _____ _____ of guitars. _____ _____ _____ _____ do you want _____ _____?

M: I _____ _____ play pop songs.

W: Then you _____ _____ a classical guitar.

M: Okay, I will _____ a _____ _____.

M: 저 좀 도와주시겠어요? 저는 기타를 하나 사고 싶어요.

W: 다양한 종류의 기타가 있어요. 어떤 종류의 음악을 연주하고 싶으신가요?

M: 저는 팝송을 연주하려고 해요.

W: 그럼 클래식 기타를 사셔야 해요.

M: 알겠습니다, 클래식 기타로 살게요.

Step2

※ 다음 우리말에 맞도록 대화를 영어로 쓰시오.

Listen & Talk 1 A-1

W: _____

M: _____

W: _____

M: _____

W: Brian, 너희 밴드는 '십 대 음악 축제'에서 연주할 거야?
M: 응, 우리는 거의 매일 연습하고 있어.
W: 너희는 올해 어떤 종류의 음악을 연주하려고 해?
M: 록 음악. 우리는 90년대 곡들을 연주할 거야.

Listen & Talk 1 A-2

W: _____

M: _____

W: _____

M: _____

W: _____

W: 나 좀 도와줄래? 나는 선을 깔끔하게 그리는 방법을 모르겠어.
M: 어떤 종류의 붓을 사용하고 있었니?
W: 이 둥근 붓이야.
M: 선을 그릴 때는 납작한 붓이 더 나아. 이것을 써 봐.
W: 알았어, 고마워.

Listen & Talk 1 B

W: _____

M: _____

W: _____

M: _____

W: _____

M: _____

W: _____

W: (전화벨 소리) 안녕, Steve.
M: 안녕, Anna. 우리 내일 1시 30분에 예술 축제에서 만나는 거 맞지?
W: 맞아. 먼저 어떤 종류의 공연을 보고 싶어?
M: 난 힙합 댄스 공연을 먼저 보고 싶어.
W: 좋은 생각이야. 체육관에서 오후 2시에 하는 거 맞지?
M: 응, 그리고 오후 4시에 '로미오와 줄리엣' 연극을 보는 건 어때?
W: 아, 체육관 근처 대강당에서 하는 연극 말이지? 좋아!

Listen & Talk 2 A-1

M: _____

W: _____

M: _____

W: _____

M: _____

M: 지나야, 너 무엇을 읽고 있니?
W: '파이 이야기'라는 소설이야. 한 소년과 호랑이에 대한 이야기이지.
M: 훌륭한 책이야. 나는 그것을 영화로도 봤어. 나는 소설보다는 영화가 더 좋아.
W: 왜 영화가 더 좋은데?
M: 장면이 매우 아름다워. 그리고 호랑이가 매우 진짜같이 보이거든.

Listen & Talk 2 A-2

W: _____

M: _____

W: _____

M: _____
_____

W: 너는 Jane의 새 노래인 '여자 친구'를 들어 봤니?

M: 응, 정말 멋져. 기타 부분이 굉장하지.

W: 앨범에는 그 노래의 댄스 버전도 있어.

M: 나는 그것을 들었는데 댄스 버전보다는 기타 버전이 더 좋아. 그 버전이 그녀의 목소리와 더 잘 어울리거든.

Listen & Talk 2 B

W: _____

M: _____

W: _____

M: _____
_____

W: _____

W: 나 미술 책에서 흥미로운 그림을 봤어. 이것 봐.

M: 와, 그것은 다빈치의 '모나리자'처럼 보이는데.

W: 사실 이 그림은 페르난도 보테로의 '모나리자'야. 넌 어느 것이 더 마음에 드니?

M: 나는 보테로의 그림보다 다빈치의 모나리자가 더 좋아. 다빈치의 '모나리자'에는 흥미로운 미소가 있어. 너는 어때?

W: 음, 나는 다빈치의 모나리자보다는 보테로의 모나리자가 더 좋아. 그의 '모나리자'는 귀엽고 현대적으로 보여.

Communication

M: _____
_____

W: _____

M: _____

W: _____

M: _____

W: _____

M: _____

W: _____

M: _____

M: 안녕하세요, 저희는 학교 축제를 계획 중이고, 그래서 학생들이 어떤 종류의 공연을 좋아하는지 알고 싶습니다. 몇 가지 질문을 해도 될까요?

W: 물론이죠.

M: 어떤 종류의 공연을 가장 좋아하나요?

W: 저는 음악 공연을 가장 좋아해요.

M: 알겠습니다. 그러면 록과 힙합 중 어떤 것을 더 좋아하나요?

W: 저는 힙합보다 록을 더 좋아해요.

M: 가장 좋아하는 뮤지션은 누구인가요?

W: 제가 가장 좋아하는 뮤지션은 TJ입니다.

M: 좋습니다. 답변해 주셔서 감사합니다.

Wrap Up 1

M: _____

W: _____

M: _____

W: _____

M: _____

M: 저 좀 도와주시겠어요? 저는 기타를 하나 사고 싶어요.

W: 다양한 종류의 기타가 있어요. 어떤 종류의 음악을 연주하고 싶으신가요?

M: 저는 팝송을 연주하려고 해요.

W: 그럼 클래식 기타를 사셔야 해요.

M: 알겠습니다, 클래식 기타로 살게요.

※ 다음 우리말과 일치하도록 빈칸에 알맞은 것을 골라 쓰시오.

1 _____ _____ the World Art Museum _____ .
    A. tour   B. to   C. welcome

2 _____ you go to an art museum, how _____ time do you spend _____ at _____ painting?
    A. much   B. looking   C. when   D. each

3 Many visitors _____ at one painting _____ only a _____ seconds before they move _____ .
    A. few   B. on   C. for   D. glance

4 But you _____ _____ the important details of paintings _____ it is hard to _____ them right away.
    A. since   B. notice   C. miss   D. might

5 Today, we'll look _____ two paintings _____ and I'll _____ you _____ interesting details.
    A. closely   B. see   C. at   D. help

6 _____ _____ this painting _____ .
    A. at   B. look   C. first

7 The _____ landscape is so _____ and beautiful, _____ ?
    A. isn't   B. peaceful   C. seaside   D. it

8 The _____ of this painting _____ *Landscape* _____ *the Fall of Icarus*.
    A. is   B. title   C. with

9 So, can you see _____ _____ _____ ?
    A. Icarus   B. where   C. is

10 Do you see two legs _____ are _____ _____ of the water _____ the ship?
    A. out   B. near   C. sticking   D. that

11 This is Icarus _____ the _____ in Greece.
    A. myth   B. famous   C. in

12 In the myth, Icarus' father made _____ for him with _____ and wax and told him to _____ _____ from the sun.
    A. away   B. feathers   C. wings   D. stay

13 _____ , Icarus _____ _____ .
    A. didn't   B. however   C. listen

14 He _____ too _____ the sun.
    A. close   B. flew   C. to

15 So, the wax _____ and he _____ the water.
    A. into   B. melted   C. fell

---

1 세계 미술관(the World Art Museum)에 오신 것을 환영합니다.

2 미술관에 갈 때 여러분은 각각의 그림을 보는 데 얼마나 많은 시간을 보내나요?

3 많은 방문객들은 이동하기 전에 하나의 그림을 몇 초간만 힐끗 봅니다.

4 하지만 그림의 중요한 세부 사항들을 즉시 알아채는 것은 어렵기 때문에 여러분들은 그것들을 놓칠 수 있습니다.

5 오늘 우리는 두 개의 그림을 자세히 살펴볼 것이고, 여러분이 흥미로운 세부 사항들을 볼 수 있도록 제가 도와드리겠습니다.

6 먼저 이 그림을 보세요.

7 바닷가 풍경이 매우 평화롭고 아름답죠, 그렇지 않나요?

8 이 그림의 제목은 '추락하는 이카루스가 있는 풍경'입니다.

9 그러면 이카루스가 어디에 있는지 보이나요?

10 배 근처에 물 밖으로 나와 있는 두 다리가 보이죠?

11 이것이 그리스의 유명한 신화에 나오는 이카루스입니다.

12 신화에서 이카루스의 아버지는 그를 위해 깃털과 밀랍으로 날개를 만들어 주었고 그에게 태양을 가까이 하지 말라고 말했습니다.

13 하지만 이카루스는 듣지 않았습니다.

14 그는 태양에 너무 가깝게 날았습니다.

15 그래서 밀랍이 녹았고 그는 물에 빠졌습니다.

16 Now, _____ _____ the _____ painting again.

    A. at   B. entire   C. look

17 _____ the tragedy of Icarus, people are _____ _____ with their _____ activities.

    A. on   B. despite   C. going   D. everyday

18 Does the painting _____ _____ _____ ?

    A. look   B. still   C. peaceful

19 _____ do you _____ the artist is _____ to tell us?

    A. trying   B. think   C. what

20 Now, let's _____ _____ _____ the next painting.

    A. on   B. move   C. to

21 Do you _____ the artist _____ the _____ canvas?

    A. behind   B. see   C. large

22 He is Diego Velázquez, and he _____ _____ this picture.

    A. painted   B. actually

23 _____ do you _____ _____ _____ painting?

    A. think   B. is   C. he   D. who

24 _____ a quick _____ .

    A. look   B. take

25 The young princess _____ _____ be the _____ person _____ she is in the center of the painting.

    A. to   B. main   C. seems   D. because

26 But the _____ of the _____ is *The Maids of Honour*.

    A. painting   B. title

27 Then, is the artist _____ the two women _____ the _____ ?

    A. beside   B. drawing   C. princess

28 _____ a _____ look.

    A. close   B. take

29 It will _____ _____ _____ about the painting more.

    A. wonder   B. make   C. you

30 _____ to see _____ _____ the artist is looking at.

    A. direction   B. try   C. which

31 Can you _____ the king and the queen _____ the _____ in the _____ of the painting?

    A. background   B. in   C. see   D. mirror

32 _____ do you _____ he _____ painting now?

    A. is   B. think   C. who

16 이제, 그림 전체를 다시 보세요.

17 이카루스의 비극에도 불구하고 사람들은 일상의 활동을 계속하고 있습니다.

18 그림이 여전히 평화로워 보이나요?

19 화가가 우리에게 무엇을 말하려 한다고 생각하나요?

20 이제, 다음 그림으로 넘어갑시다.

21 커다란 캔버스 뒤에 있는 화가가 보이나요?

22 그는 Diego Velázquez이고, 그가 실제로 이 그림을 그렸습니다.

23 그가 누구를 그리고 있다고 생각하나요?

24 재빨리 봅시다.

25 어린 공주가 그림의 중앙에 있기 때문에 주인공처럼 보입니다.

26 하지만 그림의 제목은 '시녀들'입니다.

27 그렇다면 화가는 공주 옆에 있는 두 여인을 그리고 있나요?

28 자세히 보세요.

29 그림에 대해 더 궁금해하게 될 겁니다.

30 화가가 바라보고 있는 방향을 보려고 노력해 보세요.

31 그림의 배경에 있는 거울 속 왕과 왕비가 보이나요?

32 이제 여러분은 그가 누구를 그리고 있다고 생각하나요?

Step2

※ 다음 우리말과 일치하도록 빈칸에 알맞은 말을 쓰시오.

1 _____ _____ the World Art Museum _____ .

2 _____ you _____ _____ an art museum, _____ _____ _____ do you _____ _____ _____ each painting?

3 Many visitors _____ _____ one painting _____ only _____ _____ seconds before they _____ _____ .

4 But you _____ _____ the important details of paintings _____ it is hard _____ _____ _____ right away.

5 Today, we'll _____ _____ two paintings _____ and I'll _____ _____ _____ interesting _____ .

6 _____ _____ this painting _____ .

7 The _____ _____ is so _____ and beautiful, _____ _____ ?

8 The _____ _____ this painting _____ *Landscape with the Fall of Icarus.*

9 So, can you see _____ _____ _____ ?

10 Do you see two legs that _____ _____ _____ _____ _____ _____ the ship?

11 This is Icarus _____ _____ in Greece.

12 In the myth, Icarus' father _____ _____ _____ _____ _____ and wax and told him _____ _____ _____ _____ the sun.

13 _____ , Icarus _____ .

14 He _____ _____ _____ to the sun.

15 So, the wax _____ and he _____ _____ the water.

1 세계 미술관(the World Art Museum)에 오신 것을 환영합니다.

2 미술관에 갈 때 여러분은 각각의 그림을 보는 데 얼마나 많은 시간을 보내나요?

3 많은 방문객들은 이동하기 전에 하나의 그림을 몇 초간만 힐끗 봅니다.

4 하지만 그림의 중요한 세부 사항들을 즉시 알아채는 것은 어렵기 때문에 여러분들은 그것들을 놓칠 수 있습니다.

5 오늘 우리는 두 개의 그림을 자세히 살펴볼 것이고, 여러분이 흥미로운 세부 사항들을 볼 수 있도록 제가 도와드리겠습니다.

6 먼저 이 그림을 보세요.

7 바닷가 풍경이 매우 평화롭고 아름답죠, 그렇지 않나요?

8 이 그림의 제목은 '추락하는 이카루스가 있는 풍경'입니다.

9 그러면 이카루스가 어디에 있는지 보이나요?

10 배 근처에 물 밖으로 나와 있는 두 다리가 보이죠?

11 이것이 그리스의 유명한 신화에 나오는 이카루스입니다.

12 신화에서 이카루스의 아버지는 그를 위해 깃털과 밀랍으로 날개를 만들어 주었고 그에게 태양을 가까이 하지 말라고 말했습니다.

13 하지만 이카루스는 듣지 않았습니다.

14 그는 태양에 너무 가깝게 날았습니다.

15 그래서 밀랍이 녹았고 그는 물에 빠졌습니다.

16 Now, _____ _____ the _____ painting again.

17 _____ the tragedy of Icarus, people are _____ _____ _____ their _____ _____.

18 Does the painting _____ _____ _____?

19 _____ _____ _____ the artist is _____ _____ tell us?

20 Now, let's _____ _____ _____ the next painting.

21 Do you _____ the artist _____ the large canvas?

22 He is Diego Velázquez, and he _____ _____ this picture.

23 _____ _____ _____ _____ _____ _____ painting?

24 _____ a _____ _____.

25 The young princess _____ _____ _____ the main person _____ she is _____ _____ _____ of the painting.

26 But the _____ of the _____ is *The Maids of Honour*.

27 Then, is the artist _____ the two women _____ the princess?

28 _____ a _____ _____.

29 It will _____ _____ _____ about the painting more.

30 _____ _____ see _____ _____ _____ _____ looking at.

31 Can you _____ the king and the queen _____ _____ in the _____ of the painting?

32 _____ _____ _____ _____ _____ _____ _____ painting now?

※ 다음 문장을 우리말로 쓰시오.

1 ▶ Welcome to the World Art Museum tour.

➡ _____

2 ▶ When you go to an art museum, how much time do you spend looking at each painting?

➡ _____

3 ▶ Many visitors glance at one painting for only a few seconds before they move on.

➡ _____

4 ▶ But you might miss the important details of paintings since it is hard to notice them right away.

➡ _____

5 ▶ Today, we'll look at two paintings closely and I'll help you see interesting details.

➡ _____

6 ▶ Look at this painting first.

➡ _____

7 ▶ The seaside landscape is so peaceful and beautiful, isn't it?

➡ _____

8 ▶ The title of this painting is *Landscape with the Fall* of Icarus.

➡ _____

9 ▶ So, can you see where Icarus is?

➡ _____

10 ▶ Do you see two legs that are sticking out of the water near the ship?

➡ _____

11 ▶ This is Icarus in the famous myth in Greece.

➡ _____

12 ▶ In the myth, Icarus' father made wings for him with feathers and wax and told him to stay away from the sun.

➡ _____

_____

13 ▶ However, Icarus didn't listen.

➡ _____

14 ▶ He flew too close to the sun.

➡ _____

15 ▶ So, the wax melted and he fell into the water.

➡ _____

16 Now, look at the entire painting again.

➡ _____

17 Despite the tragedy of Icarus, people are going on with their everyday activities.

➡ _____

18 Does the painting still look peaceful?

➡ _____

19 What do you think the artist is trying to tell us?

➡ _____

20 Now, let's move on to the next painting.

➡ _____

21 Do you see the artist behind the large canvas?

➡ _____

22 He is Diego Velázquez, and he actually painted this picture.

➡ _____

23 Who do you think he is painting?

➡ _____

24 Take a quick look.

➡ _____

25 The young princess seems to be the main person because she is in the center of the painting.

➡ _____

26 But the title of the painting is *The Maids of Honour*.

➡ _____

27 Then, is the artist drawing the two women beside the princess?

➡ _____

28 Take a close look.

➡ _____

29 It will make you wonder about the painting more.

➡ _____

30 Try to see which direction the artist is looking at.

➡ _____

31 Can you see the king and the queen in the mirror in the background of the painting?

➡ _____

32 Who do you think he is painting now?

➡ _____

Step4

※ 다음 괄호 안의 단어들을 우리말에 맞도록 바르게 배열하시오.

1 (to / World / the / Welcome / tour. / Museum / Art)
➡ _____

2 (you / when / to / go / art / an / museum, / much / how / do / time / spend / you / at / looking / painting? / each)
➡ _____

3 (visitors / many / at / glance / painting / one / only / for / few / a / seconds / before / on. / move / they)
➡ _____

4 (you / but / miss / might / important / the / of / paintings / details / it / since / is / to / hard / them / notice / away. / right)
➡ _____

5 (today, / look / we'll / two / at / closely / paintings / and / help / I'll / see / you / details. / interesting)
➡ _____

6 (at / look / first. / painting / this)
➡ _____

7 (seaside / the / is / landscape / peaceful / so / and / isn't / beautiful / it?)
➡ _____

8 (title / the / this / of / painting / is / *with* / *Landscape* / *the* / *Icarus.* / *of* / *Fall*)
➡ _____

9 (so, / you / can / see / Icarus / is? / where)
➡ _____

10 (you / do / see / legs / two / are / that / out / sticking / of / water / the / near / ship? / the)
➡ _____

11 (is / this / Icarus / in / famous / the / Greece. / in / myth)
➡ _____

12 (the / in / myth, / father / Icarus' / wings / made / him / for / feathers / with / wax / and / told / to / him / away / stay / from / sun. / the)
➡ _____

13 (Icarus / however, / listen. / didn't)
➡ _____

14 (flew / he / close / too / sun. / the / to)
➡ _____

15 (so, / wax / the / melted / and / fell / he / into / water. / the)
➡ _____

1 세계 미술관(the World Art Museum)에 오신 것을 환영합니다.

2 미술관에 갈 때 여러분은 각각의 그림을 보는 데 얼마나 많은 시간을 보내나요?

3 많은 방문객들은 이동하기 전에 하나의 그림을 몇 초간만 힐끗 봅니다.

4 하지만 그림의 중요한 세부 사항들을 즉시 알아채는 것은 어렵기 때문에 여러분들은 그것들을 놓칠 수 있습니다.

5 오늘 우리는 두 개의 그림을 자세히 살펴볼 것이고, 여러분이 흥미로운 세부 사항들을 볼 수 있도록 제가 도와드리겠습니다.

6 먼저 이 그림을 보세요.

7 바닷가 풍경이 매우 평화롭고 아름답죠. 그렇지 않나요?

8 이 그림의 제목은 '추락하는 이카루스가 있는 풍경'입니다.

9 그러면 이카루스가 어디에 있는지 보이나요?

10 배 근처에 물 밖으로 나와 있는 두 다리가 보이죠?

11 이것이 그리스의 유명한 신화에 나오는 이카루스입니다.

12 신화에서 이카루스의 아버지는 그를 위해 깃털과 밀랍으로 날개를 만들어 주었고 그에게 태양을 가까이 하지 말라고 말했습니다.

13 하지만 이카루스는 듣지 않았습니다.

14 그는 태양에 너무 가깝게 날았습니다.

15 그래서 밀랍이 녹았고 그는 물에 빠졌습니다.

16 (now, / at / look / entire / the / again. / painting)
➡ _____

17 (the / despite / tragedy / Icarus, / of / are / people / going / with / on / everyday / their / activities.)
➡ _____

18 (the / does / still / painting / peaceful? / look)
➡ _____

19 (do / what / think / you / artist / the / trying / is / us? / tell / to)
➡ _____

20 (now, / move / let's / to / on / painting. / next / the)
➡ _____

21 (you / do / see / artist / the / the / behind / canvas? / large)
➡ _____

22 (is / he / Velázquez, / Diego / and / actually / he / this / picture. / painted)
➡ _____

23 (do / who / think / you / painting? / is / he)
➡ _____

24 (a / take / look. / quick)
➡ _____

25 (young / the / seems / princess / be / to / main / the / because / person / is / she / the / in / center / the / painting. / of)
➡ _____

26 (the / but / of / title / painting / the / is / of / Maids / Honour. / The)
➡ _____

27 (then, / the / is / drawing / artist / the / women / two / princess? / the / beside)
➡ _____

28 (a / take / look. / close)
➡ _____

29 (will / it / you / make / about / wonder / the / more. / about / painting)
➡ _____

30 (to / try / which / direction / see / the / artist / at. / looking / is)
➡ _____

31 (you / can / the / see / king / the / and / queen / the / in / mirror / the / in / background / painting? / the / of)
➡ _____

32 (do / who / think / you / is / he / now? / painting)
➡ _____

16 이제, 그림 전체를 다시 보세요.

17 이카루스의 비극에도 불구하고 사람들은 일상의 활동을 계속하고 있습니다.

18 그림이 여전히 평화로워 보이나요?

19 화가가 우리에게 무엇을 말하려 한다고 생각하나요?

20 이제, 다음 그림으로 넘어갑시다.

21 커다란 캔버스 뒤에 있는 화가가 보이나요?

22 그는 Diego Velázquez이고, 그가 실제로 이 그림을 그렸습니다.

23 그가 누구를 그리고 있다고 생각하나요?

24 재빨리 봅시다.

25 어린 공주가 그림의 중앙에 있기 때문에 주인공처럼 보입니다.

26 하지만 그림의 제목은 '시녀들' 입니다.

27 그렇다면 화가는 공주 옆에 있는 두 여인을 그리고 있나요?

28 자세히 보세요.

29 그림에 대해 더 궁금해하게 될 겁니다.

30 화가가 바라보고 있는 방향을 보려고 노력해 보세요.

31 그림의 배경에 있는 거울 속 왕과 왕비가 보이나요?

32 이제 여러분은 그가 누구를 그리고 있다고 생각하나요?

※ 다음 우리말을 영어로 쓰시오.

1 세계 미술관(the World Art Museum)에 오신 것을 환영합니다.
➡ _____

2 미술관에 갈 때 여러분은 각각의 그림을 보는 데 얼마나 많은 시간을 보내나요?
➡ _____

3 많은 방문객들은 이동하기 전에 하나의 그림을 몇 초간만 힐끗 봅니다.
➡ _____

4 하지만 그림의 중요한 세부 사항들을 즉시 알아채는 것은 어렵기 때문에 여러분들은 그것들을 놓칠 수 있습니다.
➡ _____

5 오늘 우리는 두 개의 그림을 자세히 살펴볼 것이고, 여러분이 흥미로운 세부 사항들을 볼 수 있도록 제가 도와드리겠습니다.
➡ _____

6 먼저 이 그림을 보세요.
➡ _____

7 바닷가 풍경이 매우 평화롭고 아름답죠, 그렇지 않나요?
➡ _____

8 이 그림의 제목은 '추락하는 이카루스가 있는 풍경'입니다.
➡ _____

9 그러면 이카루스가 어디에 있는지 보이나요?
➡ _____

10 배 근처에 물 밖으로 나와 있는 두 다리가 보이죠?
➡ _____

11 이것이 그리스의 유명한 신화에 나오는 이카루스입니다.
➡ _____

12 신화에서 이카루스의 아버지는 그를 위해 깃털과 밀랍으로 날개를 만들어 주었고 그에게 태양을 가까이 하지 말라고 말했습니다.
➡ _____
_____

13 하지만 이카루스는 듣지 않았습니다.
➡ _____

14 그는 태양에 너무 가깝게 날았습니다.
➡ _____

15 그래서 밀랍이 녹았고 그는 물에 빠졌습니다.
➡ _____

16 이제, 그림 전체를 다시 보세요.

➡ _____

17 이카루스의 비극에도 불구하고 사람들은 일상의 활동을 계속하고 있습니다.

➡ _____

18 그림이 여전히 평화로워 보이나요?

➡ _____

19 화가가 우리에게 무엇을 말하려 한다고 생각하나요?

➡ _____

20 이제, 다음 그림으로 넘어갑시다.

➡ _____

21 커다란 캔버스 뒤에 있는 화가가 보이나요?

➡ _____

22 그는 Diego Velázquez이고, 그가 실제로 이 그림을 그렸습니다.

➡ _____

23 그가 누구를 그리고 있다고 생각하나요?

➡ _____

24 재빨리 봅시다.

➡ _____

25 어린 공주가 그림의 중앙에 있기 때문에 주인공처럼 보입니다.

➡ _____

26 하지만 그림의 제목은 '시녀들'입니다.

➡ _____

27 그렇다면 화가는 공주 옆에 있는 두 여인을 그리고 있나요?

➡ _____

28 자세히 보세요.

➡ _____

29 그림에 대해 더 궁금해하게 될 겁니다.

➡ _____

30 화가가 바라보고 있는 방향을 보려고 노력해 보세요.

➡ _____

31 그림의 배경에 있는 거울 속 왕과 왕비가 보이나요?

➡ _____

32 이제 여러분은 그가 누구를 그리고 있다고 생각하나요?

➡ _____

※ 다음 우리말과 일치하도록 빈칸에 알맞은 말을 쓰시오.

Listen & Talk

1. M: What _____ you _____, Sally?

2 W: I'm _____ *The Maze Runner*. It's about boys _____ are put _____ _____ _____.

3 M: It's a great story. I've _____ the movie of it, _____. I _____ the novel _____ the movie.

4 W: _____ do you _____ it _____?

5 M: The novel has _____ _____. But the movie didn't _____ some _____ _____ of the story.

Grammar in Real Life

1. Princess, please _____ me _____.

2. _____ are _____?

3. The princess _____ _____, "If you help me, I'll _____ _____ _____ the palace and _____ my friend."

4. Come here. I'll have people _____ _____ some _____ and _____.

5. No! _____ _____ him _____. I don't like him.

6. Don't _____, Frog. I'll _____ _____ _____ _____ her promise.

Think and Write C

1. Today, I went to the _____ _____ _____.

2. At the exhibition, I saw many _____ _____ _____ _____.

3. _____ them, I liked the piece _____ *Moon Tree*.

4. It _____ _____ _____ French artist, David Myriam.

5. _____, sand _____ _____ in this painting.

6. I like it _____ a tree in the moon _____ _____ _____.

7. Now I know that anything _____ _____ _____ make art.

8. _____ is _____!

1. M: Sally, 너는 무엇을 읽고 있니?
2. W: 나는 '미로를 달리는 사람'을 읽고 있어. 미로에 갇힌 소년들에 관한 내용이야.
3. M: 그건 대단한 이야기이지. 나는 그것을 영화로도 봤어. 나는 영화보다는 소설이 더 좋아.
4. W: 왜 소설이 더 좋은데?
5. M: 소설에는 다양한 이야기가 담겨 있어. 하지만 영화에서는 이야기의 중요한 몇 부분이 나오지 않았어.

1. 공주님, 저를 들어가게 해 주세요.
2. 그대는 누군가?
3. 공주님은 제게 "네가 날 도와준다면, 나는 너를 궁전에 들어오게 하고 내 친구가 되게 해 주겠어."라고 약속하셨어요.
4. 이쪽으로 오게. 내가 사람들을 시켜 자네에게 과자와 차를 가져다 주게 하겠네.
5. 안 돼요! 그를 들어오게 하지 마세요. 저는 그를 좋아하지 않아요.
6. 걱정 말게, 개구리. 나는 공주가 그녀의 약속을 지키게 하겠네.

1. 오늘 나는 놀라운 미술 전시회에 갔다.
2. 전시회에서, 나는 많은 흥미로운 예술 작품들을 보았다.
3. 그 중에서, 나는 Moon Tree라고 불리는 작품이 좋았다.
4. 그것은 프랑스 예술가 David Myriam에 의해 만들어졌다.
5. 흥미롭게도, 모래가 이 미술품에 사용되었다.
6. 달 속에 있는 나무 한그루가 내 마음을 고요하게 만들기 때문에 나는 그것이 좋다.
7. 이제 나는 어떠한 것이든 미술을 만들기 위해 사용될 수 있다는 사실을 안다.
8. 무엇이든 가능하다!

※ **다음 우리말을 영어로 쓰시오.**

Listen & Talk

1. M: Sally, 너는 무엇을 읽고 있니?
➡

2. W: 나는 '미로를 달리는 사람'을 읽고 있어. 미로에 갇힌 소년들에 관한 내용이야.
➡

3. M: 그건 대단한 이야기이지. 나는 그것을 영화로도 봤어. 나는 영화보다는 소설이 더 좋아.
➡

4. W: 왜 소설이 더 좋은데?
➡

5. M: 소설에는 다양한 이야기가 담겨 있어. 하지만 영화에서는 이야기의 중요한 몇 부분이 나오지 않았어.
➡

Grammar in Real Life

1. 공주님, 저를 들어가게 해 주세요.
➡

2. 그대는 누군가?
➡

3. 공주님은 제게 "네가 날 도와준다면, 나는 너를 궁전에 들어오게 하고 내 친구가 되게 해 주겠어."라고 약속하셨어요.
➡

4. 이쪽으로 오게. 내가 사람들을 시켜 자네에게 과자와 차를 가져다 주게 하겠네.
➡

5. 안 돼요! 그를 들어오게 하지 마세요. 저는 그를 좋아하지 않아요.
➡

6. 걱정 말게, 개구리. 나는 공주가 그녀의 약속을 지키게 하겠네.
➡

Think and Write C

1. 오늘 나는 놀라운 미술 전시회에 갔다.
➡

2. 전시회에서, 나는 많은 흥미로운 예술 작품들을 보았다.
➡

3. 그 중에서, 나는 Moon Tree라고 불리는 작품이 좋았다.
➡

4. 그것은 프랑스 예술가 David Myriam에 의해 만들어졌다.
➡

5. 흥미롭게도, 모래가 이 미술품에 사용되었다.
➡

6. 달 속에 있는 나무 한그루가 내 마음을 고요하게 만들기 때문에 나는 그것이 좋다.
➡

7. 이제 나는 어떠한 것이든 미술을 만들기 위해 사용될 수 있다는 사실을 안다.
➡

8. 무엇이든 가능하다!
➡

MEMO

MEMO

적중100

2학기

정답 및 해설

비상 | 김진완

중 2

적중100

영어 기출 문제집

적중 100

2학기

정답 및 해설

비상 | 김진완

중 2

Explore Your Feelings!

Lesson 5

시험대비 실력평가   p.08

01 (h)ate   02 ⑤   03 (1) alone   (2) lines

    (3) limit   (4) since   04 ⑤

05 (1) I can't stand the cold very well.

    (2) They talked about the matter.

    (3) Give me some advice, please.

    (4) was upset because she used my stuff without

      asking me first.   06 ④

01 주어진 관계는 반의어 관계를 나타낸다. hate: 싫어하다

02 ⑤번 문장에서 line은 '대사'를 뜻한다. rude: 무례한

03 alone: 혼자, line: 대사, limit: 제한, since: ~ 이후로

04 '누군가가 특정한 상황에서 해야 하는 것에 대한 의견 또는 제안'
을 가리키는 말은 advice(조언)이다.

05 stand: 참다, matter: 문제, advice: 조언, stuff: 물건

06 주어진 문장에서 stand는 '참다, 견디다'를 의미하며 이와 같은 의
미로 쓰인 것은 ④번이다. 나머지는 모두 '서다, 서 있다'를 의미한
다. arrogant: 거만한

서술형 시험대비   p.09

01 toothache

02 (1) lunch break(= lunch time)   (2) advice   (3) hurt

03 (1) on purpose   (2) gain weight   (3) focus on

    (4) In the end

04 (1) He sometimes puts people down.

    (2) She always points out my mistakes.

    (3) Set an alarm before you go to bed.

05 (1) Thank you for pointing out some mistakes in
      my report.

    (2) Here are your scripts, so practice your lines.

    (3) The reason I called was to ask about the
      plans for Saturday.

    (4) It is important to take measures to avoid the
      risk of fire.

01 치아의 아픔을 가리키는 말은 toothache(치통)이다.

02 lunch break: 점심시간, advice: 조언, hurt: 다치게 하다

03 on purpose: 고의로, gain weight: 체중이 늘다, focus on: ~
에 집중하다, in the end: 결국

04 put down: 깎아내리다, point out: 지적하다, set an alarm:
자명종을 맞추다

05 point out: 지적하다, script: 대본, reason: 이유, take
measures: 조치를 취하다

[교과서]
Conversation

핵심 Check   p.10~11

1 (1) nervous, What's the matter(= problem

    (2) Why do you look so sad

    (3) wrong / What should I do

2 (1) I think you should

    (2) advise

    (3) Why don't you

교과서 대화문 익히기

Check(√) True or False   p.12

1 T   2 F   3 T   4 F

교과서 확인학습   p.14~15

Listen & Talk 1-A-1

don't look, matter / wore, got / what to do

Listen & Talk 1-A-2

look down, What's the matter / haircut, funny / Take off
/ used to

Listen & Talk 1-B

tired / I didn't have breakfast this morning / too bad,
lunch break / snack bar / make, suggestion / post

Listen & Talk 2 A-1

how to do, advice / solve / solve, focus on / ones / got

Listen & Talk 2 A-2

late for, wake up / set an alarm / turn it off / far from,
That way

Listen & Talk 2 B

stop playing computer games. What should I do /
set, limit, shuts down / I think you should / out of,
into / advice

Communication

on the air / matter / sharing, with, stuff / feelings, make
some rules / I'll try that

01 (D) → (A) → (C) → (B)   02 ③   03 ②, ④

04 ②

01 (D) 자신의 고민을 이야기함 → (A) 자명종을 맞춰 두는지 질
문 → (C) 대답 → (B) 조언

02 이어지는 문장에서 매점이 있어야 하는 이유를 설명하고 있으므
로 (C)가 적절하다.

03 ⓐ는 상대방의 의견에 동의하는 표현이다.

01 ⑤   02 ①

03 her sister's favorite T-shirt

04 suggestion

05 They can post it on the suggestion board.

06 ①, ③   07 (C) → (B) → (A) → (D)

08 I think you should focus on the ones you got
wrong.   09 ⑤   10 ⓐ → playing

11 how about using a special program?   12 ④

13 She couldn't wake up in the morning.

14 Because she will have to get out of bed to turn it
off.

01 (A)는 상대방의 기분이 언짢아 보일 때 무슨 일이 있는지 묻는
표현이다. ⑤번은 직업을 묻는 표현이다.

02 언니의 티셔츠에 포도 주스를 쏟아 어찌할 바를 모르고 있는 여자
의 심정으로 worried(걱정스러운)가 적절하다.

04 '다른 누군가가 그것에 관해 생각하도록 당신이 언급한 의견 또
는 계획'을 가리키는 말은 suggestion(제안)이다.

05 Jane과 Tom은 제안 게시판에 그것을 게시할 수 있다.

06 (A)는 안타까움 또는 유감을 나타내는 표현으로 이와 바꾸어 쓸
수 있는 표현은 ①, ③번이다.

07 (C) 무슨 일이 있는지 질문 → (B) 기분이 좋지 않은 이유 설명
→ (A) 모자를 벗고 보여줄 것을 요청 → (D) 반응

09 ⑤번을 제외한 (a)와 나머지 모두는 조언해 줄 것을 요청하는 표
현이다.

10 stop+to부정사: ~하기 위해 멈추다, stop+~ing: ~하던 것을
멈추다

11 why don't you ~?는 '~하는 게 어때?'라고 제안하는 표현으
로 'how about ~?'과 바꾸어 쓸 수 있다.

13 Emily는 아침에 일어날 수 없어서 수업에 늦었다.

14 Tom이 자명종을 침대에서 멀리 놓으라고 조언한 이유는 그녀가
그것을 끄기 위해 일어날 수밖에 없기 때문이다.

01 (방송에) 연결되었습니다.

02 Because her little sister uses Amy's stuff without
asking her first.

03 tell her my feelings and make some rules with
her

04 She doesn't know how to do better in math.

05 Sujin should focus on the math problems she got
wrong.

06 (A) He can't stop playing computer games
(B) set a time limit, (C) his room, (D) the living room

01 be on the air: 전파를 타다

03 만약 내가 너라면 나는 그녀에게 내 기분에 대해 이야기하고 그
녀와 함께 몇 가지 규칙을 정할 거야.

04 Sujin은 수학을 더 잘하는 법을 모른다.

05 Sujin은 그녀가 틀린 수학 문제에 집중해야 한다.

교과서
Grammar

1 (1) has studied   (2) has, arrived   (3) have done

2 (1) which(또는 that) you made

  (2) which(또는 that) he bought

  (3) who(m)(또는 that) Helen came with

01 (1) have you left → did you leave

  (2) teach → teaches

  (3) did → have done

  (4) whom → which[that]

02 (1) Have you found the pen that[which] you lost?

  (2) Did she take the class which[that] James
taught?

  (3) I want to meet the boy whom[who/that] you
speak highly of.

  (4) Molly likes the movie which[that] Tom Cruise
starred in.

03 (1) I haven't finished my lunch yet.

  (2) She has been to the church two times.

  (3) I gave her all the money that I had.

  (4) Where is the report which we handed in?

01 (1) 의미상 그 장소를 언제 떠났는지를 묻고 있으므로 과거시제를 쓰는 것이 옳다. (2) Mr. Pang이 주어이므로 단수 동사를 쓴다. (3) 지금까지 오랫동안 이 일을 해 왔다는 것이므로 현재완료 시제를 쓴다. (4) 사물이 선행사이므로 which[that]를 쓰는 것이 옳다.

02 관계대명사 which, who(m)를 대신하여 that을 써도 무방하며, 목적격 관계대명사이므로 생략해도 좋다.

03 (2) '~에 가 보았다'라는 경험은 have been to로 표현한다.

시험대비 실력평가　　　　　　　　　　p.23~25

01 ④　　　　02 ⑤　　　　03 ③

04 like the dress which you want to buy

05 ⑤　　　　06 ②　　　　07 ③

08 whom you invited　　　09 ②　　　10 ④

11 Tell me about the people who(m) you met in the hospital.　12 ③　　　13 ②　　　14 ④

15 The letter that you sent to me has not arrived yet.

16 ④　　　17 ⑤　　　18 ③

19 Have you ever been to India before?　　20 ③

21 I have lost my cap.

22 The I-pad which[that] I got from my father was my birthday present.

23 that the children play with

01 ④ Have you ~?로 물을 때에는 Yes, I have. 혹은 No, I haven't.로 답한다.

02 'Jamie가 쓴 책'이므로 which Jamie wrote이 the book을 수식하도록 문장을 만든다.

03 현재완료가 쓰이고 있으므로 과거를 나타내는 어구는 빈칸에 쓰일 수 없다.

04 which를 대신하여 that을 써도 무방하다.

05 '~에 가 본 적이 있다'는 표현은 have been to를 쓴다. have gone to는 '~에 가고 없다'는 의미이다.

06 ② 과거를 나타내는 a few minutes ago는 현재완료 시제와 함께 쓸 수 없다.

07 현재완료 시제와 함께 쓰일 때 기간을 이끌 수 있는 전치사는 for이다. since는 특정 시점을 이끈다.

08 whom을 대신하여 who나 that을 써도 무방하다.

09 첫 번째 빈칸은 유명인을 만나본 적이 있느냐는 경험을 묻는 말이므로 현재완료 시제를 쓰는 것이 옳으며, 두 번째 빈칸에는 현재 그가 휴가를 즐기는 중이라는 말로 미루어 보아 '이탈리아에 가고 없다'는 표현이 들어가는 것이 옳다.

10 두 시간 전에 그 주제에 관하여 대화하기 시작하여 여전히 대화하고 있다는 것이므로 두 시간 동안 그 주제에 관하여 대화하고 있다는 것을 현재완료 시제로 나타낼 수 있다.

11 who(m)를 대신하여 that을 써도 무방하다.

12 모두 현재완료의 '완료' 용법이지만, ③번은 '계속'으로 쓰였다.

13 목적격 관계대명사나 '주격 관계대명사+be동사'를 생략할 수 있다.

14 사람과 동물이 함께 있는 선행사는 관계대명사 that으로 받는다.

15 '네가 나에게 보낸 그 편지'라고 하였으므로 관계대명사절 that you sent to me가 The letter를 수식하도록 문장을 쓴다.

16 (A) 특정 시점을 나타내고 있으므로 since, (B) 과거를 나타내는 last week은 현재완료와 함께 쓰일 수 없으며, (C) 지금까지 벽을 두 번 칠했다는 의미이므로 현재완료를 쓰는 것이 옳다.

17 ①~④는 주격 관계대명사로 쓰였으나 ⑤번은 목적격 관계대명사로 쓰인 that이다.

18 3년 전에 쓴 책이므로 과거시제를 쓰고 선행사가 사물이므로 which 혹은 that을 쓰는 것이 적절하다.

19 경험을 묻는 말이므로 현재완료 시제를 쓰는 것이 적절하다.

20 ③ 현재완료 시제는 명백한 과거를 나타내는 어구와 함께 쓰일 수 없다. 따라서 had로 쓰는 것이 옳다.

21 모자를 잃어버려 현재까지 그 상황이 이어지고 있으므로 현재완료 시제를 써서 한 문장으로 표현할 수 있다.

22 해석: 아버지로부터 받은 그 아이패드는 내 생일 선물이었다.

23 해석: 그 아이들이 가지고 노는 장난감은 더러워 보인다.

서술형 시험대비　　　　　　　　　　p.26~27

01 It has been sunny since yesterday.

02 which you are drinking

03 since / for / ago / since

04 The missing boy whom people were looking for came home last night.

05 have you lived / ago, have lived, for

06 (1) What is the name of the man whom[who] you want to meet?

(2) This is the car which my friend hopes to buy someday.

(3) Where is the red sweater which I put in my drawer?

07 Have you seen an elephant before?
No, I haven't.

08 (1) Did you throw a party for her yesterday?

(2) I have been to Boston many times.

(3) The sandwich which[that] he made for us is very delicious.

09 Kevin has lost his umbrella.

10 (1) isn't much information which you can get

(2) gave Tim the pants which he always liked

(3) he the man whom you respect very much

11 This is the desk which[that] my father made.

12 (1) The tennis game he played yesterday was great.

    (2) Do you know the boy talking with your sister?

    (3) The subject Jane is interested in is history and Korean.

13 that[which] she doesn't like

14 have lost

15 which you attended

01 현재완료 시제를 이용하여 어제 이후로 계속 맑다는 문장을 쓸 수 있다.

02 which 대신에 that을 써도 좋다. 또, drinking 대신에 having 을 써도 좋다.

03 특정 시점 앞에는 전치사나 접속사 since, 기간 앞에는 전치사 for 를 쓰며, ago는 과거동사와 함께 어울리는 부사이다.

04 '사람들이 찾던 그 실종 소년'이므로 The missing boy whom people were looking for라고 쓰는 것이 옳다.

05 이 집에서 얼마나 오랫동안 살았는지를 묻는 말이다. 현재완료 의 '계속' 용법을 이용하여 문장을 완성할 수 있다. 기간을 이끄 는 전치사는 for이다.

06 (1) 네가 만나기를 원하는 그 남자의 이름이 뭐야? (2) 이것이 내 친구가 언젠가 사기를 원하는 차야. (3) 내가 옷장에 넣어둔 빨간 색 스웨터는 어디에 있어?

07 경험을 묻는 말을 현재완료 시제를 사용하여 쓸 수 있다.

08 (1) 과거를 나타내는 yesterday는 현재완료 시제와 함께 쓸 수 없다. (2) '~에 가고 없다'는 의미의 have gone to는 3인 칭 주어에만 쓸 수 있다. (3) 선행사가 사물이므로 관계대명사는 which[that]를 쓰는 것이 옳다.

09 Kevin이 우산을 잃어버린 상황이 과거부터 현재까지 이어지므 로 현재완료 시제를 써서 한 문장으로 표현할 수 있다.

10 which를 대신하여 that을 써도 무방하며, whom을 대신하여 who나 that을 써도 좋다. (1) 네가 얻을 수 있는 많은 정보가 없어. (2) 나는 Tim이 항상 좋아하는 바지를 그에게 줬다. (3) 그가 네가 아주 존경하는 그 남자니?

11 '우리 아빠가 만드신 책상'이므로 관계사절이 the desk를 수식 하도록 문장을 만든다.

12 목적격 관계대명사와 '주격 관계대명사+be동사'를 생략할 수 있 다.

13 '그녀가 좋아하지 않는 음식'이므로 that[which] she doesn't like라고 쓰는 것이 옳다.

14 신발을 잃어버렸다는 결과를 나타내는 것이므로 현재완료 시제 를 이용한다.

15 which를 대신하여 that을 써도 좋다. attend a party: 파티에 참석하다, 파티에 가다

교과서
Reading

확인문제   p.28

1 T   2 F   3 T   4 F   5 T

확인문제   p.29

1 T   2 F   3 T   4 F   5 T   6 T

교과서 확인학습 A   p.30~31

01 years old, these days, going up and down

02 looks down

03 feelings, find out why'

04 What a day, yelled at, after

05 because, forgot, lines

06 that Bella made

07 could, in front of

08 did not mean to hurt

09 have been, since

10 what, saying

11 would never put

12 that, not going to be friends   13 too far, see

14 forgive, say a word   15 even look at

16 has never been

17 ate alone during   18 best friend

19 that we don't know about

20 stand, any longer   21 go, tell, about

22 to be hurt   23 let it go   24 work it out

25 that, are talking   26 talked to her

27 avoid, on purpose

28 a way to say   29 any more problems

30 part of growing up

31 Just like, face, solve them, wiser

교과서 확인학습 B   p.32~33

1 Bella is 15 years old this year and these days her feelings are going up and down.

2 Today, she looks down.

3 Let's listen to Bella's feelings and find out why.

4 What a day! I can't believe Jenny yelled at Bella after the school play.

5 Well, that's because Bella forgot her lines on stage.

5

6 Jenny pointed out the mistake that Bella made.

7 How could she do that in front of everyone?

8 But I'm sure Jenny did not mean to hurt Bella.

9 They have been best friends since elementary school. Remember?

10 That's what I'm saying.

11 A true friend would never put Bella down like that.

12 I'm worried that they are not going to be friends anymore.

13 Come on, Fear. Don't go too far. We'll see.

14 I can't forgive Jenny. She didn't say a word to Bella.

15 Jenny didn't even look at her.

16 Jenny has never been this cold before.

17 Bella ate alone during lunch today. Poor Bella!

18 Jenny is Bella's best friend.

19 I'm sure there is a reason that we don't know about.

20 I can't stand this any longer.

21 Bella should just go and tell her about her feelings.

22 I don't want Bella to be hurt again.

23 She should let it go.

24 They are good friends. They will work it out.

25 Whew! I'm so happy that they are talking again.

26 Yeah, Bella went to Jenny and talked to her first.

27 Jenny didn't avoid Bella on purpose.

28 Yeah, Jenny didn't know a way to say sorry.

29 I hope Bella doesn't have any more problems like this.

30 Me, too. But problems are part of growing up.

31 Just like this time, Bella will face the problems, solve them, and become wiser in the end.

시험대비 실력평가

p.34~37

01 down 　　02 ①, ② 　　03 실수를 지적하는 것

04 ③ 　　05 ④

06 That's because Bella forgot her lines on stage.

07 ③ 　　08 ③ 　　09 ④ 　　10 forgive

11 ⑤ 　　12 part of growing up 　　13 ①

14 Bella and Jenny are talking again. 　　15 ④

16 She feels up and down.

17 Fear is worried that Bella and Jenny are not going to be friends anymore. 　　18 ② 　　19 ③

20 ⑤ 　　21 she ate alone during lunch today

22 Anger wants Bella to go and tell Jenny about her

feelings. 　　23 ② 　　24 ④ 　　25 ②

26 wiser 　　27 have not talked

01 오늘 있었던 일로 미루어 보아 Bella의 기분이 안 좋아 보인다고 하는 것이 옳다. down: 우울한

02 사물을 선행사로 취하는 목적격 관계대명사 which 혹은 that이 들어갈 수 있다.

03 Jenny가 Bella의 실수를 지적한 것을 의미한다.

04 현재완료에서 since는 특정 시점을 이끌고, for는 기간을 이끈다. 따라서 ③번에는 for가 들어간다.

05 Bella가 무대에서 왜 대사를 잊어버렸는지는 글을 읽고 알 수 없다.

06 Jenny가 Bella에게 소리를 지른 이유는 Bella가 무대에서 그녀의 대사를 잊어버렸기 때문이라고 하였다.

07 밑줄 친 (A)는 현재완료의 '경험'을 나타내는 말이다. 따라서 ③번이 옳다.

08 ⓒ는 Jenny를, 나머지는 모두 Bella를 가리키는 말이다.

09 Fear가 말하는 let it go는 '상황을 내버려 두다'는 의미로 Bella가 Jenny를 가게 해야만 한다는 것이 아니다.

10 누군가에게 화를 내거나 비난하는 것을 멈추는 것은 '용서하다(forgive)'이다.

11 on purpose: 일부러, 고의로 ① be satisfied with: ~에 만족하다 ② give up: 포기하다 ③ take part in: ~에 참가하다 ④ come up with: (생각을) 떠올리다 ⑤ turn on: ~을 켜다

12 전치사 of의 목적어로 동명사구를 쓰는 것에 유의한다.

13 in the end는 '결국, 마침내'라는 의미이다. 따라서 ①번이 옳다.

14 Joy가 행복한 이유는 'Bella와 Jenny가 다시 이야기하게 되어서'라고 하였다.

15 (A) listen은 자동사이므로 전치사 to와 함께 쓰일 때 목적어를 받음 (B) Jenny가 Bella에게 소리를 지른 이유를 설명하고 있으므로 that's because, (C) 초등학교 때부터 현재까지 가장 친한 친구라는 의미이므로 현재완료.

16 그녀의 기분은 좋다가 안 좋다가 한다고 하였다.

17 Fear는 Bella와 Jenny가 더 이상 친구로 지내지 않을까 봐 걱정된다고 하였다.

18 ⓐ는 '(연극, 영화의) 대사'라는 의미로 쓰인 line이다. 모두 line을 풀이한 말이며 ① (표면에 그어진) 선, 줄 ② 대사 ③ 주름살 ④ 윤곽선 ⑤ 줄, 열을 의미한다.

19 ③ Joy는 Jenny가 Bella에게 상처를 주려고 했던 것은 아니라고 확신한다. intend to: ~을 의도하다

20 밑줄 친 (A)는 불완전한 문장을 이끄는 관계대명사이다. ⑤는 접속사로 완전한 문장을 이끌고 있다.

21 Sadness가 Bella를 가엾어 하는 이유는 Bella가 오늘 점심시

간에 혼자 밥을 먹어서이다.

22 Anger는 Bella가 Jenny에게 가서 자신의 감정을 말하기를 원한다.

23 ② Fear는 Bella가 다시 상처받는 것을 원치 않는다고 하였다.

24 이번처럼 Bella는 문제를 피하는 것이 아니라 직면하게 될 것이다. avoid → face

25 Joy의 첫 번째 말로 미루어 보아 두 사람은 서로 이야기를 하지 않고 있다가 다시 이야기하게 되었으므로 ②번이 가장 적절하다.

26 문제를 해결하면서 Bella는 결국 더 현명해질 것이라 하였다.

27 이틀 동안 서로 대화를 하지 않았다는 의미로 현재완료 시제를 써서 나타낼 수 있다.

서술형 시험대비 p.38~39

01 why she looks down today

02 Bella made the mistake.
Jenny pointed out the mistake.

03 They have been best friends since elementary school.

04 She forgot her lines on stage.

05 She yelled at Bella.

06 Jenny didn't say a word to Bella and she didn't even look at her.

07 I have forgiven my best friend before.

08 It's because she ate alone during lunch today.

09 She went to Jenny and talked to her first

10 that we face

11 she didn't know a way to say sorry

12 I want to tell you a problem that I have

13 have had   14 I don't know what to do.

15 my terrible math grades

---

01 Bella의 감정에 귀 기울여 보고 기분이 안 좋은 이유를 알아보자는 의미이다.

02 the mistake를 선행사로 하여 만든 문장이므로 다른 하나의 문장은 Bella made the mistake.로 쓸 수 있다.

03 초등학교 때부터 가장 친한 친구였다는 의미이므로 현재완료 시제를 써서 표현할 수 있다.

04 Bella가 저지른 실수는 무대에서 대사를 잊어버린 것이다.

05 Jenny는 Bella에게 학교 연극이 끝난 후 소리를 질렀다고 하였다.

06 Jenny는 Bella에게 한마디도 말을 안 했고 심지어 Bella를 쳐다보지도 않았다고 하였다.

07 현재완료의 '경험'을 나타내는 말로 위 글의 표현을 이용하여 영어로 쓸 수 있다.

08 Sadness가 "가엾은 Bella"라고 말한 것은 그녀가 오늘 점심시

간에 혼자 밥을 먹었기 때문이다.

09 Bella가 Jenny에게 먼저 말을 걸어서 화해를 하게 되었다.

10 관계대명사 that을 대신하여 which를 써도 무방하다. 해석: Joy에 따르면 우리가 직면하는 문제들은 우리가 더 현명해 지도록 돕는다.

11 Jenny는 사과하는 방법을 몰랐기 때문에 Bella를 피한 것이라고 하였다.

12 'I have a problem that I want to tell you.'라고 써도 좋다. that을 대신하여 which를 써도 무방하다.

13 since를 쓰며 현재의 문제를 이야기하고 있으므로 현재완료 시제를 쓰는 것이 가장 적절하다.

14 what to do: 무엇을 해야 할지

15 형편없는 수학 점수를 의미한다.

영역별 핵심문제 p.41~45

01 ②   02 ④

03 (1) You should focus on the problem at hand.
(2) We can face a problem again.
(3) Children grow up so fast these days.

04 elementary   05 ②   06 ②

07 ②   08 ③

09 (A)share my room with her, (B)advice, (C)tell my little sister my feelings and make some rules with her

10 (C) → (D) → (B) → (A)

11 ②   12 ②

13 Because he got a haircut but it's too short.

14 She thought it looked fine.   15 ①

16 ⑤   17 ②, ③

18 whom I care about most 19 ②, ⑤   20 ③

21 ⑤   22 she has gone to   23 ③

24 I will read the book which I borrowed from the library.   25 ③   26 ④

27 She forgot her lines on stage.   28 ⑤

29 ③

30 Bella and Jenny finally made up with each other.

31 ④

---

01 '당신에게 해롭게 하거나 화나게 하거나 또는 불안하게 하는 무언가를 한 사람에게 화내는 감정을 그만두다'를 나타내는 말은 forgive(용서하다)이다.

02 on purpose는 '고의로'를 의미한다.

03 at hand: 가까이에 (있는), face a problem: 문제에 직면하다, grow up: 성장하다

04 주어진 관계는 반의어 관계를 나타낸다. advanced: 상급의, 고등의, elementary: 초급의, 초보의

05 주어진 문장에서 lines는 '대사'를 나타내며 이와 같은 의미로

7

쓰인 것은 ②번이다. 나머지는 모두 '선'을 뜻한다.

06 mean은 동사로 '의미하다', 형용사로 '비열한, 인색한', means
는 명사로 '수단, 방법'을 뜻한다.

07 (A) late: 늦은, lately: 최근에, (B) turn on: ~을 켜다 turn
off: ~을 끄다, (C) close to: ~에 가까이, far from: ~에서 멀
리

09 나는 오늘도 화가 났었다. 왜냐하면 내 여동생이 내게 먼저 물
어보지도 않고 내 물건을 사용했기 때문이다. 나는 그녀와 더 이
상 방을 같이 쓰고 싶지 않았다. 이 문제를 해결하기 위해, 나는
Solomon에게 전화를 해서 내게 조언을 해 줄 것을 요청하였다.
그는 내게 내 기분을 그녀에게 이야기하고 나의 여동생과 몇 가지
규칙을 정해볼 것을 조언하였다. 이것은 내게 훌륭한 조언이었으
며 그것을 해 보기로 결정했다.

10 (C) 무슨 일이 있는지 질문 → (D) 기분이 좋지 않은 이유 설명
→ (B) 반응 및 질문 → (A) 대답

11 이어서 특별한 프로그램의 기능을 설명하고 있으므로 (B)가 알
맞다.

12 ② 위 대화를 통해 왜 Eric이 컴퓨터 게임을 멈출 수 없는지는
알 수 없다.

13 David는 머리를 잘랐는데 너무 짧아 침울하다.

14 Sora는 David의 머리가 괜찮아 보인다고 생각했다.

15 목적격 관계대명사가 생략된 문장이다. 선행사인 The watch
뒤에 위치하는 것이 옳다.

16 Mr. Kim taught the students English에서 온 문장이므로
⑤번은 옳지 않다.

17 사물을 선행사로 취하는 목적격 관계대명사이므로 that이나
which를 쓰는 것이 옳다.

18 about whom I care most라고 써도 무방하다.

19 주어진 문장은 Jason이 여행에서 집으로 돌아왔다는 것으로
Jason이 과거에 여행을 떠났다가 현재 돌아와 집에 있다는 것
을 말하는 문장이다.

20 우산을 잃어버렸지만 지금은 그것을 가지고 있다는 것이므로 '우
산을 지금까지 잃어버리고 있다'라는 두 번째 문장과 의미가 통하
지 않는다.

21 주어진 문장의 현재완료는 '경험'을 나타낸다. ①, ④ 완료 ②,
③ 계속을 나타내는 현재완료이다.

22 Sally가 집에 가서 없다는 의미이므로 have gone to를 쓴다.

23 ③ yesterday는 과거를 나타내는 어구이므로 현재완료 시제와
함께 쓸 수 없다.

24 목적격 관계대명사 which를 대신하여 that을 쓰거나 생략해도
무방하다.

25 밑줄 친 (A)는 관계대명사 that으로 불완전한 문장을 이끈다. 따
라서 ③번이 답이다.

26 Bella와 Jenny가 더 이상 친구가 되지 않을 것이라는 생각을
하지 말라는 의미이다.

27 Bella는 무대에서 그녀의 대사를 잊어버렸다고 하였다.

28 학교 연극의 이름이 무엇인지는 알 수 없다.

29 on purpose, intentionally: 고의로

30 두 사람은 마침내 화해하였다. make up with: 화해하다

31 Bella가 이러한 문제들에 직면하게 되지 않기를 바라는 것은
Fear의 희망이지, Bella가 원치 않는 것이 아니다.

단원별 예상문제
p.46~49

01 ④ 02 ⑤

03 Because he didn't have breakfast this morning.

04 They should wait for two more hours.

05 They can have a quick breakfast or snacks.

06 I think you should tell her your feelings. 07 ⑤

08 ③ 09 ②, ④

10 (B) → (D) → (C) → (A) 11 ④

12 (1) Where is the man? You cheered for him.

(2) The car is very expensive. Tony Stark drives
the car in the movie.

13 ⑤ 14 ③ 15 ⑤

16 I have lost my cell phone.

17 have seen, for 18 ③

19 I'm sure there is a reason.
We don't know about the reason.

20 ③ 21 Fear wants her not to be hurt again.

22 ⑤

23 Fear hopes that Bella doesn't have any more
problems like this. 24 ③ 25 ①, ④

26 I have had this problem since last year.

01 나머지는 모두 조언을 요청하는 표현이지만 ④번은 도움을 제안
하는 표현이다.

02 ⑤번을 제외한 (A)와 나머지는 모두 조언을 하는 표현이다.

03 Mike는 오늘 아침에 아침을 먹지 않아 피곤해 보인다.

04 Jane과 Mike는 점심시간까지 두 시간 이상 기다려야 한다.

05 Jane과 Mike는 학교에 매점이 있다면 간단한 아침이나 간식을
먹을 수 있다.

07 Amy가 그녀의 여동생과 어떻게 화해할지는 알 수 없다.

08 Kevin은 엄마의 새 안경을 깨뜨려 걱정하고 있다.

09 빈칸 (A)는 유감이나 동정을 나타내는 표현이 적절하므로 ②,
④번이 적절하다.

10 (B) Daisy에게 지각함을 알림 → (D) 사과 및 지각한 이유 설
명 → (C) 조언 → (A) 반응

11 주어진 문장은 현재완료의 '완료'를 나타내고 있다. ④번은 경험
을 나타내는 현재완료이다.

12 (1) 네가 응원했던 그 남자는 어디에 있니? (2) 그 영화에서
Tony Stark가 운전하는 차는 아주 비싸다.

13 사람과 사물을 모두 선행사로 취할 수 있는 관계대명사는 that이다.

14 ③ 관계대명사로 이어진 문장이므로 it을 쓰지 않아야 한다.

15 목적격 관계대명사 혹은 '주격 관계대명사+be동사'를 생략할 수 있다.

16 휴대전화기를 잃어버린 상황이 현재까지 지속되고 있으므로 현재완료 시제를 써서 한 문장으로 표현할 수 있다.

17 '우리는 두 시간 동안 그 영화를 보고 있다'라고 쓸 수 있다.

18 (A) Jenny가 Bella를 쳐다보지도 않았다는 의미가 적절하므로 at, (B) 명사를 이끌고 있으므로 전치사 during, (C) 타동사는 대명사 목적어를 부사 앞에 위치시키므로 work it out이 옳다.

19 a reason이 선행사임에 유의하여 문장을 둘로 나눈다.

20 Bella가 혼자 점심을 먹었다고 하였으므로 ③번은 옳지 않다.

21 Fear는 Bella가 다시는 상처받지 않기를 원한다고 하였다.

22 밑줄 친 (A)는 앞의 명사를 수식하는 형용사로 쓰인 to부정사이다. 따라서 ⑤번이 답이다.

23 Fear는 Bella에게 이번과 같은 문제가 더 이상 없기를 바란다고 하였다.

24 Jenny가 Bella를 의도적으로 피한 것이 아니라고 하였으므로 ③번은 글의 내용과 일치하지 않는다.

25 선행사가 사물이므로 that이나 which를 써서 관계사절을 만든다.

26 작년 이래로 계속 이 문제를 가지고 있다는 것이므로 현재완료 시제로 표현할 수 있다.

🐾 서술형 실전문제
p.50~51

01 What should I do?

02 The computer shuts down at the set time.

03 She advises him to move it out of his room and into the living room.

04 (1) Have you ever been to Busan?
   (2) She has gone to Busan.

05 The weight which she is lifting is not that heavy.
   The restaurant which Paul runs is crowded with people.
   The children whom I take care of are very noisy.

06 How long have you known each other?

07 The girl whom Tom is looking at is Danny's friend.

08 which[that] Jimmy is wearing

09 (A)has, played   (B)when, has played, for

10 Jenny yelled at Bella after the school play.

11 A true friend would never put Bella down like that.

12 Jenny pointed out my mistake in front of everyone

13 ⓒ-ⓐ-ⓑ

14 whom I have known since elementary school

---

02 Eric이 특별한 프로그램을 사용하여 시간 제한을 설정하면 정해진 시간에 컴퓨터가 종료된다.

03 Ms. Morris는 Eric에게 컴퓨터를 그의 방에서 거실로 옮길 것을 조언하였다.

04 (1) 현재완료 시제를 이용하여 경험을 묻는 말을 쓸 수 있고, (2) '~에 가고 없다'는 결과 역시 현재완료 시제로 표현할 수 있다.

05 which를 대신하여 that을 쓸 수 있으며 whom 대신 who나 that을 써도 좋다. 모두 목적격 관계대명사이므로 생략해도 무방하다.

06 대답으로 미루어 보아 서로를 얼마나 오랫동안 알아왔는지를 묻는 말이 들어가는 것이 옳다.

07 'Tom이 바라보고 있는 그 소녀'이므로 관계사절 whom Tom is looking at이 명사 the girl을 수식하도록 문장을 쓸 수 있다.

08 wear a helmet: 헬멧을 쓰다

09 남동생이 얼마나 오랫동안 골프를 쳐 왔는지를 묻는 말에, 일곱 살때 골프를 배워 지금까지 5년 동안 골프를 쳐 오고 있다는 대답을 하고 있다.

10 Jenny가 Bella에게 소리를 지른 것을 가리키는 말이다.

11 never는 빈도부사로 일반동사 앞, 조동사 뒤에 위치하는 것에 유의한다. put A down: A를 깎아내리다

12 Jenny는 모든 사람 앞에서 Bella의 실수를 지적하였다. in front of: ~ 앞에서

13 Bella가 자신의 대사를 잊어버리자 이를 지적하며 Jenny가 Bella에게 소리를 질렀고 Bella는 그것 때문에 슬펐다는 것이 사건의 순서이다.

14 whom을 대신하여 who 또는 that을 써도 무방하다.

🕊️ 창의사고력 서술형 문제
p.52

|모범답안|

01 (A) I didn't have breakfast
   (B) two more hours
   (C) our school should have a snack bar
   (D)the suggestion board

02 (1) I have argued with my best friend several times.
   (2) My friends have visited my house once.
   (3) I have never had a snow fight with my friend.
   (4) I have known Sumin since 2015.
   (5) I have been to a concert with my friends before.

03 (1) has lived in New York
   (2) has been to Spain
   (3) has raised Cooper since
   (4) and John have known each other since

01 나는 늦게 일어나 버스를 거의 놓칠 번했다. 다행히, 학교에 지각하지 않았다. 하지만 나는 너무 피곤하고 배고팠다. 왜냐하면 아침을 먹지 않았기 때문이다. 심지어, 나는 점심시간을 위해 두 시간 이상을 기다려야 했다. 나는 우리학교가 배고픈 학생들을 위해 매점이 있어야 한다고 생각했다. 내가 이것에 대해 Jane과 이야기 했을 때 그녀는 내 생각에 동의했다. 나는 곧 내 생각을 제안 게시판에 게시할 계획을 세웠다.

01 (1) suggestion   (2) repeat   (3) orgive   02 ⑤

03 (1) stay up late   (2) up and down   (3) wake up

    (4) work out

04 (1) explain   (2) yell   (3) worry   (4) pack   (5)fight

05 ②   06 ④   07 ③   08 ①

09 (A)breakfast, (B)hungry, (C)have a snack barin our school

10 Because she stayed up late again last night.

11 She should pack her bag the night before.

12 (1) I can't stand working with him any more.

   (2) Minho has to memorize his lines in English.

   (3) I was embarrassed when he pointed out my mistakes.   13 ③   14 ⑤

15 ④

16 I have just eaten the cake that you bought for me.

17 I have not found my gold necklace yet.   18 ④

19 No,she didn't. She pointed out my mistake in front of everyone   20 ④   21 stand

22 ③   23 they aregood friends

01 suggestion: 제안, repeat: 반복하다, forgive: 용서하다

02 since는 전치사로 '~부터, ~ 이래로', 접속사로 '~한 이래로, ~이기 때문에'를 의미한다.

03 stay up late: 늦게까지 자지 않고 있다, up and down: 좋다가 나쁘다가 하는, wake up: 잠에서 깨다, work out: 해결하다

04 explain: 설명하다, yell: 소리치다, worry: 걱정하다, pack: (짐을) 싸다, fight like cat and dog: 싸우다, 격렬하게 서로 으르렁거리다

05 위 대화에서 ⓐdown은 '우울한'을 의미하며 이와 같은 의미로 쓰인 것은 ②번이다.

06 David는 새로운 그의 머리 스타일 때문에 기분이 좋지 않다.

07 이어서 Amy가 그녀의 여동생과 방을 같이 쓰기 싫은 이유를 설명하고 있으므로 (C)가 적절하다.

08 Amy와 Solomon은 직접 마주하여 이야기를 하는 것이 아니라 통화하고 있다.

09 몇몇 학생들이 아침을 먹지 않아 배고픔을 느낀다. 우리 학교에

매점이 있어야 한다.

10 Daisy는 지난밤에 또 늦게까지 자지 않고 깨어 있었기 때문에 지각하였다.

11 Daisy는 아침에 시간을 절약하기 위해 전날 밤에 가방을 싸야 한다.

13 현재완료에서 'since+시점', 'for+기간'으로 쓰이는 것에 유의하자.

14 관계대명사가 전치사의 목적어로 쓰인 경우에 유의하자. talk about: ~에 대하여 말하다

15 어제 이후로 아무것도 먹지 않았다는 의미이므로 have eaten을 쓰는 것이 옳다.

16 '네가 나에게 사 주었던 그 케이크'이므로 the cake that you bought for me라고 쓰는 것이 옳다.

17 현재완료 시제를 이용하여 나는 아직 내 금목걸이를 찾지 못했다는 의미로 쓸 수 있다.

18 연극이 끝난 후에 Jenny가 Bella에게 소리를 질렀다고 하였다.

19 Jenny는 모든 사람들 앞에서 Bella의 실수를 지적하였다.

20 우울해 보이는 것은 Jenny가 아니라 Bella이다.

21 어려운 상황을 받아들이거나 잘 다룰 수 있는 것은 'stand(참다, 견디다)'이다.

22 Bella가 자신의 감정을 Jenny에게 말해야 한다고 Anger가 말했을 뿐, 실제로 Bella가 Jenny에게 먼저 말을 걸지는 않았다.

23 Joy는 Bella와 Jenny가 좋은 친구이므로 잘 해낼 것이라고 생각한다.

Doors to the Wild

Lesson 6

시험대비 실력평가
p.60

01 thin   02 ②   03 ④

04 (1) trunk   (2) whale   (3) Female

05 (1) Elephants rarely attack humans.

   (2) The rescue team arrived on time.

   (3) These rings symbolize our friendship

06 ④   07 ①

01 주어진 관계는 반의어 관계를 나타낸다. giant: 거대한, tiny: 작은, thick: 두꺼운, thin: 얇은

02 '볼 수 없는'을 뜻하는 말은 blind(눈이 먼)이다.

03 appear: 나타나다

04 trunk: (코끼리의) 코, whale: 고래, female: 암컷; 암컷의

05 rarely: 좀처럼 ~하지 않는, attack: 공격하다, rescue: 구조, symbolize: 상징하다

06 주어진 문장에서 bat은 '박쥐'를 뜻하며 이와 같은 의미로 쓰인 것은 ④번이다. 나머지는 모두 '방망이'를 뜻한다.

07 sense: (명) 감각, (동) 감지하다 approach: 다가가다

서술형 시험대비
p.61

01 careless   02 ①

03 (1) care for   (2) her eyes   (3) take a picture

04 (1) seem   (2) allow   (3) Female   (4) feed

   (5) probably

05 (1) The careless driver didn't see the light turn red.

   (2) Children are curious about everything around them.

   (3) My parents won't allow me to play computer games.

06 (1) I visited a local animal shelter last weekend.

   (2) He was restless at that time.

   (3) We need to be more adventurous and stronger.

01 주어진 관계는 반의어 관계를 나타낸다. careful: 주의 깊은, careless: 부주의한

02 '사람이나 동물에게 먹을 것을 주다'를 뜻하는 말은 feed(먹이다)이다.

03 care for: ~을 돌보다, keep one's eyes on ~: ~에서 눈을 떼지 못하다, take a picture of ~의 사진을 찍다

04 probably: 아마도, seem: ~처럼 보이다, feed: 먹이를 주다, female: 암컷의, allow: 허락하다

05 careless: 부주의한, curious: 호기심이 많은, allow: 허락하다

06 shelter: 보호소, restless: 가만히 있지 않는, adventurous: 모험심이 강한

교과서 Conversation

핵심 Check
p.62~63

1 (1) curious about / Let's read

  (2) blind / wonder

  (3) communicate / I'm curious about the way / find out

2 (1) big / as big as   (2) color / as red as a rose

  (3) as well as dogs / to know about them more

교과서 대화문 익히기

Check(√) True or False
p.64

1 T   2 F   3 T   4 F

교과서 확인학습
p.66~67

Listen & Talk 1 A-1

topic / I'm curious about weather change, doing

Listen and Talk 1 A-2

huge / bigger / curious about, says, insects / why

Listen and Talk 1 B

be friends / think so / friendship / curious about / raised, back, wild, a year later / touching

Listen and Talk 2 A-1

puppy / so small / as small as, much bigger / grow

Listen and Talk 2 A-2

over there / really big / as old as me / planted, was, born

Listen and Talk 2 B

give a presentation, the biggest, longer than, as heavy as, isn't it

Communication

millions of / curious, any / many, as heavy as / amazing

01 ④   02 weather change

03 (A) biggest   (B) longer   04 ④

03 (A) the+최상급: 가장 ~한, (B) 비교급+than: …보다 ~한
04 Toby의 설명에 따르면 흰긴수염고래는 농구 경기장보다 더 길다.

 시험대비 실력평가   p.69~70

01 I'm curious about weather change.   02 ⑤

03 (1) biggest   (2) about 30m   (3) a basketball court
    (4) Its tongue is as heavy as an elephant.

04 insect   05 ④   06 ②   07 ②

08 ②   09 1년 후에 사자가 자기를 키워준 두 남자를

기억한 것   10 ⑤

02 Judy가 날씨 변화에 관심이 있다는 설명은 대화의 내용과 일치
하지 않는다.

04 '6개의 다리와 3부분으로 나누어지는 몸을 가진 작은 생명체'를
나타내는 말은 insect(곤충)이다

05 대화를 통해 왜 벌레들이 커다란 꽃의 향기를 좋아하는지는 알
수 없다.

06 (A)는 'as+원급+as' 구문으로 원급인 small, (B)는 비교급을
수식할 수 있는 much, (C)는 동사를 수식하는 부사가 적절하
므로 quickly가 적절하다.

07 Dylan은 Mina에게 사진을 보여주고 있다.

08 (A) between A and B: A와 B 사이에, (B) raised와 병렬
구조이므로 sent, (C) touching: 감동적인

10 나무는 Kelly의 할머니 할아버지만큼 오래되었다는 설명은 대
화의 내용과 일치하지 않는다.

 서술형 시험대비   p.71

01 It is about 30 meters long.

02 A blue whale is longer than a basketball court.

03 It is as heavy as an elephant.

04 (A) bigger   (B) picture   (C) insects
    (D) they love the smell

05 It was about friendship between two men and a
lion.

06 She remembered the two men who had raised
her.

07 (D) → (B) → (A) → (C)

01 흰긴수염고래는 약 30미터 정도이다.

02 흰긴수염고래가 농구 경기장보다 더 길다.

03 흰긴수염고래의 혀는 코끼리만큼 무겁다.

04 Jane은 사진에서, 사람보다 큰 꽃을 발견하였다. 흥미롭게도,
이 꽃은 냄새가 고약하지만 벌레들은 그 냄새를 좋아한다. Tom
은 왜 벌레들이 그 냄새를 좋아하는지 궁금해 하였다.

05 Clare가 본 비디오는 두 남자와 사자 사이의 우정에 대한 것이다.

06 사자는 그녀를 길렀던 두 남자를 기억했다.

07 (D) 주제 선택 여부 질문 → (B) 대답 및 질문 → (A) 궁금한
것 표현하기 → (C) 반응

 교과서
Grammar

1 (1) It, to exercise   (2) It, to go   (3) It, not to use
2 (1) not as[so] poor as   (2) twice as expensive as
   (3) as well as

 시험대비 기본평가   p.74

01 (1) to being → to be
    (2) simply → simple
    (3) drive → to drive
    (4) three time → three times

02 (1) as fun as   (2) not as[so] long as
    (3) twice as warm as   (4) as sweet as

03 (1) It is important to help people in need.
    (2) It is beneficial to help each other.
    (3) He is not as foolish as you are.
    (4) The movie is not as boring as Amazing Amy.

01 (1), (3) 진주어를 to부정사로 쓰는 것이 옳다. (2) be동사의 보
어가 비어 있으므로 as ~ as 사이 에는 형용사를 써야 한다. (2)
배수사 as+원급+as: ~보다 몇 배 …한

02 (1), (4) '~만큼 …한'이란 의미의 동등비교는 'as+형용사 또는
부사의 원급+as'로 나타낼 수 있 다. (2) 두 대상이 서로 같지
않음을 나타낼 때에는 동등비교의 부정 표현을 이용한다. (3) 배
수사 +as+원급+as: ~보다 몇 배 …한

03 (1), (2) '어려움에 처한 사람들을 돕는 것', '서로를 돕는 것'이
주어이므로 이를 진주어로 만들어 문장을 쓸 수 있다. (3), (4)
동등비교의 부정인 'not as+원급+as'를 이용하여 두 대상간의
차이를 나타낼 수 있다.

01 ⑤   02 ③   03 ⑤

04 It is difficult to solve the puzzle in an hour.

05 ④   06 ②   07 ⑤

08 It is dangerous to go outside alone late at night.

09 ④   10 ④   11 ③

12 Alex gets up as early as I (do).   13 ③

14 ④   15 ⑤   16 ④

17 ④   18 are not as[so] tall as   19 ③

20 It is natural that you worry about her.   21 ④

22 ③   23 ④

24 It is safe to drink this water.

01 문맥상 as ~ as 사이에는 형용사의 원급이 들어간다. '형용사+ly'는 부사로 쓰이지만 '명사+ly'는 형용사로 쓰이는 것에 유의한다.

02 모두 가주어로 쓰인 It이지만 ③번은 인칭대명사 It으로 '그것'이라고 해석된다.

03 fast는 형용사와 부사의 형태가 같다. 따라서 '빠르게 달리다'는 것은 run fast로 표현한다.

04 '그 퍼즐을 푸는 것'이 주어이므로 이를 to solve the puzzle로 진주어의 문장을 만들 수 있다.

05 진주어는 to부정사가 가능하며, 두 번째 문장의 의미는 '잘 먹는 것은 잘 자는 것만큼 중요하다'는 것이다. be동사의 보어가 필요하므로 as와 as 사이에 형용사를 써서 문장을 완성할 수 있다.

06 위 문장을 영어로 쓰면 'It is a good exercise to ride a bike.'이다.

07 ⑤ 원급 비교 as ~ as 사이에 문맥상 형용사의 원급이 온다.

08 '밤늦게 밖에 혼자 나가는 것'이 주어이므로 이를 진주어로 하여 문장을 쓰며, to부정사를 진주어로 쓴다.

09 Jason의 몸무게는 70kg이며 Paul의 몸무게는 64kg이므로 Jason은 Paul보다 무겁다고 말하는 것이 옳다.

10 빈칸에는 명사절 접속사 that이 오는 것이 옳다.

11 It is true that John lied to me.라고 쓰는 것이 옳다.

12 Alex와 나는 똑같이 오전 6시에 일어난다. 따라서 'Alex는 나만큼 일찍 일어난다.'라는 말을 할 수 있다.

13 to부정사의 부정형은 not to V 형태이다.

14 Zach이 Clara보다 더 긴장하고 있다는 것은 Clara는 Zach만큼 긴장하고 있지 않다는 의미이다.

15 모두 to부정사의 부사적 용법 중 '목적'으로 쓰여 '~하기 위'

16 문장을 이끌고 있으므로 첫 번째 빈칸에는 진주어 역할을 하는 명사절 접속사 that이 들어가는 것이 옳으며, TV를 보는 것은 시간의 양이므로 much를 쓰는 것이 옳다.

17 진주어로 to부정사를 쓸 수 있다. obey: 따르다, 준수하다

18 남동생의 키는 170cm이므로 '너는 나의 남동생만큼 크지 않다'고 말할 수 있다.

19 '너의 시계는 나의 시계보다 더 비싸다'는 것은 '나의 시계는 너의 시계만큼 비싸지 않다'는 것이므로 My watch is not as expensive as yours.라고 쓰는 것이 옳다.

20 '네가 그녀를 걱정하는 것'은 문장으로 써야 하므로 가주어 it에 진주어 명사절 that을 써서 문장을 만드는 것이 적절하다.

21 Kelly가 Julia보다 일을 더 열심히 한다는 것은 Julia가 Kelly만큼 열심히 일하지 않는다는 것과 같다.

22 ⓐ 진주어는 to부정사를 쓴다. 따라서 to see the man make a speech, ⓑ 노래를 잘 부르는 것이므로 sing을 수식하는 부사가 들어가는 것이 옳다. 따라서 as well as, ⓔ 진주어이므로 to부정사로 만들어 to find를 쓴다.

23 David가 Gloria보다 더 많은 친구를 가지고 있으므로 Gloria는 David만큼 친구를 많이 가지고 있지 않다고 표현 하는 것이 옳다.

24 진주어로 to부정사를 써서 문장을 만든다.

01 have two times as many balloons as Jinsu has

02 It is possible to walk to the top of this mountain.

03 as much money as

04 is safe to wear a helmet

05 is not as[so] old as

06 It is hard to see something without my glasses. I am as blind as a bat without my glasses.

07 (1) It is important that we try to save energy.

  (2) It is impossible to get there in time.

  (3) It was difficult to hear her singing.

  (4) It is foolish to want to be rich without working hard.

  (5) It is unsafe to play with matches.

08 is as light as

09 (1) is not as[so] tall as   (2) are not as[so] big as

  (3) are as big as   (4) is as heavy as

  (5) is as tall as   (6) is not as[so] heavy as

10 It is necessary to protect the animals on Earth.

11 as cold as

12 easy to answer his questions

13 (1) wrong to feed animals

  (2) exciting to take a zoo tour

  (3) dangerous to enter a cage

  (4) unsafe to take pets to the zoo

14 is twice as long as / is as long as mine

15 A: Is it fun to fly a kite?

  B: is as fun as playing a computer game

01 나는 진수보다 풍선을 두 배 더 많이 가지고 있다는 말로 쓸 수 있다. two times 대신 twice를 써도 좋다.

02 가주어 it을 쓰고 진주어로 to walk를 쓴다.

03 네가 나보다 돈을 더 많이 가지고 있다는 것은 '나는 너만큼 돈을 많이 가지고 있지 않다'는 의미와 같다.

04 가주어 it을 이용하여 같은 의미의 문장을 만드는 것이다.

05 Jackson씨의 나이는 Jackson 여사의 나이만큼 들지 않았다는 문장을 쓸 수 있다.

06 가주어 it과 원급 비교 구문을 이용한다.

07 가주어 it을 이용하여 문장을 만드는 문제이다. 주어가 to부정사 구이거나 명사절 접속사 that절인 경우 긴 주어를 뒤로 보내고 가주어 it을 사용하여 주어 자리를 채울 수 있다.

08 상자가 깃털만큼 가볍다는 이야기이다. 따라서 원급비교 as ~ as를 이용하여 문장을 완성할 수 있다.

09 (1) Mike의 키는 John보다 크지 않다. (2) John의 발 크기는 Mike의 발 크기만큼 크지 않다. (3) Betty의 발 크기는 John의 발 크기만큼 크다. (4) John은 Mike만큼 무겁다. (5) Mike는 Betty만큼 키가 크다. (6) Betty는 Mike와 John만큼 무겁지 않다.

10 '지구에 사는 동물들을 보호하는 것'을 주어로 만들어 문장을 쓸 수 있다.

11 피자가 얼음처럼 차가웠기 때문에 데워야만 했다고 말하는 것이 자연스럽다.

12 대답으로 미루어 보아 '그의 질문에 대답하는 것이 쉬웠는지'를 묻고 있음을 알 수 있다.

13 가주어로 it이 나와 있으므로 진주어로 to부정사를 쓴다. (4) unsafe를 대신하여 not safe를 써도 좋다.

14 나의 밧줄은 50cm이고 너의 밧줄은 1미터이므로, 너의 밧줄은 나의 밧줄보다 두 배만큼 더 길다고 할 수 있다. 수지의 밧줄은 나의 밧줄과 같다고 하였으므로 나의 밧줄만큼 길다고 할 수 있다.

15 연을 날리는 것과 컴퓨터 게임을 하는 것이 동등하게 재미있다고 말하고 있으므로 동등 비교 표현인 as ~ as를 활용하여 답을 쓸 수 있 다.

Reading

확인문제   p.80

1 T 2 F 3 T 4 F

확인문제   p.81

1 F 2 F 3 T 4 F 5 T 6 T 7 F

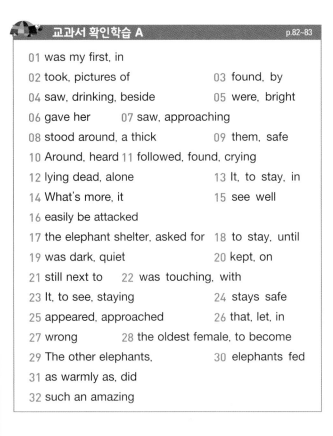

교과서 확인학습 A   p.82~83

01 was my first, in
02 took, pictures of   03 found, by
04 saw, drinking, beside   05 were, bright
06 gave her   07 saw, approaching
08 stood around, a thick   09 them, safe
10 Around, heard 11 followed, found, crying
12 lying dead, alone   13 It, to stay, in
14 What's more, it   15 see well
16 easily be attacked
17 the elephant shelter, asked for 18 to stay, until
19 was dark, quiet   20 kept, on
21 still next to   22 was touching, with
23 It, to see, staying   24 stays safe
25 appeared, approached   26 that, let, in
27 wrong   28 the oldest female, to become
29 The other elephants,   30 elephants fed
31 as warmly as, did
32 such an amazing

교과서 확인학습 B   p.84~85

1 Notes: Today was my first day in Africa.
2 I took lots of pictures of elephants.
3 This morning, I found an elephant group by a small water hole.
4 I saw a baby elephant drinking water beside her mother.
5 Her eyes were as bright as stars.
6 I gave her a name, Stella.
7 Around noon, I saw a group of lions approaching Stella.
8 The elephants stood around Stella and made a thick wall.
9 Thanks to them, Stella was safe.
10 Notes: Around sunset, I heard a strange sound.
11 I followed the sound and found Stella crying next to her mom.
12 She was lying dead and Stella was alone.
13 It is dangerous to stay alone in such a wild area.
14 What's more, it was going to be dark soon.
15 Elephants can't see well at night.
16 So Stella could easily be attacked.
17 I called the elephant shelter and asked for help.
18 I decided to stay by her until the rescue team came.
19 Notes: The night was dark and quiet.

20 I kept my eyes on Stella with my night camera.

21 Stella was still next to her mom.

22 She was touching her mom's lifeless body with her nose.

23 It was sad to see Stella staying close to her mom.

24 I hope Stella stays safe throughout the night.

25 Notes: A new elephant group appeared and Stella approached them.

26 At first, I thought that they would not let Stella in their group.

27 But I was wrong.

28 An elephant, probably the oldest female allowed Stella to become part of the group.

29 The other elephants also seemed to welcome Stella.

30 Unbelievably, one of the female elephants fed Stella.

31 She cared for Stella as warmly as Stella's mom did.

32 This was such an amazing moment!

시험대비 실력평가 p.86~89

01 ⑤　　　02 ②　　　03 The writer found an elephant group by a small water hole. 04 to stay

05 ③　　　06 ④　　　07 shelter　　08 ④

09 Seeing Stella staying close to her mom 10 ④

11 (C)−(B)−(D)−(A)　　12 ③　　　13 ②

14 ⑤　　　15 ⑤　　　16 The writer wrote it in Africa.　　17 ③　　　18 was dangerous to stay alone in such a wild area　　19 ⑤

20 It's because elephants can't see well at night.

21 ③　　　22 ④　　　23 It is interesting to see a pitcher plant eat insects.　24 warmly　　25 ④

26 ③

01 아기 코끼리가 마시고 있는 것은 엄마의 젖이 아니라 물이라고 하였다.

02 글쓴이가 기록을 한 날은 7월 8일이다.

03 글쓴이는 7월 8일 아침에 작은 물웅덩이 옆에 있는 한 코끼리 무리를 발견하였다.

04 진주어로 쓰일 수 있는 것은 to부정사이다.

05 '더욱이', '게다가'라는 의미의 연결어가 들어가는 것이 적절하다. 따라서 ③번은 적절하지 않다.

06 코끼리들은 밤에 잘 볼 수 없다고 하였다.

07 '나쁜 날씨, 위험, 또는 공격으로부터 보호를 제공하기 위해 만들어진 건물'은 '보호소'이다.

08 빈칸 (A)에는 전치사 on이 들어간다. ① turn off: ~을 끄다 ② look forward to: ~을 기대하다 ③ be full of: ~으로 가득 차 있다 ④ put on: ~을 입다, 쓰다 ⑤ pick up: ~을 태우러 가다

09 Stella가 그녀의 엄마 가까이에 머물고 있는 것을 보는 것이 슬픈 일이었다고 하였다.

10 글의 내용으로 보아 Stella의 엄마가 죽었음을 알 수 있다

11 (C) 글쓴이는 Stella가 무리에게 거절당할 것이라고 예상 - (B) 그러나 가장 나이 많은 코끼리가 Stella를 받아 줌 - (D) 나머지 코끼리도 Stella를 환영 - (A) 심지어 Stella에게 젖을 먹이는 코끼리도 있음

12 'such+a(n)+형용사+명사'의 어순이 옳다.

13 Stella는 새로운 코끼리 무리에 다가갔다고 하였다. 따라서 ② 번이 글의 내용과 일치한다.

14 much는 셀 수 없는 명사를 수식한다.

16 글쓴이는 이 글을 아프리카에서 썼다.

17 Stella라고 이름을 지어준 것은 아기 코끼리였다.

18 가주어 it을 활용하여 같은 의미의 문장을 쓸 수 있다.

19 (B)는 비인칭 주어로 날씨, 날짜, 거리, 명암 등을 나타낼 때 쓰이는 주어이다. ⑤번은 가주어 It이다.

20 Stella가 밤에 공격을 받기 쉬운 이유는 코끼리들이 밤에 잘 볼 수 없기 때문이다.

21 글쓴이가 전화를 건 곳은 코끼리 보호소였다.

22 벌레잡이 식물은 글쓴이의 손만큼 길다고 하였다.

23 it을 가주어로 하고 진주어로 to부정사를 쓴다.

24 동사를 수식하는 부사가 들어가는 것이 적절하다.

25 stay는 보어로 형용사를 취하는 2형식 동사이다. 따라서 safe라고 쓰는 것이 옳다.

26 글쓴이는 코끼리들이 Stella를 자신의 무리로 받아들이지 않을 것이라고 생각했다. 따라서 Unlike가 아닌 Like라고 쓰는 것이 옳다.

서술형 시험대비 p.90~91

01 Her eyes were as bright as stars.

02 They stood around Stella and made a thick wall.

03 see a group of lions

04 It was scaring to see a group of lions approaching Stella.

05 I decided to stay by her

06 He found Stella crying next to her mom.

07 Stella가 야생 지역에 혼자 남아 있고, 코끼리들은 밤에 잘 볼 수 없어서 공격받기 쉽기 때문에

08 I am as blind as elephants at night.

09 She cared for Stella as warmly as her mother did.

15

01 그녀의 눈이 밝았고 별같이 밝았다고 하였으므로 '그녀의 눈은 별처럼 밝았다'는 표현을 할 수 있다.

02 코끼리들은 Stella 주위에 둘러서서 두꺼운 벽을 만들어 Stella를 보호하였다.

03 정오 즈음이라고 답하는 것으로 보아 언제 한 무리의 사자를 보았는지 묻는 말이 들어가는 것이 옳다.

04 it을 가주어로 하고 to부정사를 진주어로 쓴다.

05 '나는 그녀 곁에 머물기로 결정했다'는 의미이다.

06 이상한 소리를 따라간 글쓴이는 Stella가 자신의 엄마 옆에서 울고 있는 것을 발견했다.

07 야생 지역에 혼자 남은 Stella는 코끼리의 특성상 밤에 잘 볼 수 없기 때문에 공격을 당하기 쉬우므로 글쓴이는 코끼리 보호소에 전화를 걸어 도움을 요청한 것이다.

08 blind: 앞이 안 보이는

09 그녀는 Stella를 Stella의 엄마만큼 따뜻하게 돌보았다는 문장으로 쓸 수 있다.

10 가주어 It을 활용하여 같은 의미의 문장을 쓸 수 있다.

11 새로운 코끼리 무리를 가리키는 대명사이다.

12 Stella는 코로 엄마의 죽은 몸을 어루만지고 있었다고 하였다.

13 Stella 앞에 새로운 코끼리 무리가 나타났다고 하였다.

14 글쓴이는 처음에 코끼리 무리가 Stella를 받아주지 않을 것이라고 생각하였다.

15 벌레잡이 풀은 글쓴이의 손만큼 길다고 하였고, 벌레잡이 풀의 길이는 대략 15cm라고 하였다.

16 식물은 항아리 같이 생겼다고 하였다.

영역별 핵심문제
p.93~97

01 ①   02 ③

03 (1) rescue (2) tail (3) strength   04 ②

05 (1) Do you know the girl next to the little boy?

    (2) Millions of people around the world use the Internet.

    (3) She loves to take a picture of her daughter.

06 (A) give (B) tell (C) keep

07 ⓑ → bigger   08 ①

09 (B) → (D) → (C) → (E) → (A)

---

01 '입안에서 이리저리 움직이는, 맛을 보거나 삼키거나 말을 하는 데 사용되는 부드러운 부분'을 지칭하는 말은 tongue(혀)이다.

02 thick: 두꺼운

03 rescue: 구조, tail: 꼬리, strength: 힘

04 주어진 문장에서 approach는 '다가가다'를 의미하며 이와 같은 의미로 쓰인 것은 ②번이다. 나머지는 모두 '접근, 접근법'을 뜻한다.

05 next to: ~ 옆에, millions of: 수백만의, take a picture of ~: ~의 사진을 찍다

06 give a presentation 발표하다, tell the difference: 차이를 구별하다, keep one's eyes on: ~에서 눈을 떼지 않다

08 Jane과 Tom이 정원에서 커다란 꽃을 보고 있다는 설명은 대화의 내용과 일치하지 않는다.

09 (B) 질문에 대한 대답 → (D) 비디오 소개 → (C) 궁금함을 표현 → (E) 비디오 내용 설명 → (A) 반응

11 빈칸 (A)에 비교급을 강조하는 표현이 들어갈 수 있다. very는 비교급을 강조할 수 없다.

13 위 대화를 통해 Dylan이 강아지를 돌보기 위해 무엇을 해야 하는지는 알 수 없다.

14 진주어로 쓰일 수 있는 것은 to부정사나 명사절 접속사 that이다. that의 경우 주어와 동사가 있는 문장을 이끌어야 한다.

15 진주어이므로 to부정사를 쓰는 것이 옳다.

16 ③ to부정사구 주어는 단수 취급한다. 따라서 is라고 쓰는 것이 옳다.

17 '물 없이 사는 것'이 주어이므로 to live without water를 진주어로 하여 문장을 만든다.

18 표에서 오렌지를 좋아하는 여성들이 15명이고, 남성들이 8명이라고 하였으므로 여성은 남성보다 오렌지를 더 좋아한다고 답했음을 알 수 있다.

19 '그녀가 노래 부르는 것을 듣는 것'이 주어이므로 'to hear her singing[sing]'을 주어로 하여 문장을 만들 수 있다.

20 모두 가주어로 쓰인 It이지만 ⑤번은 인칭대명사 It이다.

21 James의 개와 나의 개는 둘 다 세 살이다. 따라서 James의 개는 나의 개만큼 나이가 들었다고 말할 수 있다.

22 진주어로 to부정사가 적절하다

23 (A) 지각동사+목적어+동사원형 혹은 Ving (B) be동사의 보어가 필요하므로 형용사 (C) 지칭하는 대상이 the elephants로 복수 명사이므로 them

24 글쓴이는 아기 코끼리에게 Stella라는 이름을 지어주었다.

25 몇 마리의 사자가 Stella에게 다가가고 있었는지는 알 수 없다.

26 코끼리들이 아기 코끼리 주위를 둘러서서 두꺼운 벽을 만든 이유는 사자로부터 아기 코끼리를 보호해 주기를 원해서이 다.

27 새로운 코끼리 무리가 Stella를 받아주지 않을 것이라고 생 각했던 것이 틀렸고, Stella는 무리의 일원이 되었다는 흐름 이 자연스럽다.

28 (A) Stella는 엄마 옆에 있었다는 의미이므로 beside (B) approach는 타동사로 전치사 없이 목적어를 받아주므로 approached (C) 일반동사를 받아주는 동사이므로 did를 쓰는 것이 옳다. besides: 게다가

29 B의 말로 미루어 보아 암컷 코끼리 중 한 마리가 Stella에 게 젖을 준 것을 말하는 것이다.

30 Stella는 코로 엄마의 죽은 몸을 어루만지고 있었다.

단원별 예상문제   p.98~101

01 (1) humorous (2) careless (3) wild
   (4) blind (5) sheet
02 (1) Wild animals can be dangerous.
   (2) We need to have a sense of humor.
   (3) Don't feed the animals in the zoo.
03 ③　　　　　04 해룡은 꼬리가 곧지만 해마는 그렇지 않다.
05 ③　　　　　06 ⑤
07 (A) that (B) as (C) planted　　　　08 ⑤
09 They're talking about the science project topic.
10 He is wondering about weather change.
11 ③　　　　　12 ③
13 It was possible to see the object at night.
14 ③　　　　　15 ②
16 This room is about two times as large as that one.
17 It was wonderful to see fish swim in the water.
18 It is dangerous to stay alone in such a wild area.
19 ④　　　　20 ③　　　　21 ⑤　　　　22 ②, ④
23 The writer heard a strange sound.
24 It is interesting that the plant attracts insects and
   eats them.
25 ④

01 careless: 부주의한, humorous: 재미있는, sheet: (종이) 한 장, blind: 눈 먼, wild: 야생의
02 wild: 야생의, sense: 감각, feed: 먹이를 주다
03 밑줄 친 (A)는 '구별하다'라는 의미로 쓰였으며 이와 같은 뜻으로 쓰인 것은 ③번이다. 나머지는 모두 '말하다'를 의미한 다.

05 주어진 문장은 궁금증을 표현하고 있고 Dr. Watson의 연구에 대한 소개에 대한 반응으로 자연스러우므로 (C)가 적절하다.

06 자이언트 캥거루는 사람 세 명만큼 무거웠으므로 자이언트 캥거루가 세 명보다 더 무거웠다는 설명은 대화의 내용과 일치하지 않는다.

07 (A) 지시형용사 that이 알맞다. (B) 'as+원급+as' 구문이므로 as가 적절하다. (C) plant는 '심다'를 나타내는 동사로 과거시제로 나타내야 하므로 planted가 적절하다.

08 위 대화를 통해 Kelly의 할아버지가 2004년에 무슨 나무를 심었는지는 알 수 없다.

09 Judy와 Ryan은 과학 프로젝트 주제에 대해 이야기하고 있다.

10 Ryan은 날씨 변화에 대해 궁금해 하고 있다.

11 주어진 문장의 밑줄 친 부분은 가주어 It이다. ① 인칭대명사 ② 비인칭 주어 ③ 가주어 ④ 비인칭 주어 ⑤ 인칭대명사

12 가주어로 쓰일 수 있는 것은 It이다.

13 '밤에 그 사물을 보는 것'이 주어이므로 to see the object at night을 진주어로 하여 문장을 만든다.

14 Jill이 나보다 많은 사람들을 알고 있다는 것은 결국 나는 Jill만큼 많은 사람들을 알지 못한다는 의미가 된다.

15 진주어가 쓰일 자리이므로 to부정사를 쓰는 것이 옳다.

16 '배수사+as+원급+as: ~보다 …배 더 ~한 / as를 추가한다.

17 swim을 대신하여 swimming을 써도 좋다.

18 '이러한 야생 지역에서 혼자 있는 것'이 주어이므로 진주어로 to stay alone in such a wild area를 쓸 수 있다.

19 (A) 죽은 엄마 옆에서 Stella가 울고 있는 소리를 들었으므로 strange (B) 글쓴이가 사건을 목격한 시점은 해질녘으로 곧 어두워진다고 말하며 코끼리가 밤에 잘 볼 수 없음을 걱정하는 말이 들어가는 것이 자연스러우므로 dark (C) Stella의 엄마가 죽어 있었다고 하였으므로 lifeless가 옳다.

20 (D)는 가주어로 사용된 It이다. 모두 가주어 It이지만 ③번은 '그 것'이라고 해석되는 인칭대명사 It이다.

21 오후 10시 40분에도 Stella는 엄마 곁에 남아 있었으므로 ⑤ 번은 글의 내용과 일치하지 않는다.

22 Stella는 홀로 남아 있었고 구조팀이 도착

23 해질녘에 글쓴이는 이상한 소리를 들었다고 하였다.

24 '그 식물이 곤충을 끌어들이고 그것들을 먹는 것'이 주어이 므로 진주어 that절을 활용하여 문장을 만든다.

25 식물이 곤충을 끌어들이는 방법은 알 수 없다.

서술형 실전문제   p.102~103

01 ⓐ old ⓑ was born
02 It is thirteen years old.
03 He planted the tree when Kelly was born.
04 It is important to be kind to your classmates.
05 A yellow pencil is as cheap as a green pencil.

06 possible to live without electricity

07 goes to bed as early as

08 as well as

09 as white as

10 My eyes are not as[so] bright as her eyes.

11 A group of lions approached Stella.

12 ⑤번 → safe

13 She cared for Stella as warmly as Stella's mom did.

14 Stella become part of the group

15 would let Stella in

01 'as+원급+as' 구문이므로 원급인 old가 적절하다. be born: 태어나다

02 빨간 집 옆에 있는 나무는 수령이 13년 되었다.

03 Kelly의 할아버지는 Kelly가 태어났을 때 나무를 심었다.

04 '학급 친구들에게 친절하게 대하는 것'이 주어이므로 to be kind to your classmates를 진주어로 하여 문장을 만든다.

05 두 색깔의 연필이 가격이 같으므로 '노란색 연필은 초록색 연필만큼 싸다.'는 문장을 쓸 수 있다.

06 대답으로 미루어 보아 전기 없이 사는 것이 가능한지 묻는 말이 들어가는 것이 적절하다.

07 두 사람은 같은 시간에 잠든다. 따라서 'Brian은 June만큼 일찍 잠자리에 든다.'는 문장을 완성할 수 있다.

08 대화의 내용상 '그들만큼 축구를 잘하지 못했다'는 말이 들어가는 것이 적절하다.

09 Helen의 얼굴은 종이만큼 하얗다는 문장을 완성할 수 있다.

10 'as hers'라고 써도 무방하다.

11 Stella에게 다가간 것은 한 무리의 사자들이다.

12 Stella 주변을 둘러서서 보호해 준 코끼리들 덕분에 Stella는 안전했다고 말하는 것이 적절하다.

13 as ~ as 사이에는 형용사나 부사의 원급이 쓰일 수 있다. 앞 문장에서 She cared for Stella라는 완전한 문장이 쓰였고 '따뜻하게 보살피다'라는 의미이므로 부사 warmly를 써서 문장을 쓰는 것에 유의한다.

14 '사역동사(let)+목적어+동사원형' 형태에 유의하여 답을 쓴다.

15 글쓴이는 새로운 코끼리 무리가 Stella를 새로운 일원으로 받아주는 것이 불가능하다고 생각했다.

창의사고력 서술형 문제
p.104

|모범답안|

01 (A) lions (B) friendship (C) raised her

02 (1) It is interesting to see elephants protect a baby elephant.

   (2) It is amazing to read that the female elephant took good care of Stella.

(3) It was really touching to see the new elephants accept Stella as a group member.

03 moss ball, dark green, like, about 4cm, as big as, it floats up when it gets enough sunlight

단원별 모의고사
p.105~108

01 (D) → (A) → (C) → (B)

02 He studies animals that lived millions of years ago.

03 It lived in Australia.

04 It was as heavy as three men.

05 ③   06 ⑤

07 She is curious about the huge flower in the picture.

08 It smells very bad.

09 (1) tell the difference   (2) become part of

   (3) give a presentation   (4) next to

   (5) Thanks to

10 that tree is as old as me 11 ②

12 (C) → (B) → (D) → (E) → (A)   13 ④

14 as long as, twice as long as

15 ⑤   16 ⑤

17 It is important to listen to what he says. It's because his opinion is as important as yours.

18 ③   19 ③   20 ④   21 ②

22 the elephant shelter / alone / to stay alone / dark

23 ⑤

24 He saw a baby elephant with her mother.

25 We will be there as soon as possible.

01 (D) 자신의 새 강아지 소개 → (A) 반응 → (C) 작은 강아지 설명 → (B) 강아지가 빨리 자란다는 사실 설명

02 Dr. Watson은 수백만 년 전에 살았던 동물들을 연구한다.

03 자이언트 캥거루는 호주에서 살았었다.

04 자이언트 캥거루는 3명의 사람만큼 무거웠다.

05 주어진 문장은 궁금증을 표현하고 있으므로 이어서 구체적인 설명을 요구하는 (C)가 적절하다.

06 Todd가 두 남자와 사자 사이에 우정에 대한 이야기에 감동 받았다는 설명이 위 대화의 내용과 일치한다.

07 Jane은 사진에 있는 커다란 꽃에 대해 궁금해 하고 있다.

08 커다란 꽃의 냄새는 매우 나쁘다.

09 become part of: ~의 일원이 되다, give a presentation: 발표하다, thanks to: ~ 덕분에, next to: ~ 옆에, tell the difference: 차이를 구별하다

11 위 대화에서 Kelly와 George는 빨간 집 옆에 있는 나무에 대해 이야기하고 있다.

12 (C) 연구 소개 요청 → (B) 연구 소개 → (D) 궁금증 표현 및 연구에 대한 질문 → (E) 질문에 대한 대답 및 연구 결과 설명 → (A) 놀라움 표현

13 주어진 문장의 밑줄 친 부분은 진주어로 쓰인 to부정사이다. ① 부사적 용법 중 목적 ② 형용사적 용법 ③ 부사적 용법 중 목적 ④ 진주어 ⑤ 부사적 용법 중 목적

14 세 사람의 공부 시간을 보면, Smith는 Clara만큼 오랜 시간 공부하지 않고, Clara는 Zach보다 두 시간 더 공부한다고 말할 수 있다.

15 'so ~ as'로 쓰는 경우는 부정일 때이며 긍정의 경우는 'as ~ as'로 쓴다.

16 가주어가 될 수 있는 것은 It이며, 진주어는 to부정사가 적절하다. 'as soon as possible'은 'as soon as you can'과 같다.

17 yours를 대신하여 your opinion이라고 써도 좋다.

18 코끼리들이 Stella 주위에 둘러서서 두꺼운 벽을 만든 이유는 사자들로부터 Stella를 보호하기 위한 것이다.

19 '그들 덕분에'라는 의미가 적절하다. ①, ④ ~에도 불구하고 ② ~ 대신에 ③ ~ 덕분에 ⑤ ~을 제외하고

20 구조팀이 올 때까지 그녀 곁에 머물기로 하였다고 말하는 것이 가장 자연스럽다.

21 밑줄 친 (B)는 가주어로 쓰인 It이다. ①, ③, ⑤ 인칭대명사 ② 가주어 ④ 비인칭 주어

22 코끼리 보호소에 전화한 글쓴이는 아기 코끼리가 혼자 있다고 말하자 야생에서 혼자 있는 것은 위험하다고 답하고, 곧 어두워져서 코끼리가 걱정된다고 말하는 것이 글의 내용과 일치한다.

23 Stella의 엄마가 왜 죽었는지는 위 글을 읽고 알 수 없다.

24 글쓴이는 아기 코끼리가 그녀의 엄마와 함께 있는 모습을 보았다.

25 as soon as we can이라고 써도 좋다

Art around Us

시험대비 실력평가   p.112

01 melt   02 ①   03 ⑤
04 (1) took   (2) glanced
    (3) artworks   (4) soap bubbles
05 (1) myth   (2) landscape   (3) details
    (4) wax   (5) wings
06 ①

01 주어진 단어의 관계는 반의어 관계이다. melt: 녹다, freeze: 얼다

02 특히 자연적이거나 역사적인 사건을 설명하기 위해 만들어진 고대의 이야기를 가리키는 말은 myth(신화)이다.

03 despite: ~에도 불구하고

04 (1) take a look at: ~을 보다 (2) glance at: ~을 힐끗 보다 (3) artwork: 미술 작품 (4) soap bubble: 비눗방울

06 주어진 문장에서 notice는 '알아차리다'라는 의미를 나타내며 이와 같은 의미로 쓰인 것은 ①번이다. 나머지는 모두 '통지, 공고'라는 의미로 썼다.

서술형 시험대비   p.113

01 princess
02 (1) melts   (2) exhibition   (3) feathers
03 (1) landscape   (2) notice   (3) stick
    (4) promise   (5) seaside
04 (1) I wonder why he invited me to his party.
    (2) Production of new cars will start next month.
    (3) Nobody noticed me at first.
05 melt
06 (1) Stay away from windows during a storm.
    (2) May I take a look at your movie ticket?
    (3) I called the police right away.

01 prince: 왕자, princess: 공주

02 melt: 녹다, exhibition: 전시회, feather: 깃털

03 notice: 알아차리다, landscape: 풍경, stick: 내밀다, promise: 약속하다, seaside: 해안가

05 열을 가함으로써 고체에서 액체로 변하는 것을 가리키는 말은 melt(녹다)이다.

06 (1) stay away from: ~을 가까이 하지 않다 (2) take a look at: ~을 보다 (3) right away: 즉시, 바로

Conversation

p.114~115

1 (1) What kind of concert
  (2) movie do you want to see   (3) type
2 (1) Which do you prefer
  (2) taking photos, drawing pictures
  (3) I prefer dogs to cats

교과서 대화문 익히기

Check(√) True or False   p.116

1 T   2 F   3 T   4 T

교과서 확인학습   p.118~119

Listen & Talk 1 A-1

going to play / almost every day / What kind of music / play songs

Listen & Talk 1 A-2

how to paint clean lines / What kind of brush / flat , better, Try

Listen & Talk 1 B

meeting, right / do you want to watch first / want to / Sounds, right / watching the play / the one

Listen & Talk 2 A-1

a story / of it, prefer, to / like, better / scenes, real

Listen & Talk 2 A-2

Have, listened / cool, part / dance version / I prefer the guitar version / matches

Listen & Talk 2 B

interesting painting / looks like / Which do you prefer / prefer, to / How about you / prefer, to / modern

Communication

so, find out, May, ask / What kind of performance / do, prefer / prefer rock to hip-hop / favorite musician / Thank, for

---

Wrap Up 1

Can, help / various kinds, What kind of music / want to / should get

시험대비 기본평가   p.120

01 ①, ④   02 What kind of brush were you using?
03 (A) *Life of Pi*   (B) the movie   04 ④

01 (A)는 도움을 요청하는 표현이다.
04 ④ Minsu는 소설보다 영화를 더 선호한다.

시험대비 실력평가   p.121~122

01 ⑤   02 (A) Jane's new song (= Girl Friend)
(B) a dance version   (C) the guitar version
03 ④   04 ⑤   05 (A) Jack   (B) Mina
(C) It has an interesting smile.   (D) His Mona Lisa is
cute, and it looks modern. 06 ③   07 which
do you prefer 08 She likes rock better.   09 (C) →
(B) → (D) → (A)

03 ④ Tony는 Jane의 목소리가 기타 버전에 잘 어울린다고 생각한다.
04 ⑤ Steve가 '로미오와 줄리엣' 연극 볼 것을 왜 제안하는지 는 알 수 없다.
08 Emily는 록을 더 좋아한다.
09 (C) 어떠한 종류의 음악을 연주하고 싶은지 질문→ (B) 대답 → (D) 기타 추천 → (A) 구매

서술형 시험대비   p.123

01 (A) ⓑ   (B) ⓒ   (C) ⓐ
02 They have listened to Girl Friend .
03 Because he thinks that the guitar version matches Jane's voice better.
04 I prefer the movie to the novel.
05 It's about a boy and a tiger.
06 It's because he thinks that the scenes are very beautiful and the tiger looks so real.

02 Tony와 Sue가 Jane의 앨범에서 들은 노래는 *Girl Friend* 이다.
03 Tony는 기타 버전이 Jane의 목소리와 더 잘 어울린다고 생각하기 때문이다.

04 prefer A to B: A를 B보다 선호하다

05 *Life of Pi* 는 소년과 호랑이에 관한 이야기이다.

06 민수가 소설보다 영화를 더 선호한 이유는 장면이 매우 아름 답고 호랑이가 매우 진짜처럼 보이기 때문이다.

Grammar [교과서]

핵심 Check   p.124~125

1 (1) me watch   (2) him use   (3) my dad come
2 (1) who she is   (2) why you study   (3) where you went

시험대비 기본평가   p.126

01 (1) to read → read
   (2) was the weather → the weather was
   (3) buying → buy
   (4) were you → you were
02 (1) Oliver wanted to ask if[whether] she was satisfied with his service.
   (2) Can you tell me where we are going?
   (3) I'd like to know what you do during your free time.
   (4) I wonder how often you water the plant.
03 (1) The boss made him stay in the office.
   (2) Did you let your friend borrow your bicycle?
   (3) We had him wear a straw hat.
   (4) Please let me see the answer.

01 (1), (3) 사역동사의 목적격 보어는 동사원형 형태이다. (2), (4) 의문사가 이끄는 문장이 명사 역할을 할 때 '의문사+주어+동사'의 어순임에 유의하자.

02 의문사가 없는 경우는 if나 whether를 사용하여 간접의문문을 만들

03 사역동사 make, have, let은 목적격 보어로 동사원형 형태를 사용한다. 이때 목적어와 목적격 보어의 관계는 주어와 서술어의 관계가 성립하여 '목적어가 ~ 하도록 시키다'라고 해석한다.

시험대비 실력평가   p.127~129

01 ⑤   02 ③   03 ④   04 ⑤
05 come   06 will   07 ③   08 ③
09 Who do you suppose broke the window?
10 ②   11 ③

---

12 Why do you think she made you do it again?
13 I made him repair my watch.
14 ④   15 ④   16 ③   17 ③
18 ④   19 ⑤   20 ③   21 ④
22 what you do when you are free
23 ③   24 ②
25 I want to know if[whether] she liked the present.

01 want는 목적격 보어로 to부정사를 취하는 동사이다.

02 '목적어가 ~하도록 시키다'는 의미로 쓰이는 동사는 사역동사이다.

03 간접의문문의 의문사를 문두에 배치하는 동사는 추측동사로 think, imagine, guess, suppose, believe 등이 이에 속한다.

04 모두 목적격 보어로 동사원형 형태를 취할 수 있는 동사이지만, allow는 목적격 보어로 to부정사를 취하는 동사이다.

05 make는 사역동사이므로 목적격 보어로 동사원형 형태를 취한다.

06 주어진 문장을 영어로 옮기면 'I wonder when you will arrive here.'이다.

07 ⓑ when they will call me ⓒ let me wear라고 쓰는 것이 옳다.

08 간접의문문을 만드는 문제이다. 간접의문문의 어순은 '의문사+주어+동사'이다.

09 suppose가 있는 문장에서 간접의문문의 주어를 문두에 배치하는 것에 유의한다.

10 '누가 한글을 만들었는지'라는 의미이므로 who made Hanguel이라고 쓰는 것이 옳다.

11 사역동사의 목적격 보어는 동사원형의 형태를 취하며, '너의 부모님이 집에 없는 동안 너를 누가 돌볼 것인지를 말해 달라'는 것이므로 간접의문문을 이용하여 who will take care of you라고 쓰는 것이 옳다.

12 think가 있는 문장이므로 간접의문문의 의문사를 문두에 배치해야 한다.

13 '그가 내 시계를 고치게 했다'는 것은 사역동사를 이용하여 나타낼 수 있다.

14 주어진 말을 영어로 쓰면 What time do you think it is?이다.

15 allow는 목적격 보어로 to부정사를 취하는 동사이다. help는 목적격 보어로 to부정사나 동사원형 형태를 취한다.

16 간접의문문의 어순은 '의문사+주어+동사'임에 유의한다.

17 사역동사로 쓰인 make이므로 목적격 보어로 동사원형 형태를 쓴다.

18 3형식, 4형식, 5형식으로 모두 쓰이면서 목적격 보어로 동사원형 형태까지 취할 수 있는 것은 동사 make이다.

19 Who do you guess built the building?이라고 쓰는 것이 옳다.

20 대답으로 미루어 보아 몇 학년인지를 묻는 말이 들어가는 것이 가장 적절하다. 간접의문문의 어순인 '의문사+주어+동사'에 유의한다.

21 목적격 보어로 동사원형 형태를 취하는 동사는 사역동사이다.

22 답변으로 보아 여가 시간에 무엇을 하는지를 묻는 말이 들어가는 것이 적절하다.

23 think가 있는 문장이므로 Who do you think you are? 라고 쓰는 것이 옳다.

24 엄마가 내게 무언가를 하라고 말하는 것이므로 ②번이 내용상 가장 적절하다.

25 의문사가 없는 문장의 간접의문문은 if 혹은 whether를 써서 만든다.

01 Mom made me and my sister clean the house.

02 Who do you think stole the money?

03 Can you tell me when they let you go home?

04 (1) me drive his car

(2) him bring her

(3) me look at

05 Brad made me accept the job.

06 (1) I don't know where he lives.

(2) How old do you guess he is?

(3) Can you tell me why you were absent from school?

(4) I want to know when you met him for the first time.

(5) When do you think the concert starts?

(6) Why do you imagine the baby is crying?

(7) Do you know if(또는 whether) Charley was sleeping at that time?

07 I helped my cousin (to) do his homework.

08 (1) play   (2) published   (3) take

(4) work   (5) will report

09 the oranges are / how many oranges he wants to buy

10 The woman lets the man drink water.

11 The suit makes me look fancy.

12 A: How do you think the movie was?

B: It made me feel sleepy.

13 Do you know who drove the car yesterday?

14 (1) Can you tell me when she wrote this book?

(2) You can lead a horse to water, but you can't make him drink.

(3) I wonder if(또는 whether) he is full or not.

01 make는 '목적어에게 ~하도록 시키다'라는 의미의 사역동사이다. 따라서 목적격 보어로 동사원형 형태를 써서 문장을 만든다.

02 think가 있는 문장에서는 간접의문문의 의문사를 문두에 배치한다. 이 문장에서 who는 의문사이자 주어 역할을 동시에 하고 있음에 유의한다.

03 tell의 직접목적어로 간접의문문을 쓰며, '그들이 너를 집에 가게 했다'고 하였으므로 사역동사를 이용하여 문장을 만들 수 있다.

04 위 문장에서 let, make, have는 모두 사역동사로 쓰이고 있으므로 목적격 보어로 동사원형 형태를 쓰는 것에 유의한다.

05 force+목적어+to부정사: 목적어가 ~하도록 강요하다

06 의문사가 이끄는 문장이 절 내에서 주어, 목적어, 보어 역할을 할 때 이를 간접의문문이라고 한다. 간접의문문의 어순은 '의문사+주어+동사'의 어순이며 think, believe, suppose, imagine, guess와 같은 동사가 있을 때에는 의문사를 문두로 배치한다.

07 help는 목적격 보어로 to부정사나 동사원형 형태를 취한다.

08 (1), (3), (4) 사역동사의 목적격 보어는 동사원형의 형태를 취한다. (2) 작년에 이 책을 누가 출간했는지를 궁금해 하는 내용이므로 과거 시제를 쓴다. (5) 내일 무엇을 보고할 것이라고 생각하느냐는 문장이다. 내용에 맞게 미래 시제를 써서 나타낸다.

09 Andy는 오렌지 가격이 얼마인지 알고 싶어한다. 그래서 Paul은 Andy에게 얼마나 많은 오렌지를 사길 원하는지 묻는다.

10 사역동사 let은 목적격 보어로 동사원형 형태를 취한다.

11 정장이 나를 멋지게 보이도록 하는 것이므로 주어는 the suit, 목적어는 me로 하여 사역동사를 써서 문장을 완성할 수 있다.

12 Do you think?와 How was the movie?를 하나의 문장으로 만들어 How do you think the movie was?를 만들 수 있다.

13 who가 의문사와 주어 역할을 동시에 하고 있으므로 who drove the car의 어순으로 쓸 수 있다.

14 의문사가 있는 간접의문문은 '의문사+주어+동사'의 어순을 쓰고 의문사가 없는 경우 if나 whether를 써서 간접의문문을 나타낼 수 있다. 사역 동사는 목적격 보어로 동사원형 형태를 취한다.

🐦 [교과서]
Reading

📎 **확인문제**   p.132

1 F   2 T   3 T   4 F   5 F

📎 **확인문제**   p.133

1 F   2 T   3 T   4 T   5 T   6 F

🌐 **교과서 확인학습 A**   p.134~135

01 Welcome to

02 when, go to, how much time, looking

03 glance at, for, a few, on

04 might miss, since, to notice them

05 look at, closely, help you see　06 at, first

07 seaside landscape, peaceful, isn't it

08 title, is　　　09 where Icarus is

10 are sticking out of the water

11 in the famous myth

12 made wings for him, to stay away from

13 However, listen　　14 flew too close

15 melted, fell into　　16 at, entire

17 Despite, going on with

18 still look peaceful

19 What do you think　　20 move on to

21 see, behind　22 actually painted

23 Who do you think he is　24 Take

25 seems to be, because　26 title, painting

27 drawing, beside　28 Take

29 make you wonder

30 which direction the artist is

31 see, in the mirror, background

32 Who do you think he is

1 Welcome to the World Art Museum tour.

2 When you go to an art museum, how much time do you spend looking at each painting?

3 Many visitors glance at one painting for only a few seconds before they move on.

4 But you might miss the important details of paintings since it is hard to notice them right away.

5 Today, we'll look at two paintings closely and I'll help you see interesting details.

6 Look at this painting first.

7 The seaside landscape is so peaceful and beautiful, isn't it?

8 The title of this painting is *Landscape with the Fall of Icarus*.

9 So, can you see where Icarus is?

10 Do you see two legs that are sticking out of the water near the ship?

11 This is Icarus in the famous myth in Greece.

12 In the myth, Icarus' father made wings for him with feathers and wax and told him to stay away from the sun.

13 However, Icarus didn't listen.

14 He flew too close to the sun.

15 So, the wax melted and he fell into the water.

16 Now, look at the entire painting again.

17 Despite the tragedy of Icarus, people are going on with their everyday activities.

18 Does the painting still look peaceful?

19 What do you think the artist is trying to tell us?

20 Now, let's move on to the next painting.

21 Do you see the artist behind the large canvas?

22 He is Diego Velázquez, and he actually painted this picture.

23 Who do you think he is painting?

24 Take a quick look.

25 The young princess seems to be the main person because she is in the center of the painting.

26 But the title of the painting is *The Maids of Honour*.

27 Then, is the artist drawing the two women beside the princess?

28 Take a close look.

29 It will make you wonder about the painting more.

30 Try to see which direction the artist is looking at.

31 Can you see the king and the queen in the mirror in the background of the painting?

32 Who do you think he is painting now?

01 ①　　　　02 notice　　03 ③

04 We will look at two paintings closely.

05 Can you see where Icarus is?

06 ①　　　　07 ②

08 It is *Landscape with the Fall of Icarus*.

09 ③　　　　10 ④　　　11 wonder　12 ③

13 The young princess seems to be the main person because she is in the center of the painting.

14 We can find him behind the large canvas.

15 ⑤　　　16 ②

17 It takes them only a few seconds to see one painting.

18 ③　　　19 ③　　　20 ⑤　　　21 ②

22 ⑤

23 He told Icarus to stay away from the sun.

24 ③　　　25 ④　　　26 ④

27 The young princess is in the middle of the painting.

28 ②

01 문장에서 since는 이유를 나타내는 접속사로 쓰였다. 따라서 ① 번이 옳다.

02 '무언가를 혹은 어떤 사람을 인식하게 되다'는 '알아차리다 (notice)'이다.

03 (B)는 진주어로 쓰인 to부정사이다. ① 명사적 용법 중 목적어 ② 부사적 용법 중 감정의 원인 ③ 명사적 용법 중 진주어 ④ 형용사적 용법 ⑤ 명사적 용법 중 보어

04 두 개의 그림을 자세히 살펴볼 것이라고 하였다.

05 간접의문문을 만드는 문제이다. '의문사+주어+동사'의 어순에 유의하여 문장을 만든다.

06 이카루스의 비극에도 불구하고 사람들은 일상의 활동을 계속하고 있다는 의미가 가장 자연스럽다. 따라서 despite와 같은 의미인 in spite of를 쓰는 것이 옳다.

07 이카루스의 아버지는 날개를 만들어 주며 태양에 가까이 가지 말라고 말했지만 이카루스는 그의 말을 듣지 않았다는 순서가 자연스러우며 ②번 이하의 문장은 주어진 문장의 결과 이다.

08 그림의 제목은 '추락하는 이카루스가 있는 풍경'이라고 하였다.

09 그림에서 이카루스는 물에 빠져서 두 다리만 보이는 상황이다. 따라서 ③번은 그림에서 찾아볼 수 없다.

10 이카루스의 날개는 그의 아버지가 만들어 준 것이다.

11 사역동사의 목적격 보어 자리이다. 따라서 동사원형 형태를 쓰는 것이 옳다.

12 (B)는 진행형을 만드는 현재분사이다. 모두 동명사이지만 ③번은 현재분사이다.

13 seem to부정사: ~인 것 같다

14 두 번째 그림의 화가는 커다란 캔버스 뒤에 있다고 하였다.

15 그림이 얼마나 큰지는 글을 읽고 알 수 없다.

16 (A) 시간은 셀 수 없으므로 how much (B) the important details of paintings를 가리키므로 복수 대명사 them (C) help는 목적격 보어로 to부정사나 동사원 형 형태를 취한다.

17 많은 방문객들은 이동하기 전에 하나의 그림을 몇 초간만 힐끗 본다고 하였다. It takes+사람+시간+to V: 사람이 … 하는 데 ~만큼의 시간이 걸리다

18 두 개의 그림을 자세히 살펴보며 흥미로운 세부 사항들을 볼 수 있게 도와준다고 하였으므로 ③번이 가장 적절하다.

19 아버지가 태양에 가까이 가지 말라고 이야기했지만 이카루스는 그의 말을 듣지 않고 태양에 가깝게 날았다는 내용이므로 However가 옳다.

20 이카루스가 어디에 보이는지 물음 - (C) 그림 속에서 이카루스가 어디에 있는지 설명하며 이카루스는 그리스 신화에 나오는 인물임을 언급함 - (B) 그리스 신화에 나오는 이카루스의 이야기 - (A) 아버지의 말을 듣지 않은 이카루스는 물에 빠짐

21 의문사가 이끄는 문장이 절 내에서 명사 역할을 하는 간접의문문의 어순은 '의문사+주어+동사'의 어순이다.

22 이카루스는 아버지의 말을 듣지 않고 태양 가까이로 날았다가 밀랍이 녹아 물에 빠졌다고 하였다.

23 이카루스의 아버지는 그에게 태양에 가까이 가지 말라고 이야기 하였다.

24 make는 목적격 보어로 동사원형을 취하는 사역동사이며 feel은 형용사를 보어로 취하는 감각동사이다.

25 ④ David Myriam이 그의 작품에서 사용한 것은 모래라고 하였다.

26 추측동사 believe, think, guess, imagine, suppose가 있는 문장에서는 간접의문문의 의문사를 문두로 배치한다. know는 이러한 동사에 해당하지 않는다.

27 그림의 중앙에 있는 사람은 공주라고 하였다.

28 커다란 캔버스 뒤에 있는 화가가 Diego Velázquez이므로 그가 그림에 등장하지 않는다는 것은 글의 내용과 일치하지 않는다.

서술형 시험대비
p.142~143

01 how much time you spend looking at each painting.

02 the important details of paintings

03 I'll help you (to) see interesting details.

04 What do you think the artist is trying to tell us?

05 tragedy

06 He made wings for him.

07 melt

08 where Icarus is, are sticking out of the water

09 actually

10 Diego Velázquez painted the picture.

11 그림을 자세히 보는 것

12 They are the king and the queen.

13 I wonder who actually painted this picture.

14 what the artist used

15 Because a tree in the moon makes the writer feel calm.

01 간접의문문을 완성하는 문제이다. '의문사+주어+동사' 어순에 유의하여 답을 쓴다.

02 그림의 중요한 세부 사항들을 가리키는 말이다.

03 help는 목적격 보어로 to부정사나 동사원형을 모두 쓸 수 있는 준사역동사이다.

04 문장의 동사가 think인 경우 간접의문문의 의문사를 문두에 배치하는 것에 유의하여 답을 쓴다.

05 화가가 그림을 통해 말하려는 것은 우리는 타인의 비극을 알 수 없다는 것이다.

06 이카루스의 아버지는 그를 위하여 날개를 만들어 주었다고 하였다.

07 무엇이 밀랍을 녹게 만들었느냐는 질문을 쓰는 것이 옳다. 사역동사의 목적격 보어 자리이므로 동사원형 형태를 쓰는 것에 유의한다.

08 두 사람의 대화로 미루어 보아 A는 이카루스가 어디에 있는지 묻고 있으며 B가 알려주는 중임을 알 수 있다.

09 동사를 수식하므로 부사로 고쳐야 한다.

10 그림을 그린 사람은 Diego Velázquez라고 하였다.

11 It은 앞 문장 전체인 'Take a close look.'을 가리킨다.

12 그림의 배경에 있는 거울 속 사람들은 왕과 왕비라고 하였다.

13 간접의문문을 이용하여 문장을 만들 수 있다. 여기에서 who는 의문사와 주어 역할을 동시에 하는 것에 유의한다.

14 답변으로 미루어 보아 작가가 그림에 무엇을 사용했는지 묻는 말이 들어가는 것이 옳다.

15 글쓴이가 그 그림을 좋아하는 이유는 달에 있는 나무가 차분 한 기분을 느끼게 해 주어서라고 하였다.

01 tragedy   02 ⑤   03 ④

04 (1) tourists   (2) stick   (3) novelist

05 (1) I prefer the novel to the poem.

    (2) My family will take a trip to the seaside.

    (3) The war was a tragedy for the whole world.

06 ②   07 ①   08 ⑤   09 ③

10 What kind of performance do you want to watch first?

11 ⑤   12 ③   13 ③   14 ⑤

15 She doesn't know how to paint clean lines.

16 She will use a flat brush. 17 ③   18 ⑤

19 ④   20 Where do you think she is now?

21 ②   22 ③   23 ⑤

24 help, do   25 ①

26 The monster made the children scream.

27 (1) I didn't hear what you said.

    (2) I'd like to know if you are friends with Jina.

28 ①, ②   29 ③

30 They were made of feathers and wax. 31 ⑤

32 if the painting still looks peaceful

33 tragedy   34 (A) looking   (B) a few   (C) closely

35 We might miss the important details of a painting.

36 ③

01 주어진 단어의 관계는 반의어 관계이다. comedy: 희극, tragedy: 비극

02 특히 죽음과 관련된 매우 슬픈 사건을 가리키는 말은 tragedy(비극)이다.

03 flat: 평평한

06 주어진 문장은 '내밀다'라는 뜻을 나타내며 이와 같은 의미로 쓰인 것은 ②번이다. ①, ④ ~을 붙이다, ③, ⑤ 막대기

07 direct: ~으로 향하다, (길을) 안내하다[알려주다], direct flight: 직행 항공편

08 주어진 문장은 소설을 더 좋아하는 이유로 적절하므로 (E)가 알맞다.

09 ③ Jean이 Sally와 함께 영화 *The Maze Runner* 를 보았다는 설명은 대화의 내용과 일치하지 않는다.

13 주어진 문장은 영화를 선호한다는 것으로 다음에 이유를 질문하는 문장에 자연스럽게 이어지므로 (C)가 적절하다.

14 대화를 통해 민수가 언제 영화를 봤는지 알 수 없다.

15 Sora는 선을 깔끔하게 그리는 방법을 모른다.

16 Sora는 선을 그릴 때 납작한 붓을 사용할 것이다.

17 파티에 초대한 주체가 who이므로 who invited you의 어순이 옳다.

18 조건절과 명사절을 동시에 이끌 수 있는 접속사는 if이다.

19 let은 사역동사로 목적격 보어로 동사원형 형태를 취한다. 따라서 use라고 쓰는 것이 옳다.

20 Do you think?와 Where is she now?를 하나로 만든 문장이다.

21 주어진 문장을 영어로 쓰면 I wonder who made you send me this flower.이다.

22 Who kicked the ball?에서 Who는 의문사이자 주어 역할을 동시에 하고 있으므로 ③번이 가장 적절하다.

23 tell은 목적격 보어로 to부정사를 취하는 동사이다.

24 help는 목적격 보어로 to부정사나 동사원형 형태를 모두 쓸 수 있는 동사이다.

25 ⓐ who you are talking with ⓑ have them go to school ⓓ what Jason does ⓔ if(또는 whether) you have brothers or sisters라고 쓰는 것이 옳다.

26 '아이들이 비명을 지르게 하는 것'이므로 사역동사를 이용하여 문장을 만들 수 있다. 사역동사의 목적격 보어는 동사원 형 형태임에 유의한다.

27 (2)번은 if를 대신하여 whether를 써도 좋다.

28 의문사가 없는 의문문에는 whether나 if를 써서 간접의문문을 만든다.

29 모두 이카루스를 지칭하는 말이지만 ③번은 이카루스의 아버지를 가리키고 있다.

30 이카루스의 날개는 깃털과 밀랍으로 이루어졌다고 하였다. be made of: ~으로 이루어지다

31 밀랍과 깃털로 이루어진 날개를 달고 태양 가까이 날아간 것 때문에 이카루스는 물에 빠지게 되었다. 따라서 ⑤번은 옳지 않다.

32 의문사가 없는 문장의 간접의문문은 if나 whether를 써서 만든다.

33 '특히 죽음과 관련된 아주 슬픈 사건'은 '비극(tragedy)'이라고 한다.

34 (A) spend+시간+Ving: V하는 데에 시간을 쓰다 (B) 셀 수 있는 seconds를 수식하므로 a few (C) '자세히'라는 의미의 부사가 적절하므로 closely

35 하나의 그림을 몇 초간만 힐끗 보는 것의 문제는 그림의 중요한 세부 사항들을 놓칠 수 있다는 것이다.

36 ⓐ는 가주어로 쓰인 it이다. ① 비인칭 주어 ② 비인칭 주어 ③ 가주어 ④ 인칭대명사 ⑤ 인칭대명사

01 (D) than→ to　　　　　　　02 ⑤

03 What kind of performance do you like best?

04 Which musician do you like best?

05 ④　　　　　　06 performance

07 (A) 2:00 p.m.　(B) gym　(C) Play　(D) Main Hall

08 ④　　　　　09 ⑤

10 (C) → (B) → (E) → (D) → (A)　　　　11 ③

12 ④　　　　13 what you wore　　　14 ⑤

15 ③　　　　16 ②

17 My parents let me sleep late on weekends.

18 ④　　　　19 ③　　　　20 ②　　　　21 ①

22 what happened to Icarus

23 I wonder if you saw many interesting pieces of art.

24 ④

01 prefer A to B: A보다 B를 선호하다

02 Tony가 Girl Friend 의 댄스 버전에 대해 어떻게 생각하는지는 알 수 없다.

08 주어진 문장은 상대방의 의견을 물어보는 표현이므로 (D)가 적절하다.

09 왜 보테로의 '모나리자'가 현대적으로 보이는지는 알 수 없다.

10 (C) Jina가 무엇을 읽고 있는지 질문 → (B) 대답 → (E) 자신은 영화도 보았다며 소설보다 영화를 더 선호함을 말함 → (D) 이유 질문 → (A) 이유 대답

11 '누가 너에게 그 비밀을 말해 줬는지'이므로 who가 간접의문문의 주어 역할을 하는 것이 옳다.

12 사역동사의 목적어와 목적격보어가 능동 관계일 경우 목적격보어로 동사원형 형태를 쓴다. drop by: ~에 들르다

13 간접의문문의 어순은 '의문사+주어+동사'이다. 과거시제를 사용하고 있으므로 what you wore라고 쓰는 것에 유의한다.

14 목적격보어로 동사원형 형태를 취할 수 있는 것은 사역동사와 help이다.

15 사역동사 let의 목적격 보어로 동사원형 형태를 쓰는 것이 옳다.

16 What kind of fruit do you like most?를 간접의문문으로 만든 것이므로 '의문사+주어+동사' 어순에 맞는 것을 답으로 고른다.

17 let은 목적격보어로 동사원형 형태를 취하는 사역동사이다.

18 화가가 그리려고 했던 대상이 그림의 중앙에 있는 공주처럼 보이지만 그림의 제목이 '시녀들'이라면 화가가 그리려던 대상이 공주 옆에 있는 두 여인일지 묻는 말로 이어지는 것이 가장 자연스럽다.

19 그림의 제목이 '시녀들'이라고 말하며 '그렇다면 화가는 공주 옆에 있는 두 여자를 그리고 있나요?'라고 하였으므로 시녀들은 두 명임을 알 수 있다.

20 그림에서 왕자는 등장하지 않는다.

21 태양으로 가까이 간 결과 밀랍이 녹아서 물에 빠졌다는 것이다. 따라서 결과를 이끄는 연결어가 나오는 것이 옳다.

22 간접의문문을 이용하여 답을 쓸 수 있다. 이때 what은 의문사와 주어 역할을 동시에 하는 것에 유의한다.

23 if를 대신하여 whether를 써도 무방하다.

01 They will go to the arts festival.

02 They will watch it at the gym.

03 It is at 4. p.m. at the Main Hall.

04 (1) Tell me where Maria lives.

　(2) I wonder if you are married.

　(3) May I ask if he is alone?

　(4) Can you tell me who drove your car?

05 Nothing will make me change my mind.

06 who opened the door

07 to know how many books you read last year

08 (A) melted　(B) fell into

09 What do you think the artist is trying to tell us?

10 near the ship, sticking out of the water

11 He couldn't make his son stay away from the sun.

12 flew, close, wax, melted

13 (D)–(A)–(C)–(B)

14 ⓐ on　ⓑ in

01 Anna와 Steve는 예술 축제에 갈 것이다.

02 Anna와 Steve는 체육관에서 힙합 댄스 공연을 볼 것이다.

03 로미오와 줄리엣은 4시에 Main Hall에서 공연한다.

04 (2), (3)번은 if를 대신하여 whether를 써도 무방하다.

05 make를 사역동사로 사용하고, 마음을 바꾸는 주체가 '나'이므로 이를 목적어로 사용하여 문장을 완성한다.

06 의문사가 주어 역할을 겸하고 있는 간접의문문이다. 이때 동사가 바로 이어져 나올 수 있다.

07 작년에 얼마나 많은 책을 읽었는지 알고 싶다는 문장을 완성 할 수 있다.

08 태양에 의해 밀랍이 녹아 물에 빠졌다고 하는 것이 적절하다.

09 think가 있는 문장에서는 간접의문문의 의문사를 문두로 보낸다.

10 이카루스는 배 가까이에 있으며 그의 두 다리가 물 밖으로 나와 있다고 하였다.

11 아들이 태양에서 멀리 떨어지도록 시키지 못했다는 것이므로 사역동사의 목적어로 his son, 목적격보어로 동사원형 형태를 써서 문장을 만들 수 있다.

12 이카루스는 태양에 너무 가깝게 날아서 날개의 밀랍이 녹았다.

13 주어진 글의 질문에 이어 (D)에서 Velázquez라고 답하고 누구를 그리려고 했는지 질문하고 (A)에서 공주가 주인공인 것처럼 보인다고 답하며 (C)에서 But으로 상반되는 제목을 소개하며 그림을

더 자세히 보라고 말하며 (B)에서 궁금하게 만들 것이라고 언급한 뒤. 화가가 보고 있는 방향을 보라고 한 후 누구라고 생각하는지 묻는 것이 자연스럽다.

14 move on to: ~으로 옮기다, in the background of: ~의 배경에

 창의사고력 서술형 문제   p.156

|모범답안|

01 (A) da Vinci's *Mona Lisa*   (B) Botero's
   (C) an interesting smile   (D) Botero's *Mona Lisa*

02 what grade you are in / how often you go to a museum / what kind of museum you like to go to / how long you usually spend time in the museum

01 오늘 나는 미술책에서 재미있는 그림을 보았다. 그것은 다빈치의 '모나리자'처럼 보이는데 사실은 페르난도 보테로의 '모나리자'였다. 둘 중에, Jack은 보테로의 그림보다 페르난도의 '모나지라'를 더욱 좋아하였다. 왜냐하면 다빈치의 '모나리자'에 있는 흥미로운 미소 때문이었다. 그와 반대로, 나는 보테로의 '모나리자'가 훨씬 더욱 좋았다. 왜냐하면 그의 모나리자는 귀엽고 현대적으로 보였기 때문이었다.

 단원별 모의고사   p.157~160

01 ⑤
02 (1) Melt   (2) Despite   (3) tourist
   (4) direction   (5) wonder
03 Can you give me a hand?
04 What kind of music do you want to play?
05 ③   06 ②   07 ⑤
08 (C) → Which   09 ⑤   10 nearly
11 What kind of music are you going to play this year?
12 nineties   13 ⑤
14 Good music will make you feel better.
15 ⑤
16 (1) Do you remember where you found this bag?
   (2) Can you tell me why Kelly wants to become a dancer?
17 ④   18 ③
19 They were just doing their everyday activities.
20 ②   21 why Icarus' wings melted
22 ②   23 ⑤   24 canvas   25 ⑤

01 brush: 붓; ~을 닦다
05 기타를 추천하고 구매하는 상황이므로 손님과 점원의 관계가 적

절하다.

06 (A) a few: 몇몇의, few: 거의 없는, (B) 이어지는 대답에서 가장 좋아하는 공연의 종류를 설명하고 있으므로 most, (C) 둘 중에 어느 것을 더 좋아하느냐고 묻고 있으므로 or(또는)가 적절하다.

07 위 대화에서 왜 Emily가 TJ를 가장 좋아하는지 알 수 없다.

08 '어느 것을 더 좋아하니?'라는 의미의 선호를 물어보는 질문이 적절하므로 'which'가 적절하다.

10 almost = nearly: 거의

12 ninety: 90, nineties: 90년대

13 라푼젤의 엄마는 라푼젤이 탑 안에 머물게 했다는 의미이다. make는 목적격보어로 동사원형 형태를 쓰는 사역동사이다.

14 '네가 기분이 더 좋아지도록 만들다'이므로 사역동사 make 를 활용하여 문장을 만들 수 있다. 기분이 좋아지는 주체는 you이므로 이를 목적어로 사용한다.

15 what made Tom upset이라고 쓰는 것이 옳다. 간접의 문문에서 의문사가 주어 역할을 동시에 하는 경우에 유의한다.

16 간접의문문의 어순은 '의문사+주어+동사'임에 유의한다.

17 의문사가 주어인 경우이므로 who turned off the lights라고 쓰는 것이 옳다.

18 빈칸 (A)에는 전치사 from이 들어간다. ① listen to: ~을 듣다 ② take care of: ~을 돌보다 ③ suffer from: ~으로 고통받다 ④ turn off: ~을 끄다 ⑤ be satisfied with: ~에 만족하

19 They were going on with their everyday activities.'라고 써도 무방하다.

20 이카루스의 다리는 물 밖으로 나와 있다.

21 대답으로 미루어 보아 이카루스의 날개가 녹은 이유를 묻는 말이 들어가는 것이 옳다. 간접의문문을 이용하여 답을 쓸 수 있다.

22 화가가 누구를 그리고 있는지를 추측하는 내용이 이어지고 있으므로 ②번이 적절하다.

23 간접의문문이므로 '의문사+주어+동사' 어순으로 써야 한다. 따라서 which direction the artist is looking at이라고 쓰는 것이 옳다.

24 '그림을 그리기 위해서 미술가들에 의해 사용되는 두꺼운 헝겊 조각'은 '화폭, 캔버스(canvas)'이다.

25 '시녀들'의 작가는 그림의 배경에 있는 거울 속에 왕과 왕비를 그렸다고 하였다.

교과서 파헤치기

Lesson

5

단어 TEST Step 1   p.02

01 피하다   02 제안   03 속상한, 마음이 상한
04 걱정하다; 걱정 05 접촉, 닿음   06 조언
07 싸우다   08 이발, 머리 깎기 09 홀로, 혼자
10 물건   11 다치게 하다, 아프게 하다
12 어질러진, 더러운 13 현명한   14 공유하다, 나누다
15 점심시간   16 반복하다   17 문제
18 소리치다, 소리 지르다   19 ~부터, ~ 이후
20 의도하다, 작정하다   21 싫어하다
22 참다, 견디다   23 한계, 제한   24 설명하다
25 조언하다, 충고하다   26 아직
27 싸다, 꾸리다   28 어려운   29 용서하다
30 초보의, 초급의   31 두려움, 공포   32 이유, 까닭
33 풀다, 해결하다   34 (연극, 영화의) 대사
35 ~에 집중하다   36 잠에서 깨다
37 늦게까지 자지 않고 있다   38 체중이 늘다
39 고의로, 일부러   40 (기계가) 멈추다, 정지하다
41 해결하다   42 결국, 마침내   43 지적하다

단어 TEST Step 2   p.03

01 mirror   02 elementary   03 share
04 difficult   05 repeat   06 yell
07 contact   08 advise   09 matter
10 pack   11 fight   12 lunch break
13 haircut   14 stuff   15 hurt
16 stand   17 avoid   18 limit
19 yet   20 toothache   21 suggestion
22 alone   23 worry   24 messy
25 upset   26 reason   27 hate
28 line   29 advice   30 forgive
31 explain   32 fear   33 wise
34 solve   35 in the end   36 focus on
37 shut down   38 gain weight   39 up and down
40 stay up late 41 on purpose   42 set an alarm
43 wake up

단어 TEST Step 3   p.04

1 messy, 어질러진, 더러운   2 hate, 싫어하다
3 toothache, 치통   4 contact, 접촉
5 haircut, 이발, 머리 깎기   6 line, 대사   7 repeat, 반복하다
8 share, 공유하다   9 suggestion, 제안   10 fear, 두려움,

---

11 avoid, 피하다   12 elementary, 초급의
13 hurt, 다치게 하다   14 yell, 소리 지르다
15 advice, 조언   16 forgive, 용서하다

대화문 TEST Step 1   p.05~06

Listen & Talk 1-A-1
look, happy, matter / wore, sister's favorite, got / Did, tell / not yet, what to do

Listen & Talk 1-A-2
look down, What's the matter / got a haircut, funny / Take off, let me see, looks fine / not used to

Listen & Talk 1-B
look tired, the matter / I didn't have breakfast this morning / too bad, until lunch break / snack bar, could have / think so, too, How, make, suggestion / can post, suggestion

Listen & Talk 2 A-1
how to do better, give me some advice / solve a lot of / solve, should focus on, ones, got wrong

Listen & Talk 2 A-2
was late for class, wake up / set an alarm / turn it off / think you should, far from, That way, get out of bed

Review 1
stop playing computer games, What should I do / why don't you use, set, limit, shuts down / a good idea / I think you should move, out of, into / I think, should, for the advice

Communication
on the air / What's the matter / sharing, with, stuff without asking, What should, do / tell her your feelings, make some rules / I'll try that, Thanks for

대화문 TEST Step 2   p.07~08

Listen & Talk 1-A-1
M: You don't look so happy today. What's the matter?
W: I wore my sister's favorite T-shirt. But I got grape juice on it.
M: Oh, no. Did you tell your sister?
W: No, not yet. I don't know what to do .

Listen & Talk 1-A-2
Sora: David, you look down today. What's the matter?
David: I got a haircut but it's too short. I look funny.
Sora: Take off your hat and let me see. (pause) Oh, it looks fine.
David: Really? I guess I'm just not used to it yet.

Jane: You look tired. What's the matter?

Mike: I didn't have breakfast this morning. I'm so hungry.

Jane: Oh, that's too bad. We still have two more hours until lunch break.

Mike: Our school should have a snack bar. Then, we could have a quick breakfast or snacks.

Jane: I think so, too. How can we make that suggestion?

Mike: We can post it on the suggestion board.

Sujin: I don't know how to do better in math. Can you give me some advice ?

Jake: How do you study for tests?

Sujin: I just solve a lot of problems.

Jake: Well, don't solve everything. I think you should focus on the ones you got wrong.

Emily: I was late for class again. I just can't wake up in the morning.

Tom: Do you set an alarm?

Emily: Yeah, but I turn it off and go back to sleep.

Tom: I think you should put it far from your bed. That way, you'll have to get out of bed.

Eric: Ms. Morris, I just can't stop playing computer games. What should I do ?

Ms. Morris: Well, why don't you use a special program? When you set a time limit, the computer shuts down at that time.

Eric: Oh, that's a good idea.

Ms. Morris: And I think you should move the computer out of your room and into the living room.

Eric: I think I should. Thank you for the advice, Ms. Morris.

Solomon: Hello, you're on the air.

Amy: Hi, Solomon. I'm Amy.

Solomon: Hi, Amy. What's the matter?

Amy: I hate sharing my room with my little sister. She uses my stuff without asking me first. What should I do?

Solomon: Hmm…. I think you should tell her your feelings. And you should also make some rules with your sister.

Amy: Oh, I'll try that. Thanks for the advice.

본문 TEST Step 1   p.09~10

01 old, these, going, down   02 looks down

03 Let's, feelings, find

04 What, yelled at, after

05 because, forgot, lines   06 out, that, made

07 could, in front

08 sure, mean, hurt

09 have been, since   10 what, saying

11 never put, down

12 that, going, be   13 Don't, far, see

14 forgive, say, word   15 even look at

16 has never been

17 alone during   18 best friend

19 reason, know about

20 stand, any longer   21 go, tell, about

22 want, to, hurt   23 let, go   24 work, out

25 so, that, talking

26 went, talked, her

27 avoid, on purpose

28 didn't, way, say

29 doesn't, any more

30 too, part, up   31 like, face, wiser, end

본문 TEST Step 2   p.11~12

01 years old, these days, going up and down

02 looks down

03 Let's listen to, feelings, find out why

04 What a day, yelled at, after

05 because, forgot, lines on stage

06 pointed out, that Bella made

07 could, in front of

08 sure, did not mean to hurt

09 have been, since elementary school

10 what, saying

11 would never put, down

12 that, not going to be friends anymore

13 Don't go too far, see

14 can't forgive, didn't say a word

15 didn't even look at

16 has never been

17 ate alone during

18 Bella's best friend

19 reason that we don't know about

20 can't stand, any longer   21 go, tell, about

22 want, to be hurt

23 should let it go   24 work it out

25 that, are talking

26 went to, talked to her

27 didn't avoid, on purpose

28 a way to say sorry

29 any more problems like

30 Me, too, part of growing up

31 Just like, face, solve them, wiser, end

1 Bella는 올해 15세이고 요즘 그 애의 기분은 좋다가 안 좋다가 한다.

2 오늘 그 애는 우울해 보인다.

3 Bella의 감정에 귀 기울여 보고 그 이유를 알아보자.

4 정말 끔찍한 하루야! 학교 연극이 끝난 후 Jenny가 Bella에게 소리를 지르다니 믿을 수가 없어.

5 글쎄, 그건 Bella가 무대에서 그녀의 대사를 잊어버렸기 때문이잖아.

6 Jenny는 Bella가 저지른 실수를 지적했잖아.

7 어떻게 모든 사람 앞에서 그렇게 할 수가 있니?

8 하지만 난 Jenny가 Bella에게 상처를 주려고 했던 건 아니었다고 확신해.

9 그들은 초등학교 때부터 가장 친한 친구였잖아. 기억하지?

10 내 말이 바로 그거야.

11 진정한 친구라면 절대로 그런 식으로 Bella를 깎아내리지 않을 거야.

12 나는 그들이 더 이상 친구로 지내지 않을까봐 걱정돼.

13 자, Fear. 너무 극단적으로 생각하지 마. 곧 알게 되겠지.

14 난 Jenny를 용서할 수 없어. 그 애는 Bella에게 한마디도 말을 안 했어.

15 Jenny는 심지어 Bella를 쳐다보지도 않았어.

16 Jenny가 전에 이렇게 차가웠던 적이 없었어.

17 Bella는 오늘 점심시간에 혼자 밥을 먹었잖아. 가엾은 Bella!

18 Jenny는 Bella의 가장 친한 친구야.

19 나는 우리가 모르는 어떤 이유가 있다고 확신해.

20 나는 더 이상 이 상황을 못 참아.

21 Bella는 일단 가서 Jenny에게 자신의 감정을 말해야 해.

22 나는 Bella가 또다시 상처받는 걸 원하지 않아.

23 그 애는 그냥 내버려 두어야 해.

24 그 애들은 좋은 친구야. 그 애들이 잘 해낼 거야.

25 휴! 나는 그 애들이 다시 이야기하게 되어 무척 기뻐.

26 그래, Bella가 Jenny에게 가서 그 애에게 먼저 말을 걸었지.

27 Jenny는 일부러 Bella를 피한 게 아니었어.

28 맞아, Jenny는 사과하는 방법을 몰랐던 거야.

29 나는 Bella에게 이번과 같은 문제가 더 이상 없기를 바라.

30 나도 그래. 하지만 문제들은 성장의 일부야.

31 이번과 꼭 마찬가지로 Bella는 문제들에 직면하게 될 거고, 그것들을 해결할 거고, 그리고 결국 더 현명해질 거야.

1 Bella is 15 years old this year and these days her feelings are going up and down.

2 Today, she looks down.

3 Let's listen to Bella's feelings and find out why.

4 What a day! I can't believe Jenny yelled at Bella after the school play.

5 Well, that's because Bella forgot her lines on stage.

6 Jenny pointed out the mistake that Bella made.

7 How could she do that in front of everyone?

8 But I'm sure Jenny did not mean to hurt Bella.

9 They have been best friends since elementary school. Remember?

10 That's what I'm saying.

11 A true friend would never put Bella down like that.

12 I'm worried that they are not going to be friends anymore.

13 Come on, Fear. Don't go too far. We'll see.

14 I can't forgive Jenny. She didn't say a word to Bella.

15 Jenny didn't even look at her.

16 Jenny has never been this cold before.

17 Bella ate alone during lunch today. Poor Bella!

18 Jenny is Bella's best friend.

19 I'm sure there is a reason that we don't know about.

20 I can't stand this any longer.

21 Bella should just go and tell her about her feelings.

22 I don't want Bella to be hurt again.

23 She should let it go.

24 They are good friends. They will work it out.

25 Whew! I'm so happy that they are talking again.

26 Yeah, Bella went to Jenny and talked to her first.

27 Jenny didn't avoid Bella on purpose.

28 Yeah, Jenny didn't know a way to say sorry.

29 I hope Bella doesn't have any more problems like this.

30 Me, too. But problems are part of growing up.

31 Just like this time, Bella will face the problems, solve them, and become wiser in the end.

Wrap up 1

1. late again

2. stayed up late, last night

3. should try to, earlier

4. should also pack, save time

5. try your advice

1. upset when, pointed out, in front of others

2. mean to hurt

3. Thanks for coming up

Think & Write

1. Worry Doll

2. want to tell, have

3. worried about, math grades

4. have had, since last year

5. do better

6. try to study, can't focus on

7. what to do

8. have not had, because of

9. take, away

구석구석지문 TEST Step 2   p.20

Wrap up 1

1. Mr. Jones: Daisy, you're late again.

2. Daisy: I'm really sorry, Mr. Jones. I stayed up late again last night.

3. Mr. Jones: Well, I think you should try to go to bed earlier.

4. You should also pack your bag the night before, so you can save time in the morning.

5. Daisy: Okay, Mr. Jones. I'll try your advice.

Read & Think

1. Bella: Jenny, I was upset when you pointed out my mistake in front of others.

2. But I'm sure you didn't mean to hurt my feelings.

3. Jenny: I'm so sorry, Bella. Thanks for coming up to me first.

Think & Write

1. Dear Worry Doll,

2. I want to tell you a problem that I have.

3. I'm worried about my terrible math grades.

4. I have had this problem since last year.

5. I want to do better in math.

6. But when I try to study math, I just can't focus on it.

7. I don't know what to do.

8. I have not had a good night's sleep because of this worry.

9. Can you take my worries away?

Lesson 6

단어 TEST Step 1   p.21

01 눈 먼, 맹인인	02 죽은	03 ~처럼 보이다
04 끌다, ~을 끌어당기다		05 부주의한
06 ~ 동안, ~ 내내	07 궁금한, 호기심이 많은	
08 감각	09 위험한	10 거대한
11 두꺼운	12 나타나다	13 생강
14 먹이를 주다	15 공격하다	16 보호소
17 구조	18 거대한	19 가만히 못 있는
20 혀	21 우정	22 (코끼리의) 코
23 힘	24 꼬리	
25 재미있는, 유머러스한		26 곤충, 벌레
27 허락하다	28 믿을 수 없을 정도로	
29 고래	30 죽은, 생명이 없는	31 다가가다, 다가오다
32 아마	33 암컷의	34 모험심이 강한
35 ~ 덕분에	36 ~에서 눈을 떼지 않다	
37 태어나다	38 ~을 돌보다	39 차이를 구별하다
40 수백만의	41 ~의 일원이 되다	42 발표하다
43 ~ 옆에		

단어 TEST Step 2   p.22

01 giant[huge]	02 appear	03 rescue
04 curious	05 dead	06 adventurous
07 allow	08 dolphin	09 friendship
10 snake	11 dangerous	12 approach
13 ginger	14 lifeless	15 attack
16 hole	17 careless	18 sense
19 humorous	20 throughout	21 female
22 tongue	23 sheet	24 insect
25 language	26 restless	27 unbelievably
28 strength	29 blind	30 feed
31 shelter	32 attract	33 thick
34 trunk	35 thanks to	36 next to
37 care for	38 become part of	
39 millions of	40 give a presentation	
41 be born	42 keep one's eyes on	
43 tell the difference		

단어 TEST Step 3   p.23

1 dead, 죽은   2 trunk, (코끼리의) 코

3 blind, 눈 먼, 맹인인   4 curious, 호기심이 많은

5 feed, 먹이를 주다   6 adventurous, 모험심이 강한

7 approach, 다가가다   8 friendship, 우정   9 insect, 곤충
10 whale, 고래   11 rescue, 구조하다   12 shelter, 보호소
13 tongue, 혀   14 allow, 허락하다   15 careless, 부주의한
16 tail, 꼬리

대화문 TEST Step 1   p.24~25

Listen & Talk 1 A-1

choose, topic / How about / I'm curious about
weather change, thinking about doing / interesting
topic

Listen and Talk 1 A-2

Look at, huge / bigger than / curious about, says,
smells, bad, insects / wonder why

Listen and Talk 1 B

be friends / don't think so / watched, friendship
between, and / curious about / raised, sent, back,
wild, a year later / touching

Listen and Talk 2 A-1

Look at, puppy, two weeks / so small / as small as,
much bigger, few months / grow

Listen and Talk 2 A-2

over there, grandparents' / by, really big / as old as
me / How, know / planted, was, born

Listen and Talk 2 B

going, give a presentation, the biggest, How big,
longer than, Another interesting thing, as heavy as,
isn't it

Communication

tell us / millions of years ago / curious about, any /
many, giant, as heavy as, couldn't jump / amazing

대화문 TEST Step 2   p.26~27

Listen & Talk 1 A-1

Ryan: Judy, did you choose a topic for your science
project?

Judy: Not yet. How about you, Ryan?

Ryan: I'm curious about weather change. So I'm
thinking about doing the project on that.

Judy: That's an interesting topic!

Listen and Talk 1 A-2

Jane: Look at this picture of a huge flower.

Tom: Wow, it is bigger than a person.

Jane: Yeah. I'm really curious about this flower. It
also says here that the flower smells very bad,
but insects love the smell.

Tom: Hmm, I wonder why.

Listen and Talk 1 B

Clare: Do you think we can be friends with lions,
Todd?

Todd: No, Clare. I don't think so.

Clare: Well, I watched a video clip about friendship
between two men and a lion.

Todd: Really? I'm curious about the story. Can you
tell me more?

Clare: The two men raised a baby lion and sent her
back into the wild. When the men and the lion
met a year later, she remembered them.

Todd: Wow, that's so touching.

Listen and Talk 2 A-1

Dylan: Look at this picture, Mina. We got a new
puppy yesterday. He's only two weeks old.

Mina: Oh, Dylan, he's so small!

Dylan: Yeah. He's as small as my hand now, but he'll
get much bigger in a few months.

Mina: Wow, puppies grow very quickly.

Listen and Talk 2 A-2

Kelly: George, that red house over there is my
grandparents' house.

George: Wow, the tree by the house is really big.

Kelly: Actually, that tree is as old as me, thirteen
years old.

George: How do you know that, Kelly?

Kelly: My grandfather planted the tree in 2004 when I
was born.

Listen and Talk 2 B

Toby: Hi, I'm Toby. I'm going to give a presentation
about the blue whale. It's the biggest sea
animal in the world. How big is it? Well, it's
about 30m long. That means it's longer than a
basketball court. Another interesting thing is
that its tongue is as heavy as an elephant!
Surprising, isn't it?

Communication

Emily: Hello, Dr. Watson. Can you tell us about your
study?

Dr. Watson: I study animals that lived millions of
years ago.

Emily: Oh, I'm curious about those animals. Were
there any interesting ones?

Dr. Watson: Yes, there were many. This is the giant
kangaroo. It lived in Australia. It was as heavy
as three men and it couldn't jump well.

Emily: That's amazing!

01 my first, in   02 took, pictures of

03 found, by, hole

04 saw, drinking, beside

05 were, bright as

06 gave her, name

07 Around, saw, approaching

08 stood around, thick

09 Thanks to, safe

10 Around, heard, sound

11 followed, found, crying

12 lying dead, alone

13 It, to stay, such

14 What's more, going   15 can't see well

16 easily be attacked

17 called, shelter, asked for   18 stay by, until

19 dark, quiet   20 kept, on, with

21 still next to   22 touching, lifeless, with

23 to see, staying

24 stays safe throughout

25 new, appeared, approached

26 thought that, let, in

27 But, wrong   28 oldest female, become part

29 other seemed, welcome

30 Unbelievably, one, female, fed

31 cared for, warmly, did

32 such, amazing moment

01 was my first, in

02 took lots, pictures of

03 found, by, water hole

04 saw, drinking, beside

05 were as bright as

06 gave her a name

07 saw, approaching

08 stood around, made a thick wall

09 Thanks to them, safe

10 Around sunset, heard

11 followed, found, crying next to

12 lying dead, alone

13 It, to stay, in such a wild area

14 What's more, it, be dark

15 see well at night

16 easily be attacked

17 the elephant shelter, asked for   18 to stay, until

19 was dark, quiet   20 kept, on, with

21 still next to   22 was touching, with

23 It, to see, staying close to

24 stays safe throughout

25 appeared, approached

26 thought that, let, in

27 was wrong

28 the oldest female, to become part of

29 The other elephants, seemed

30 Unbelievably, elephants fed

31 cared for, as warmly as, did

32 such an amazing moment

1 기록: 오늘은 내가 아프리카에 온 첫날이었다.

2 나는 코끼리 사진을 많이 찍었다.

3 오늘 아침에 나는 작은 물웅덩이 옆에 있는 한 코끼리 무리를 발견했다.

4 나는 아기 코끼리 한 마리가 엄마 옆에서 물을 마시고 있는 것을 보았다.

5 그 코끼리의 눈이 별처럼 밝았다.

6 나는 그 코끼리에게 Stella란 이름을 붙여 주었다.

7 정오 즈음에 나는 사자 한 무리가 Stella에게 다가가는 것을 보았다.

8 코끼리들은 Stella 주위에 둘러서서 두꺼운 벽을 만들었다.

9 그 코끼리들 덕분에 Stella는 안전했다.

10 기록: 해질녘에 나는 이상한 소리를 들었다.

11 나는 그 소리를 따라갔고 Stella가 자신의 엄마 옆에서 울고 있는 것을 발견했다.

12 엄마는 죽어서 누워 있었고, Stella는 혼자였다.

13 이러한 야생 지역에서 혼자 있는 것은 위험하다.

14 더욱이 곧 어두워질 것이었다.

15 코끼리들은 밤에 잘 볼 수 없다.

16 그래서 Stella는 쉽게 공격을 받을 수 있었다.

17 나는 코끼리 보호소에 전화를 해서 도움을 요청했다.

18 나는 구조대가 올 때까지 Stella 곁에 머물기로 결정했다.

19 기록: 밤은 어둡고 조용했다.

20 나는 야간용 카메라를 이용해서 Stella를 계속 지켜보았다.

21 Stella는 여전히 엄마 곁에 있었다.

22 Stella는 코로 엄마의 죽은 몸을 어루만지고 있었다.

23 Stella가 엄마 가까이에 머물고 있는 것을 보는 것은 슬픈 일이었다.

24 나는 Stella가 밤새도록 안전하게 있기를 바란다.

25 기록: 새로운 코끼리 무리가 나타났고, Stella는 그 무리에 다가갔다.

26 처음에 나는 그 코끼리들이 Stella를 자신의 무리로 받아들이지 않을 것이라고 생각했다.

27 그러나 내 생각이 틀렸다.

28 아마도 가장 나이가 많은 암컷인 듯한 코끼리 한 마리가 Stella가 그 무리의 일원이 되도록 허락했다.

29 다른 코끼리들도 Stella를 반기는 것처럼 보였다.

30 믿을 수 없게도, 암컷 코끼리 중의 한 마리가 Stella에게 젖을 먹였다.

31 그 코끼리는 Stella의 엄마만큼 따뜻하게 Stella를 보살폈다.

32 이것은 너무나 놀라운 순간이었다.

28 An elephant, probably the oldest female allowed Stella to become part of the group.

29 The other elephants also seemed to welcome Stella.

30 Unbelievably, one of the female elephants fed Stella.

31 She cared for Stella as warmly as Stella's mom did.

32 This was such an amazing moment!

본문 TEST Step 4 ~ Step 5   p.34~37

1 Notes: Today was my first day in Africa.

2 I took lots of pictures of elephants.

3 This morning, I found an elephant group by a small water hole.

4 I saw a baby elephant drinking water beside her mother.

5 Her eyes were as bright as stars.

6 I gave her a name, Stella.

7 Around noon, I saw a group of lions approaching Stella.

8 The elephants stood around Stella and made a thick wall.

9 Thanks to them, Stella was safe.

10 Notes: Around sunset, I heard a strange sound.

11 I followed the sound and found Stella crying next to her mom.

12 She was lying dead and Stella was alone.

13 It is dangerous to stay alone in such a wild area.

14 What's more, it was going to be dark soon.

15 Elephants can't see well at night.

16 So Stella could easily be attacked.

17 I called the elephant shelter and asked for help.

18 I decided to stay by her until the rescue team came.

19 Notes: The night was dark and quiet.

20 I kept my eyes on Stella with my night camera.

21 Stella was still next to her mom.

22 She was touching her mom's lifeless body with her nose.

23 It was sad to see Stella staying close to her mom.

24 I hope Stella stays safe throughout the night.

25 Notes: A new elephant group appeared and Stella approached them.

26 At first, I thought that they would not let Stella in their group.

27 But I was wrong.

구석구석지문 TEST Step 1   p.38

Read and Think

1. tried to attack

2. thick, to protect

3. was crying next to

4. watched, all night

5. oldest female, allowed, to become part of

Think & Write C

1. Plant Diary

2. June 15th

3. what you saw

4. saw, is called

5. bright, looks like

6. As, its size , about, as long as

7. It, that, attracts insects

Wrap Up 1

1. Isn't, sea horse

2. Actually, sea dragon

3. curious about , between

4. Look at, carefully, straight one, does not

5. tell the difference

구석구석지문 TEST Step 2   p.39

Read and Think

1. Some lions tried to attack Stella.

2. The elephant group made a thick wall to protect her.

3. Stella was crying next to her dead mother.

4. I watched her all night.

5. The oldest female elephant of a new group allowed Stella to become part of them.

Think & Write C

1. Plant Diary

2. Date: June 15th , 2019

3. Write about what you saw :

4. Today, I saw a plant. It is called a pitcher plant.

5. It is bright green and red. It looks like a pitcher.

6. As for its size, it is about 15cm long. It is as long as my hand.

7. It is interesting that the plant attracts insects and eats them.

Wrap Up 1

1. Minho: Look! Isn't that a sea horse?

2. Sue: Actually, no. It's a sea dragon.

3. Minho: Oh, really? I'm curious about the difference between them.

4. Sue: Look at the tail carefully. A sea dragon has a straight one, but a sea horse does not.

5. Minho: Oh, I can tell the difference now!

Lesson 7

단어 TEST Step 1 p.40

01 왕자	02 클래식의	03 녹다
04 생산하다	05 방향	06 전시하다
07 깃털	08 예술가, 미술가	09 약속하다
10 붓	11 풍경	12 소설
13 ~에도 불구하고	14 예술 작품	15 십 대
16 미로	17 생산	18 ~을 알아차리다
19 궁금해하다	20 납작한	21 해변, 바닷가
22 세부 사항	23 비극	24 더 좋아하다
25 날개	26 현대의	27 왕비, 여왕
28 록 음악	29 진짜의, 현실적인	30 소설가
31 ~ 때문에, ~이므로		32 신화
33 관광객	34 (어떤 것의) 변형	35 밀랍, 왁스
36 화폭, 캔버스	37 A를 B보다 더 좋아하다	
38 ~을 보다	39 ~을 힐끗 보다	
40 ~을 가까이하지 않다		41 즉시, 바로
42 ~을 보다	43 ~로 이동하다, 넘어가다	

단어 TEST Step 2 p.41

01 melt	02 produce	03 feather
04 wing	05 direction	06 queen
07 artist	08 brush	09 prince
10 exhibit	11 frog	12 maze
13 promise	14 novel	15 despite
16 modern	17 flat	18 teen
19 notice	20 landscape	21 art work
22 version	23 detail	24 myth
25 production	26 tragedy	27 prefer
28 wonder	29 real	30 canvas
31 tourist	32 wax	33 rock
34 novelist	35 comedy	36 since
37 seaside	38 move on	39 prefer A to B
40 glance at	41 take a look[look at]	
42 stay away from		43 right away

단어 TEST Step 3 p.42

1 feather, 깃털   2 seaside, 해변, 바닷가   3 melt, 녹다

4 tragedy, 비극   5 direction, 방향   6 wonder, 궁금해하다

7 landscape, 풍경   8 notice, 알아차리다   9 stick, 내밀다

10 artist, 예술가   11 wing, 날개   12 detail, 세부 사항

13 exhibit, 전시하다   14 rock, 록 음악

15 canvas, 화폭, 캔버스   16 myth, 신화

Listen & Talk 1 A-1

going to play / practicing almost every day / What kind of music / play songs, nineties

Listen & Talk 1 A-2

how to paint clean lines / What kind of brush, using / round brush / When, paint, flat, better, Try

Listen & Talk 1 B

meeting, right / performance do you want to watch first / want to, performance / Sounds, right / about watching the play / the one, near

Listen & Talk 2 A-1

are, reading / a story / seen, of it, too, prefer, to / Why, like, better / scenes, looks, real

Listen & Talk 2 A-2

Have, listened / cool, part, great / dance version / listened to, I prefer the guitar version, matches, better

Listen & Talk 2 B

interesting painting, Look at / looks like / Which do you prefer / prefer, to / smile, How about you / prefer, to / looks modern

Communication

are planning, so, fine out, May, ask, a few questions / What kind of performance / performances best / do, prefer / prefer rock to hip-hop / favorite musician / favorite musicia / Thank, for

Wrap Up 1

Can, help, to buy / various kinds, What kind of music, to play / want to / should get / take, classical guitar

Listen & Talk 1 A-1

W: Brian, is your band going to play at the Teen Music Festival?

M: Yes, we're practicing almost every day.

W: What kind of music are you going to play this year?

M: Rock music. We'll play songs from the nineties.

Listen & Talk 1 A-2

W: Can you help me? I don't know how to paint clean lines.

M: What kind of brush were you using?

W: This round brush.

M: When you paint lines, a flat brush is better. Try this one.

W: Okay, thank you.

Listen & Talk 1 B

W: (ringing) Hello, Steve.

M: Hi, Anna. We're meeting at the arts festival tomorrow at 1:30, right?

W: Right. What kind of performance do you want to watch first?

M: I want to watch the hip-hop dance performance first.

W: Sounds good. It's at 2 p.m. at the gym, right?

M: Yeah, and how about watching the play, Romeo and Juliet, at 4 p.m.?

W: Oh, the one at the Main Hall near the gym? Sure!

Listen & Talk 2 A-1

M: What are you reading, Jina?

W: The novel, Life of Pi. It's a story of a boy and a tiger.

M: It's a great book. I've seen the movie of it, too. I prefer the movie to the novel.

W: Why do you like it better?

M: The scenes are very beautiful. And the tiger looks so real.

Listen & Talk 2 A-2

W: Have you listened to Jane's new song, Girl Friend ?

M: Yeah, it's really cool. The guitar part is great.

W: There is also a dance version of the song on the album.

M: I've listened to it, but I prefer the guitar version to the dance version. It matches her voice better.

Listen & Talk 2 B

W: I saw an interesting painting in an art book. Look at this.

M: Wow, it looks like da Vinci's Mona Lisa .

W: Actually, it's Mona Lisa by Fernando Botero. Which do you prefer?

M: I prefer da Vinci's to Botero's. Da Vinci's Mona Lisa has an interesting smile. How about you?

W: Well, I prefer Botero's to da Vinci's. His Mona Lisa is cute, and it looks modern.

Communication

M: Hi, we are planning a school festival, so we want to find out students' favorite types of performances. May I ask you a few questions?

W: Sure.

M: What kind of performance do you like best?

W: I like music performances best.

M: Okay. Then, which do you prefer, rock or hip-hop?

W: I prefer rock to hip-hop.

M: Who's your favorite musician?

W: My favorite musician is TJ.

M: Great. Thank you for your answers.

Wrap Up 1

M: Can you help me? I want to buy a guitar.

W: There are various kinds of guitars. What kind of music do you want to play?

M: I want to play pop songs.

W: Then you should get a classical guitar.

M: Okay, I will take a classical guitar.

본문 TEST Step 1 — p.47~48

01 Welcome to, tour
02 when, much, looking, each
03 glance, for, few, on
04 might miss, since, notice
05 at, closely, help, see
06 Look at, first
07 seaside, peaceful, isn't it
08 title, is, with
09 where Icarus is
10 that, sticking out, near
11 in, famous myth
12 wings, feathers, stay away
13 However, didn't listen
14 flew, close to
15 melted, fell into
16 look at, entire
17 Despite, going on, everyday
18 still look peaceful
19 What, think, trying
20 move on to
21 see, behind, large
22 actually painted
23 Who, think he is
24 Take, look
25 seems to, main, because
26 title, painting
27 drawing, beside, princess
28 Take, close
29 make you wonder
30 Try, which direction
31 see, in, mirror, background
32 Who, think, is

본문 TEST Step 2 — p.49~50

01 Welcome to, tour
02 when, go to, how much time, spend looking at
03 glance at, for, a few, move on
04 might miss, since, to notice them
05 look at, closely, help you see, details

06 Look at, first
07 seaside landscape, peaceful, isn't it
08 title of, is
09 where Icarus is
10 are sticking out of the water near
11 in the famous myth
12 made wings for him with feathers, to stay away from
13 However, didn't listen
14 flew too close
15 melted, fell into
16 look at, entire
17 Despite, going on with, everyday activities
18 still look peaceful
19 What do you think, trying to
20 move on to
21 see, behind
22 actually painted
23 Who do you think he is
24 Take, quick look
25 seems to be, because, in the center
26 title, painting
27 drawing, beside
28 Take, close look
29 make you wonder
30 Try to, which direction the artist is
31 see, in the mirror, background
32 Who do you think he is

본문 TEST Step 3 — p.51~52

1 세계 미술관(the World Art Museum)에 오신 것을 환영합니다.

2 미술관에 갈 때 여러분은 각각의 그림을 보는 데 얼마나 많은 시간을 보내나요?

3 많은 방문객들은 이동하기 전에 하나의 그림을 몇 초간만 힐끗 봅니다.

4 하지만 그림의 중요한 세부 사항들을 즉시 알아채는 것은 어렵기 때문에 여러분들은 그것들을 놓칠 수 있습니다.

5 오늘 우리는 두 개의 그림을 자세히 살펴볼 것이고, 여러분이 흥미로운 세부 사항들을 볼 수 있도록 제가 도와드리겠습니다.

6 먼저 이 그림을 보세요.

7 바닷가 풍경이 매우 평화롭고 아름답죠, 그렇지 않나요?

8 이 그림의 제목은 '추락하는 이카루스가 있는 풍경'입니다.

9 그러면 이카루스가 어디에 있는지 보이나요?

10 배 근처에 물 밖으로 나와 있는 두 다리가 보이죠?

11 이것이 그리스의 유명한 신화에 나오는 이카루스입니다.

12 신화에서 이카루스의 아버지는 그를 위해 깃털과 밀랍으로 날개를 만들어 주었고 그에게 태양을 가까이 하지 말라고 말했습니다.

13 하지만 이카루스는 듣지 않았습니다.

14 그는 태양에 너무 가깝게 날았습니다.

15 그래서 밀랍이 녹았고 그는 물에 빠졌습니다.

16 이제, 그림 전체를 다시 보세요.

17 이카루스의 비극에도 불구하고 사람들은 일상의 활동을 계속하고 있습니다.

18 그림이 여전히 평화로워 보이나요?

19 화가가 우리에게 무엇을 말하려 한다고 생각하나요?

20 이제, 다음 그림으로 넘어갑시다.

21 커다란 캔버스 뒤에 있는 화가가 보이나요?

22 그는 Diego Velázquez이고, 그가 실제로 이 그림을 그렸습니다.

23 그가 누구를 그리고 있다고 생각하나요?

24 재빨리 봅시다.

25 어린 공주가 그림의 중앙에 있기 때문에 주인공처럼 보입니다.

26 하지만 그림의 제목은 '시녀들'입니다.

27 그렇다면 화가는 공주 옆에 있는 두 여인을 그리고 있나요?

28 자세히 보세요.

29 그림에 대해 더 궁금해하게 될 겁니다.

30 화가가 바라보고 있는 방향을 보려고 노력해 보세요.

31 그림의 배경에 있는 거울 속 왕과 왕비가 보이나요?

32 이제 여러분은 그가 누구를 그리고 있다고 생각하나요?

본문 TEST Step 4~Step 5   p.53~56

1 Welcome to the World Art Museum tour.

2 When you go to an art museum, how much time do you spend looking at each painting?

3 Many visitors glance at one painting for only a few seconds before they move on.

4 But you might miss the important details of paintings since it is hard to notice them right away.

5 Today, we'll look at two paintings closely and I'll help you see interesting details.

6 Look at this painting first.

7 The seaside landscape is so peaceful and beautiful, isn't it?

8 The title of this painting is *Landscape with the Fall of Icarus.*

9 So, can you see where Icarus is?

10 Do you see two legs that are sticking out of the water near the ship?

11 This is Icarus in the famous myth in Greece.

12 In the myth, Icarus' father made wings for him with feathers and wax and told him to stay away from the sun.

13 However, Icarus didn't listen.

14 He flew too close to the sun.

15 So, the wax melted and he fell into the water.

16 Now, look at the entire painting again.

17 Despite the tragedy of Icarus, people are going on with their everyday activities.

18 Does the painting still look peaceful?

19 What do you think the artist is trying to tell us?

20 Now, let's move on to the next painting.

21 Do you see the artist behind the large canvas?

22 He is Diego Velázquez, and he actually painted this picture.

23 Who do you think he is painting?

24 Take a quick look.

25 The young princess seems to be the main person because she is in the center of the painting.

26 But the title of the painting is *The Maids of Honour.*

27 Then, is the artist drawing the two women beside the princess?

28 Take a close look.

29 It will make you wonder about the painting more.

30 Try to see which direction the artist is looking at.

31 Can you see the king and the queen in the mirror in the background of the painting?

32 Who do you think he is painting now?

구석구석지문 TEST Step 1   p.57

Listen & Talk

1. are, reading
2. reading, who, in a maze
3. seen, too, prefer, to
4. Why, like, better
5. various stories, show, important parts

Grammar in Real Life

1. let, in
2. Who, you
3. promised me, let you enter, be
4. serve you, cookies, tea
5. Never let, in
6. worry, make the princess keep

Think and Write C

1. Amazing Art exhibition
2. interesting pieces of art
3. Among, called
4. was made by
5. Interestingly, was used
6. because, makes me feel calm
7. can be used to
8. Anything, possible

Listen & Talk

1. M: What are you reading , Sally?

2. W: I'm reading The Maze Runner. It's about boys who are put in a maze.

3. M: It's a great story. I've seen the movie of it, too. I prefer the novel to the movie.

4. W: Why do you like it better?

5. M: The novel has various stories. But the movie didn't show some important parts of the story.

Grammar in Real Life

1. Princess, please let me in.

2. Who are you?

3. The princess promised me, "If you help me, I'll let you enter the palace and be my friend."

4. Come here. I'll have people serve you some cookies and tea.

5. No! Never let him in. I don't like him.

6. Don't worry, Frog. I'll make the princess keep her promise.

Think and Write C

1. Today, I went to the Amazing Art exhibition.

2. At the exhibition, I saw many interesting pieces of art.

3. Among them, I liked the piece called Moon Tree.

4. It was made by French artist, David Myriam.

5. Interestingly, sand was used in this painting.

6. I like it because a tree in the moon makes me feel calm.

7. Now I know that anything can be used to make art.

8. Anything is possible!

MEMO

적중100

영어 기출 문제집

정답 및 해설

비상 | 김진완